The One Year®
Mother Daughter Devo

Dannah Gresh
with Janet Mylin

 Tyndale House Publishers, Inc., Carol Stream, Illinois

For my sweet niece Rebecca,
who I pray will love God's voice as much as I do.

—Aunt Dannah

For my mom, Rachel, and my mother-in-law, Fran—
I love how you love God.

—Janet

Hi, Moms and Daughters!

I love devos!

Since my mom gave me my first daily devotion book when I was in elementary school, I have loved opening up the Bible every day to hear the special things God wants to tell me.

I hope you'll love it too. Whether you're a well-practiced daily student of the Bible or this is the first time you've given it a try, my greatest prayer is that this will be fun for you. If you like it, you'll want more, and daily Bible reading will become a lifelong practice.

My dear friend Janet Mylin helped me write these for you. We worked really hard to make this book unlike any other daily devotion you've ever used. Our answer was to put some fun and unique elements together to help you study the Bible.

Bible Blast: The Bible Blast at the beginning of each devotion is optional. If you really want to dig in deep, open your own Bible and read the Bible Blast Scripture offered just under the date and title of the day's devo. It'll be referenced in the devotion that day and will give you a little extra meat to chew on, but the reading is not necessary. Mom, you might want to use this if you have an older daughter. It's great for building the discipline of opening your own Bible each day.

Language Lab: The Language Lab devotions are easy-to-swallow theology lessons for both of you. You'll learn what big and important words in the Christian faith mean and how God wants you to apply them in your life. You'll find one or two each month.

Amazing Animals: What girl doesn't love animals? Each month includes one or two Amazing Animals devos. On those days, you'll meet some pretty amazing creatures and dig into the Bible to see what they can teach us about God.

Kickin' Kraft: If you love crafts, you'll love these devos. (And if you don't, relax! They're easy and optional.) A couple of times a month, a craft project made from everyday items that you'll find around your house will provide a simple object lesson or reminder to go along with your devotion.

Meditation Moments: It's great that you're doing devotions. I'm so proud of you. Since I also want you to be able to have devotions without my help, we'll take some time to practice meditating on God's Word. Meditation is what I do when I write a devotion for you. I study a Bible verse and then let God guide my thoughts about it through prayer. Meditation is easy, and it's a great habit to form if you love reading your Bible.

So what are we waiting for? Let's dig in!

Dannah

Can You See Where You Are Going?

Bible Blast: Read Genesis 12:1-7

Your word is a lamp to guide my feet and a light for my path.
PSALM 119:105

I have *the* best dog in the world. She is a huge chocolate Labradoodle named Stormie. She brings me my newspaper every morning and cuddles on my feet when I'm writing books. She's my constant companion. As wonderful as she is, Stormie has one fault: she's a scaredy-cat! Once, my husband, Bob, took her on a survival camping trip. Stormie was scared silly! She whimpered and whined into the wee hours of the morning. Realizing he wasn't going to get any rest, my husband finally stood up and said, "Let's go home, Stormie." Eager to leave, she tore off in the direction of the car. Bob ran after her, jumping over branches and avoiding holes by using his flashlight. Suddenly, Stormie stopped and stood dead still! Bob knew something was wrong. Ever so carefully, he moved the light toward the spot where Stormie was staring. Imagine his shock to find a porcupine hanging on the side of a tree and staring right back at him! He slowly moved toward Stormie, and together they walked *around* the danger.

The Bible is like a flashlight for you and me. It shows us the way to walk in a world that's full of darkness. The Bible is the light to show us where to walk so we won't stumble into things that could hurt us—like that porcupine!

When Abram obeyed God and headed out to the Promised Land, he didn't know where it was. He had to listen to God's voice. He didn't even know he'd gotten to a place where he could see the land until God told him he was there. Pretty cool to have God's voice as your guide, huh? Well, you can have it too! Just read your Bible, and you'll hear God telling you what to do from day to day.

On this first day of the year, make a promise to *use* the Bible together—as mom and daughter—to guide you in every decision you make.

Girl Gab: Mom, share a time when you had a difficult decision to make and the Bible was a "light for your path," giving you a clear answer. Daughter, talk to your mom about a situation at school or in your family that is difficult for you right now. Pray about that situation together and start looking for direction from God in the pages of your Bible.

A Tall-Icy-Glass-of-Red-Kool-Aid Story

Bible Blast: Read Genesis 12:10-20

Don't lie to each other. COLOSSIANS 3:9

Girl Gab: Mom, can you remember a time when you told a lie that made things difficult for you? Share that with your daughter. Daughter, tell your mom about a time when you lied and how it made you feel. Pray together and thank God for his forgiveness and make a decision to tell the truth!

Do you know what it's like for a fib to grow out of control? I do. It all started one hot summer afternoon when I was a kid. I needed to use the typewriter in my dad's office. (What's a typewriter? Ask your mom!) I just couldn't stand how hot it was, so I broke the "no food allowed" rule. I made myself a nice tall, icy glass of red Kool-Aid and placed it next to the typewriter. Big mistake. You see, typewriters have this thing called a "return." It's a big clunky piece of metal that "returns" to a starting position when you finish a line of writing. Well, when I hit the "return" button, that thing returned right into my tall, icy glass of red Kool-Aid. I scrubbed and scrubbed and tried my best to hide any trace of the tragedy, but my dad *knew*. (Parents have a sixth sense!) I was so afraid that the punishment would be more than I could stand. When he asked who had spilled Kool-Aid in his office, I said I didn't know. He just smiled knowingly. And then the fib started growing. Oh, it never really came up again. But in my heart that lie was like an inflating balloon just waiting to burst. I'd wake up in the morning and think about it. I'd pour a glass of Kool-Aid and remember. I'd hear my dad coming home from work, and I just knew that this terrible lie stood between us. Finally, I couldn't stand it. I told my dad the truth. He just smiled and said, "Yeah, I knew it was you, but you were doing such a good job punishing yourself that I felt no need to help!" Then he forgave me.

In the Bible, we learn that Abram lied. Why? Because he was afraid! And it caused a lot of trouble. Many people got sick. Abram almost lost his wife to Pharaoh, and Abram and Sarai had to leave Egypt. Lying makes life difficult. That's why God doesn't want you and me to lie. Lying also proves that we've lost faith in God's ability to work things out for us.

Got a tall-icy-glass-of-red-Kool-Aid story in your life? Get rid of the guilt. Confess it today. I'm sure your mom will forgive you just like my dad forgave me.

Language Lab: What Does "Hallelujah" Mean?

Bible Blast: Read Revelation 19:1-8

I heard what sounded like a great multitude, like the roar of rushing waters and like loud peals of thunder, shouting: "Hallelujah! For our Lord God Almighty reigns. Let us rejoice and be glad and give him glory! For the wedding of the Lamb has come, and his bride has made herself ready."

REVELATION 19:6-7 (NIV)

Have you ever been on a roller coaster? Do you remember going slowly up, up, up the first big hill as your heart started beating faster and butterflies swirled around in your stomach? When you finally began plunging down going super fast, you probably screamed something like "Wa-Hooooooo!"

Hallelujah is like "Wa-Hooooooo!" But you use *hallelujah* to express your excitement and love for God. You can think of it as a special word reserved just for telling your Creator how awesome he is.

Hallelujah means "to be bright, to shine." It has to do with radiance. The word *radiant* always makes me think of *Charlotte's Web* when Charlotte weaves that word into her web for everyone to see. Wilbur the pig was definitely clean after his milk bath, but I don't think he actually glowed! When we praise God, it doesn't just please him; it changes us. It causes our lives to be radiant. Matthew 5:14 says that you are the light of the world. How can you give off light?

Light is something that helps people see clearly in a dark place. Some lights even give off warmth. When you live a life of hallelujah—a life of praising the Lord—other people will see that you're different. They may even ask why you're not complaining all the time like everyone else. When you tell them about the hope of Jesus, that's being a light! People who don't know Jesus are living in darkness because they haven't seen the truth. When they begin to see him for who he really is, they begin to walk in light.

So the next time you sing, "Hallelujah," tell others to put on their sunglasses. You might be radiating!

Girl Gab: Do you know someone who lives a "Hallelujah Life"—a life that glows with praising God in every circumstance? Come up with a creative way to encourage that person today! Listen to or sing a song with the word *hallelujah* in it.

God's Secret Name for You

Bible Blast: Read Genesis 17:1-15

I will give to each one a white stone, and on the stone will be engraved a new name that no one understands except the one who receives it. REVELATION 2:17

Girl Gab: Mom, get on the Internet with your daughter and look up both of your names. Just Google "meaning of names," and you'll find lots of Web sites to choose from. Write your names and their meanings on a piece of paper, and put it on your fridge! Daughter, pray for your mom! Ask God to give her confidence to walk in the power of her name. Sometimes moms need you to do the praying!

Names are pretty cool, and they have a lot of meaning. If your name is *Emily*—the number one girl's name in the United States for the past decade—it means "revival" or "rebirth." Is your name *Brianna*? That means "noble, strong, and pure." I like that one a lot and encourage you to live up to your name. *Alexis* is a favorite of mine because I gave it to my own daughter. It's from ancient Greece and means "defender." Any girl named *Alexis* should be a defender of God's truth. I also love the name *Natalie*. It comes from Italy, where the saying "Buon Natale" means "Merry Christmas." So every time someone says, "Natalie," they are mentioning the birth of our Savior!

When Abram was ninety years old, he still wasn't a dad. Whoa! Had God forgotten him? No way! In fact, God appeared to remind Abram of the promise that he would be the father of many. And then God did something really cool. He gave Abram a new name: *Abraham*. His first name—Abram—meant "high father." What a funny thing that this childless man carried a name about being a dad. (Maybe that's one reason he wanted to be one so badly.) God changed it to Abraham. Bible scholars say that the new name is hard to understand. Stumped as they are, scholars conclude that the new name means "father of a multitude" and that God made the name by taking the *h* in God's own Hebrew name, Yahweh, and placing it into Abram's name. See that? AbraHam. God did that with Sarai, too, when he changed her name to *Sarah*, which means "princess." Wow! From that day on they'd be saying God's name when they said their own names!

Do you know that God has a special name for you, too? The book of Revelation tells us that one day, you'll be given that new name on a white stone. I wonder what yours will be. How very much God loves us to be so personal with us!

Amazing Animals: Jessica the Hippo

Bible Blast: Read 2 Corinthians 11:12-15

I am not surprised! Even Satan disguises himself as an angel of light. So it is no wonder that his servants also disguise themselves as servants of righteousness. In the end they will get the punishment their wicked deeds deserve. 2 CORINTHIANS 11:14-15

It's a sunny, warm day, and you're lying on a blanket in your backyard reading a good book. Curled up next to you is your cute, snuggly pet . . . hippo.

Not what you were thinking? Well, for Tonie in South Africa that's exactly how life is. In the year 2000, a newborn baby hippo washed up on Tonie's lawn. He adopted the lost animal and named her "Jessica." Today Jessica—weighing almost a ton—fits right in with the pet dogs. She loves coffee and sweet potatoes, and she will even wander inside looking for a snack.

Hippos seem so gentle and adorable. Other than its size, a hippo would be the perfect pet. Right? *Wrong!* Did you know that in Africa, hippos kill more humans than any other wild animal? This is a great mystery because hippopotami are herbivores, plant eaters.

Sometimes the things in life that appear to be harmless are the most dangerous things around. Like, if you get a book from the library, you may not pick the one with the creepy dude on the cover because you know that book will have some seriously evil stuff inside. Instead you pick a book that has a happy boy and girl on the cover. As you read that story, you find yourself thinking that you *need* a boyfriend to be happy or cool, when you know the Bible says true joy is found in the Lord, not in boy-craziness (see Nehemiah 8:10). So even though some things seem harmless, they're putting wrong ideas in our heads. We really need something called "discernment" from God when we're making choices. Discernment is the ability to know what's good and what's evil.

Girl Gab: Mom, you can find some great footage of Jessica the Hippo online. After you watch a clip of this amiable beast, talk with your daughter about some things that appear to be good on the outside but aren't good on the inside. This is a great time to discuss why you don't allow her to indulge in certain TV shows, movies, books, music, or friendships. Daughter, ask God to give you discernment so you can make godly choices every day.

Girl Gab: Mom, using discernment about what your daughter can understand and handle, share a need that you and your daughter can pray for together in expectation that God will provide through his riches. Daughter, from this day on, every time you begin to wonder if God will provide what your mom has decided you will pray for, you can just say, "God will provide _____ for my mom."

Bible Blast: Read Genesis 22:1-13

This same God who takes care of me will supply all your needs from his glorious riches, which have been given to us in Christ Jesus. PHILIPPIANS 4:19

One of the wealthiest men to ever live was Alexander the Great! At one point, he actually owned many civilizations, which added up to what he thought was the entire world. Let's try to wrap our heads around his wealth by checking out his schooling. When Alexander was thirteen, his dad began to search for a tutor. But he didn't want just any tutor, so he hired the great Aristotle. To top it off, Alexander's dad bought him a temple to serve as his private schoolhouse. (This is homeschooling on steroids, girls!) Aristotle's fee? Aristotle wanted Alexander's dad to build him a city! Now that's a dad who will do anything to meet the needs of his child.

Alexander's wealth was nothing compared to the riches God has. He actually does own the entire world and the universe, too. Every morsel of food, every dollar, every medication, every airplane, and every piece of property is God's, first and foremost. (We're just helping him manage it.)

Abraham's faith had become so solid that the truth of God's ability to provide for his needs was like a rock in the bottom of his heart. Nothing would shake it. So when God came to him with a startling request—to sacrifice his only son—Abraham humbly obeyed. When Isaac asked his dad where the lamb was that they would sacrifice, Abraham just said, "God will provide a lamb, my son." Abraham trusted God to provide. To Abraham, God was like a father who owned the entire world and would give his son what was needed at just the right time. God is not like an earthly father, but he is our Father. And he is the richest dad ever! He's got what it takes, but he might need you to climb up a mountain like Abraham did to demonstrate your faith.

God will provide for you, too, my friends. Whatever your need is today, take that need to him with confidence.

Kickin' Kraft: Check the Label

Bible Blast: Read 1 Samuel 18:1-7

David replied to the Philistine, "You come to me with sword, spear, and javelin, but I come to you in the name of the LORD of Heaven's Armies—the God of the armies of Israel, whom you have defied." 1 SAMUEL 17:45

Lisa was in fourth grade, and she wanted to be the spelling bee champion. But she had a problem: Jeffrey. He'd been the class bully ever since she'd known him.

One day in third grade, Lisa had gotten a bad grade on a spelling test. Jeffrey found out and started chanting, "Lisa's dumb! She can't spell!" It was as if he took a big label that said, "Loser Lisa," and attached it to her shirt. Lisa pretended the bullying didn't bother her, but it really did.

One year later, Lisa's mom asked her if she wanted to sign up for the spelling bee. Lisa looked down at her feet and said quietly, "I used to want to." Her mom said, "That's wonderful!" Lisa burst into tears and said, "I can't! I'm dumb! I'm a loser!" Lisa's mom grabbed her by the shoulders, looked her in the eyes, and said, "You are not dumb, Lisa. You are a very intelligent girl who God created! If you want to be in the spelling bee, God will give you the strength to do it!"

That day it was like Lisa's mom tore off the label of "Loser Lisa" that Lisa had secretly been wearing since first grade and put on a new label of "Smart Girl." With her mom's encouragement and help, Lisa knew she could compete in the Spelling Bee.

The Bible teaches that when David was a young boy, he tended the sheep while his brothers were in King Saul's army. David's brothers put the label of "Shepherd" on him, but God had other labels for David in mind. To God, David was "Commander" and "Warrior."

Names people call us when we're little can affect us during our whole lives if we let them. Ask God today to tear off any bad labels you're wearing. Then start calling yourself the opposite of that label. For example, if you feel like you're wearing a label that says, "Weak," start calling yourself "Strong in the Lord!"

Kickin' Kraft:
Radical Reflections!

(Check out p. 367 for a great mother-daughter craft that helps reinforce today's devo.)

Mushy Marshmallows

Bible Blast: Read Genesis 25:27-34

Be self-controlled and alert. 1 PETER 5:8 (NIV)

Many years ago Stanford University conducted the Great Marshmallow Experiment. They took four-year-olds individually into a room with a marshmallow sitting on the table. The scientist told each child that he needed to leave the room for a moment and that he or she could eat the marshmallow. But if the child waited, he or she could have two marshmallows instead when the scientist returned. Some of the kids grabbed that mushy marshmallow the moment the door closed. Others waited—sometimes for twenty minutes—so they could have two.

Fourteen years later, the scientist compared the children who ate the marshmallow right away and those who waited. Guess what? The ones who waited scored higher on tests. They also tended to be more self-controlled and became teens making positive, good choices as opposed to poor decisions like shoplifting, cheating, or drinking underage. Learning to wait is a critical skill for lifelong success.

Esau traded the lasting benefits of his birthright—or family inheritance—for an immediate pleasure, a bowl of stew. (Sounds a lot like those kids who could not keep their hands off the marshmallow.) Esau exaggerated his hunger when he said, "I'm about to die." He wasn't going to die, and he could have waited. Instead, he acted impulsively and did not pause to consider what his choice would mean in the long run. It meant that the honor of continuing the family leadership now belonged to Jacob. From that day on, it was destined that we would refer to God as the "God of Abraham, Isaac, and Jacob." Esau lost a lot when he slurped up that bowl of soup.

It's easy to be like Esau. Sometimes we just see something and want it, so we go after it. But it's better to think things over and consider what will happen.

If that experiment were conducted today, which group would you be in: the group that took one marshmallow or the group that waited and got the reward of having two?

Girl Gab: Mom, tell your daughter if you're a one-marshmallow girl or a two-marshmallow girl. Then ask her what she thinks she is. Take some time to discuss this, and make suggestions so you can both be more self-disciplined. Daughter, grab some marshmallows out of the cupboard, and enjoy a whole handful! (Or put them on Mom's shopping list.)

Don't Let a Grudge Hold You

Bible Blast: Read Genesis 27:41-45

Do not seek revenge or bear a grudge against a fellow Israelite, but love your neighbor as yourself. LEVITICUS 19:18

Kim was only nine years old when her village was raided. She remembers running down a street after fire had burned off her clothing. The photo of her running terrified and naked through the streets is a famous image from the Vietnam War. When Kim returned home from the hospital, everything was gone. She was also told she could no longer attend school, destroying her dream of one day becoming a doctor. Headaches, hatred, and anger consumed her until she began to spend hours in the library reading books, including the Bible. Through that book, she met Jesus and made him Lord of her life and learned to forgive those who hurt her. Today she is living a happy and healthy life because she chose to stop holding a grudge against those who hurt her and to live in forgiveness.

God wants you and me to forgive people, no matter how badly they hurt us. It would have been best if Esau had forgiven his brother for getting the birthright that he actually gave away for a bowl of stew, but he didn't. The Bible tells us that he held a grudge.

How can you know if you are holding a grudge? Here are three questions I ask myself. 1.) Am I planning evil in my mind? These are not necessarily plans you intend to carry out, but you enjoy thinking about how to get revenge. 2.) Am I running away from the relationship? If your heart is clean, you'll hope that you can eventually work it out. 3.) Do I find myself lying to make this person look worse? If you answered yes to any of these, you may be holding a grudge.

But here's the deal: I'm not sure if we hold grudges or they hold us. You see, the Hebrew word for grudge is *satam*. Sound similar to a name you know? It means "to hate," and it is the root word for *Satan*. We have to be very careful to guard against grudges, because they are really Satan holding on to us and using us. That thought often gets me on my knees asking for forgiveness and being willing to extend it.

Girl Gab: Spend a moment in quiet prayer asking God if there is anyone you need to forgive. Mom, after the silence, ask your daughter if there is a relationship she'd like to talk about. Coach her through the process of truly forgiving and letting go.

XOXO

Bible Blast: Read Genesis 33:1-12

Esau ran to meet Jacob and embraced him; he threw his arms around his neck and kissed him. And they wept.
GENESIS 33:4 (NIV)

Ever wonder how XOXO came to mean "kisses and hugs"? The X symbol was traditionally a symbol for the Christian cross and for the first letter of the Greek word for Christ, *Xristos*. Could there be a more awesome symbol of love than Jesus? The O is believed to be a symbol that looks like two people's arms meeting for a hug.

Imagine the hug between Esau and Jacob. Remember how Esau traded his family inheritance for that pot of stew? What came after that was the grudge. When it had been many years since they last saw one another, Jacob decided to go back to his homeland with his family. As he drew near, he suddenly saw Esau coming to meet them with *four hundred* men! Jacob didn't know if he was going to live or die. He put his children in front of him, hoping Esau would be merciful, and he got down on the ground behind them to bow before his brother. Bowing seven times was commonly associated with a sign of respect for a king. Jacob didn't want to take any chances! But when Esau saw him, he ran to him and hugged him!

Imagine how hard this reunion must have been for both of them. For Esau, Jacob was the man he'd once wanted to kill. And Jacob was hugging the man who had wanted to kill him! But time had allowed the bitter wounds to heal, and the brothers were able to see that their relationship was more important than their real estate. They'd finally learned to share and to love each other.

You might not have an inheritance, but you have real estate. Your room is your "real estate." Your hairbrush is your property. The family computer is shared property. Do you value your relationship with your brothers and/or sisters as more important than those things?

Maybe today would be a good day to share some of Jesus' love and some hugs by sharing what is "yours."

Meditation Moment: Psalm 145:1-10

Study this Book of Instruction continually. Meditate on it day and night so you will be sure to obey everything written in it. Only then will you prosper and succeed in all you do. JOSHUA 1:8

When I say "meditation," you might picture a yoga guru with her legs crossed and her fingers making circles. But that's not real meditation. That's just a fake for something better. True meditation is something God asks you and me to do so that we can feel closer to him and learn from him. I think it is one of the most important skills you can learn as you develop a habit of daily devotions.

What is meditation? I like to say that meditation is when studying the Bible and praying crash into each other. Basically, it's a math equation. Studying + Praying = Meditation Moment.

In our Meditation Moments, you will study a word or concept in the verse. Then you will have time just to pray, asking God for clarity. After that it's time just to sit and wait. When you have a story, thought, idea, prayer, or picture in your head, then you are really meditating! Just like I do when I write a devotion, you may want to write something down as well, so that you can remember what God is speaking to you as you meditate. You might want to scribble right in this book, or choose another journal or notebook for this purpose.

Why not start by meditating on the idea of meditation? Read Joshua 1:8 above with that word in it. Think about it. Pray. And then wait and write.

Girl Gab: Share with each other what you heard from God as you meditated on Joshua 1:8. (And then, Mom, friend me on Facebook so you and your daughter can tell me how the first meditation went. I love to hear about what God says to my reading friends.)

Language Lab: What Is "Grace"?

Bible Blast: Read Romans 6:14-16

Since God's grace has set us free from the law, does that mean we can go on sinning? Of course not! ROMANS 6:15

Girl Gab: Mom, share a time when you really experienced God's grace—when he gave you something you didn't deserve. Daughter, tell your mom what you think grace is. Then, thank God for his grace.

Grace is one of the most powerful words you'll ever encounter. It means "joy, favor, acceptance . . . a favor done without expectation of return. Unearned and unmerited favor." Those definitions are big, fancy words for getting something that we don't deserve.

One of my favorite stories is about a girl who was really, really bad during church one Sunday. (And her dad was the *pastor!*) Twila was disrespectful and made noise on purpose, just to be bad. Her mom drove her straight home after church and sat her on the porch. Twila knew she would be in big trouble when her dad got home. She waited for what seemed like forever. And then he came.

"Twila," said her dad. "Get in the car." She obeyed.

He drove without saying a word, and she was scared. She knew she deserved a big punishment, but where could he be taking her? They stopped at the grocery store. He took her inside and bought the biggest package of Tootsie Rolls you've ever seen. They were Twila's favorite candy of all time.

They drove home in silence. Then her dad took her back to the porch where he opened the bag of candy.

"I want to share these Tootsie Rolls with you, Twila," said her dad. "Come over here and sit closer to me so we can enjoy them together."

After munching for a long time, her dad said, "Twila, I want you to remember this. Today you were bad and you deserved a punishment, but instead I decided that because I love you, I would get you Tootsie Rolls. That's what God calls *grace*. He gives us something we don't deserve."

God's grace is much bigger than any sin you will ever commit. He sent his Son to die on the cross for your sins, and he is always ready to forgive you when you ask for his forgiveness. And the grace God gives us is always better than Tootsie Rolls!

When You Can't Find the Words

Bible Blast: Read 2 Corinthians 10:3-6

Put on salvation as your helmet, and take the sword of the Spirit, which is the word of God. EPHESIANS 6:17

"Dear God, um, like, I don't really know how to, like, pray for this thing, so like, I guess, just, you know, do something. Like, change stuff and make it better and . . . and . . . um, Amen, I think."

Have you ever prayed like that before? Sometimes when we have something really big to pray about, our words get jumbled up. I used to get that way, but not anymore because I've learned about a secret weapon God's given us. Well, it's not really a secret, but it's so amazing and powerful, it's like finding a buried treasure! Here it is: I can take Bible verses and turn them into prayers! And so can you!

Second Corinthians 10 talks about how the weapons Christians use to fight evil aren't the same weapons the world uses. For instance, if a girl who doesn't love Jesus gets hurt by someone, she may think the best way to handle that hurt is to hurt that person back and make her feel terrible for what she did. But if a Christian is hurt by someone, she can go to the Bible to find out what to do. Luke 6:27-28 says, "Love your enemies! Do good to those who hate you. Bless those who curse you. Pray for those who hurt you." See? Christians' weapons are totally different from the world's weapons, and our weapons are more effective.

The Bible is one of the greatest weapons we have. Today's focus verse even tells us that the Bible is a *sword!* The book of Hebrews says that God's Word is alive and powerful. We know that God's Word can show us what to do in tough situations, but did you know that his words are always the right thing to say when you pray? When I don't really know what to pray or how to pray, I take God's words and make them my prayers. If I was hurt by someone and wanted to use Luke's writing to pray, I might say, "Dear Lord, you say to love my enemies. Help me love that girl who hurt me. I want to do good to her and bless her. Show me how."

Isn't that cool? Go ahead and give it a try.

Girl Gab: Mom, show your daughter how to use the concordance in the back of a Bible. Ask her which subject to look up and instruct her how to do it. For instance, if she says, "I'm having trouble waiting to find out where Dad's new job is going to be," look up the word *patience* in the concordance and help her find a Scripture that she can pray as she waits. Then let her help you find a Scripture to pray for something you're dealing with right now.

Megan's Music

Bible Blast: Read Psalm 121

I look up to the mountains—does my help come from there? My help comes from the LORD, who made heaven and earth!
PSALM 121:1-2

Girl Gab: Mom, is there a time when you can remember choosing to worship God even though you didn't feel like it? Tell your daughter about it. Daughter, what are some ways God can help you when you feel blue? How can you help a friend who's feeling that way? Thank God for his help.

Do you know what it means to have "the blues"? It's kind of like feeling blah or lonely or just kind of sad like Eeyore, Winnie the Pooh's donkey friend.

I know a girl named Megan who has chocolate brown hair and dark, smiling eyes. She's a gifted guitarist and singer, and she loves Jesus with her whole heart. When Megan feels "the blues" coming on, she sits in her room and strums her guitar. Sometimes she sings worship songs from church, and other times she writes her own songs to Jesus. To Megan, praising Jesus is more comforting than hugging a big, fluffy pillow.

I'm so proud of Megan because she knows where to get help when she feels kind of blah. She goes to Jesus. According to today's focus verse, our help will never come from any other place. When we're upset, it's not always easy to praise and thank Jesus, is it? It might be easier to eat a ton of food, watch TV, or climb into bed and pull the covers over our heads. But to get real help, we need to turn to him.

If you're like me, you may not have the ability to play the guitar or write songs. I love to put on my headphones and blast one of my favorite worship songs while I sing along. Are you a writer? Take time to write, telling God why you feel so blue. Do you love the outdoors? Go on a hike, and talk to Jesus out loud as if he were walking right beside you. Does art excite you? Grab a canvas or some paper, and create a picture that expresses your emotions. Are you a reader? Pick up the Bible, and start reading some psalms. You can even turn those psalms into prayers. Try Psalm 121!

When we feel like Eeyore, it's super important to keep talking to God. He'll give us strength and perseverance to get past "the blues." He may even teach us something new about himself in the process.

I Have a Dream . . .

Bible Blast: Read Galatians 3:26-28

You are all children of God through faith in Christ Jesus.
GALATIANS 3:26

I have a dream that one day this nation will rise up and live out the true meaning of its creed: "We hold these truths to be self-evident: that all men are created equal."

I have a dream that one day on the red hills of Georgia the sons of former slaves and the sons of former slave owners will be able to sit down together at a table of brotherhood.

I have a dream that one day even the state of Mississippi, a desert state, sweltering with the heat of injustice and oppression, will be transformed into an oasis of freedom and justice. I have a dream that my four children will one day live in a nation where they will not be judged by the color of their skin but by the content of their character. I have a dream today.

Martin Luther King Jr. spoke these words in one of the most famous speeches ever written. Born on this day in 1929, he led the famous March on Washington in 1963. Thousands of people from different races and religions gathered to take a stand against prejudice—"hatred or unfair treatment toward a person or group without cause or reason."[1]

Some prejudices are really obvious, like disliking people with a different skin color. But some prejudices aren't so easy to see. What about a person who thinks poor people aren't hard workers? Have you ever thought someone with a different accent wasn't smart? If you have a negative experience with one person, it can be easy to misjudge an entire group of people.

God created everyone. He doesn't play favorites, and he's more concerned with our hearts than with our outside (see 1 Samuel 16:7). Ask him to show you if you have any prejudices and to replace them with his great love for all people. Remember John 3:16 says that God loved the *world*!

---

1 See www.wordsmyth.net.

Girl Gab: With your mom's help, go online and find a video of Martin Luther King Jr.'s speech at the March on Washington in 1963. It's a little more than fifteen minutes long. Watch the video together. Take some time to thank God for his love for you and everyone.

16 January

Girl Gab: Make a list of your favorite fruits, and get them at the grocery store the next time you're out. Make a point to eat more fruit during these next nine Fruit of the Spirit devo days. You could even try a funky fruit you've never eaten before, like star fruit. When you slice it, it makes little star shapes. So cool!

Fresh Fruit: The Fruit of the Spirit

Bible Blast: Read Romans 8:9-11

The Holy Spirit produces this kind of fruit in our lives: love, joy, peace, patience, kindness, goodness, faithfulness, gentleness, and self-control. There is no law against these things!
GALATIANS 5:22-23

When you hear people mention the "fruit of the Spirit," they're talking about these nine things: love, joy, peace, patience, kindness, goodness, faithfulness, gentleness, and self-control. Picture the fruit of the Spirit as a beautiful, juicy cluster of grapes. Love, joy, peace, and the others are individual grapes in that cluster. Let's consider why God decided to call them fruit.

Have you ever heard the phrase, "You reap what you sow"? Did you know that's from the Bible? In Galatians 6:7-9, God says that whatever you plant, you'll grow. If you plant a watermelon seed, you will get watermelons, not strawberries. When we "plant" the Holy Spirit in our lives, we "grow" love, joy, peace, patience, kindness, goodness, faithfulness, gentleness, and self-control.

Planting the Holy Spirit means that we let him guide us. Look at Galatians 5:16-17. "Let the Holy Spirit guide your lives. Then you won't be doing what your sinful nature craves. The sinful nature wants to do evil, which is just the opposite of what the Spirit wants. And the Spirit gives us desires that are the opposite of what the sinful nature desires. These two forces are constantly fighting each other, so you are not free to carry out your good intentions." So if we just went around doing whatever we felt like doing, we would not have the Spirit's fruit hanging from our vines. We would have things like hatred, worry, stress, selfishness, and laziness growing in our lives. Fruits like those are rotten from the moment they're planted.

As we look at the fruit of the Spirit for the next nine days, ask yourself, "Is this something that grows in my life?" If the answer is no, then go searching for that fruit with all you've got.

Fresh Fruit: Love

Bible Blast: Read Mark 12:28-31

The Holy Spirit produces this kind of fruit in our lives: LOVE, joy, peace, patience, kindness, goodness, faithfulness, gentleness, and self-control. There is no law against these things!
GALATIANS 5:22-23

Let's say you're a big fan of the artist Pablo Picasso. You tell people that you love absolutely everything about Picasso. You rave about him and tell everyone they should love him too. *But . . .* you hate his artwork and criticize it all the time. How can you say you love "absolutely everything" about him, but you hate what he's created?

It's the same with God. If you truly love him, then you will also love the people he's created, including yourself.

The first fruit of the Spirit listed in Galatians 5 is love, and I can see why it's first. The fruit of love is the key to all the others. In Mark 12:28-31, a teacher asked Jesus, "Of all the commandments, which is the most important?" Jesus answered, "You must love the LORD your God with all your heart, all your soul, all your mind, and all your strength.'" Then he told the man, "Love your neighbor as yourself." And in 1 Corinthians 13:13, it says, "Three things will last forever—faith, hope, and love—and the greatest of these is love."

Above everything else, God wants us to display love. If we love God with all our heart, soul, mind, and strength, we're giving him absolutely everything, holding back nothing.

Directly connected to our love for God is our love for others. Look at 1 John 4:20-21: "If someone says, 'I love God,' but hates a Christian brother or sister, that person is a liar; for if we don't love people we can see, how can we love God, whom we cannot see? And he has given us this command: Those who love God must also love their Christian brothers and sisters."

If we're fans of God, we've also got to love his artwork—people! So the next time you're tempted to say, "Oh, I hate her!" or "I just can't stand that girl," you may want to consider the Artist you're criticizing.

Girl Gab:
Daughter, who do you think Jesus is talking about when he says, "Love your neighbor"? Who is your neighbor? Are neighbors just the people who live next door? Mom, tell your daughter what you think it means to "love your neighbor as yourself."

18 January

Girl Gab: Mom, do you think a joyful person has a smile on his or her face 24/7? Daughter, how can Christians be joyful even during really unhappy times? Ask God to make eternal joy more real to you.

Fresh Fruit: Joy

Bible Blast: Read Psalm 4:7-8

The Holy Spirit produces this kind of fruit in our lives: love, JOY, peace, patience, kindness, goodness, faithfulness, gentleness, and self-control. There is no law against these things!
GALATIANS 5:22-23

My friend Janet makes the most amazing chocolate cake with peanut butter icing. When I say it is amazing, you need to understand: It's über-amazing! The first time I ever tasted it Janet brought me one single piece to cheer me up. I was not prepared for my bad day to become one of the best days ever with just one bite! Oh, wow! The chocolate cake was extra moist. The middle tasted like one of my mom's homemade peanut butter eggs. I suddenly felt . . . happier! (In fact, it made me so happy that I wanted you to be happy, too, so I included the recipe in our Wacky Appendix at the back of this book. It's full of wacky things to do together as mom and daughter.)

It seems like a lot of times if I have a good day, my heart feels happy. But if I have a bad day, I don't feel happy. I know God wants us to be joyful all the time, so that must mean that joy and happiness are two different things.

Happiness is something anybody can have. It's a temporary feeling that depends on circumstances. You'll probably feel happy when you taste Janet's cake. But happiness is far from you when you find out your friend is moving away.

Joy is not like that. It's not temporary, and it doesn't change with circumstances. Joy planted by the Holy Spirit is eternal, forever, and never-ending. True joy happens in the heart of a Christian because it springs from knowing that God loves me and wants what is best for me. In Psalm 4:7-8, David sang, "You have given me greater joy than those who have abundant harvests of grain and new wine. In peace I will lie down and sleep, for you alone, O Lord, will keep me safe." David had a lot of bad days. But even then, he slept well because he had joy. Joy doesn't depend on what is going on *around* you. It's based on God's Spirit living *in* you.

Fresh Fruit: Peace

Bible Blast: Read Philippians 4:6-7

The Holy Spirit produces this kind of fruit in our lives: love, joy, PEACE, patience, kindness, goodness, faithfulness, gentleness, and self-control. There is no law against these things!
GALATIANS 5:22-23

Okay, pretend you are at your doctor's office. You've come because you need a cure. You tell him your symptoms: a rash you can't stop itching, a headache that won't stop throbbing, and a mind that won't sleep at night. He thinks and then writes out a prescription:

Medication Name: PEACE
Dosage: Take every second of every day for the rest of your life.
Possible Side Effects: No more worry.

Peace is a cure—a cure for worry. Philippians 4:6-7 says, "Don't worry about anything; instead, pray about everything. Tell God what you need, and thank him for all he has done. Then you will experience God's peace, which exceeds anything we can understand. His peace will guard your hearts and minds as you live in Christ Jesus."

Real peace comes from God. It's not something we can completely understand, but peace is there for us always—if we choose to take it. Philippians 4 is our prescription. Think of God as your Great Physician to cure whatever ails you. All you need to do is tell him your symptoms. You might say: "Dear God, today I need help with my math test. Math is really hard for me, and I am worried that I won't get a good grade. I could also use some help with my friends. We just keep fighting about silly things. These things are causing a lot of worry. Please help me. In Jesus' name, Amen!"

You'll be surprised at just how much better you will feel if you stop worrying and start praying. As you pray more and more, you'll find yourself experiencing more and more of God's peace.

Girl Gab: On separate pieces of paper, each of you write a list of all the things that are worrying you. Then pray about each item on your list for a few moments. When you are done, rip the list into little shreds. Now those things are on God's list, and you can count on him to take care of them.

Girl Gab: Consider
renting a movie
entitled *Faith
like Potatoes*. It's
an amazing true
story about faith.
It involves a lot
of patience—and
potatoes! You'll love
it, and it'll give you a
lot of great things to
gab about as mother
and daughter!

Fresh Fruit: Patience

Bible Blast: Read Proverbs 25:15

The Holy Spirit produces this kind of fruit in our lives: love, joy, peace, PATIENCE, kindness, goodness, faithfulness, gentleness, and self-control. There is no law against these things!
GALATIANS 5:22-23

Potatoes are amazing. One potato can feed one person or many people. How could you feed several people with one potato? You'd have to plant it, which requires some patience. First you have to "chit" the potato by cutting it into pieces and letting them rot for a couple of days. Then you put them in a warm place. After a week, the pieces will grow sprouts or "eyes." Then you plant them in a trench. The potatoes will be ready to harvest in a couple of months. One seed potato may produce up to ten potatoes! If you need to eat right now, one potato will satisfy your hunger. But if you have the time, you could plant that potato and feed your entire family.

"Good things come to those who wait." It's so true—and not just with gardening. Most of the world isn't willing to wait for anything. If people have to wait too long for a meal at a restaurant, they demand their money back. Instead of waiting until they have the cash to buy something, people use a credit card so they can have it right away.

When we're impatient, we're telling the world that we deserve better. It's really a way of saying, "I'm too important to wait." That ugly thing called pride starts taking over. But waiting isn't always bad. It often produces *more* for us, not *less*.

This year, my son needed to have an operation that cost $15,000 dollars. We didn't have $15,000, and our insurance company had never paid for this specific surgery. We were worried, but we decided to pray. It took a lot of patience, but one month later we got a letter saying they had approved the payment. Better than giving us the money, God took the bill away entirely! He does great things like that when we pray and wait patiently.

Fresh Fruit: Kindness

Bible Blast: Read Ephesians 4:29-32

The Holy Spirit produces this kind of fruit in our lives: love, joy, peace, patience, KINDNESS, goodness, faithfulness, gentleness, and self-control. There is no law against these things!
GALATIANS 5:22-23

Girl Gab: Plan your own random act of kindness. What act of kindness can you do for someone? Does someone need his driveway shoveled? Could you take an ill woman's dog for a walk? Is there a mom who really needs a night out but doesn't have the money for a babysitter? Plan your act of kindness and follow through on the plan. Just something simple can make a big difference.

When my son, Rob, was in high school, he had to do a random act of kindness as an assignment. He and some of his buddies decided to bake cookies, knock on doors, and give them away to brighten people's day. At one of the houses, a middle-aged mom and her teenaged daughter were home. The woman could not believe that three high school boys were doing something kind.

"Why are you doing this?" she demanded.

"It's actually an assignment from our school, Grace Prep," said one of them.

"We just want to show God's love in a practical way," said another.

She grabbed the cookies and slammed the door.

A week later, a letter arrived at the school with an apology from the woman. You see, a few weeks earlier her husband and the father of her teenaged daughter had died. That very morning she and her daughter had prayed, "God, if you really see us and our pain, please show us in some simple way today." It was a desperate cry for hope. And God heard it. The woman just wanted to say thanks and to note that "no one shows kindness like that these days," so she knew that what they had done was from God.

Being kind to other people is a way of recycling God's kindness to us. Ephesians 4:31-32 says that we need to "get rid of all bitterness, rage, anger, harsh words, and slander, as well as all types of evil behavior. Instead, be kind to each other, tenderhearted, forgiving one another, just as God through Christ has forgiven you."

In a world where many people are mean, kindness really stands out.

Fresh Fruit: Goodness

Bible Blast: Read Genesis 1:1-10

The Holy Spirit produces this kind of fruit in our lives: love, joy, peace, patience, kindness, GOODNESS, faithfulness, gentleness, and self-control. There is no law against these things! GALATIANS 5:22-23

The first few days when our earth was created were a pretty big deal! Basically God had six amazing days. He invented planets, sunshine, zebras, and the crazy Blue-footed Booby birds. (They're real. I promise.) He romped with giraffes, soaked his toes in the first few waves of the earth's oceans, and viewed the first-ever sunset and sunrise. He figured out how to make living beings out of the tiniest of atoms and created his best friend, Adam. And then, he said, "What I've created is good."

Just "good"? "Good" seems like such a blah way to describe the creation of the whole universe. I mean, macaroni and cheese is good. The world and all its creatures are *great* or *awesome* or *totally and incredibly amazing!*

I don't think when God said it was "good" that he was saying, "Well. That's okay. I'll just go with that." He had used great care and precision in crafting each and every cell. Our world was a perfect, complete place where God and his creation were together all the time, with no misunderstandings or problems coming between them. It was completely good. God was saying, "I did my best. This is 'good.'"

Do you do your best? When you are given an assignment from school, do you put your whole heart into it so that it's "good"? When your mom or dad asks you to clean your room, do you dig in with the vacuum cleaner and dust rag so that the finished job is "good"?

Goodness means "done well."

Take some time today to write down a few things you each do really well, and a few you each want to start doing better. Some of the things you think of will already be good. Other areas are ones you can aspire to "be good." Give yourself some encouragement, and identify an area in which you can start working to improve right away.

Fresh Fruit: Faithfulness

Bible Blast: Read Romans 1:20-22

The Holy Spirit produces this kind of fruit in our lives: love, joy, peace, patience, kindness, goodness, FAITHFULNESS, gentleness, and self-control. There is no law against these things!
GALATIANS 5:22-23

I was walking through New York City with a group of students from Grace Prep, the Christian high school my husband started. We were there simply to pray with people. I was asking God who I should pray with when I saw a teenaged boy and his girlfriend who looked kind of, well, unhappy.

"Hi, guys," I said. "My name is Dannah. Do you guys have anything you need prayer for? I'd love to pray for you."

"I don't believe in God," said the guy. "Why do you? You can't see him. You have no evidence that he exists."

I wasn't prepared for that. Most people in the New York subway are really hungry for prayer when we approach them. They love it. They don't get angry like this guy did. I didn't know what to say, so I prayed quietly for help. Almost without thinking, I said, "Do you believe the wind is real?"

"Of course," he said. When I asked why, he said, "Because you can see it."

"No, you can't," I said. "You can't see the wind. It is invisible. But you can see what it touches. The trees bend, and flowers dance when the wind touches them. I can see God because I see the lives he touches. I know he's real."

The boy's girlfriend asked me if I would pray for them.

My friend's dad says, "Faith is looking at the invisible and seeing something." It takes faith to trust God and serve him. Believing in God is kind of like believing in the wind. Even though you can't see the actual wind, you know it's there and you believe wind exists.

Being faithful can mean being filled with faith. How have you seen God in other people's lives—and in your own? Remembering what God has done can help you be filled with faith.

Girl Gab: Talk about who you have seen God touch, helping you to believe that he exists. Take a moment to write that person a quick note of encouragement for boosting your faith today.

24 January

Fresh Fruit: Gentleness

Bible Blast: Read 1 Peter 3:14-15

The Holy Spirit produces this kind of fruit in our lives: love, joy, peace, patience, kindness, goodness, faithfulness, GENTLENESS, and self-control. There is no law against these things! GALATIANS 5:22-23

Girl Gab: Talk about how you can share the gospel of Jesus in a gentle, but truthful, way. Make a point to try to be gentle toward everyone you meet today.

Have you ever seen a toddler "pet" a cat? Usually, it's more of a slapping motion causing the irritated cat to hiss and escape to an out-of-reach windowsill. If the child had been gentle, the cat would have probably liked being touched and spent a little time arching his back for a good rubbing. Instead, the cat runs, and the toddler cries.

Some Christians forget about gentleness when they share Jesus. I heard of a girl who told her friend that she was going to hell if she didn't believe in Jesus. She could have been gentler. Maybe she could have told her friend how she feels loved by Jesus, invited her to a fun event at church, or offered to pray for her. Those would be gentle ways to share Jesus, and that is how God desires for us to share our faith.

Gentleness isn't a weak or wimpy thing. Just because someone is gentle does not mean she's not strong. Actually, God calls us to be strong in the Lord and in his mighty power (see Ephesians 6:10) even though we are also called to be gentle.

It's important to tell people what you believe, and that takes a lot of strength and courage. But you need to do it with gentleness. "Even if you suffer for doing what is right, God will reward you for it. So don't worry or be afraid of their threats. Instead, you must worship Christ as Lord of your life. And if someone asks about your Christian hope, always be ready to explain it. But do this in a gentle and respectful way" (1 Peter 3:14-16).

Cats don't like to be pushed around, and neither do people. Speak gentle words, and treat all people, unbelievers and friends and family, with respect and love. This will be much more effective in bringing them to Christ than if you try to yell or scare the truth into their hearts.

Fresh Fruit: Self-Control

Bible Blast: Read Proverbs 16:32

The Holy Spirit produces this kind of fruit in our lives: love, joy, peace, patience, kindness, goodness, faithfulness, gentleness, and SELF-CONTROL. There is no law against these things!
GALATIANS 5:22-23

Did you know that kids have less self-control today than they did in the 1940s? Waaaaayyyy back then, some experimenters asked girls about the age of seven to stand still for as long as possible. Almost all of them were able to stand still for as long as they wanted, while five-year-olds could only stand still for three minutes. In more recent years, some people re-created the experiment, and guess what? Seven-year-olds could only stand still for about three minutes, like the five-year-olds of the past. Today's seven-year-olds don't have as much self-control as kids that age once had. That's not good!

Self-control helps us our whole lives. When I was in middle school, self-control helped me not to cheat on tests. (It would have been easier to cheat.) When I was in high school, self-control kept me from going to bad parties. (It would have been fun to go.) When I was in college, self-control kept me from dating way too many boys. (It was popular to date that way.) Now, self-control helps me to be a good mom and wife.

You can practice self-control today. You can sit quietly and wait for your mom when she's taking too long to shop. You can wait until after dinner to eat those cookies. These opportunities build your self-control "muscle" for bigger things that will come your way.

People who give in to every single desire are not strong. If there's a plate of cookies on my table, and every time I walk by I eat one, that's weakness. A girl who has the ability to say no is a strong person. There's a lot of power and strength in that little word *no*. When you say no to a desire that's not God's best for you, you're saying that you're not going to give in because you know that God has something better.

Girl Gab:
Daughter, just for fun, while Mom is cooking dinner, let her time you to see how long you can stand still. Mom, tell your daughter one area where she is strong because she has self-control. Talk about it, and thank God together for helping her develop that self-control muscle.

You Can Do It!

Bible Blast: Read Genesis 21:1-7

All glory to God, who is able, through his mighty power at work within us, to accomplish infinitely more than we might ask or think. EPHESIANS 3:20

Girl Gab: Mom, can you recall a miracle that you've witnessed or heard about? Tell your daughter about it. Daughter, it is said that someone who has never seen a flower would think a dandelion was a great miracle. Go find a flower or plant, and bring it to your mom. Study it, and discuss how it recalls a miracle of God's creation.

Recently, I learned about a man from New Zealand named Craig Marsh. He was in great pain and had to have surgery on his stomach. The surgeons discovered a horrible cancer. Eventually, Craig had to have so many stomach surgeries, he couldn't digest food properly. Eating was painful so he ate as little as possible. Soon he began wasting away. He was not expected to live long.

One day, some men gathered around Craig and began to pray for him. For many hours they prayed, while Craig lay on the floor with his stomach making strange noises. Then, suddenly he was hungry. That was the first miracle. You see, his stomach no longer produced the acid that makes a person feel hungry. Craig had not felt hunger for months. His friends took him to eat. Only a few hours later, Craig wanted to eat again—and again and again and again. Doctors were amazed, and they are still perplexed. It's been more than a decade since God healed Craig, whose stomach functions as if it were totally normal. God can do anything.

The Bible is full of stories about God doing amazing things. For instance, God made Abraham a father at the age of one hundred! That was a miracle. It's a greater miracle that he made Sarah's body function properly to produce a child when she was ninety! Every single baby born is a beautiful work of God, but creating a baby with two old bodies is a miracle!

Abraham and Sarah's miracle didn't stop with having the baby. Next they had to raise the baby as old parents. In obedience, they did it through the strength that God offered to them.

Doing the impossible is God's everyday business. Big, impossible things don't seem too difficult when you consider that you can do "everything" through Christ's strength. What difficult thing do you need to do?

Meditation Moment: Psalm 139

O LORD, you have examined my heart and know everything about me. You know when I sit down or stand up. You know my thoughts even when I'm far away. You see me when I travel and when I rest at home. You know everything I do. You know what I am going to say even before I say it, LORD. You go before me and follow me. You place your hand of blessing on my head. Such knowledge is too wonderful for me, too great for me to understand! PSALM 139:1-6

Sometimes we don't let people know us completely because we are afraid they won't like us or accept us if they do. That can never be the case with God. He knows everything about us. *Everything?* Yep, everything. Even how many hairs are on your head (see Matthew 10:30). You don't even know that about yourself!

Okay, it's time to muscle up and meditate. Read and reread Psalm 139:1-6, thinking about what it really says. Next, take some time to pray, using the ideas in this passage to help you praise and thank God. Then wait for God to give you a story, picture, thought, or idea to write down. You can do it!

Girl Gab: Share with each other what God spoke into your heart as you meditated on his Word today. What do you need to do in response to that?

Keep Asking

Bible Blast: Read Genesis 25:19-26

Never stop praying. 1 THESSALONIANS 5:17

In 2001, I started to have endless thoughts about Africa, especially while I was praying. I didn't even know anyone who lived on that continent, but I was suddenly burdened or called to pray for the countries of Africa. I could not stop being obsessed with the many needs of the people there, so I finally went to my mom and my husband. I asked them to pray for God to open the door for me to do what God wanted me to do in Africa. The calling became so powerful that I begged God to show me his plan before December of that year, but he did not. Did I stop praying? No. I kept on praying. Another entire year went by before December of 2002, when I received an e-mail I will never forget. It began, "Greetings in the name of our Lord and Savior Jesus Christ." It was a request to write a curriculum to teach purity and to share the message of salvation in the government schools of Zambia, a country in Africa. The man had been praying for someone like me to come, and I had been praying for a way to go to Africa. Finally, God answered our prayers and helped us find each other. Together we reached 75,000 students with the message of purity and with the Good News of salvation through Jesus. I'm so glad that I kept praying!

Look at Genesis 25:20. How old was Isaac when he first married Rebekah? He was forty. We find out in Genesis 25:26 how old he was when he finally had a baby with Rebekah. He was sixty. So how many years did he pray for a baby? Twenty years! That's a long time to keep on praying, but that's just what God wants you and me to do.

Sometimes God doesn't answer us right away because he wants us to have a better understanding of what we need or what we are asking for. Sometimes he waits so we can really be grateful for the gift when it comes along. Other times God makes us wait because we simply are not ready and we need to mature. Only God knew the reasons Isaac needed to wait. But while he waited, Isaac kept on praying.

Amazing Animals: The Cheetah

Bible Blast: Read 1 Corinthians 9:23-25

Don't you realize that in a race everyone runs, but only one person gets the prize? So run to win! 1 CORINTHIANS 9:24

Can you tell the difference between a cheetah and a leopard? A leopard has a thick, muscular build. The cheetah is long and lean. A leopard has white lining under its eyes to help it see better for nighttime hunting. The cheetah has black lines running from its eyes down the sides of its nose and mouth to help keep the sun out of its eyes for better daytime hunting. Leopards have larger heads and ears than cheetahs, because cheetahs have small heads for better aerodynamics when they run. The cheetah has black spots all over its body. The leopard's fur pattern has spots that are outlined in black, but are not solid spots.

The cheetah is the fastest land animal God created. It can run up to seventy-five miles per hour. That's faster than most legal speed limits! When an animal does something really special, I love to see exactly how God designed that animal to be so unique.

Cheetahs have long legs that help them cover more ground more quickly than any other animal. Their claws aren't retractable (except for one hunting claw) like a dog's are, so they're always ready to grip the ground for running. The cheetah's tail is long and strong with a flattened end. This specially designed tail helps the cheetah steer and stay balanced when it turns at high speeds. Enlarged nostrils, sinuses, lungs, and heart allow the cheetah to take in more oxygen when sprinting.

God truly designed the cheetah to run. He designed us to run, too, but instead of running after a gazelle, we run after a different prize—bringing people to Christ. When the apostle Paul wrote 1 Corinthians 9:24, he was talking about a race to bring people to Jesus. Part of giving your life to Jesus is running as fast as you can to help those who don't know him. Just like the cheetah, you should always have your feet ready to sprint to anyone who needs Christ (see Ephesians 6:15). With his help, you'll be able to cover a lot of ground.

Girl Gab: Find video clips of a cheetah in action. Notice how its body moves, especially the tail. Are you ready to run this race of bringing people to the knowledge of Jesus Christ?

Mom, I'll bet there has been a time in your life when God really did what he promised you he would do. Share that with your daughter. Daughter, maybe you need faith that God will heal you or someone you love. Maybe you need faith that God will either give you a friend or be a friend. Ask your mom to pray for you about a situation in which you need some extra faith.

Faith in the Utterly Impossible

Bible Blast: Read Genesis 15:1-6

Even when there was no reason for hope, Abraham kept hoping—believing that he would become the father of many nations. For God had said to him, "That's how many descendants you will have!" ROMANS 4:18

A few years ago, God called my family to adopt a thirteen-year-old girl from China named Qiu Yun (Cho-yoon), which means Autumn Cloud. She was almost fourteen years old and only months away from being without a family for the rest of her life. We felt God leading us to adopt her. The only problem was that we needed $25,000 within just a few weeks. A family friend gave us $12,000 to get started, but we still needed $13,000. It seemed impossible! With no hope other than hope in what God can do, we began to pray for $13,000. One day, my accountant called and told me that my tax records were messed up. That sounded like awful news, but we kept praying. Later, my accountant called back and said, "Good news. The IRS owes you $13,060.00." We had the check within a few weeks. In August of 2007, Autumn Gresh became a part of our family.

Abram was in a similar situation in Genesis 15. When Abram died he would pass all his belongings on to his servant Eliezar. Though Abram loved Eliezar very much, he wanted a son to carry on the family name. It seemed "utterly impossible" that he'd ever have a child since he was already very old, but God came to him and promised him that he would. And Abram believed God's promise against all hope.

Romans 4:3 says, "Abraham believed God, and God counted him as righteous." It was faith that made Abraham right before God. Even though going to church, reading your Bible, and praying are important, those are only outward actions. They don't make us right with God. Only faith—that God is who he says he is, that he will do what he has promised, and that he has saved us by Christ's blood—makes us right with God.

So what about you? Do you have faith that God can do the utterly impossible?

Kickin' Kraft: Ebenezer (Not the Scrooge)

Bible Blast: Read 1 Samuel 7:7-12

Samuel then took a large stone and placed it between the towns of Mizpah and Jeshanah. He named it Ebenezer (which means "the stone of help"), for he said, "Up to this point the LORD has helped us!" 1 SAMUEL 7:12

Kickin' Kraft:
Excellent Ebenezer Stones!

(Check out p. 367 for a great mother-daughter craft that helps reinforce today's devo!)

I've been writing in a journal since I was about nine years old. (I called it a diary back then.) Every time I look through one of my old journals, it's a big ol' trip down memory lane. I giggle when I look at the "cool" words I used to say. I feel a little twinge of pain when I read about some of the arguments my friends and I used to get into. I feel warm fuzzies when I read about the different things my parents and I used to do together. And I roll my eyes when I read about the crushes I had. But the best part about that trip down memory lane is seeing how God helped me through all the circumstances from the time I was a tween until now. That kind of remembering helps me have faith in difficult times, because I know if God helped me then, he'll keep on giving me the strength I need now.

I feel as if every page of my journal is an Ebenezer stone, like the one Samuel set up that's mentioned in today's focus verse. At the top of every page of my journal, I could write, "Up to this point, the Lord has helped me!" One line from the song "Come Thou Fount of Every Blessing" says, "Here I raise my Ebenezer; Here by Thy great help I've come." Now you know what that means: "Right now I remember that God's help has brought me here." Cool, huh?

Take a minute and think of "Ebenezer stones" in your life. Those are the times when you saw God provide for you. He helps us with healing, money, food, safety, joy, problem solving, inspiration, relationships, and in many, many other ways. Can you think of at least three "Ebenezers"? Good! You're going to need them for today's Kickin' Kraft!

Girl Gab: Okay, girls! Time to brainstorm! Make a list of at least ten things you can do to serve others. Think about your school, church, family, neighbors, and friends. Now put your love into action!

Big Love!

Bible Blast: Read John 13:31-38

I am giving you a new commandment: Love each other. Just as I have loved you, you should love each other. JOHN 13:34

"I love you."

"*Je t'aime.*"

"*Te amo.*"

Professing your love in any language is a beautiful thing, isn't it? Let's face it. We use the word *love* all the time.

"I totally loved that movie!"

"Fluffy, I love you! You're the best cat in the world!"

"I *love* homework!"

Okay. That last one may have been a stretch, but we do say that we love lots of things. Saying "I love you" might be easy, but showing it can be a lot harder.

I can't find anywhere in Scripture where Jesus says, "Just tell people you love them. That's enough." God wants us to put hands and feet to those words!

Today's Bible Blast is so interesting because Jesus tells the disciples how the world will know they love him. Apparently, people will be so shocked by the extravagant love Christians will demonstrate to one another that they'll know it must be God that helps the believers love that way!

So now we know we need to love each other and that our love will be a witness to those around us. But how do we love so extravagantly? Do we send lots of candy in heart-shaped boxes? Or write poems to our BFFs? Should we constantly hug everyone?

John 13:34 answers our question. Jesus said, "Just as I have loved you, you should love each other." How did Jesus love us? He served. Look at Mark 10:45. It says, "Even the Son of Man came not to be served but to serve others and to give his life as a ransom for many."

If Jesus came to serve, and he wants us to love others by serving them, what are some ways we can do that? That's what you'll be talking about in today's Girl Gab!

Get Your "Phil" of Laughter

Bible Blast: Read Luke 12:22-31

She is clothed with strength and dignity, and she laughs without fear of the future. PROVERBS 31:25

Punxsutawney. It's pronounced "punks-a-tah-nee," and it's a town in Pennsylvania. It is a small town with businesses, restaurants, and parks just like any other town, but it has one thing no other town has: Phil, the groundhog.

Since the 1800s, folks in Punxy have carried on a tradition of watching this groundhog come out of his hole on February 2, Groundhog Day. The story goes that if he sees his shadow on that day, winter's *not* over yet. If he doesn't see it, winter's over, and spring is on its way. On February 2nd, Punxsutawney Phil is *the* groundhog to watch. If you can't get there to see him in person—I mean, in rodent—don't worry. You can watch him come out of his hole live on TV.

As it turns out, Phil's shadow isn't the most secure way of forecasting the weather, but a lot of people have a great time celebrating that furry little guy.

So many people want to know what's going to happen in the future. They don't want any surprises, but a woman of God doesn't live that way. As our focus verse for today says, "she laughs without fear of the future." When we live a life of faith in God, there's no need to look for someone to predict the future. The Bible tells us over and over not to worry, and Matthew 6:34 specifically tells us not to worry about the future: "Don't worry about tomorrow, for tomorrow will bring its own worries. Today's trouble is enough for today."

When the woman in Proverbs 31 is laughing "without fear of the future," it means she's joyful about what *is* happening now instead of obsessing about what *might* happen in the future.

Is there something you have been worried about recently? You probably won't find the answer in a groundhog, but you could find some peace if you just focus with joy on today and tell God that whatever he has for tomorrow will be okay, as long as you have him.

Girl Gab: Mom, say this tongue twister as fast as you can three times in a row: "How much wood could a woodchuck chuck if a woodchuck could chuck wood?"

All right, Daughter, now it's your turn. Now both of you do it again while holding onto the tip of your tongue with your fingers. As you laugh together, remember God wants you to be a woman who laughs in spite of what the future may hold.

Daughter, put a blindfold on your mom. Make sure she can't see! Now hold her hands and guide her through some of the rooms of the house. See how well you can guide her with your words and actions. Mom, if you feel very trusting, let your daughter guide you up or down the steps! Thank God for the guidance of the Holy Spirit.

No Fear

Bible Blast: Read Acts 16:6-8

Coming to the borders of Mysia, they headed north for the province of Bithynia, but again the Spirit of Jesus did not allow them to go there. ACTS 16:7

Nineteen-year-old Janet was a missionary in the Ukraine. Her experience there was amazing and difficult, all at the same time. The Ukrainian people were beautiful and unforgettable, but it was hard to be away from family. Janet decided to take a break and fly home for a couple of weeks. While she was there, Janet was praying and asking God if she should return to the mission field.

The day came for her return, and Janet still had not felt clear leading from God about what she should do. But she got up, packed her bags, and went to the airport. As she walked around still feeling unsure, she heard her name called out over the loudspeaker: "Janet Harding, please pick up a courtesy phone." Worried that something was wrong, she went to the nearest phone and picked it up. On the other end was the voice of her mom. "Sweetie, you don't need to worry. Just take a step onto the plane. If that seems right, then sit down. If that seems right, then fly back to the Ukraine. You don't need to worry or be afraid because God knows you want to do his will, and he loves you too much to let you go the wrong way."

With new courage and comfort, Janet got on the plane and flew back to the mission field. There she did great things for God with the Ukrainian people for another year.

Today's focus verse should help Christians get rid of their fear. It's encouraging that Paul and Silas tried to go somewhere but the Holy Spirit didn't let them, so they went somewhere else. To me that says, "If you love God and obey him, you don't need to be afraid of the next step for your life. He will stop you from going somewhere he doesn't need you to be."

God doesn't want us to go through life full of fear and anxiety about where we're going or what we're doing. Walk with confidence, knowing his Spirit guides those who love him.

Kickin' Kraft: Anne and Helen

Bible Blast: Read John 1:1-5

He uncovers mysteries hidden in darkness; he brings light to the deepest gloom. JOB 12:22

Johanna (Anne) Mansfield Sullivan was born in 1866 and had an extremely difficult childhood. Her mom was really sick all the time, and her alcoholic father was abusive. By the time she was seven years old, Anne was almost blind because of an untreated eye infection. She lived in darkness. Her mom died when Anne was just eight, and then her dad abandoned her and her brother, Jimmie. The two children were sent to live in a place like an orphanage. While they were there, Jimmie died. Her last hope was getting enrolled in Perkins School for the Blind in Massachusetts. There, she learned very quickly. Before long she could read, write, and use sign language, eventually graduating close to the top of her class. Then she received an invitation that would eventually make her famous.

The Keller family asked Anne Sullivan if she would come and work with their daughter, Helen. Maybe you've heard of Helen Keller. Helen was deaf and blind. She was wild and hard to control. It took some time for Anne to gain Helen's confidence and trust, but once she did, Helen finally learned how to communicate and enjoy life. Anne would run water on one of Helen's hands while she signed the word *water* in her other hand to help Helen understand. Because of Anne's work, Helen was able to live a long, fulfilling life of writing, traveling, and speaking. The movie *The Miracle Worker* tells the story of Anne Sullivan and Helen Keller.

Imagine being like Helen, never seeing the bright sunshine and blue sky on a clear day or hearing the birds chirp on a spring morning. Sometimes, we may feel like we'll always have gloomy, cloudy days—we might be sad about a fight we had with a friend or a bad grade on a quiz. But our focus verse says that God "brings light to the deepest gloom." We need to be patient, but we can count on him to rescue us as he did both Anne and Helen. We'll see the sunshine again!

Kickin' Kraft:
A Slammin' Sunglasses Case!

(Check out p. 368 for a great mother-daughter craft that helps reinforce today's devo!)

Girl Gab: When people around you are negative, do you join them, or do you ask God for help? Are you a complainer? Ask God to wash away the grumpy germs and replace them with contagious thankfulness!

The Grumpy Germ

Bible Blast: Read Exodus 16:2-3, 13-15, 31

They began to speak against God and Moses. "Why have you brought us out of Egypt to die here in the wilderness?" they complained. "There is nothing to eat here and nothing to drink. And we hate this horrible manna!" NUMBERS 21:5

Cecelia is a happy girl. She smiles a lot and always says *please* and *thank you*—until she hangs out with Lily. Lily complains . . . a lot. The last time Lily came to Cecelia's house to watch a movie, Cecelia found herself whining about the popcorn and yelling at her brother. She even scowled at her dad when he asked her to turn the volume down a little while he was on the phone.

After Lily went home, Cecelia and her dad had a talk:

Dad: "Cecelia, do you have anything you want to say?"

Cecelia: "Yeah. I'm really sorry for being such a rude whiner tonight."

Dad: "We forgive you, but why do you think you acted like that?"

Cecelia: "I don't know . . . maybe because Lily complains all the time. I feel like when I'm with her I have to complain too."

Dad: "But you don't have to be like that. You can choose to be different. Honey, complaining is like a contagious grumpy germ. When one person has it, she can easily spread it to others. But do you know what else is contagious?"

Cecelia: "What?"

Dad: "Thankfulness. The next time you're with Lily or someone like her, try to let your thankful heart be louder than her whining."

The Israelites complained almost all the time. As you read today in the book of Exodus, they complained that they didn't have food, so God provided meat and manna for them. Then Numbers 21 reports that they complained about the manna! Moses was constantly dealing with negative words from the people he was leading from captivity in Egypt, but he didn't join in their complaining. When he got tired of their whining, he went to the Lord and asked for help.

Amazing Animals: Bolas Spiders

Bible Blast: Read Genesis 1:20-25

God said, "Let the earth produce every sort of animal, each producing offspring of the same kind—livestock, small animals that scurry along the ground, and wild animals." And that is what happened. GENESIS 1:24

Imagine a cowgirl up on her horse chasing after a calf. She lifts up her lasso, swings it around and around, releases it, and—*bam*! She catches a calf! It's an amazing skill that is a lot harder than it looks. Professional cattle ropers practice using lassos for years to perfect the art.

But there's one tiny creation that's born knowing how to use a lasso. It's called a bolas spider. They're named after a weapon called a "bolas"—a rope with heavy balls on the ends of it. When a hunter or cowboy throws it at an animal, it wraps around the animal's legs to force it to stop running.

Bolas spiders have a favorite meal: moths. (Yuck, right?) Instead of weaving a web for the moth to fly into and get caught, the bolas spider makes a long string with a sticky ball on the end of it. The ball has a special scent that moths totally love. When the moth comes flying near, the bolas spider carefully swings the sticky ball and sticks its prey.

It is truly one of the most unbelievable things I've ever seen an animal do. When I think about the bolas spider, I wonder, *Why didn't God just make all spiders do the same thing, with the same kinds of webs? Why did he make a spider that catches moths like that?* I guess the answer is, Why not?

God isn't just a creator; he's *the* Creator. The One who creates. I absolutely believe he found perfect joy in creating each animal—from the ginormous blue whale to the tiny bolas spider. If you had the opportunity to create anything and everything, wouldn't you have fun with it? Wouldn't you want to create a spider that throws a rope to catch moths? Or an elephant that uses an extremely long nose to grab food? Or a dog that can learn how to shake hands and roll over?

God loves his creation. The little bolas spider makes me say, "Thank you, God, for your creativity! I totally enjoy it!"

Girl Gab: You probably know what I want you to do, don't you? That's right! Grab your mom and head to the computer. You can find short videos of the bolas spider in action. You won't believe your eyes! Thank God for his creativity!

You Can Do Anything

Bible Blast: Read Joshua 6:1-20

Not that I was ever in need, for I have learned how to be content with whatever I have. I know how to live on almost nothing or with everything. I have learned the secret of living in every situation, whether it is with a full stomach or empty, with plenty or little. For I can do everything through Christ, who gives me strength. PHILIPPIANS 4:11-13

When Ben Underwood was three, doctors had to remove his eyes to save him from cancer. Imagine the incredible grief in his mom's heart when Ben awoke from the surgery and cried, "Mommy, I can't see."

His mom bravely responded, "No, you can't see with your eyes, but you still have your ears and your nose and your mouth. You'll learn to use them instead." And Ben did.

Ben learned to use echolocation. By clicking his tongue and then listening, he could hear the echoes bounce off objects to help him determine where and what they were. His skill was so sharp that he could tell you exactly *what* he was walking around. You can see video footage of Ben online as he skateboards, wins pillow fights, and even plays video games using his gift.

Sadly, Ben's cancer returned, and he died when he was just sixteen. Still his mom was able to rejoice that he was with Jesus in heaven. In a letter to the world, she said, "God has used Ben's life in such a way that his life has blessed people of every walk of life, all around the world." That's because of the joy with which Ben clicked his tongue. It was like praise to his God!

Ben was a lot like Joshua, who conquered a well-fortified city with just the blast of trumpets. In some places the city had walls up to twenty-five feet high and twenty feet thick. But the loud praise from the trumpets brought the walls down! God used this to set the stage to win every other battle that Israel needed to win to gain the Promised Land.

Sometimes the great things God wants you to do require you to step up and act in faith. What does God want you to do today? Why not start with just some praise?

Mirror, Mirror on the Wall . . .

Bible Blast: Read James 1:19-25

If you listen to the word and don't obey, it is like glancing at your face in a mirror. You see yourself, walk away, and forget what you look like. JAMES 1:23-24

Imagine that there was a church where all the people were on their knees. They all scooted to church on their knees, and the pastor was on his knees as he began to speak to them. He said, "Church, I've discovered something amazing! I have *legs*!" And he very shakily stood up on his feet and showed everyone how he could walk on legs. The people were absolutely shocked at the sight of their pastor standing up so tall. The pastor said, "And you have legs too! Come on! Try to stand up!" The people were scared and nervous, but they helped each other stand up and were very happy to discover that they had legs. They jumped up and down and danced around on their new legs. The pastor then prayed, "Dear God, thank you for our legs! Help us use our legs every day to serve you. Amen." The people all said, "Amen," and began to walk out of the church waving good-bye to the pastor. But as they left, one by one, they dropped back down on their knees again and scooted out while the pastor shook his head in disbelief and frustration.

The focus verse for today says that people who read God's Word and don't obey what it teaches are just like a girl who looks in a mirror and then forgets what she looks like. Or maybe the girl learns from the Bible that God wants her to do something, and she gets excited about it and tells other people about it but never actually does it—just like the people in that church who wouldn't keep using their legs.

If God tells you something, it's a good thing. His guidance and direction are meant to change your life. His Word is meant to make you more like him, to cause you to fall more in love with him. One thing that makes a woman strong is when she knows God's Word and does what it says. She doesn't forget who she is, but she pays attention to God's truth.

Girl Gab: Daughter, get up right now and go look in a mirror for two seconds, then come back. Go ahead. Now, tell your mom what you look like. Tell her what color your hair is and whether it's rumpled or neat. Tell her the color of your eyes and if they look happy or sad today. Describe how you look right now. Wouldn't it be silly if you glanced in the mirror and then totally forgot what you look like? Let's promise not to be like that when we "glance" at God's Word.

9 February

Girl Gab: Take time to pray for each person on your list. Over the next few weeks, remind each other to pray for these three friends and encourage one another as you watch for opportunities to share Jesus' love with them.

Language Lab: What Is "The Great Commission"?

Bible Blast: Read Matthew 28:16-20

Go and make disciples of all the nations, baptizing them in the name of the Father and the Son and the Holy Spirit. Teach these new disciples to obey all the commands I have given you. And be sure of this: I am with you always, even to the end of the age.
MATTHEW 28:19-20

When I was about your age, my mom often handed me a big, round, light blue glass bowl. Then she would say, "Go pick some of Grandma's strawberries for me, so I can make strawberry shortcake." Oh, I loved that job! I loved going to Grandma Barker's strawberry patch for my mom. Basically, when my mom assigned me to pick strawberries, she was giving me a commission. A commission is something we're told to do.

After Jesus was crucified and rose from the dead, he saw his disciples one last time on earth and gave them the great commission. We read about it in Matthew 28:18-20. He told them to go everywhere they could and teach people about him and make sure the new believers got baptized.

The great commission isn't just about missionaries going to another country. The great commission is for every Christian, in every place. So it is your commission too. When Jesus said "make disciples of all nations," that included potential disciples in your neighborhood, school, and family. Everywhere you go, there are people who need to learn the truth about salvation through Jesus. You can fulfill the great commission, no matter where you are or who you are.

Make a list of three people you would like to see become disciples of Jesus Christ:

1.
2.
3.

Sing a New Song

Bible Blast: Read 1 Samuel 16:14-23

He has given me a new song to sing, a hymn of praise to our God. Many will see what he has done and be amazed. They will put their trust in the LORD. PSALM 40:3

This morning I was in a bad mood. I decided to go out to my old childhood home and take a walk on the gravel road. Incredible! The only sound I could hear out there were birds. Dozens of different kinds of birds chirped in a chorus that would have made Mozart jealous. I stood for a moment and just listened to each distinct note and sound. Twenty minutes later, I left feeling radically, totally, unbelievably giddy.

Did you know that music *can* actually change your mood and make you healthier? It had that effect on Saul. Whenever Saul was depressed and angry, the young shepherd David was called upon to play his harp—and Saul became happy.

In the 1970s, botanist Dorothy L. Retallack did a study of the effect of music on plants by placing them near music and monitoring the results. She found that the plants exposed to happy and pleasant music tended to thrive and grow toward the music. Plants exposed to noise and "negative" sounding music tended to grow away from the music and shrivel up. Some even died. Similar studies have been done with animals, verifying that God's creation responds well to good music. Some of the newest studies confirm that well-written, positive music can perhaps heal the brain of many problems, including depression.

God created us—and perhaps all of creation—to be soothed and sometimes even healed by *good* music. Music is not neutral. It is either having a positive effect or a negative effect on our spirits. Consider the lyrics and the emotional feel of what you listen to regularly. Make sure what you choose sends good messages to your mind and heart.

If you're feeling a little blue, you might consider putting on some praise tunes or just taking a walk to hear the birds sing. It did wonders for me today.

Girl Gab: Mom, surprise your daughter with a concert of praise to God. You choose where and how—maybe a walk outside to hear the birds or maybe a jam session with her rock star dad—but worship your hearts out! Then, take time to talk about how it made you feel. Make it a goal to sing a new song to God when you feel down.

Bible Bucks, Allowance, and Candies

Bible Blast: Read Hebrews 11:1-6

It is impossible to please God without faith. Anyone who wants to come to him must believe that God exists and that he rewards those who sincerely seek him. HEBREWS 11:6

Have you ever earned a really cool "reward" for doing something good? I remember when my son Rob earned some "Bible Bucks" in Sunday school for memorizing verses. Lexi and Autumn get an allowance for doing their daily chores. Maybe when you were really small, your mom gave you some candy for being quiet during church. Did you know that God loves to reward us, too?

I've experienced God's reward system my whole life. I remember being a teenager and deciding to volunteer for a Christian ministry. All my other friends got jobs and got paid. It didn't look as if I was going to have a fun summer at all, but I knew God wanted me to serve him by teaching the Bible to little kids. It turned out to be my best summer of high school.

But the best reward I ever received happened just a few years ago. Remember how I wrote about God calling me to Africa for some missions work? He provided an amazing invitation to write lesson plans for schools in Zambia, Africa. It would require me to take my spring break to write the lessons, and our family would need to use our vacation money for the trip. But did God have an amazing reward for me! An African safari filled with more adventure than I ever thought I would experience in my lifetime! I spent four days in one of the world's largest wildlife preserves, Kruger National Park in South Africa.

Tomorrow I will share another adventure story and the lesson God taught me through it. Today's lesson is this: God *loves* to reward us. He doesn't always reward us, and we can't expect it. Our motivation for choices we make cannot be what good thing God might do for us. But when he sees us trying our best to glorify him, he often knocks our socks off with good stuff.

Don't Miss the Signs!

Bible Blast: Read John 12:35-41

Despite all the miraculous signs Jesus had done, most of the people still did not believe in him. JOHN 12:37

"I'm pretty sure this is really dangerous," piped nine-year-old Lexi Gresh as we crunched through the tall African grass. But we—her dad, her big brother Robby, and I—didn't believe her.

That night, we were staying at Hippo Hollow, which was world famous for the hippos that came to play beneath the dining area. But dinner had come and gone without any hippo sightings. So we took matters into our own hands. Armed with nothing but a disposable flashlight, the Gresh family was exploring the banks of the river.

"I don't think this is a good idea," Lexi had warned as we got started. "I think hippos kill people! I learned it in school."

But off we went. At one point, we could hear hippos in the river on the other side of some very tall grasses. We were about ten feet away.

Finally, we found the hippos. As soon as we directed our flashlights toward them, they ran off toward the water. It was one of the most exciting things I've ever experienced.

And one of the dumbest. The next morning we were told that what we had done was very dangerous. Although we couldn't see them in the dark, signs were posted, saying, "Danger: Hippos. Enter at Your Own Risk."

This is a lot like the experience of people who don't know Jesus. They're walking around in the dark and just can't see the "signs" to believe in him. God has given us many "signs." One of these signs is the Bible, which is actually written down for us, like those signs we didn't see in the dark. He's also given us preachers, like Lexi crying out truthful warnings for us. But some people can't see or believe them because they are "in the dark."

Be patient with people who don't know Jesus yet and don't see his "signs." He loves them and may just protect them and open their eyes one day, just as he did for our family on our hippo-hunting night!

Girl Gab:

Remember the three names you wrote down awhile back—people you know who don't seem to understand Jesus or be able to see his "signs." Write this list on some paper and put it on your fridge so you can remember to pray for them.

13 February

"Coincidence" or God's Perfect Timing?

Bible Blast: Read Luke 12:6-7

See how very much our Father loves us, for he calls us his children, and that is what we are! But the people who belong to this world don't recognize that we are God's children because they don't know him. 1 JOHN 3:1

In the middle of the night during a winter snowfall in Wasilla, Alaska, an eighty-three-year-old woman, Joyce Peldo, decided to go for a walk. Joyce was a healthy person except for one thing: she had Alzheimer's disease, a brain disorder that affects the memory. A person with Alzheimer's may have trouble remembering where she lives, who her family is, and how to perform daily tasks. She may even "forget" to wear warm clothes when it's snowing. Joyce did just that. Wearing only a nightgown, light jacket, and slippers, she went for a winter walk.

At about 5:00 a.m., a man named Phillip Allison was driving to work. He had been in a hurry that morning and didn't brush the snow off his headlights before he left. Soon he had to stop to clear off his lights so he could see better.

As Phillip did that, he heard a faint voice saying, "Help me." He looked around with his flashlight until he found Joyce lying in the snow about fifty feet away. He quickly took Joyce to the hospital, where her frantic family found her.

Joyce's son was quoted as saying about Phillip Allison, "He was there by the grace of God. It's pretty much a . . . miracle." But not everyone felt it was a miracle of God's timing and love. Many people used words like *luck, coincidence,* and *chance.*

Today's focus verse points out something that "people who belong to this world" don't recognize: that "we are God's children." Those who don't know our heavenly Father don't get it when things like Phillip finding Joyce in the snow happen. When miraculous stories like this are shared, they don't see God's timing and his love for his children. But the Peldos and the Allisons know exactly what happened—and who was controlling the events—that wintry morning.

Girl Gab: Do you think Christians should say things like "What a coincidence!" or "I'm so lucky!" or "What a great twist of fate"? From now on try to give God the credit when you see his perfect timing at work in someone's life. Discuss what phrases you can use instead of these, and then pray that God will bring them to mind so you can use them.

Meditation Moment: 1 Corinthians 13

Love is patient and kind. Love is not jealous or boastful or proud.
1 CORINTHIANS 13:4

Happy Valentine's Day! I hope you got some really cool valentines from your friends. I used to love getting valentines—and giving them. I still have some of the ones that I received in first grade. Crazy, huh? But true love isn't buying a box of thirty-two valentines for your classmates, is it? Though giving cards is a lot of fun, true love is much more difficult than that.

First Corinthians 13 is often called "The Love Chapter" because it teaches us so much about love. Verse four alone tells us five things about true love. It starts with patience. True love is patient. In the original language of the New Testament, it actually said something more like this: "Love is slow to boil." What a powerful word picture! When our love is tested, we don't just blow off steam like a pot of water about to whistle. Instead, we are "slow to boil."

Okay, now that you've studied a little piece of 1 Corinthians 13:4 with me, go ahead and pray. Then, meditate on how love is patient, and wait for God to give you a story, picture, idea, or thought to write down.

Girl Gab: Mom, start with a big "I love you" Valentine's Day hug, and then tell your daughter what God said to you during the meditation. Daughter, how about a kiss on the cheek for Mom before you share your thoughts on 1 Corinthians 13:4?

15 February

Girl Gab: Mom, go online and look up Jason McElwain. The video of those miraculous four minutes can be found in many different places. Watch Jason's story together. Grab the tissues! It's a tearjerker!

An Unlikely Hero

Bible Blast: Read Psalm 104:31-34

May the glory of the LORD continue forever! The LORD takes pleasure in all he has made! PSALM 104:31

Jason "J-Mac" McElwain is highly functional in spite of having autism, a brain disorder that made him what some might call disabled. In high school, the basketball coach, Jim Johnson, heard that J-Mac loved the game. He asked Jason to be the team manager, figuring it would be too difficult for him to be a player. Jason served in his position faithfully. He got water bottles for the players, helped out during practice, and was a fantastic motivator for the team before a game. He also spent many hours in the empty gym shooting baskets by himself.

For the last game of the season in Jason's senior year, Coach Johnson let J-Mac suit up (put on a team uniform), figuring that would help Jason feel like he was more a part of the team. With four minutes to go in the game, Coach Johnson did something shocking. He stood up and pointed to Jason, telling him to get in the game. Their team had racked up a big lead, and the coach wanted to let Jason play. When J-Mac bounded out onto the court, the crowd went wild.

The first shot he threw was way off. The second shot missed too. But on the third shot, Jason nailed a three-pointer! And that's not the end of it.

Jason hit three point shots again—and again—and again—and again—and again! And he made one two-pointer! That's right! This autistic teenager made twenty points in four minutes!

When the buzzer sounded, the crowd was in a frenzy trying to get to Jason. They lifted him up on their shoulders, cheering, clapping, and crying for their hero.

Every time I watch the video of Jason making those shots, I get tears in my eyes. When I see the crowd fly off the bleachers, going crazy for Jason, I know that God was jumping up off his throne, dancing in circles for him too. God takes such pleasure in us. He loves it every time you achieve something because he made you and he loves his creation!

Rooftop Kitties

Bible Blast: Read Psalm 91

He will cover you with his feathers. He will shelter you with his wings. His faithful promises are your armor and protection.
PSALM 91:4

I've heard of animals having their babies in peculiar places: shoe closets, sock drawers, laundry baskets. But this story is a first and, I hope, a last.

When Annie was little, her family's pet cat was pregnant and almost ready to deliver her kitties. Annie was playing upstairs when she looked out the window and saw their cat nursing her newborn kittens out on the roof! She watched with wonder and relief as her mom carefully crawled out and brought the little kitties in to safety.

It's hard to imagine why a cat would go up on the roof to produce a family! Generally, animals have great instincts about keeping their babies safe. Maybe Annie's cat wanted to get away from the noise of the house. My guess is she was taking a walk on the roof when the kitties said, "Ready or not! Here we come!"

Unlike Annie's cat, God knows how to take care of you. He is our perfect protection. Proverbs 18:10 says that God's name is like a strong tower where we can find safety.

Knowing God protects us doesn't mean we'll never have a broken arm or a broken heart. There are times when God definitely steers us out of harm's way, but there are other times when bad things happen. God's protection means that no matter what we go through, our hearts can still be full of hope and faith. And even better than that, we are headed to the ultimate protection of eternity with God. So even in death, we have hope because we'll live forever with him after we leave this earth.

The Bible says we are like sheep and Jesus is our Good Shepherd. It says, "He gathers the lambs in his arms and carries them close to his heart" (Isaiah 40:11, NIV).

Little lamb, don't be afraid. He's carrying you close to his heart.

Girl Gab: Mom, can you think of a time when God very clearly protected you or someone you know? Daughter, are you going through something right now where you need to know God is protecting you? Ask him to show you his protection today.

17 February

Girl Gab: This is a great time to talk about biblical fasting with your mom. Do you think Christians fast as much now as they did in Bible times? Why or why not? Do you think fasting would be hard or easy? When someone gives up food for a time so she can pray, what do you think her actions tell God?

What Fasting Is

Bible Blast: Read Matthew 6:16-17

When you fast, don't make it obvious, as the hypocrites do, for they try to look miserable and disheveled so people will admire them for their fasting. I tell you the truth, that is the only reward they will ever get. MATTHEW 6:16

One of my favorite stories in the Bible is how Queen Esther saved the Jewish people by asking the king not to allow his soldiers to slaughter them as was planned.

In presenting herself to the king, who was her husband, without a specific invitation, she was risking immediate death. Queen Esther asked the Jewish people to fast on her behalf because she had to risk her life to save her people. "Esther sent this reply to Mordecai: 'Go and gather together all the Jews of Susa and fast for me. Do not eat or drink for three days, night or day. My maids and I will do the same. And then, though it is against the law, I will go in to see the king. If I must die, I must die'" (Esther 4:15-16).

Miraculously, the King did not punish her or kill her for coming to his throne room uninvited, and she won his heart with her wise approach. She asked that her people be spared, and her husband gave her what she asked.

When the Bible talks about "fasting," it's talking about not eating food in order to focus on prayer and worship. As you read the Scriptures, you'll find many instances of people fasting in the Old and New Testament, both men and women, young and old, for short times and long times. Even Jesus fasted for forty days and forty nights. Matthew 4:2 points out that "After fasting forty days and forty nights, he was hungry" (NIV). Wow! I usually need a snack after forty *minutes*! I can't imagine how Jesus felt after forty *days*!

Fasting helps us shift our focus off our own needs and get in touch with what God wants. You might not be ready to fast just yet. I was much older when I began, but maybe you and your mom could begin to talk about fasting and understand it for a future time when you feel God prompting you to fast for the first time.

I Deserve It!

Bible Blast: Read Luke 18:9-14

Those who exalt themselves will be humbled, and those who humble themselves will be exalted. LUKE 18:14

When you want your parents to get you something or take you somewhere, do you try to "butter them up" first? Like, is this how you ask your mom if you can do something?

"Hi, Mom! Your hair looks really nice like that. Also, I'm pretty sure you've lost weight. Good for you! Just so you know, I cleaned the litter box, made my bed, did my homework, swept the porch, and put my laundry away. I even ate carrot sticks instead of cookies for a snack. So do you think I could go to Marie's slumber party Friday night?"

It's as if you think if you list all the good things you've done, your parents will suddenly be overwhelmed with love for you and let you do what you want. Just so you know, I don't think that approach works very well, but you can keep trying if you don't believe me!

You definitely can't butter up God by reminding him of all the good things you've done for him. Today's Bible Blast passage describes a Pharisee who was proud of all he did for God, including fasting from food twice a week. He even let God know that he wasn't like the tax collector! Now take a look at those verses again. Which man did God say was right in his eyes? Whose prayer did God honor? That's right. The tax collector. The Pharisee's prayer was rooted in pride, not in humility and love for God. The Pharisee was saying, "Notice me! Look at what I've done! I've been so obedient. I'm better than this other guy!" God wasn't impressed. That's because God doesn't love us because of the things we do. He loves our hearts.

God knows exactly what you do all the time. You don't need to remind him of anything. When you approach God in prayer, tell him what's on your heart, just like the tax collector did. He was just honest with the Lord. He hadn't done anything "great" for God, and he knew it. He just wanted to be forgiven for his sins, which actually was a great thing after all.

Girl Gab: Go and make some toast. Spread some butter on it and sprinkle a little sugar and cinnamon on it. Yum! While you eat it, talk about the phrase "buttering someone up." Do you think it's an honest way of speaking with someone? Ask God to help you and your mom communicate in honesty to each other.

Kickin' Kraft:
Jazzy Jars!

(Check out
p. 368 for a great
mother-daughter
craft that helps
reinforce today's
devo!)

Kickin' Kraft:
The Jar Is Always Half-Full

Bible Blast: Read 1 Kings 17:8-16

*There was always enough flour and olive oil left in the containers,
just as the LORD had promised through Elijah. 1 KINGS 17:16*

The widow of Zarephath and her son were almost
starved to death when they met Elijah. There was just
one meal's worth of flour and oil to cook. Then came
Elijah, asking the widow to give him some of their last
meal. When she explained their desperate situation, he told
her not to worry because God would keep filling her jars with
flour and oil—and not just for one meal but until the rain
came and the crops grew again. The widow decided to believe
Elijah, and she fed him. The next morning, she went to her
cupboard, looked in her jars, and saw more flour and oil. It was
a miracle. God had blessed the widow for giving even when
she felt she had nothing to give.

I was on a ministry trip in South America with teen
magazine editor Susie Shellenberger a few years ago. Some
teenagers on that trip decided to give their peanut butter sandwiches away in a village with dozens and dozens of children.
The teenagers didn't have dozens and dozens of peanut butter
sandwiches. It took faith to give them away and trust God.
They were risking a riot if they ran out. Do you know that
dozens and dozens of starving little Spanish-speaking children
ate and ate and ate, and the teens never ran out until the last
child's face was smeared with jelly?

I'm convinced it's always a good idea to give to someone in need, even if you don't feel like you have much—or
enough—to offer. A hungry person would be so grateful for a
peanut butter sandwich. It's not really our job to supply the
need. It's our job to *see* the need and respond.

Whatever!

Bible Blast: Read Psalm 26:2-3

Whatever is true, whatever is noble, whatever is right, whatever is pure, whatever is lovely, whatever is admirable—if anything is excellent or praiseworthy—think about such things.
PHILIPPIANS 4:8 (NIV)

It seems like every time I turn around, someone is saying, "Whatever!" In our culture, it is another way of saying, "I don't really care. It doesn't matter." I would say most of the time it's not a very appropriate or respectful response. Wouldn't you agree? I usually think of that word as a sign of major attitude. But when God's Word uses *whatever* to point out what your mind should dwell on, God's definition of *whatever* actually means, "I really, really care, and it definitely matters!"

A couple of years ago my pastor preached a whole series of messages on Philippians 4:8. Every week we would go to church and study what each of these words mean: *true, noble, right, pure, lovely, admirable, excellent,* and *praiseworthy*. If God wants us to think about these things, we should know what they mean. At the end of the sermon series, he gave everyone in the congregation a black bumper sticker with white letters that simply said, "Whatever." A bunch of us put them on our vehicles so that when we would see that word on someone else's car as we drove around town, we would be challenged and reminded to fix our thoughts on things that honor God.

When I see one of those stickers now, I try to investigate my thoughts and make sure they're in order with Philippians 4:8. One thing that's really helpful in keeping my mind fixed on good things is having my girlfriends ask me questions like, "How has your thought life been lately? Are you focused on God things or Dannah things?" It's hard when I have to fess up and tell someone sinful thoughts I might have, but I feel so clean afterward. It's so great to hear someone say, "I'm going to pray that God helps you turn your thoughts to whatever is true, noble, right, pure, lovely, and admirable."

Girl Gab: One good way to really understand what a word means is to figure out what the antonym, or opposite, of that word is. Pick one word—*true, noble, right, pure, lovely, admirable, excellent,* or *praiseworthy*—and talk about its opposite. Then pray together asking God to help you be "whatever" he wants.

21 February

Obedience Is Good

Bible Blast: Read Colossians 2:6-8

Just as you accepted Christ Jesus as your Lord, you must continue to follow him. COLOSSIANS 2:6

Girl Gab:

Daughter, pick one family rule that is hard for you to obey—maybe cleaning your room every Saturday or not walking to the nearby gas station alone. Tell your mom why you don't like that rule. Mom, explain to your daughter how that rule is meant to keep her safe.

We had just entered Kruger National Park, one of Africa's best safari destinations. Nearly five million acres of lions, elephants, zebras, giraffes, and more awaited the Gresh family. We couldn't wait to get to our campsite. Maybe that's why my husband, Bob, was driving a little fast on the dirt road. Suddenly we hit a bump so hard that my head clunked the roof of our Land Rover.

"Cool!" beamed Rob from the backseat.

"Hmmm. Not so cool," said Bob. "Actually, it's kind of getting hot."

A needle on the car's dashboard told Bob that the car was almost instantly overheating. Whatever had happened under our feet wasn't good. We got about a mile further, and then the car just shut down.

We were in the middle of wild Africa, and the signs just outside the park said, "Stay in your vehicle at all times." So we stayed in the car, as the temperature in it was rising. We called our campsite, but the others in our group never picked up. We waited for almost an hour, and no one drove by.

"I'm getting out. I'll walk to the nearest camp," said Bob.

"No," I begged him to stay. "We have to obey those signs. Someone will find us."

Finally, a man did drive by. He was the repairman coming to fix the phone at our campsite! He could drive us right to it, and he did.

Later we found out how wise it had been that we'd obeyed the signs. A hungry lion had been spotted near the place we'd broken down just that morning. Bob would have been in terrible danger if he'd have walked off on his own. We learned that day that obedience is good.

Just like those signs were there to protect us, God's rules—and your parents' rules—are for your protection. Obedience is always good, even if it is hard.

Amazing Animals: Chook, the Superb Lyrebird

Bible Blast: Read 1 Corinthians 9:22-23

I try to find common ground with everyone, doing everything I can to save some. 1 CORINTHIANS 9:22

Say you're walking through the forest with friends when suddenly you hear a car alarm. Huh? Then you stop in your tracks because you hear a baby crying and construction workers hammering. You and your friends search all over until you finally find the source of the sounds: a bird.

The Superb Lyrebird lives in Australia, and it is a master at mimicking sounds, especially when it's trying to attract a mate. It can copy the sounds of any other bird it hears but also any other noise. It's amazing!

There's a lyrebird named Chook who lives at the Adelaide Zoo in Australia. Chook amazes visitors and workers at the zoo by perfectly mimicking sounds from the construction of a panda exhibit. When you check out the video of Chook online for your Girl Gab, you'll hear sounds of saws, hammers, and whistling from the construction workers! It's just unbelievable!

I wonder what's in the throat or voice box of the lyrebird to give it the ability to make those sounds. It's almost as if it has a little recorder in it! And even beyond its mimicking abilities, the lyrebird is a super fancy bird with long, extravagant tail feathers. The male lyrebird goes into the most complicated songs it can make to see if it can attract a lovely female lyrebird.

The apostle Paul knew it was important to try to reach every kind of person with the gospel of Jesus Christ. Like it says in today's focus verse, he did what he could to find a common ground with everyone he came across in order to bring each one to salvation. Paul didn't try to become exactly like the people he was around, like the lyrebird, but he did try to make them feel welcome in his conversation with them because doing so might provide an opportunity to share Christ.

Girl Gab: First, check out a video of Chook the Superb Lyrebird at the Adelaide Zoo online. Next, think if there's anybody you know who you don't have much in common with, but you really want to tell about Christ. Ask God for a creative connection with that person.

23 February

Loving Mean People

Bible Blast: Read Matthew 5:43-48

I say, love your enemies! Pray for those who persecute you!
MATTHEW 5:44

Girl Gab: Mom, tell your daughter about some of the "Fionas" and "Daniels" from when you were a kid. Be honest and tell her how you dealt with those difficult kids. Pray with her about some of the kids in her life that are hard to love.

She couldn't believe it. Sadie's teacher changed the seating chart in class, and she had to sit beside a mean person—again. The last two times Mrs. Johnston changed their seats, Sadie had to sit with Fiona. Fiona was mean, and she talked all the time. Mrs. Johnston would hear talking coming from their desks and yell at both of them, even though Fiona was always the one talking. And now Sadie was assigned to sit with Daniel. He called people names and got into fights all the time.

When Sadie told her dad about the new seating arrangement, he was sad for her. "I'm sorry, Sadie. I know you're disappointed, but did you ever think about *why* Mrs. Johnston might be seating you with the difficult kids?"

"Because she wants me to learn to be friends with them?" Sadie said.

"I wonder if it's something more than that. When we have your parent-teacher conferences, Mrs. Johnston always remarks about how kind you are, how you notice when kids are sad and try to cheer them up. Do you think maybe your teacher thinks you can be a positive influence on kids like Fiona and Daniel? Like maybe you'll show love to those kids?"

"But how do I show love to someone like Daniel? I don't want other kids to think I have a crush on him or anything."

Her dad chuckled. "Right. Why don't you just say hi to him in the mornings? Also, pray for a chance to talk to him about why he's so angry. He may have something going on at home that causes him to feel mad a lot of the time."

"That's true," Sadie agreed. "I'll give it a shot."

Our focus verse says we're supposed to love those who persecute us or treat us unfairly. Those people might live in the home next to you, or they might be the people who sit next to you on a bus or in school. How can you love those people?

Meditation Moment: 1 Corinthians 1:10

I appeal to you, dear brothers and sisters, by the authority of our Lord Jesus Christ, to live in harmony with each other. Let there be no divisions in the church. Rather, be of one mind, united in thought and purpose. 1 CORINTHIANS 1:10

Did you know that *church* isn't just a building that you go into on Sundays to learn more about God? The church really is about all the people around the world who love God and serve him with their whole hearts. Here in the United States, I'm part of the church—and so is a lady I've never met who loves Jesus all the way in Mongolia. The church is about people, not a building. So when you read today's Scripture, you could replace the phrase "the church" with "followers of Jesus everywhere."

God doesn't want us to just express love to the Christians in our own church or family. He wants his followers all over the world to be united in their love for him and each other.

Now that we've studied the verse above, it's time for you to pray. Bow your head and then wait for God to show you a picture, story, thought, or idea that teaches you something from today's Scripture. Write about it here or in a journal.

Girl Gab: How did your Meditation Moment go today? Share what God spoke into your heart with each other! Mom, do you see a budding devotional author in your daughter?

25 February

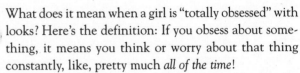

Are You Totally Obsessed?

Bible Blast: Read Matthew 6:28-32

Why worry about your clothing? Look at the lilies of the field and how they grow. They don't work or make their clothing, yet Solomon in all his glory was not dressed as beautifully as they are.
MATTHEW 6:28-29

What does it mean when a girl is "totally obsessed" with looks? Here's the definition: If you obsess about something, it means you think or worry about that thing constantly, like, pretty much *all of the time*!

Lots of girls and women are really obsessed with how they look. I know women who exercise 24/7 because they aren't happy with their bodies. I've cried with girls who are so afraid of gaining weight, they don't eat anything at all.

Quiz time! Answer a few questions to see if you're in danger of "totally obsessing"!

1. Does your desire to wear the perfect outfit keep you from being on time?
2. Are you a mirror junkie?
3. Do you constantly exercise? I mean, do you eat, sleep, and breathe on the treadmill?
4. Do you only want clothes from certain "cool" stores?
5. Do you try to eat healthy foods? Or do you just eat tiny bits of things because you're afraid of gaining weight?
6. Do you constantly look at magazines or Web sites with pictures of celebrities to see what they're wearing?
7. Do you make fun of other girls who are a different size than you, either to their faces or behind their backs?

If you answered yes to most or all of these, consider talking to someone specially trained to help you get a better view of your beauty and value. Your body was given to you in order to glorify God! The Holy Spirit lives in our bodies (see 1 Corinthians 6:19). Since that's true, we'd better make sure we do our best to take care of ourselves and be thankful for the bodies we've been given, don't you think?

Girl Gab:

Daughter, if you answered yes to a bunch of those quiz questions, talk to your mom about it. Believe it or not, she totally understands and may even have some of the same struggles you have. What about you, Mom? Do you struggle with overattention to body image and outward appearance? Pray together about this and agree to encourage each other.

A Holy Time-out for Sibling Rivalry

Bible Blast: Read Numbers 12:1-16

So Moses cried out to the LORD, "O God, I beg you, please heal her." NUMBERS 12:13

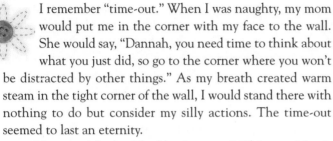

I remember "time-out." When I was naughty, my mom would put me in the corner with my face to the wall. She would say, "Dannah, you need time to think about what you just did, so go to the corner where you won't be distracted by other things." As my breath created warm steam in the tight corner of the wall, I would stand there with nothing to do but consider my silly actions. The time-out seemed to last an eternity.

Not so with the "double time-out." This was Mom's punishment when my brother and I got into a fight. She'd put *each* of us in a separate corner. This common experience bonded us together. I remember sneaking peeks at my brother. We had an unspoken code-language that we'd developed and used from corner to corner. The giggles were held in as quietly as possible until our sentence was over, and then we'd fall to the floor in hysterical laughter.

Numbers 12 shows a sort of holy "time-out" for sibling rivalry. Aaron and Miriam are grumbling because Moses is hearing God's voice and they are not. So they start to say bad things about him. God calls for Aaron and Miriam. And then he punishes Miriam by letting her get sick enough that she has to go out of the community. Moses can't stand to watch her suffering. He loves Aaron and Miriam. Soon Moses cries out to God to "please heal her."

Even if you don't get along with your brothers and sisters very well, you still need to show love for them by not attacking them with your words or actions. Maybe the next time you're tempted to have an argument, don't say anything at all. It's really hard for two people to fight when one of them isn't saying something mean. I bet if you do this, the amount of yelling in your house will go way down.

Isn't it funny how we fight with our siblings? And isn't it amazing that when we get in trouble for it, we sometimes realize that we actually love them?

Girl Gab: Mom, share with your daughter how you feel when she fights with her siblings (or friends, if she is an only child). Talk to her about why you do whatever it is that you do to intervene when they fight!

27 February

John's BFF

Bible Blast: Read John 13:21-26

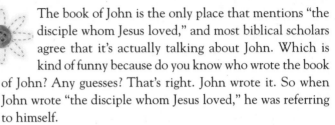

One of them, the disciple whom Jesus loved, was reclining next to him. JOHN 13:23 (NIV)

Girl Gab: For a moment, close your eyes and try to imagine what it would have been like to be John leaning against Jesus' chest. What do you think you would have noticed about Jesus? Pray for each other that you would both have a greater sense of Jesus' love for you.

The book of John is the only place that mentions "the disciple whom Jesus loved," and most biblical scholars agree that it's actually talking about John. Which is kind of funny because do you know who wrote the book of John? Any guesses? That's right. John wrote it. So when John wrote "the disciple whom Jesus loved," he was referring to himself.

Does that sound kind of conceited to you? Let's keep looking at it. Several passages in the Bible suggest that although Jesus loved all of the disciples, he was a bit closer to Peter, James, and John. And in your Bible Blast (if you chose to read it), you read that John was actually leaning against Jesus! Can you imagine being so close to Jesus that you could actually feel his heartbeat?

John knew Jesus was the King of kings. He knew that for Jesus to live as a human on earth was a really big deal. He respected Jesus and honored his position. So for Jesus to actually be fantastic friends with John was a great privilege. When John called himself "the disciple whom Jesus loved," he wasn't bragging as if to say, "Look who *I'm* friends with!" He was humbly telling the world that this all-powerful King actually loves a human like John . . . and a human like you and a human like me.

John 19:26 describes Jesus on the cross just before his death. Jesus looks down and sees his mom, Mary, and his wonderful friend John. He tells his mom and John to take care of each other. Jesus must have thought a lot of John to trust him to be like a son to Mary.

Have you ever been around a person who made you feel as if you're the most important person in the universe? I believe that's how Jesus made John feel. In Jesus' presence, John was consumed by a big love: the love of his Savior.

Language Lab: What Is a "Hypocrite"?

Bible Blast: Read Matthew 23:25-26

How can you think of saying, "Friend, let me help you get rid of that speck in your eye," when you can't see past the log in your own eye? Hypocrite! First get rid of the log in your own eye; then you will see well enough to deal with the speck in your friend's eye. LUKE 6:42

Marion Jones was "the fastest woman on earth," and she proved it by winning five medals at the 2000 Olympics in Sydney. She ran so fast that a lot of people accused her of using drugs to help her body perform. She denied it. In her 2004 autobiography she wrote, "I am against performance-enhancing drugs. I have never taken them, and I never will take them."

In 2007, Jones confessed. Yes, she had used performance-enhancing drugs. That's illegal for an athlete, not to mention very unhealthy. She had to go to jail for six months and do some community service as punishment. She said she was sorry and ended up being truthful.

What makes her a hypocrite? When she told everyone publicly that drugs are bad but privately used them, she became a hypocrite. A hypocrite is someone who says she believes something but doesn't live that belief out in her personal and private life.

In Greek, the word *hypocrite* is used to describe a stage actor who wears a mask to impersonate, or pretend to be, someone else.

One type of hypocrisy girls sometimes struggle with is gossip. On the bus you might hear Junie say, "I totally hate it when people gossip!" And then at lunch you hear her whispering about other girls. Junie is saying one thing but doing the opposite thing.

If you feel like someone's being hypocritical, don't tell anyone else about it. Instead, pray for that person in private and ask God to help her. Most importantly, examine your own life to be sure that how you are living in private matches up with what you say you believe in public.

Girl Gab: Mom, share with your daughter a time when you realized that you weren't practicing what you preached. Daughter, pray for both you and your mom to be more careful about living what you believe.

Kickin' Kraft:
Bodacious Bookmarks!

(Check out p. 369 for a great mother-daughter craft that helps reinforce today's devo!)

Kickin' Kraft: What's *He* Looking For?

Bible Blast: Read Mark 12:38-44

They gave a tiny part of their surplus, but she, poor as she is, has given everything she had to live on. MARK 12:44

A widow is a woman who was married but her husband has died. The Bible speaks often of the importance of taking care of widows. It can be very difficult for a widowed woman to live without the income of her husband, and this was especially true back when the Bible was written. In today's Bible Blast, you may have read about a widowed woman who was very poor, but she put two little coins in the offering plate at "church." It was all she had—and she gave it.

It took more faith and trust for the widow to give her coins than it did for the rich man to give his money because of sacrifice. The widow's gift was a great sacrifice. The rich man didn't have to give up any of his needs or desires in order to give some money because he gave what was extra.

The widow knew God would take care of her either by a miracle or through his people. She trusted him enough to give everything she had.

Jesus didn't observe the people's giving at the Temple so he could see who gave the most money. He wanted to teach the disciples that giving isn't about the *amount of money*. It's about the *value* of what you give. As with everything in his Kingdom, value comes from the heart.

Wrapped Up

Bible Blast: Read Proverbs 5:21-23

An evil man is held captive by his own sins; they are ropes that catch and hold him. PROVERBS 5:22

Grab a spool of thread and your mom. Today I'm going to show you how sin can be like a rope that holds you. As I tell you a story, your mom's going to use the thread to illustrate it.

There was a six-year-old girl who went shopping with her mom. She really, really wanted some gum, but her mom had told her no. So while her mom was paying, the little girl grabbed a pack of bubble gum and stuck it in her pocket.

Now stand up, arms down at your sides, and have your mom wrap thread around your arms and body one time.

Later on the little girl started to feel bad about what she did. She confessed her sin to her mom and to God. She promised never to do it again.

Use your arms to "break free" from the thread. Pretty easy, right?

As the little girl grew, she started seeing other things she wanted but didn't have the money to buy. It became easy for her to steal books, lip gloss, nail polish, and magazines. She always felt guilty, but it became harder for her to say no to something she wanted.

Have your mom wrap the thread around your arms four times. Now try to break free. Was it harder this time?

When she grew into a teenager, stealing began to take over. She downloaded movies and music illegally online. She stole her friend's ring. She even took money from her parents' wallets. She never felt guilty anymore. It was a habit.

This time have your mom wrap the thread around you twenty times! Now do your best to break free from the string. Can you do it? Or does your mom need to grab some scissors?

This is what sin does to us if we let it. We get all tangled up in its "ropes" until we can't break free anymore. When this happens, the only one who can get you out of it is Jesus—but he doesn't have to use scissors!

Girl Gab: Mom, let your daughter wrap you in the thread and see if you can break free from it. Talk to each other about how sin keeps you from doing God's will. Pray for God's strength to stand against temptations to sin.

3 March

Liquids vs. Solids

Bible Blast: Read Hebrews 5:12-14

Solid food is for those who are mature, who through training have the skill to recognize the difference between right and wrong.
HEBREWS 5:14

Girl Gab: Okay, this will be some fun girl gab. Where do you think you are—spiritually speaking—amidst these choices? Pick one and tell your mom (or daughter) why that's where you think you are: 1) milk only 2) mashed-up baby food 3) getting on solids 4) eating soft meat 5) T-bones daily.

Does your mom have any pictures of you slopped up with baby food in a high chair? I have a picture of my daughter Lexi that I just love. She's about a year old, sitting in her high chair. The table is covered in mushy baby food, as is her face.

The only thing a newborn baby can eat is mom's milk or formula. Gradually, as a baby gets older and stronger, you can start giving her vegetables and fruit that have been pureed into an unappetizing, runny consistency. Soon enough she can eat Cheerios, and eventually she's on her way to sinking her teeth into a thick, juicy steak.

When someone first gives her heart to Jesus, she probably isn't ready to dive right into some of the more "meaty" things of the faith, like premillennialism vs. amillennialism. (Huh? Don't worry. Most adults don't know those words. But your pastor probably does.)

It would be wise for a "baby believer" to begin by learning about prayer and studying the Bible, some of the more simple practices of Christianity, like reading the Gospels or 1 Corinthians 13. The idea of a new Christian drinking "milk" is that she needs to understand and believe the basic truths of her new faith in God before she can go on to tackling some of the more complicated ideas.

On the other hand, those who have been walking with Christ for a while shouldn't still be drinking milk. The more you grow up in Christ, the more you'll be able to understand more of the "solid food" of the faith. That's why your mom probably reads books about her faith and your pastor can define big words. They are "meat eaters." They've grown up and can digest deeper things of the faith.

Make it a goal to grow up in your faith and become a "meat eater."

Reduce! Reuse! Recycle!

Bible Blast: Read Hebrews 12:1-4

Since we are surrounded by such a huge crowd of witnesses to the life of faith, let us strip off every weight that slows us down, especially the sin that so easily trips us up. And let us run with endurance the race God has set before us. HEBREWS 12:1

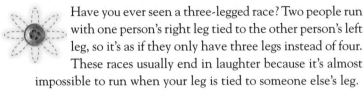

Have you ever seen a three-legged race? Two people run with one person's right leg tied to the other person's left leg, so it's as if they only have three legs instead of four.

These races usually end in laughter because it's almost impossible to run when your leg is tied to someone else's leg.

Today as I thought about running the race of our Christian life, I thought of what it would be like to tie myself to someone who struggled with sin. Here's a practical example of how sin might slow you down in your walk with God:

Sholanda and Rebekah were friends. Rebekah had a major problem telling the truth, but Sholanda still liked to hang out with her. One night, Sholanda's parents told her they didn't want her to hang out with Rebekah anymore because she lied so often and may be a bad influence on her. Sholanda was heartbroken and angry. She went into her room, slammed the door, and decided she would be friends with Rebekah anyway. Sholanda and Rebekah kept spending time together on the bus and at school, and eventually Sholanda started lying, too. She lied to teachers about her homework. She lied to her parents about who was going to be at slumber parties. On top of all of that, she stopped spending time with Jesus and only prayed before meals.

Sholanda was tripped up by sin. Instead of running for Christ, she chose to "tie" herself to Rebekah's sinful way of living. The only way Sholanda could get back into the race was to obey her parents and "cut off" her friendship.

Running the race God has set before you isn't always easy, but it's always the right thing to do. If you get tripped up by friendships, it's time to "reduce" the clutter so you can focus on your relationship with God.

Girl Gab: Daughter, tell your mom if you have any friends like Rebekah who might be bad to be "tied" to. Mom, listen lovingly and let your daughter guide the conversation about what to do with that friendship. Support her and pray with her.

Reduce! Reuse! Recycle!

Bible Blast: Read Psalm 126

They weep as they go to plant their seed, but they sing as they return with the harvest. PSALM 126:6

Girl Gab: Mom, show your daughter one of your favorite Bible verses. Hide that verse in your hearts, and apply it to your lives. Later on in the day, remind each other of the verse and what you learned.

One of the sweetest memories from my childhood is my mother's garden. Even though I didn't love every vegetable, I always thought they looked wonderful as they grew.

As much as I loved the garden, I also really hated two things about it: seeding and weeding. Major yuck. I don't think I know anyone who is crazy about pulling weeds out of a garden.

By "seeding" I mean planting seeds. It was always really boring for me. What's satisfying about taking a little dried up pea and making it disappear in dirt? Later on as the seed starts to sprout it gets interesting, but until then—yawn.

You may be wondering why the people in Psalm 126 were weeping while they went to plant their seed. Sure, maybe some of them cried because they were bored like I was as a child gardener, but there was another, more meaningful reason.

As you read this psalm, you may have noticed that the people were poor but God "restored their fortunes." When someone is in need of food, it's hard to be patient. They cried when they put the seed in the ground because they were so hungry. They could have just eaten the seeds and been satisfied for the moment. But they knew if they hid the seed in the soil, watered it, and waited until the plants grew, the harvest would be great, and many would have nourishment for a much longer time than if they would have just eaten the seed.

It's the same with God's Word. Psalm 119:11 says, "I have hidden your word in my heart, that I might not sin against you." When you read the Bible, you have a choice. You can just read it and say, "Wow. That's cool," and go on with life *or* you can read it and hide it deep in your heart, allowing it to change your life. In this way, you are preparing yourself to "reuse" the truth time and time again.

Reduce! Reuse! *Recycle!*

Bible Blast: Read 2 Corinthians 1:3-7

He comforts us in all our troubles so that we can comfort others. When they are troubled, we will be able to give them the same comfort God has given us. 2 CORINTHIANS 1:4

Janet Mylin, who is helping me write this book for you, had a very sad day recently. She had to have her cat, Jasmine, "put to sleep." Jasmine was a beautiful fifteen-year-old Persian, but she was in too much pain and couldn't live any longer. So Janet was at the vet's office saying good-bye to her beloved cat. As my friend waited in the vet's exam room, holding her kitty, she prayed, "God, I'm all alone here today, and I feel so sad. Can you send someone to be with me as I go through this?" She immediately felt God speak to her heart, "I'm here with you." It was then that she noticed a sign on the door with a carving of a cat hanging from a branch. It said, "Hang in there—It will be over soon." The humor was a strange blessing. Suddenly Janet realized that her pain wouldn't last forever. She received great comfort that day from the Lord through his voice and through a little sign on the vet's door.

One reason God comforts us is so that we can pass that comfort on to others. Just as the focus verse says, he offers us a grand Comfort Recycling Program! Take Janet's experience at the vet—now when she learns of a friend going through the same thing, she can remind her that the pain isn't forever. God comforted my friend. My friend can take that same comfort and give it to her friend, and on and on and on.

When you're going through a hard time, the most meaningful help comes from those who have been through what you're experiencing. When they look you in the eyes and say, "I know this hurts. I know what you're going through," it means so much. I've had friends not say anything at all when I'm sad, but they hold me and cry with me.

We're all going to have hard things happen in life. When those things happen, remember today's focus verse from 2 Corinthians because God has extraordinary comfort for you.

Girl Gab: Have you experienced something difficult that God could use to comfort someone else? Share that with each other, and then look for opportunities to be a Comfort Recycler!

Language Lab: What Is "Righteousness"?

Bible Blast: Read Psalm 18:20-24

Everything he does reveals his glory and majesty. His righteousness never fails. PSALM 111:3

When my sweet daughter Lexi was about seven or eight years old, she came to me with a little black-and-white Beanie Baby cat. Lexi loved Beanie Babies and had about as many as the factory, I think! So the fact that I didn't remember buying it didn't surprise me. But Lexi had a confession. I hadn't bought it for her. She had stolen it—from the church nursery!

She asked if God could forgive her, and I told her yes. We prayed together, and I believe that at that very moment God made her right with him. Then I asked her what we should do. She decided to write a letter of apology to the pastor and mail it to him, along with a new Beanie Baby cat to replace the stolen one.

That day Lexi Gresh was "righteous."

What's that mean anyway?

Does *righteous* mean sinless? Nope. God's Word says, "Everyone has sinned; we all fall short of God's glorious standard" (Romans 3:23). Based on our sin, there is no one righteous.

Was Lexi righteous because she took the Beanie Baby back and bought a new one? No. That just means she was good and made restitution. Giving another Beanie Baby to the church nursery was a really good thing to do. It made her feel better, and it was right. But restitution is not righteousness.

Righteousness is being made right through Jesus Christ. We can't do anything to make ourselves like that. Only Jesus' blood can do it. A righteous person isn't one who never sins. It's not one who makes up for her sin with good acts. A righteous person is one who confesses her sin and calls on Jesus to make her right with God.

Good Dirt

Bible Blast: Read Matthew 13:1-9

Still other seed fell on good soil, where it produced a crop—
a hundred, sixty or thirty times what was sown.
MATTHEW 13:8 (NIV)

Farming is tricky business. So much depends on things that are out of the farmer's control. It's like telling people about Jesus. You can talk about Jesus' plan for salvation, but it's up to the people who hear the words to decide if it makes any difference in their lives.

Let's break down the parable of the sower together. Whenever I ask you a question, stop for a minute and answer it out loud with your mom. **The questions will be in bold.** As you go, remember that the "seeds" are a symbol of God's truth and the "soil" is a symbol of people who hear the truth.

Some of the seeds fell along the path. Picture a path in your head. **What is the dirt like?** It's packed down and hard so the seeds just rest on top of it. Since the seeds have no camouflage, the birds grab them all for dinner. **Have you ever met someone who had a really hard heart?** She may hear the truth but doesn't accept it. The truth just lies there until she forgets about it entirely. It gets snatched away because she doesn't hold onto it.

Other seeds fell among rocks. **Do you find a lot of good, deep soil where there are lots of rocks?** No, the seeds in that shallow, rocky soil grew up quickly and got burned by the sun because their roots weren't deep. I know people who gave their hearts to Jesus and got excited right away, but they never got in the Word and let their "roots" get deep in their relationship with him. When things got hard, their faith wasn't deep enough to stand up against the pain of their disappointments, and they withered away.

The third kind of seed fell where the plants were choked by thorns. **Have you ever been pricked by a thorn or gotten stuck in a briar bush?** Ouch! Some plants can't live beside other plants because one will overpower the other.

But when God's Word falls onto a tender, willing heart, the fruit it bears is endless.

Amazing Animals: Nubs the Dog

Bible Blast: Read Matthew 7:7-11

If you sinful people know how to give good gifts to your children, how much more will your heavenly Father give good gifts to those who ask him. MATTHEW 7:11

Marine Major Brian Dennis first met the German shepherd–Border collie mix on the snowy desert of the Iraq-Syria border. He was a wild dog looking for food from American soldiers as they patrolled war-torn villages. The scrappy dog's ears had been brutally clipped, which is why the soldiers named him "Nubs."

The soldiers' patrol brought them into the area every week for three months, and each time they were greeted by scavenging dogs. The local people didn't like the dogs, but the American soldiers enjoyed their company and were kind to them. One very cold day, the dogs came over to the soldiers, who noticed Nubs wasn't doing well. He was shaking and could hardly stand up. When Brian checked him out, he noticed a hole in the side of his chest. The villagers told them someone had actually stabbed the sweet dog with a screwdriver. The soldiers got the team doctor to check Nubs and treat him.

Soon Brian and the other soldiers had to leave. They were being moved seventy miles away. As they drove off, they looked back and saw Nubs slowly following their vehicles. They watched him until they couldn't see him anymore.

Two days later, when Brian Dennis was in a meeting, one of his men ran in and said, "You're not going to believe who's outside!" When Brian stepped outside, he couldn't believe his eyes. It was Nubs! He had tracked the soldiers across seventy miles of wilderness in the cold! What a great gift he was to the soldiers, who missed their families. Brian arranged to have Nubs vaccinated and flown to the United States to live with him in California.

Even something as interesting as a dog who tracks you down for seventy miles in the desert is a great gift from God. Every good gift is from God.

But I'm So Tired!

Bible Blast: Read Proverbs 6:6-11

Take a lesson from the ants, you lazybones. Learn from their ways and become wise! PROVERBS 6:6

The Brooklyn Tabernacle is a huge church located in the heart of Brooklyn, New York. It's the home of the famous Brooklyn Tabernacle Choir, which is made up of 250 people and has recorded many albums. If you ever get the chance to visit New York City, try to visit. It's an amazing place to worship God.

But as big and as beautiful as the Brooklyn Tabernacle is, it certainly wasn't easy to establish or to keep it running. The church, which began in 1847, was destroyed by a fire in 1869. They rebuilt the church in 1873, and that building was destroyed by a terrible thunderstorm in 1889. So they built again. This new building could seat 6,000 people, but sometimes they crowded 7,000 people into it. You may not believe this, but *that* building was burned by a fire in 1894! The Brooklyn Tabernacle went through a few more changes until it finally landed where it is today, in a theater on Smith Street.

It's easy to give up, isn't it? Some things are really easy to do and work right away. Other projects are very difficult, and we have to keep on trying and trying and trying. I bet the people who started Brooklyn Tabernacle were discouraged when the first church building was destroyed. But can you imagine how they must have felt when it happened two more times? Probably some of them wanted just to give up, but those who believed in the project kept pushing and building and praying to make the church what it is today.

When you believe in something and it feels as if it's constantly getting "burned down," ask God for perseverance. Perseverance means you don't give up even when things get tough, just like the people of the Brooklyn Tabernacle.

When God asks you to do something, it won't always be an easy, quick task. There will be times when you really have to work to obey God, but the end result will be glorious.

Girl Gab: Get a stack of some sort of playing cards. Have a contest with your mom to see who can build the tallest house of cards. See if you can build it to three stories high! As you build the card houses, talk about times when you've wanted to give up. Was there ever a time when you persevered and were amazed by the results?

Meditation Moment: Ephesians 1

Even before he made the world, God loved us and chose us in Christ to be holy and without fault in his eyes. EPHESIANS 1:4

Ephesians is one of my favorite books of the Bible. Written by Paul, it outlines who we are and what God wants us to be. In the verse above, we learn that God "chose us." I think Paul wrote this so we could be reminded that our salvation depends totally on God. Another thing I love about this verse is *when* he chose us: before he made the world. Whoa! Did that just blow your mind? Before he even made this world he was thinking about Y-O-U!

Now that I've helped you consider the truth in this Bible verse, why don't you give meditation another try? If you haven't found meditating on God's Word to be very easy, don't stop trying. Everyone meditates a little differently, and you'll find your groove. Stop, pray, and wait. When God gives you a picture, idea, thought, or story write it down so you will remember.

Everything We Have Is His

Bible Blast: Read 1 Chronicles 29:10-20

Who am I, and who are my people, that we could give anything to you? Everything we have has come from you, and we give you only what you first gave us! 1 CHRONICLES 29:14

King David was close to the end of his life. He had reigned as king of Israel for about forty years and was making preparations for his son Solomon to be the next king. God had told David that he would not be the one to build the Temple, but that his son would build it. Once David heard this, he began gathering all the materials and people needed for Solomon to erect this amazing Temple. Among the resources King David gathered from his own riches and from the leaders of Israel were 10,000 gold coins, 300 tons of gold, 637 tons of silver, 675 tons of bronze, and 3,750 tons of iron! (To give you an idea of how much that is, an average car weighs about 1.5 tons. So this stuff weighed about as much as 7,000 cars!)

In 1 Chronicles, it says that "the people rejoiced over the offerings, for they had given freely and wholeheartedly to the Lord, and King David was filled with joy" (29:9). So these people had given literally tons of their riches for the building of God's Temple, and they were totally pumped about it!

The focus verse today includes King David's personal words of praise to the Lord after he and his workers had everything collected and ready for Solomon to build the Temple. He didn't say, "God, look at all the stuff we have given for your Temple! We've sacrificed so much! Just look at all this gold!" He was very aware that anything the people had came from the Lord to begin with.

When we realize that all the blessings we have are from the Lord, it's much easier to give them away for his work or his people. It's because of God's provision that we have jobs, money, talents, food, health, freedom, or even an earth to live on. Once you really have it in your head that it's all God's stuff, you'll find it's much easier to give it away.

Girl Gab: Take some time to thank God for all your family has. Ask him if there's anyone who's in need that you can give to. Then take great delight in giving it!

13 March

Finding Your Inner Poet

Bible Blast: Read Psalm 63:2-4

Because your love is better than life, my lips will glorify you.
PSALM 63:3 (NIV)

Girl Gab: Why not try creating a psalm together? Write a mother/daughter psalm of praise for your relationship. Your finished product doesn't have to be perfect. Just express your gratitude to God for giving you each other.

When I was in first grade, I won a national poetry contest. I won first place out of more than a thousand entries. Here's the poem that still hangs on my mom's wall:

The Woodpecker makes his nest in a tree
He pecks all day no matter what we say,
So I'd better go away
Before he pecks me,
Little tree!

Goodness gracious! How did *that* win?

The book of Psalms is a whole book of songs and poems inspired by God. What a gift to have 150 to choose from when I'm looking for words to describe how I feel! Every now and then, I'll read a psalm out loud to God as if I wrote it myself because it's exactly what I feel like telling him in that moment. Have you ever tried to write your own psalm? You can! Just write down how you feel about God and his love for you. You can make it rhyme or not. It's totally up to you. If you play an instrument you could even set it to music.

Here's a psalm that Janet wrote:

Lord, you are faithful.
I will never have a reason to say you're not.
Our intimacy is special and it will never end.
Your love jumps toward me in leaps energized by joy
And excitement and a longing desire to be my Friend.
No matter where you lead me, Lord,
I'll just close my eyes, stretch my hands out,
And let you guide me on my knees.
For I know without you I can do nothing.
But with you I truly have everything
My heart could ever dream of and more.

Do You See What I See?

Bible Blast: Read 1 Samuel 16:4-13

The LORD doesn't see things the way you see them. People judge by outward appearance, but the LORD looks at the heart.
1 SAMUEL 16:7

The people of Israel told Samuel, the prophet who heard from God, that they wanted a king to rule over them. God reluctantly told Samuel that he would provide a man to be king. Then he sent Samuel to meet Saul and make him Israel's first king.

Saul started out pretty well, but soon he made bad decisions. Finally, God told Samuel that he had someone else lined up to be the next king—one of the sons of a man named Jesse.

Now, Saul is recorded as being the tallest, most handsome Israelite, so it's possible that Samuel assumed the son who most resembled Saul would be the one God had chosen to be king. But God said: "Don't judge by his appearance or height, for I have rejected him. The LORD doesn't see things the way you see them. People judge by outward appearance, but the LORD looks at the heart."

So which son of Jesse did God choose as Israel's next king? Jesse brought seven of his sons in front of Samuel. But Samuel said, "The Lord hasn't chosen any of these. Do you have any more sons?" Jesse told him that he had one more son, the youngest. The Lord said to Samuel, "This is the one; anoint him." Samuel took oil and anointed, or set apart, this young boy named David to be king over Israel.

Have you ever heard the saying, "Don't judge a book by its cover"? That's basically what God was telling Samuel. When our Creator looks at you, he doesn't just look at your cute haircut, your new glasses, or your sweet boots. He looks past all of that right into your heart. Of course, God created you and loves how he shaped you, but when he assigns different gifts, talents, and jobs to you, he doesn't take into consideration what you look like. He focuses on what's going on in your heart.

Girl Gab: Does it make you feel comforted or worried to know God sees right into your heart? Do you ever feel as if God would only choose "pretty people" to do really important things for him? Ask God to help you see people as he sees them. Ask him to help you see the hearts of other people.

The Trouble with King Saul: Part 1

Bible Blast: Read 1 Samuel 14:47–15:23

What is more pleasing to the LORD: your burnt offerings and sacrifices or your obedience to his voice? Listen! Obedience is better than sacrifice. 1 SAMUEL 15:22

Girl Gab:

Daughter, are you obedient? Answer that question, and tell your mom what's in your heart when—and if—you disobey. Mom, affirm your daughter in the areas where she is obedient.

In the Old Testament you'll find lots of war stories that teach us about God's creativity and strategy in overcoming evil. Today's Bible Blast tells the story of King Saul, who thought his own ideas were better than God's commands. Samuel, the prophet, gave Saul a message from God that he needed to attack the Amalekite people. He told Saul to completely destroy *all* the Amalekites and *everything* they had—crops, livestock, everything. But when Saul and his army attacked the Amalekites, they destroyed everybody except for King Agag, and they only got rid of the livestock and crops that were of poor quality. They wanted the rest for themselves.

When Samuel confronted Saul regarding his disobedience, Saul didn't seem to understand how he had failed to do exactly what God had directed. He said, "I did obey God. I did kill everybody, except for the king, and I only kept the best animals to sacrifice to the Lord your God."

I could just see Samuel shaking his head as he stated the words in our focus verse today. His heart was broken because this human king of Israel didn't understand the importance of obeying his Creator, the King of all kings. Isn't it funny how Saul said, "But I did obey God" when he clearly didn't?

I remember making similar almost-true statements to my parents. If Mom told me to clean my room, maybe I would make my bed and shove everything on the floor into a big pile in the corner. When Mom would say, "I thought I told you to clean your room," I would say, "But I did clean my room, mostly. I'll put that big pile away later." That's not obedience. It's rebellion.

When God—or your mom—asks you to do something, do it exactly as you are instructed. That's obedience.

The Trouble with King Saul: Part 2

Bible Blast: Read 1 Samuel 14:47, 15:24-29

You can make many plans, but the LORD's purpose will prevail.
PROVERBS 19:21

Saul was a power-hungry king. Some translations of 1 Samuel 14:47 say that he "secured his grasp" on the throne. Saul was really into the idea of being king of Israel, and he didn't want anybody to change that. Let's look at how things turned out for him after Samuel told him about the importance of obedience.

Saul eventually admitted that he had sinned because he didn't do exactly what the Lord had commanded him to do. Samuel's response to Saul's confession must have given Saul chill bumps all the way down to his royal sandals: "The LORD has torn the kingdom of Israel from you today and has given it to someone else—one who is better than you" (1 Samuel 15:28).

King Saul forgot that God was the one who had made him king of Israel. Saul thought if he held onto the throne tightly enough, even God wouldn't be able to tear it from his hands. He grew to love his kingly power more than he loved the One who gave it to him.

Throughout your life God will assign you different tasks, jobs, and roles. When that happens, always remember who gave them to you so if he ever needs to take them from you, you won't be completely devastated. God knows more than you. In fact, he knows everything. Did you catch that? *Everything.* When you realize this, it should help you not to worry or be afraid. Realizing that God knows all things in the past, present, and future should give you amazing peace.

Is there anything that you are holding on to that you need to let go of? A lot of girls your age start to "secure a grasp" on boyfriends. Some girls start to "secure a grasp" on sports. Still others "secure a grasp" on popular friends. These aren't things that are bad, but if they aren't from God—and the timing isn't right—it's going to hurt when God makes you let go.

Girl Gab: Mom, tell your daughter about a time in your life when you were worried about what God was doing but now you see what his purpose was. Hold out your hands with your palms facing up, and thank God for his great love and wisdom.

17 March

The Feathery Tongue

Bible Blast: Read James 3:1-12

People can tame all kinds of animals, birds, reptiles, and fish, but no one can tame the tongue. It is restless and evil, full of deadly poison. JAMES 3:7-8

Girl Gab: Mom, can you think of a time when you were hurt by someone else's words as a child? Tell your daughter about that. Daughter, tell your mom if you have been hurt by gossip or if you have hurt others with your words. Spend some time asking forgiveness from God for your hurtful words and forgiving those who have hurt you. If you need to ask someone to forgive you, make plans to do that.

There is a Roman story of a little girl who went to see a wise man, Saint Philip Neri. She wasn't a bad girl, but she had a major problem with gossip. Saint Philip said to her, "Little girl, it isn't right for you to gossip. I have two things I want you to do to help you destroy that terrible habit." The girl knew she had a problem, so she agreed to do whatever he said. "First," Saint Philip said, "buy a bird at the town market. Then as you are leaving town, pluck every feather out of the bird and drop them on the road until all the feathers are gone."

The young girl did exactly as Saint Philip said. She went to town, bought a bird, and plucked all its feathers out as she walked, dropping them on the ground. She returned to Saint Philip and said, "Sir, I have done as you said with the bird. What is the second thing I need to do?" He looked down at her and said, "You must go back the way you came and pick up every feather you dropped."

"But, sir," she exclaimed, "that's impossible! Feathers are so light and easily tossed by the breeze! None of them will be where I dropped them! I might be able to find some of them, but there's no way I could gather them all!"

Saint Philip smiled warmly at her. "Dear child, you are right. Do you see how the feathers are like your hurtful words? When you gossip behind someone's back, don't those words travel from ear to ear to ear all over the village until they're too widespread for you to take them back?"

"Yes, sir. I see what you mean. Now what do I do?" she said with a quiet voice.

The wise man got down on his knee and looked her in the eyes. "My dear child, the next time you are tempted to speak mean things about someone else, keep your mouth closed. Don't scatter the feathers. Just keep them on the bird."

Abracadabra!

Bible Blast: Read Psalm 37:1-5

Take delight in the LORD, and he will give you your heart's desires. PSALM 37:4

The story of Aladdin and the magic lamp is fun to think about, isn't it? A poor boy living on the streets finds a magic lamp. When he rubs it, a genie pops out and offers him three wishes. When I was a kid, I probably would have wished for my own horse, all the gold in the world, and maybe a trip to the moon. Now, I would probably wish that all the children in Africa would be healthy and have loving families or that my dog, Stormie, would be able to talk. I guess my wishes have changed since I was a kid.

You know, I used to think the promise in Psalm 37:4 that God would give me my heart's desire meant that God is like a magic genie in a lamp—as if just by saying the right words or doing the right things then he'd give me a new car or a fabulous vacation in the Caribbean. But it didn't take long to figure out that's not how God works.

Delighting yourself in the Lord means being totally caught up in his love, and wanting nothing but just that. When you live a life of delighting in him, several things happen. You talk about him whenever you can. You become more like him. You hate what he hates—like unkindness or television shows that are bad for you—and begin to avoid that stuff. You take advantage of any opportunity to worship and praise him. Most important, you begin to want what he wants. When you delight in God, your desires change. You don't become consumed with all the "stuff" that you want. Your heart is filled with brand new desires—God's desires.

God's desires are revealed to you in many different ways, but the Bible is the easiest place to find them. In the Bible you learn to love God with everything you have within you and to treat those around you the way you'd want to be treated (see Matthew 22:37-40). And that's not the only thing you can learn from digging into God's Word. Read it whenever you can, and ask God to change your heart to want the same things he wants.

Girl Gab: If you were granted three wishes, what would each of you wish for? What godly desires do you have in your heart? Pray for each other's desires today.

19 March

Language Lab: What Is "Tithing"?

Bible Blast: Read Malachi 3:6-12

A tithe of everything from the land, whether grain from the soil or fruit from the trees, belongs to the LORD; it is holy to the LORD.
LEVITICUS 27:30 (NIV)

Girl Gab: Mom, talk to your daughter about your family's habits of tithing. Daughter, do you get an allowance or money for babysitting? Ask your mom how you can begin tithing 10 percent of that to your church. If you make $10, you can give $1 to your church. God's not interested in how much you give. He wants to see your obedient heart.

Tithe literally means "one-tenth," so giving a tithe means you're giving 10 percent of something. God was asking the people for 10 percent of their income and their livestock. What does this mean for you and me today? Most of us don't have land or livestock! But we may earn money from an allowance or babysitting. Most churches today teach that we still need to be tithing 10 percent of our income to the church.

God doesn't ask us to tithe because he needs the money. He wants us to grow as givers. He knows we need money to live, but he also promises to take care of us if we make a habit of giving, instead of storing up stuff and being selfish with our money and belongings. God has given us many Scriptures about the importance of giving, such as Proverbs 11:24-25: "Give freely and become more wealthy; be stingy and lose everything. The generous will prosper; those who refresh others will themselves be refreshed."

About ten years ago my church sent out a challenge to tithe 10 percent of the money we made. My husband and I made a commitment to do just that, but it was scary. When it came time to write that check, my hand was shaky. But out of obedience, I sent the check in. Just a couple days later, I received a check in the mail for the exact same amount! God showed me how he takes care of my family and me when we're obedient to him.

The Bible speaks so much about money; actually about one-fourth of the Bible deals with money, tithing, or giving. Two-thirds of the parables that Jesus told were about money. As you study what God says in the Bible about money, you'll see it's very different from what the world will tell you.

The world says, "Get as rich as you can." But God says, "Give it away to those in need, and I'll take care of you."

Tall—On the Inside

Bible Blast: Read 1 Samuel 17:32-37

Some nations boast of their chariots and horses, but we boast in the name of the LORD our God. PSALM 20:7

The story of David and Goliath in 1 Samuel 17 is so cool. Goliath was a big, strong giant and a trained warrior, so when he challenged the Israelites to fight, it's no wonder they were scared to death.

Every day Goliath made fun of the Israelites and challenged them, and every day nobody took him up on the challenge. Even King Saul's mightiest warriors were afraid to battle the giant.

You probably know the story. A shepherd boy said he would defeat Goliath, and that's exactly what he did—with a sling and a stone and his greatest weapon: his faith in God. David quickly became famous for his victory over Goliath, which eventually led to King Saul's intense jealousy of him.

Sometimes I imagine the Israelite soldiers looking around to see which of them was the tallest, the most likely Israelite to be able to fight the giant. And guess who that would probably have been: King Saul.

In 1 Samuel 10:23 the Bible describes how Saul "stood head and shoulders above anyone else." So Saul, their king, was the tallest guy around. When the Israelites' tall, strong king wouldn't go out to fight Goliath, no wonder his shorter, less powerful soldiers didn't think they could defeat him.

Even though Saul may have been physically tall enough to fight Goliath, he was short in humility and trust. While he was king, he failed to listen to God and obey him. He wanted to do things his own way and missed out on God's great love because of it. In 1 Samuel 15:11, God even said, "I am sorry that I ever made Saul king, for he has not been loyal to me and has refused to obey my command."

God was David's strength. King Saul was King Saul's strength. That's why David was able to defeat the giant and King Saul wasn't.

As it turns out, because of his trust in God's power and love, a young shepherd boy was "taller" than the king.

Girl Gab:
Daughter, who's taller, you or your mom? How much taller? Do you think you will be taller someday, if you aren't already? Just for fun, have a thumb-wrestling match, and see who wins! Today commit your thoughts to God's strong love for both of you.

21 *March*

Sometimes Dogs Are Gross

Bible Blast: Read Romans 7:21-25

As a dog returns to its vomit, so a fool repeats his foolishness.
PROVERBS 26:11

Can you believe this verse is in the Bible? If you're weak stomached, don't worry. We'll get the gross stuff out of the way first.

God has designed our bodies so perfectly. When there's something stuck in our throats, we cough to clear it out. When an eyelash gets stuck in our eyes, we automatically produce tears that flush it out. And when we eat something that's harmful to our bodies, our intestines start contracting and, well, out it comes. It's yucky but amazing!

As much as I hate getting sick, I'm always impressed at how much better I feel after throwing up. However, I don't think dogs have that same thought process after they vomit. You see, after a dog vomits, it'll walk right back over to the vomit and . . . eat it! Disgusting! Why would a dog get rid of whatever is making it sick and then go put it right back into its body again? That doesn't make any sense.

The Bible says that when a "fool repeats his foolishness," he's doing the same thing that dogs do. Let me tell you a little story that shows what this verse means.

Caroline had good friends, but she really wanted to be friends with Sophia. Sophia was pretty and cool and lived in a really big house, but Sophia was mean. Whenever Caroline talked to her, Sophia would say things to her like, "You need to get new shoes so you don't look poor" or "I can't believe you ride the bus to school. My nanny drives me." Caroline always felt terrible after she spent time with Sophia, but she kept going back to her. This is a good example of a fool repeating her foolishness.

Caroline knew that Sophia made her feel awful about herself and her family, but she kept trying to earn her friendship. Do you see how that's like a dog returning to its vomit? If something or someone makes you feel unhealthy, physically or in your mind, don't go back to it! Go somewhere else.

Girl Gab: Mom, did you ever have someone in your life that you kept talking to even though that person wasn't good for you at all? Daughter, do you see fools returning to their foolishness at school? Ask God to help you not return to things that make you "sick."

Kickin' Kraft: God's Breath

Bible Blast: Read Genesis 2:4-7

The LORD God formed the man from the dust of the ground and breathed into his nostrils the breath of life, and the man became a living being. GENESIS 2:7 (NIV)

Do you know how many breaths you take during a day? Let's see if we can find out. Stop right here and count how many times you take a breath in one minute. Ready? Go! When I did this, I counted twenty. How many did you get? Multiply that amount times sixty to get how many times you breathe in an hour. My number was 1,200 times an hour. Next, I multiplied by twenty-four because that's how many hours there are in one day. The answer? I took 28,800 breaths in one day! Of course, this is only an average, because during some hours of the day I might be exercising—and breathing more rapidly. And during the night hours of each whole day, I'm sleeping—and breathing much more slowly. But probably 28,800 breaths in one day is a good average for me. That's a lot of breathing! And isn't it amazing that we breathe all those breaths without even thinking about it? All night long my body breathes while I'm dreaming. Our Creator is truly awesome!

Do you know what is the most amazing breathing ever? When God created Adam and breathed the breath of life into his body. I wonder what that sounded like. Did the sound of God's breath blend into the sound of Adam's first breath? Beautiful.

When you look at the Hebrew language for "breath of life," it doesn't mean that God just gave Adam the ability to stand up and walk around. He gave Adam *everything* he needed. He gave Adam his personality, health, mind, and spirit in that one fantastic breath.

God also has breathed into you to make you exactly who you are so that you can be and do wonderful things for his Kingdom and glory. Breathe deeply today knowing God made you on purpose.

Kickin' Kraft:
Egg-Stravagance!

(Check out p. 369 for a great mother-daughter craft that helps reinforce today's devo!)

23 March

Learning to See the Poor

Bible Blast: Read Matthew 19:16-23

If I gave everything I have to the poor and even sacrificed my body, I could boast about it; but if I didn't love others, I would have gained nothing. 1 CORINTHIANS 13:3

In 2009 Kevin and Audrey packed up their three children and moved to Haiti to serve God as missionaries. Audrey told this story from their first three months of living in Haiti.

"There was an old woman in the market selling small brown biscuits. She looked up at me and with a toothless grin pitched her wares. A friend explained to me that they were dirt cookies. The shock and disbelief left me speechless, and my heart sank. I am praying I will soon have a grasp on the Creole language so that I can build relationships with the people I meet, who desperately need to know and experience the blessings of a life in God."

During very desperate times in Haiti, the people are actually mixing clay with salt and some sort of butter or vegetable shortening to make dirt cookies. They bake them in the hot sun and sell them in the market to support their families. Haitians have been using dirt cookies as a health remedy for many years, but some families are actually eating them for every meal because they can't afford anything else.

Living in America, we can easily just think the rest of the world lives pretty much the way we do. But that isn't true.

At least 80 percent of people on the earth live on less than $10 a day.[2] That's about $310 a month, which is less than many Americans' monthly car payments.

So how do we deal with such poverty if we don't live overseas like Audrey and Kevin do? First you can pray for people in other countries, even if you don't know much about them. You can pray that they have enough to eat and stay healthy. When you hear of an earthquake, immediately pray for those people.

You may not be able to move to another country to care for the poor, but you can do a lot for them by praying.

---

2 See www.globalissues.org.

Meditation Moment: Revelation 21

He will wipe every tear from their eyes, and there will be no more death or sorrow or crying or pain. All these things are gone forever. REVELATION 21:4

Have you ever wondered what heaven will be like? Well, God allowed one of his beloved disciples, John, to have a dream. In that dream, God was able to show John what heaven would be like. Today's focus verse is part of John's description of what he saw. Imagine a place where you'll never cry again and there's no more death or sorrow or pain. That's what heaven will be like.

All right, it's time to meditate. Just pray for a moment, and then roll this verse around in your mind as you wait for God to speak to you. Wait until you think of a story, picture, idea, or thought to write down. This is one Meditation Moment that might lend itself to drawing a cool picture of what you see.

Girl Gab: Share with each other what God showed you about heaven. Then talk about whether or not you feel you'll get to live in heaven and why.

Should I Be Afraid of God?

Bible Blast: Read Proverbs 31:25-31

Charm is deceptive, and beauty does not last; but a woman who fears the LORD will be greatly praised. PROVERBS 31:30

I'm not afraid of heights. I don't freak out in small spaces. Snakes don't bother me. The threat of sharks doesn't keep me from enjoying the ocean. But there is one thing that I just can't handle. I am *totally* afraid of spiders! I have been known to completely freak out at the sight of one of those eight-legged creatures. I'm not even sure why I'm so afraid of them. I don't even recall any horrific spider bite incidents. Whatever the reason, spiders cause great fear to rise up in me. But I do have one heroic story of triumph over the biggest spider I've ever seen in my life.

I was a camp counselor, and I was spending time with my campers in our cabin. We were chatting away, and everything was fine until I spotted "It"—the most gigantic spider I've ever seen in my entire life. I remember its being at least six inches wide with horrible spiky legs. As I stood there paralyzed by fear, I realized there was no big strong man around to take care of this problem for me. I was in charge.

I'm not really sure how I did it, but somehow I gathered up the courage to trap the spider and take it outside. That's right. I didn't even kill it. Aren't you so proud of me?

We usually think of fear as a totally negative thing. But let me teach you about a different kind of fear. The Bible often talks about fearing God or the fear of the Lord. This fear isn't the same feeling I get when I see a spider. It's a positive sense of reverence or awe for God. Fearing God means you recognize that he is the all-powerful King of kings and that you live your life in respect and wonder for him.

You may have stopped to watch an amazing sunset and thought, *Wow! God did that!* That's a fear-of-the-Lord experience. Have you ever been really uncomfortable and maybe even angry when someone else spoke disrespectfully about God? That's the fear of the Lord rising up in you. Fearing the Lord isn't being terrified of him. It's acknowledging him as the ultimate power in the universe.

Amazing Animals: The Honey Badger

Bible Blast: Read 1 Corinthians 15:50-58

When our dying bodies have been transformed into bodies that will never die, this Scripture will be fulfilled: "Death is swallowed up in victory. O death, where is your victory? O death, where is your sting?" 1 CORINTHIANS 15:54-55

Honey badgers are relatively small, weighing about thirty pounds, but they are among the most fearless animals in the world. I heard of one honey badger who got into a fight with a puff adder—a very poisonous snake. With one blow, the puff adder injected poison into the fearless ball of fur. After it was bitten, the honey badger ripped off the head of the snake and began to eat it. (I know. Gross, right?) Soon, the venom worked its way through the badger's body, and it fell over, appearing to be dead. But after just a few hours, the honey badger got up, went back over to the headless viper, and continued to eat it for dinner. Here's the thing: Honey badgers are relatively tiny creatures, but they are fearless and often win battles against insurmountable odds.

When the Roman soldiers crucified Jesus on the cross, they must have thought, *Ha! We did it! We ended his life, and he won't bother us again.* Imagine their surprise when just a few days later, Jesus wasn't in the tomb anymore because he was alive!

For those who follow Jesus, death isn't the end. The end of physical life on earth marks the beginning of eternal life with other believers and God in heaven. Our life on earth is an incredible time of loving God and teaching others about him, but it's not our forever home.

When I get discouraged by the world around me, I remember that I have a perfect, sinless home waiting for me in heaven. Knowing that gives me such hope and joy. It makes me kind of like that honey badger—fearless! I can even survive the attacks of the serpent we call the devil! The next time you feel "poisoned" by stuff going on around you, remember the honey badger and let the hope of eternity with God help you get back up again and keep on living.

Girl Gab: Find something in your house that weighs thirty pounds—your overweight cat, a frisky cocker spaniel, or a toddler brother or sister. If you can't find something living, go get a few ten-pound sacks of flour or sugar. Take note of how small thirty pounds is, and remember that you are never too small to fight to win in God's Kingdom!

Girl Gab: Time for a treasure hunt. Mom, hide your Bibles and this book somewhere, and play a nice game of hot and cold. Then, change roles. Daughter, you get to hide the stuff. Time each other. The faster "treasure hunter" gets a foot rub (to be followed by prayer, of course).

Let the Hunt Begin!

Bible Blast: Read Proverbs 2:1-8

Tune your ears to . . . Wisdom; . . . Searching for it like a prospector panning for gold, like an adventurer on a treasure hunt. Believe me, before you know it . . . you'll have come upon the Knowledge of God. PROVERBS 2:1, 4-5 (THE MESSAGE)

A few weeks after my boyfriend proposed to me and gave me a beautiful diamond ring, I lost it. As I was driving to work, I looked down to admire the ring on my left hand and realized that it was gone. I was frantic! I didn't care if I was late to work. I turned my car around and headed straight for my tiny apartment. Inside, I ripped through piles of laundry, tugged all the sheets and blankets off my bed, stuck my hand down pipe drains, and turned over carpets. The place looked like a tornado had come through it, and I still hadn't found that ring! Then I remembered the chocolate cream pie! I'd just made it. I ran to the fridge, pulled it out, and wasted no time in digging through it. Nothing. Suddenly I had an amazing, revolutionary idea: maybe it was in my jewelry box! And it was.

God wants us to look for his truth in the same way that I looked for that ring, with wild passion to find it. But we aren't going to find it in a chocolate cream pie. We also aren't going to find wisdom in the advice of friends, television shows with good morals, fiction books written by Christian authors, or a great Christian rock download. Those are all decent places where we might find some truth, but there's a proper place where you can always, 100 percent guaranteed, find truth. It's right where it belongs: in the Bible.

Proverbs 2 describes looking for the truth in the Bible like being on a treasure hunt. When I read that, I felt really excited. Treasure hunts are hard work, but they are fun. Digging into God's Word should be fun. I hope you're having fun digging into God's Word with me this year, and I hope you'll keep it up your whole life long.

Think about it: Your whole life can be one fantastic treasure hunt!

The Greatest Sin Shredder

Bible Blast: Read Psalm 103:8-14

His unfailing love toward those who fear him is as great as the height of the heavens above the earth. He has removed our sins as far from us as the east is from the west. The LORD is like a father to his children, tender and compassionate to those who fear him.
PSALM 103:11-13

A pastor called all the children in the church to come up and sit on the floor in the front of the church for a special children's message. He talked to them about sin and had them write down their sins on a piece of paper. Then he brought out a square little machine and plugged it in. Most of the children had no idea what it was. The pastor took a piece of paper and fed it into the machine. The children watched as the paper was turned into tiny strips. That's right. The little machine was a paper shredder.

The pastor told the children that God forgives us for sinning when we ask him to. The kids were wide-eyed as he explained that when God forgives something, he doesn't even remember it anymore. It's like he has a great big, God-sized paper shredder in heaven. The children lined up to put their papers through the shredder, a symbol of God's totally forgiving them and not remembering their sin.

Did you know that's true? God, who knows everything, really doesn't remember your sin after he's forgiven you. Read today's focus verses again. How far exactly is the east from the west? Where do east and west begin and end? East and west go on and on, and they can't be measured! God throws our sins so far from us that we can't even measure the distance!

Don't you wish you had the ability totally to forget bad things? I know I have some things I would like never again to remember! All we have to do is confess our sins to him. Look at 1 John 1:8-9: "If we claim we have no sin, we are only fooling ourselves and not living in the truth. But if we confess our sins to him, he is faithful and just to forgive us our sins and to cleanse us from all wickedness."

Girl Gab: Mom and daughter, do you have something you've done that you still feel really bad about? If you haven't confessed it to God, then take time to do it now. Now write it on a piece of paper and run it through a paper shredder. If you don't have one, a nice pair of scissors will do the job. As you watch your sins "disappear," say a prayer thanking God for not remembering them anymore.

Bible Blast: Read Philippians 1:12-14

Don't worry about anything; instead, pray about everything.
Tell God what you need, and thank him for all he has done.
PHILIPPIANS 4:6

Girl Gab: Mom, has there ever been a time when you have dealt with anxiety? If so, talk to your daughter about how anxiety paralyzes a person. Daughter, what do you worry about the most? Take time to tell God about your worries and then thank him for all the good he has done in your lives.

The book of Philippians is a letter Paul wrote to the people who lived in a city called Philippi. Paul and the Philippian people had great love for each other because of all they had gone through together for the sake of Christ. They had been through some pretty terrible things.

In fact, where was Paul when he wrote this book? (If you read the Bible Blast today, you know the answer.) He was in prison! Paul had been thrown in jail because he told people about Jesus and stood up for righteous things, not because he stole something or hurt anybody. Just imagine what it would have been like for the Philippians to have someone who led them and loved them be put in jail for doing good things! And not only was Paul imprisoned, but his life was in danger. Later on in chapter one, Paul talks about the possibility of being killed for his faith. There were probably other reasons the Philippians had to be worried and anxious, but I'm guessing Paul's imprisonment was at the top of their list. They must have felt so out of control and helpless and confused. They must have felt worried.

Paul told them they shouldn't worry but pray—and even more than that, they should be thankful to God for everything he had done. If we could turn all our worries into prayers and thankfulness, wouldn't that make us strong in the Lord? As humans we go through many different situations that could make us get rolled up in worry: hard times in school, sickness, moving to a new house, divorce, bad dreams, and anything else that makes us want to worry. Our friends and family go through hard times, and we don't know what to say or do to help, but Paul says the best thing we can do is tell God about it and thank him for the good he has done.

A Powerful Weapon

Bible Blast: Read Philippians 4:10-13

I can do everything through Christ, who gives me strength.
PHILIPPIANS 4:13

I used to be really bad at speaking in public. I was the queen of saying, "and . . . uh . . . " I could've put cranky babies to sleep with how boring my presentations were.

But God asked me to start telling my story about how he rescued my heart. I was so terrified. This was the one thing I never, ever wanted to do. "No, God! You can't want me to speak in public," I cried in prayer. But he did, and I knew it. I had to memorize Philippians 4:13 and verses like it. I would repeat them over and over again before I got on a stage to speak. Somehow God helped me get through. Not only that, but a lot of girls and teens have been rescued because I just told my story.

You really can do anything through Christ who gives you strength. You can pass that upcoming math test. You can find a way to love someone who has hurt you. You can even tell people about how God has rescued you.

I once heard someone say that when you feel afraid and feel as if you cannot do something, picture the cross of Jesus. Then, picture a hole in the cross and—in your mind's eye—crawl right "through" that hole *before* you do what causes fear. That's how it was for me. I had to crawl "through" Jesus' love and power right before each encounter on a public stage. Would you believe it—today I actually really like speaking up there!

Draw a picture on a sheet of paper of you crawling "through" Jesus' love and power before facing a situation that's worrying you.

Girl Gab: Can you think of a time when you were afraid and God rescued you through a friend or his Word or prayer? Take time to memorize today's focus verse. Use it like a weapon every time you get afraid.

Girl Gab: God isn't impressed with how we pray. He's more concerned with why we pray. Applying what you learned from the Lord's Prayer, pray to God about your day.

Who Does God Listen To?

Bible Blast: Read Matthew 6:5-8

When you pray, don't babble on and on as people of other religions do. They think their prayers are answered merely by repeating their words again and again. MATTHEW 6:7

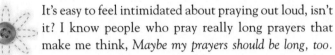

It's easy to feel intimidated about praying out loud, isn't it? I know people who pray really long prayers that make me think, *Maybe my prayers should be long, too.*

I know people who pray with flowery words almost like poetry, and I think, *I wish I could pray so beautifully.* And I've heard people pray loudly, and I think, *They really mean business! Maybe I should pray louder!*

Everyone has different styles of communicating with God. We are all unique, and God likes to hear all of our different voices in prayer.

Jesus isn't concerned with how many words you say or how loudly you say them, he just wants you to talk from your heart. He even gave an example in Matthew 6:9-13. We call it the Lord's Prayer.

"Our Father in heaven, may your name be kept holy. May your Kingdom come soon. May your will be done on earth, as it is in heaven. Give us today the food we need, and forgive us our sins, as we have forgiven those who sin against us. And don't let us yield to temptation, but rescue us from the evil one."

After each line of this simple prayer, talk to your mom about what it means. Copy each line below onto a separate piece of paper and write down what you believe Jesus was saying about how we should pray.

"Our Father in heaven, may your name be kept holy."
"May your Kingdom come soon."
"May your will be done on earth, as it is in heaven."
"Give us today the food we need."
"Forgive us our sins, as we have forgiven those who sin against us."
"Don't let us yield to temptation."
"Rescue us from the evil one."

A Satisfying Hunger

Bible Blast: Read Psalm 145:8-21

Satisfy us each morning with your unfailing love, so we may sing for joy to the end of our lives. PSALM 90:14

They don't have a lot of delicious food in Zambia. What they do have is a lot of *nshima*. To make *nshima*, the Zambians dry out big ears of corn and then smash the kernels into a dry powder. They put some of this powder into boiling water until it becomes a pasty, white substance, which is bland and not very satisfying.

On one of my trips, I'd had *nshima* for fourteen days straight! I was so tired of it, I just wanted to be home where I could eat meatloaf, mashed potatoes, and blueberry muffins! That's what I craved. Instead, I was boarding a tiny missionary plane to go out into the African bush to help some missionaries train nursing students. When I got there, missionary Sherri Letchford took me directly into her home. You won't believe this, but I thought for sure I smelled meatloaf! "Wow! Sherri, it smells so nice in here. I feel like I'm home," I said, not daring to ask if it was meatloaf I was actually smelling.

"I thought some American comfort food might be just what you needed after two weeks in Zambia," she said. "I made meatloaf balls, mashed potatoes, and mango muffins for you." No food has ever satisfied me like Sherri's simple feast of love! (I've included her mango muffin recipe in our Wacky Appendix. You'll love 'em!)

Sometimes when I feast on God's Word, it's just good and nutritious. But other times, it is like that feast with Sherri: out-of-this-world amazing and delicious because it is just what I needed! These are moments when I can really feel God's presence and he meets the needs of my heart in powerful ways. During these times, I just want to jump around and shout, "I'm so full of Jesus! Yahoooooo!"

Psalm 34:8 says, "Taste and see that the LORD is good. Oh, the joys of those who take refuge in him." Make sure that you have a lot of wonderful, satisfying times with God to "feast" on his Word and his presence.

Girl Gab: Talk about this question together: How can you "feast" on God? Add the ingredients for Sherri's amazing mango muffins to your shopping list. And think about this: Sherri has to go pick her own mangos because she can't go to the grocery store, and her flour has to be shipped from Americans who love her enough to send her care packages. Finally, if she wants butter for those muffins . . . . you guessed it, she has to make it!

Meditation Moment: Isaiah 53

He was oppressed and treated harshly, yet he never said a word. He was led like a lamb to the slaughter. And as a sheep is silent before the shearers, he did not open his mouth. ISAIAH 53:7

Isaiah was a prophet of God who lived a long time before Jesus did. But God gave this man a vision of Jesus as our ultimate payment for sin through his death on the cross.

How could the prophet help an Old Testament person understand the idea of Christ dying for us? He used the idea of a lamb being slaughtered, to help them look ahead to the kind of suffering that the future Messiah would experience.

As we experience this Resurrection season, it's not very fun to think about the horrible death that Jesus died for us, but it is a central focus of our faith. What is God saying to you about it today? First pray, then just sit quietly while you wait for God to speak to you with a picture, story, thought, or idea for below or in your journal.

Roosters

Bible Blast: Read John 18:15-27

Again Peter denied it. And immediately a rooster crowed.
JOHN 18:27

If you live near someone who has a rooster, *cock-a-doodle-doo* may be the first sound you hear in the morning. But did you know that welcoming the day is not really what they're doing when they crow?

Roosters are really hung up on their territory. When a rooster wakes up in the morning, he starts cock-a-doodling to let everyone know this is his territory and anyone had better not come near it.

When Jesus told Peter that he would deny that he knew Christ three times before the rooster crowed the next morning, Peter probably didn't believe him. He believed that he would stick by Jesus no matter what happened. But in fact, he did deny knowing Jesus three times.

The first time to a servant girl. (see John 18:17)

The second time to some men who were warming their hands by a fire. (see John 18:25)

The third time to a servant of the high priest. (see John 18:26)

And then . . . *Cock-a-doodle-doo!*

The sound of the crowing must have sent chills down Peter's back. *Jesus was right! I did deny him three times, and now the rooster has crowed!* As much as the rooster's crowing may have caused Peter to cringe, maybe it also reminded him that it was the start of a brand new day.

After refusing to admit that he knew Jesus three times, Peter needed a fresh start, especially with Jesus' crucifixion right around the corner. Psalm 30:5 says, "His anger lasts only a moment, but his favor lasts a lifetime! Weeping may last through the night, but *joy comes with the morning*" (emphasis added). Every morning is like another second chance. I have had some seriously bad days, when I flop into bed at night and say, "Thank goodness this day is over!" Knowing I will wake up to a brand-new twenty-four hours is energizing and fills me with hope.

Girl Gab: Mom and daughter, show each other your very best "Cock-a-doodle-doo!" You get bonus points if you act like a rooster while you do it! Thank God for his faithfulness and mercy, which are new every morning.

4 April

Girl Gab: Mom, have your daughter close her eyes while you read Luke 23:26-46 out loud. Daughter, while you listen to the words describing the Crucifixion, ask God to give you a new view of the Cross and Calvary. Thank him for going to the "Place of the Skull" for you.

Language Lab: What Is "Calvary"?

Bible Blast: Read Luke 23:26-46

When they came to a place called The Skull [Calvary], they nailed him to the cross. And the criminals were also crucified—one on his right and one on his left. LUKE 23:33

The word *Calvary* makes an appearance in many of the songs we sing in church, but did you ever wonder just what Calvary is? Basically *Calvary* refers to the name of the mountain or hill on which Jesus was hung on the cross to die. Another name for the hill is *Golgotha*; some versions of the Bible call it *Calvary*, and some call it *Golgotha*. Both words mean the same thing: "skull." The hill that held the cross was referred to as the "Place of the Skull." This could be for a couple of different reasons. Some believe it was called that because it was a place of execution, and there were many skulls and bones that covered it. Some believe the hill was named for its rocks that were bleached by the sun, causing them to resemble skulls. Others say there's a possibility that from a distance something about the shape of the hill actually looked something like a giant human skull. Freaky, huh?

One thing is definitely true about Calvary: It was not pretty. It wasn't a rich, grassy park, where families would take picnic baskets and spend the afternoon. When Jesus was making his way up to Calvary, he wasn't caught up in the beauty of the wildflowers growing around the base of the cross. When Jesus stumbled up the hill, the only beautiful thing that surrounded him was his great love for every human—his great love for you.

And because of Calvary, you and I have the opportunity to receive God's free gift of eternal life with him.

Because of Calvary, I know my sins are forgiven.

Because of Calvary, I'm pure and clean.

Because of Calvary, I have access to his power to live a victorious life.

Because of Calvary, hope cannot be taken away from me or from you.

Kickin' Kraft: I Lost Count!

Bible Blast: Read Isaiah 40:12-15

How precious are your thoughts about me, O God. They cannot be numbered! I can't even count them; they outnumber the grains of sand! And when I wake up, you are still with me!
PSALM 139:17-18

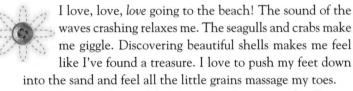

I love, love, *love* going to the beach! The sound of the waves crashing relaxes me. The seagulls and crabs make me giggle. Discovering beautiful shells makes me feel like I've found a treasure. I love to push my feet down into the sand and feel all the little grains massage my toes.

Yes. The shore of the ocean is truly spectacular. Except as much as I adore the sand, it gets *everywhere*! No matter how much I rinse off, dust off, and shake off, I still manage to take buckets of sand home in my suitcase every single time.

Have you ever tried to count a handful of grains of sand? How many did you count before you gave up? No one's been able to find out exactly how many grains of sand there are in the world. Some have guessed, but they couldn't come up with anything definite. All the grains of sand are absolutely uncountable, just like God's thoughts about you.

He has so many thoughts about you that you couldn't even begin to count them all. It's entirely overwhelming. Knowing that your Creator is that crazy for you should make you feel like you're all wrapped up in a cozy blanket today.

Kickin' Kraft:
Million-Zillion
Journals!

(Check out p. 370 for a great mother-daughter craft that helps reinforce today's devo!)

Bible Blast: Read Isaiah 44:13-17

Since this is true, we shouldn't think of God as an idol designed by craftsmen from gold or silver or stone. ACTS 17:29

Girl Gab: Pray first and ask God to help you to see anything that might be an idol in your life. It might be that you need to adjust how much time you give to something so you can be more focused on worshiping the one true God. Daughter, talk to your mom about ways you can make sure idols don't get in the way of worshiping God.

There once was a wood-carver. He was the best in the land. He took care to select only the finest trees for each task at hand. For a chair he would select a hard, lovely cherry wood. For cooking his food, he would find aromatic cedar planks. For warming his home, he would cut down a slow-burning pine tree. At the end of the day, he was so thankful for wood that he cut down just one more tree, carved a statue, and worshiped it!

Hmmm? Sounds ridiculous, but that's the story that Isaiah 44:13-17 tells. And God tells us how this idol worship makes him feel: "The person who made the idol never stops to reflect, 'Why, it's just a block of wood! I burned half of it for heat and used it to bake my bread and roast my meat. How can the rest of it be a god? Should I bow down to worship a piece of wood?' The poor, deluded fool feeds on ashes. He trusts something that can't help him at all. Yet he cannot bring himself to ask, 'Is this idol that I'm holding in my hand a lie?'" (Isaiah 44:19-20)

Basically, Isaiah is saying that the wood-carver never stops to think that he is worshiping a block of stinkin' wood! He's not even aware of it. This story makes me want to ask you a good question: Do you think that sometimes people worship things without even thinking about it? We "worship" anything that rules or masters how we spend our time and affection. Some people spend way too much time watching TV. Some girls spend way too much time being boy-crazy. Some spend way too much time thinking about how to get rich. Some spend too much time texting. All of these people have made idols and aren't even aware of it.

Can you think of any idols in your life?

Amazing Animals: Neelix the Cat

Bible Blast: Read Job 5:9-11

He does great things too marvelous to understand. He performs countless miracles. JOB 5:9

Nora Schmidt's cat, Uno, gave birth to four premature kittens. Three of them died in spite of the vet's help. Uno brought the surviving tiny kitten to Nora and laid it in her lap, as if she was asking Nora to take care of it. Nora named the kitten Neelix and bottle-fed him and took care of him. She even slept with Neelix curled up on her chest to make sure he was okay during the nights. Soon enough, he grew into a big tabby cat with eyes the color of gold. He was very intelligent, so it didn't surprise Nora when he learned how to open the door to let himself in and out of the house.

One day when Neelix was older, Nora got the flu and was really sick with fever and aches. Nora took her flu medicine and lay back in her recliner to rest. Neelix, although huge at this point, curled up on her chest and fell asleep just like he had always done.

When Nora woke up, she wasn't in her house anymore. She was in the hospital with a tube coming out of her mouth and an IV in her arm.

The medication Nora took that morning caused a bad reaction with another medication she was taking. The bad combination caused her to go into a semi-coma. That morning, Nora's neighbor heard a terrible howling sound. When she investigated, she found Neelix on her front porch. She couldn't get Neelix to stop, so she took him home. There, he ran to where Nora was on the recliner and began meowing wildly at the neighbor. The neighbor felt Nora's wrist and barely felt a pulse. She called the ambulance and got Nora to the hospital.

Nora knows it's a miracle that Neelix saved her life.

God can do miracles without human or animal help, but sometimes he uses critters like Neelix to help him perform miracles. The important truth is this: Our God performs countless miracles!

Girl Gab: Talk to your mom about miracles. Have you ever seen or heard of a miracle happening to someone you know? Ask God to help you believe him for miraculous things for yourself and others.

Time of Need

Bible Blast: Read Proverbs 17

A friend is always loyal, and a brother is born to help in time of need. PROVERBS 17:17

My daughter Autumn had a bad night.

Apparently some of the members of her sports team were less than tender when they pushed her to be a better athlete. They spent the whole practice yelling things like, "You have to be there, Autumn! Aren't you listening? What's *wrong* with you?" It can be a good sign of leadership to push your team members to give more, but in this case tenderness was sadly lacking.

I found Autumn crying in her bedroom, but she wasn't alone. She was wrapped in the arms of her sister, Lexi. When I found out how the afternoon had gone, I went downstairs to make what Autumn loves for dinner—lots of vegetables—and Lexi helped her plan her wardrobe for the next day, offering one of her own dresses for Autumn to wear. What started as a really bad night ended up being good for Autumn, mostly because her sister soothed her. Lexi was a loyal friend in Autumn's time of need.

You know, your friend doesn't have to have her house burn down to be in a "time of need." She might just be feeling overwhelmed with her homework. (You could help her by doing yours with her so she's not alone.) Or she could be feeling like the outfit she picked to wear to school looks dumb. (You could trade shirts.) Or maybe her brother said something really mean before she walked out the door that morning. (You could write her a note that tells her "Ten Totally Amazing Things about You!") Even these everyday problems can represent a "time of need."

How do you respond when your friend or a sibling is having a "time of need"? Do you slow down and try to find a practical way to make her feel better? Or do you skip over it without helping?

God says that a true friend is always loyal and helps in time of need.

Do you?

Pick Me! Pick Me!

Bible Blast: Read Mark 10:35-45

They replied, "When you sit on your glorious throne, we want to sit in places of honor next to you, one on your right and the other on your left." MARK 10:37

A man named Zebedee had at least two sons, James and John. These brothers were two of the twelve disciples who followed Jesus closely. In Matthew 4:21-22, it tells how James and John came to follow Jesus:

"A little farther up the shore he [Jesus] saw two other brothers, James and John, sitting in a boat with their father, Zebedee, repairing their nets. And he called them to come, too. They immediately followed him, leaving the boat and their father behind."

In today's Bible Blast, we learn that James and John wanted something from Jesus. They wanted to sit next to him in heaven. They even agreed to suffer as Christ would suffer, thinking that would buy those special seats of honor. Basically they were saying, "Oh! Oh! Pick me! Pick me!"

Jesus said, "I have no right to say who will sit on my right or my left. God has prepared those places for the ones he has chosen."

When the rest of the disciples got upset at James and John's request, Jesus gave them a little teaching on humility and serving. He wanted them to understand that they should not be aiming at being the greatest, but they should be trying to take on the role of a servant. For us, that might mean, instead of requesting the special seats, we need to be content to sit on the floor. It also means that we probably say things like, "Hey, pick her! Pick her!"

Who is "her"? She might be the girl on the school bus no one ever sits with, and God wants you to sit with her. She might be the last one picked for kickball at recess, and God wants her to be the first one you pick when you are captain. She might be the girl who smells bad, and God wants you to spend time with her.

How can you show humility and a servant's heart today?

Girl Gab: Are you happy for others when they receive special honors, or are you usually jealous? Pray this prayer: "Lord, I know you want me to be a servant. Help me to not always want a 'seat of honor.' Let me be content and joyful to serve others."

10 April

The Duke

Bible Blast: Read Joshua 1:1-9

This is my command—be strong and courageous! Do not be afraid or discouraged. For the LORD your God is with you wherever you go. JOSHUA 1:9

John Wayne was one of the most famous cowboy film stars of all time. From the 1920s until the 1970s, he made 170 movies. His name was Marion Mitchell Morrison, but the film producers thought John Wayne was a better name for a movie star. Actually, a lot of people just called him "The Duke," a name that came about when John was little and went absolutely everywhere with his huge dog, Duke.

The Duke used to say, "Courage is being scared to death but saddling up anyway." I love that. If anyone in the Bible could relate to that quote, it would be Joshua.

When Joshua came on the scene as Israel's leader after Moses' death, he had some pretty big shoes . . . er . . . sandals to fill. So when God repeatedly said, "Be strong and courageous," he was speaking right to this young leader's heart. Joshua was scared to death, but he "saddled up" anyway.

God told Joshua, "I have given you Jericho, its king, and all its strong warriors" (Joshua 6:2), but Joshua and his men would have to work for the victory. God told Joshua to walk with his men and seven priests around the city once a day for six days. On the seventh day, they were to walk around the city seven times, while the priests blew their horns. When the priests gave one long blast of the horns, the people were told to shout at the top of their lungs. As they shouted, the walls came tumbling down!

Conquering a city like Jericho was likely a scared-to-death situation for Joshua and the people he was assigned to lead. But Joshua made the choice to follow God in spite of his fears, and the Israelites were able to win the battle.

Being scared doesn't mean you don't love God. It's okay to be scared, but dig down deep inside of yourself to "saddle up" for God and to be strong and courageous.

Girl Gab: Is there something God wants you to do, but you're feeling really scared or nervous about it? I get scared sometimes when I know God wants me to share about Jesus with a stranger. Tell God you're scared and ask him for the courage to do the right thing in spite of your fear.

The Armor of God

Bible Blast: Read Ephesians 6:10-13

Put on every piece of God's armor so you will be able to resist the enemy in the time of evil. Then after the battle you will still be standing firm. EPHESIANS 6:13

The cartoon character Popeye was a smallish kind of sailor who was difficult to understand and had a funny, distinctive chuckle. His true love was a tall, lanky lady named Olive Oyl. Just like any other hero, he had an enemy: Bluto. Bluto was much bigger than Popeye, and he had a thing for Olive Oyl. Popeye got into fights with Bluto all the time. Now you would think that little Popeye would lose a battle with big, bombastic Bluto, but Popeye won every time. How? Popeye had a secret weapon: a can of *spinach*! Whenever Popeye ate spinach, his muscles got huge, and he had tons of energy so he could beat anyone who wanted to fight him, including Bluto.

As you may have read in your Bible Blast today, you're in a battle against the devil and his plans for your life. He wants you to get discouraged and afraid and to turn away from God. So he fights against you through circumstances, people, entertainment, thoughts, and all sorts of other sly schemes.

But just like Popeye, we have a secret weapon: the full armor of God! (No, it's not a can of spinach.) The full armor of God may not be something you're familiar with so we'll go through each piece mentioned in Ephesians 6 for the next six days. By the end of it, you'll know that you're a soldier of the King! Just like Popeye was left standing at the end of every fight, with Bluto lying on the ground wondering what had hit him, your faith can remain strong after every spiritual battle you encounter in life.

As we study the belt of truth, breastplate of righteousness, shoes of peace, shield of faith, helmet of salvation, and sword of the Spirit, we'll talk about what the actual piece of armor does, and then apply that to our lives. This is going to be a lot of fun!

Girl Gab: Mom, talk to your daughter about how our enemy the devil shows up in your life. Maybe he makes you feel sad and lonely, or maybe he causes problems in your relationships. Talk about what the battle actually looks like since it's not fought with bows and arrows!

12 April

The Armor of God: Belt of Truth

Bible Blast: Read Ephesians 6:10-18

Stand your ground, putting on the belt of truth. EPHESIANS 6:14

Girl Gab: Mom, brainstorm with your daughter some ways we get to know the truth of God. Daughter, what's one way you can learn more of God's truth today? Now get out there and gird up your loins, girlfriend!

I'm a big fan of belts. One of my favorite belts has a fancy peacock feather over the buckle. Yes, I am definitely a belt girl! It's easy for me to picture the Belt of Truth as being brown leather with shiny silver studs on it. But as I looked more into the original Greek of the New Testament, I found out that's not really the kind of belt Scripture is talking about. In the original language it says something more like, "have your loins gird about with truth."

"Loins" basically refers to the hips and pelvis area of your body. "Gird about" is something that we don't really do very much in our culture. In the Bible days, the people wore a piece of clothing called a tunic, something like a dress or robe. Over top of that they wore a belt-like thing called a girdle. The girdle kept the tunic in place throughout the day, and at night they loosened it for comfort while they slept. Sometimes the tunic's length got in the way of work or battle. So the people would "gird up their loins" by bringing up the bottom of their tunic and tucking it into the girdle (belt). This way they wouldn't trip on the long fabric of the tunic.

Have you ever gotten tripped up when you wear something long and "flowy"? When I wear a really long skirt, I have to be careful not to trip on it, especially when I'm going up and down steps. It sure would be handy if I could just grab the bottom of my skirt and tuck it up in my belt!

We need to make sure we know the truth of God's Word, or we can be easily tripped up by all the lies floating around us. Like, if you don't know the truth about the creation of the world in the book of Genesis, you might be tempted to believe it was made from a big explosion millions and millions of years ago.

When we're told to put on the belt of truth, the Bible is really telling us that we need to know the truth of God so that when times of battle come, we'll be ready to fight!

The Armor of God: Breastplate of Righteousness

Bible Blast: Read Psalm 9:7-9

Stand your ground, putting on . . . the body armor of God's righteousness. EPHESIANS 6:14

In one of my favorite movies, the hero of the film is a young peasant man attempting to join in the battle of sparring with knights born as royalty. Using long lances made of wood, the knights ride their horses as fast as they can toward each other and pound the tip of the lance directly into the other knight's chest. This would kill a guy—and sometimes did—if it weren't for the thick breastplate of steel that covered the knights' torsos.

In the movie, the hero meets a girl who says she can make him a better breastplate, but when she brings it to him, it seems too flimsy because it is light and easy to wear. So she dares him to let her and her friends hang a tree trunk from some chains and drive it into his chest. He's just dumb enough to try it, and the scene finds him flying through the air after he takes the blow. But then he laughs in disbelief and says, "I didn't feel a thing!"

A breastplate of righteousness is just like that. It's light and you hardly know you're wearing it, but it's so powerful that when Satan knocks you silly with something difficult, you'll be able to laugh and say, "I didn't feel a thing!"

What is it? It's something only God can give us. You see, "righteousness" is from him. He makes us righteous. Your good deeds do not make you righteous. There's nothing you can do to be righteous, but by God's forgiveness you can be made righteous and get yourself some standard-issue breastplate armor.

If there is anything you can "do" to put on God's righteousness, it would be to examine your heart daily for any trace of sin that God needs to wash away. Confess your sins to him every day and stay covered in his breastplate of righteousness.

Girl Gab: Take some time right now to confess your sin to God, and let him cover you in your own personal breastplate of righteousness. Be sure to thank God for his armor as you pray.

14 April

The Armor of God: Shoes of Peace

Bible Blast: Read John 16:32-33

For shoes, put on the peace that comes from the Good News so that you will be fully prepared. EPHESIANS 6:15

Girl Gab: Mom, let your daughter try on all your shoes, even the super high heels you only wear once a year! Daughter, pick which pair of your mom's shoes that would be the best "battle shoe."

Ahh, *shoes.*

Yesterday, my husband, Bob, wanted to do something special for me and Lexi, so he took us to this amazing shoe store in town and invited us to pick out something a little crazy. He likes to be spontaneous, and shoes are a great way to go crazy. I picked a pair of red patent leather Mary Janes. Lexi picked a pair of canvas Toms. We laughed as we talked about how we actually name our shoes—that is, "Mary Jane" and "Tom"—because we like them so much!

Remember how you read that we're in a battle against the devil's schemes? Well, if we're going to battle we need the right shoes! (Probably not Mary Janes!) Can you list some things a good "battle shoe" should have or not have? I can think of a few! It should be flat so I won't wobble when I fight. It should be secure on my foot, not like a flip-flop. I would like the shoe to cover my toes to protect them.

The Bible says that we need shoes made of the peace that comes from "the Good News." The Good News is that God sent Jesus to die for our sins and rise again three days later so we can spend eternity in heaven with him. Knowing that Jesus has done that for us gives us great peace because we know that because of his great love for us, he's always for us, on our side of every battle. And if God is for us, who can be against us? (see Romans 8:31)

Look at Romans 5:1. "Therefore, since we have been made right in God's sight by faith, we have peace with God because of what Jesus Christ our Lord has done for us."

When we wear shoes that have the readiness of the gospel of peace, it means that we're ready for anything because the gospel message lets us know that God is on our side. We don't run and hide from the enemy; we're prepared to stand and fight with God's strength, wearing our fabulous Shoes of Peace!

The Armor of God: Shield of Faith

Bible Blast: Read Job 42:1-6

In addition to all of these, hold up the shield of faith to stop the fiery arrows of the devil. EPHESIANS 6:16

The boy was in really bad shape. He was so sick. His father really wanted Jesus to heal the boy, but his daddy's heart was so sad that he was having a hard time believing that Jesus could actually do it. This is how the conversation went between the boy's father and Jesus:

"Have mercy on us and help us, if you can."

"What do you mean, 'If I can'?" Jesus asked. "Anything is possible if a person believes."

The father instantly cried out, "I do believe, but help me overcome my unbelief!"

The man admitted that he had been attacked with unbelief. Jesus loved how this man was so honest about struggling with faith. Jesus healed the boy.

The word *devil* means "to throw, the accuser." That's totally what the devil does! He's constantly throwing lies at us and accusing us of things. They are like fiery arrows aimed at us all day long, causing us to not really believe God is who he says he is and we are who God says we are. What does Ephesians 6 say is the best defense against these "fiery arrows" the enemy throws our way? A shield of faith.

The other pieces of armor do a good job of protecting, but a shield can be moved to block the arrows from striking any part of the body. We can move that shield of faith to exactly where the enemy is attacking. So if the breastplate of righteousness is protecting our hearts, imagine how much more protected we are when we add the shield of faith to the mix! Righteousness and faith are an unbeatable team!

When you feel like you're having lies thrown at you but you don't have the faith to un-believe them, tell God. He understands. He knows that sometimes it's tough. Say, "Jesus, I believe in you, but right now I need some help with my unbelief!" Then raise up your shield, because you're protected!

Girl Gab: Mom, encourage your daughter today. Let her know areas in which her faith is growing. Daughter, you have an extra protection! Your mom's shield of faith also helps protect you! Did you know that? If your faith is running low, ask your mom to pray for you.

16 April

The Armor of God: Helmet of Salvation

Bible Blast: Read Romans 8:5-8

Put on salvation as your helmet. EPHESIANS 6:17

Girl Gab: With your mom's help and approval search for "crazy hat photos" online. You won't believe some of the headgear people wear! I even saw one shaped like a giant jalapeño pepper! Mom, put your hands on your daughter's head and pray for her mind today.

I can't believe it! We got to talk about belts and shoes and now *hats*! I know a girl named Anna who sports all sorts of cute headwear. But of all the adorable, funky hats Anna may wear, I've never seen her wear a helmet!

Now I'm going to ask you a really brainy question. What part of the body would a helmet protect in battle? Of course, it's the head! It seems to me that's a pretty important part to protect. Let's make a list of everything your head does. (Don't forget the parts that are on your head, like ears and eyes.) My head allows me to think, hear, see, smell, speak, eat, listen to music, nod—the list goes on and on. But the helmet of salvation is mainly there to protect what we think.

Did you know that we don't really think very clearly about God and the Bible until we ask Jesus to be the Lord of our lives and embrace salvation? At that moment, God sends his Holy Spirit to guide us and teach us. He whispers into our ears and minds in ways that we could not even hear or understand before. It's not that he makes us smart! He just makes us able to understand. Maybe that's why the piece of armor that protects our thoughts is the helmet of *salvation* because we need salvation in order to be able to think clearly.

Do you have the helmet of salvation? Romans 10:9 says, "If you confess with your mouth that Jesus is Lord and believe in your heart that God raised him from the dead, you will be saved." If you haven't given your heart to Jesus, you can do that today—even right now! Talk to your mom about it. Then you can pray together asking God to forgive your sins. Tell your heavenly Father that you want to start totally living for him. Start spending time talking to him and reading his Word. It's the beginning of the most exciting journey you'll ever go on! If you have given Jesus your heart, spend some time today celebrating that with your mom.

The Armor of God: Sword of the Spirit

Bible Blast: Read Hebrews 4:12-13

Take the sword of the Spirit, which is the word of God.
EPHESIANS 6:17

Have you seen the Disney animated movie *Sleeping Beauty*? Before the prince entered into battle against the evil Maleficent (who turns into a ginormous dragon), one of the little fairies gave him two things: a Shield of Virtue and a Sword of Truth. She said, "The road to true love may be barriered by still many more dangers, which you alone will have to face. So arm thyself with this enchanted Shield of Virtue, and this mighty Sword of Truth, for these Weapons of Righteousness will triumph over evil."

When the prince was in the heat of battle, he finally threw his sword at the dragon's chest as the fairy said, "Sword of Truth, fly swift and sure, that evil die and good endure." And, of course, the dragon is destroyed, the prince kisses the sleeping Aurora, and they live happily ever after.

I know *Sleeping Beauty* is just a fairy tale, but I love the symbolism of it. It's always good to be reminded that good triumphs over evil.

The Sword of the Spirit is literally God's Word. Every word God speaks or has had written down is like an offensive weapon that can damage the enemy. When you feel attacked by sadness or anger, grab your Bible and speak out some truth. It's easy to do; you just "rewrite" a Bible verse into a prayer. When God's Word says, "God has not given us a spirit of fear and timidity, but of power, love, and self-discipline" (2 Timothy 1:7), you could pray, "God, I know this fear is not from you. Give me power, love, and a mind at ease. In Jesus' name, Amen." The Bible is a weapon God has given you, so you know it's perfect and strong enough for the task.

As you grow in your knowledge of God's Word and in the ability to hear his voice, you'll realize the amazing power you have when you wave that sword around. So grab onto the handle and hold it high! You're a mighty warrior!

Girl Gab: Mom, if it's okay with you, have your daughter open her Bible to the title page where it says "Holy Bible" and have her write "The Sword of the Spirit" under it. Now take time to put on the whole armor of God. Together with your daughter, symbolically put on each piece as you read through Ephesians 6. Pray that God would help you both be faithful warriors for his Kingdom.

UFOs in the Fridge

Bible Blast: Read Psalm 139:11-12

Even in darkness I cannot hide from you. To you the night shines as bright as day. Darkness and light are the same to you.
PSALM 139:12

Cleaning out the fridge is one of the most disgusting jobs. The first step is removing everything from the fridge. For the most part, that's not too terrible. I usually find expired bottles of salad dressing and maybe a rotting bag of lettuce. But always, always, always there is one container I'll call the UFO—Unidentified Food Object.

The UFO is usually found inside a plastic container. When I remove the UFO from the fridge, I take it to the sink and hold my breath. When the lid is pulled back, a weird, whitish, greenish, purplish fuzz reveals itself, along with a wretched smell. Quickly, I toss it down the garbage disposal. I often can't tell what the food was before it turned into a UFO. Baby carrots? Brussels sprouts? Soup?

Sometimes I treat sin kind of like that UFO in the fridge. If I've done something wrong, I have a choice: I can either confess that sin to God right away, or I can ignore it and the guilt I feel about it, hoping it will just disappear. That's a lot like sticking something in a sealed container and shoving it way to the back of the fridge!

What happens to sin when we hide it away? It makes it very difficult to have a close relationship with Jesus. David talked about how sin gets in the way of prayers in Psalm 66:18: "If I had cherished sin in my heart, the Lord would not have listened" (NIV). Jesus and sin can't mix.

You may forget a sin that you "stuffed away." Like the UFO in the fridge, you may even forget where the sin came from, but God remembers. He will keep bringing it up until you finally "get it out of the fridge and dump it down the garbage disposal"—meaning you confess your sin to God and turn away from doing it again. Once you do that, he throws your "UFO" as far as the east is from the west (see Psalm 103:12).

Meditation Moment: Psalm 37

The wicked borrow and do not repay, but the godly are generous givers. PSALM 37:21

You can tell a lot about people by the way they handle money. Have you ever been around a friend who never has money to help share the cost of a pizza, but always wants an extra slice? How about someone who always refuses to pitch in a buck for the coach's gift that the whole team is supposed to be giving? That isn't a good quality to have. They demonstrate a tremendous lack of generosity. Their focus is all on themselves.

God's Word says that we are always to repay anything we borrow and that we are supposed to give generously. Can you see those qualities of financial integrity and open-handed generosity in your daily living?

Take a moment to apply this verse to your life. First, read the focus verse and then pray, asking God to speak to you through it. Finally, wait for him to reveal a thought, idea, picture, or story. Write or draw it below or in a journal.

Girl Gab: Think about what things you own that you find really hard to share with anyone else. Explain the difficulty to each other, and then take a minute to pray that both of you will grow into "godly, generous givers."

Girl Gab: Talk about a time when you cried really hard. Were you angry, sad, confused, happy, or scared? Ask God to increase your faith to believe he can do anything.

Bible Blast: Read John 11:28-44

Jesus wept. JOHN 11:35 (NIV)

Saint Francis of Assisi, a Christian man who lived long ago and devoted much of his life to prayer for others, is said to have gone blind from crying too much over the needs of others. I don't know if that's true, but I know crying is a strange phenomenon. It is one of the most complicated functions of the brain and body, and while animals have tears that cleanse their eyes, they don't cry emotional tears the way humans do. We're unique.

People do have tears that are for cleansing our eyes. If you ever get dust in your eyes or cut up an onion, you'll experience that kind of crying. Did you know that those kinds of tears and the tears we cry when we are sad are made up of completely different kinds of chemicals? Sad tears have hormones and even a painkilling chemical in them.

What scientists do know is that we seem to cry to release stress. We cry because our bodies cannot possibly physically contain the emotion that's inside of us. It's healthier for those feelings to come out.

So why did Jesus weep when his dear friend Lazarus was dead? What emotion was in him that had to come out? Some of it was sadness, even though he was going to raise Lazarus from the dead. Perhaps there was another emotion inside of him too. Could it have been anger?

When the people didn't believe in God's power to raise Lazarus, Jesus could have been angry over the people's unbelief. Maybe it was this holy anger that caused Jesus to shout with a loud voice, "Lazarus, come out!" What happened then was truly a miracle: A man who had been dead for four days came walking out of the tomb.

I bet Mary's and Martha's weeping eyes popped right out of their heads! Within minutes, they went from deep mourning and wailing over the loss of their brother to extreme rejoicing because he was alive again!

We don't ever have to doubt God's power and love. Anything is possible with him (see Matthew 19:26).

You Can't Take It with You

Bible Blast: Read Matthew 6:19-24

Don't store up treasures here on earth, where moths eat them and rust destroys them, and where thieves break in and steal.
MATTHEW 6:19

Hold on to your handlebars! You aren't going to believe this one. *National Geographic Kids* actually reported on a sweet ride that cost more than $116,000—and I'm not talking about your grandpa's four-wheeled convertible sports car. There is actually a bike for sale that costs six digits. The gold-plated ride features 24-carat gold and 600 Swarovski crystals, a hand-sewn leather seat, and leather handlebars.

Who needs a bike like that?

The book of Matthew records that Jesus basically said, "Don't buy too much expensive stuff here on earth. Those things will eventually wear out, and what will you have then? Or if it doesn't wear out, thieves might steal what you've stocked up."

I read about a pretty dumb thief in Lynchburg, Virginia, who decided to have a snack while he was robbing a house. Too bad for him he left his greasy fingerprints all over the orange juice. Once the police had the prints, he was a cinch to catch!

My point is this: We've gotten greedy.

More and more, our culture presses you and me into believing that we "need" things that are ridiculous. Do we *really* need another pair of designer jeans? Is it absolutely necessary that we have the crystal-encrusted cover for our iPod? It's not that these things are bad, but the question is this: Are you storing up treasures in heaven? If you've sent a little bit of money to a missionary this month, then heartily enjoy downloading yet another song for your iPod. But if you've forgotten to give and have been more consumed with "getting," it's probably time to say no to the next gold-plated "must have" that comes your way.

Girl Gab: Have a chat with your mom about what your family thinks about money and "getting more stuff." What are some practical things you could do to make sure you keep God as more important than temporary things? Pray about that together.

Kickin' Kraft:

Quick-Change Butter Jars!

(Check out p. 370 for a great mother-daughter craft that helps reinforce today's devo!)

Kickin' Kraft: Metamorphosis

Bible Blast: Read 2 Corinthians 5:13-17

This means that anyone who belongs to Christ has become a new person. The old life is gone; a new life has begun!
2 CORINTHIANS 5:17

Butterflies are an extraordinary type of insect. They begin life as rather unattractive, slimy, worm-like creatures often covered in thorns. Their first act of life is to eat their own eggshell. Then they begin to disruptively eat anything in their path—sometimes creating problems for the greenery around them.

But two to four weeks into their food fest, these unbelievable creatures latch onto a leaf and begin a process that at first appears to be a shedding of the skin. They are really building a little house—or pupa—to live in for a while as they go through a process called metamorphosis. Inside the pupal case, the caterpillar is transformed into an adult. But this adult looks nothing like the selfish creature that went into the pupa. Out comes an often vivid-colored, winged creature of tremendous beauty. It's changed from the inside out.

I grew up catching the caterpillars of monarch butterflies and watching them transform. What a wonder! If you've never seen it, consider checking out our Wacky Appendix for a way to order some caterpillars and a kit so that you can watch them transform!

When we belong to Christ, we really do become entirely new people from the inside out. Sure, some aspects of our outside appearance may change when we give our lives to Christ, but that's because our brand-new heart wants to please God above all else. When someone truly loves Jesus, she is changed. She becomes different from the world around her. She has experienced a spiritual metamorphosis.

The Compass

Bible Blast: Read Hebrews 12:12-17

Trust in the LORD with all your heart; do not depend on your own understanding. Seek his will in all you do, and he will show you which path to take. PROVERBS 3:5-6

Do you know how to use a compass? It's so cool because if you're lost in the middle of the wilderness, a compass can help. How? If you hold it steady, the needle will always point north, which can be really helpful for finding your way back home. It works because the earth's core is like a big magnet that causes the compass needle to point toward the North Pole.

God's truth—like the North Pole—never changes. The truth in the Bible doesn't disappear depending on your mood. God's Word is like a compass to direct our behaviors and decisions.

But a compass doesn't do any good unless you actually take it out of your backpack, look at it, and follow its direction. That's the same with God's Word. If you don't study the Bible in your daily life, you won't know the right way to go. James 1:22 says, "Don't just listen to God's Word. You must do what it says. Otherwise, you are only fooling yourselves."

Just recently I felt like God wanted me to speak out against the actions of someone who's really popular among tween girls but was doing some really uncool stuff in God's eyes. I knew some people might not like it, but I went to God and said, "God, is this a 'me thing' or a 'you thing'? I need you to tell me if this is okay." Then I opened my Bible to have my devotional time, and staring back at me was Matthew 5:11: "God blesses you when people mock you and persecute you and lie about you and say all sorts of evil things against you because you are my followers." I knew then I had to do what was right, even if it meant some people wouldn't like what I had to say.

There may be circumstances when God says he wants you to do something difficult. During those times, remember that God's loving guidance will never point you in the wrong direction.

Girl Gab: Your assignment today is to find a compass! If you or your mom doesn't have one, ask other family members if you can borrow one for a day. You can even go online and learn how to make one out of simple household objects. Some cars have a compass in them. Take some time learning how to use it. Try to figure out if your house is north, south, east, or west of your school or church. Be reminded that you aren't alone when you make decisions.

Amazing Animals: Man o' War

Bible Blast: Read Matthew 20:1-16

The last will be first, and the first will be last. MATTHEW 20:16 (NIV)

Maybe you've heard sportscasters—or your dad—talking about a "major upset" in which a team that's supposed to win ends up losing. Did you know that turn of phrase started with a beautiful horse named Man o' War? He won twenty out of twenty-one races, which is *almost* a perfect record. The story of that one loss at the Sanford Memorial Stakes is where the "major upset" began.

In the early 1900s racetracks didn't have starting gates the way they do now. The horses used to just line up behind a webbed barrier until it was lifted. At this particular race when the barrier was raised, Man o' War wasn't even facing the right direction! All the other horses took off at high speeds, while Man o' War was trying to get turned around. In spite of a late start, Man o' War still came in second place! He only lost by half a length (about four feet) to a horse named "Upset." Because of that, sports announcers now use the phrase "This is a major upset!" when they're talking about a game in which an "underdog" unexpectedly comes up and beats the expected winner.

God's Kingdom is a little like that horse named Upset.

Everything God asks of us is unexpected and upside down compared to what the world tells us we should do. It seems like we won't "win" at life if we don't have money, friends, power, and possessions. God's wisdom points to just the opposite of that. Here's what the Bible teaches:

Live to serve God and others (see Mark 10:43-45). Use your gifts to build and encourage (see 1 Corinthians 14:12). No matter what you do, do it with all of your heart (see Colossians 3:23). Don't pursue power and greatness in life (see Luke 14:8-10). Go after loving God and loving others (see Mark 12:30-31).

May you live your life a little like Upset, embracing those things that are not of this world and that seem like they won't let you win. They will!

Language Lab: What Does "Redemption" Mean?

Bible Blast: Read Ephesians 4:29-31

Do not bring sorrow to God's Holy Spirit by the way you live. Remember, he has identified you as his own, guaranteeing that you will be saved on the day of redemption. EPHESIANS 4:30

In New Zealand, where there are more sheep than people, everyone knows about a practice called "lambing." Each spring hundreds of thousands of baby lambs are born, but unfortunately some of them die. At the same time, some of the lambs who live have mama sheep die giving birth. It seems like it would be a great idea for the mamas who have lost their babies to adopt the orphaned lambs, but mama sheep are very particular. They identify their own lambs by smell, and they will only take care of *their* babies.

New Zealand farmers are smart, though. They take the skin of the mama's dead baby and hang it on the back of an orphaned baby. The mama thinks, "Smells like my baby. Looks like my baby. This must be my baby." And then she loves, protects, and raises the lamb as her own.

We are like that orphaned lamb. Our lives are sure to end up in eternal death, unless God the Father claims us as his own. Jesus has died, though, and has draped us with his death. When God looks down on this earth, he sees you or me wrapped in Jesus' blood, and he says, "Looks like my Son. This one is mine."

Now you've probably heard phrases like "Jesus is our Redeemer." What that really means is that he has "bought" you with his death. It's kind of like "lambing" in New Zealand. It cost that dead baby lamb dearly, but the orphaned lamb lives and enjoys the benefits of family *because of the other lamb's death.*

Redemption is "buying back." Jesus is our Redeemer because he gave his life as the payment for our sin and then identified us as his own. He then, with our permission, wrapped us in his blood, so that God the Father will recognize us as his.

Girl Gab: What a great day to praise God for sending his Son Jesus to set us free from sin! Why don't you do this together today by picking a favorite song about Christ's death to sing in gratitude. I would probably pick "In Christ Alone."

The Romans Road: Part 1 of 5

Bible Blast: Read Romans 3:21-26

Everyone has sinned; we all fall short of God's glorious standard.
ROMANS 3:23

Girl Gab: Draw a picture of a target on a piece of paper. Make sure you draw the bull's-eye in the center. You may want to write something like "God's Truth" in the middle of the bull's-eye. On the outside of the bull's-eye, write some things down that "miss the mark" of God's best for you—things like lying, complaining, cheating, and laziness. Take some time to pray with your mom, asking God to help you do what you know you should do during times of temptation to sin.

Have you ever thought about what sin is? Take a minute to think of your definition of sin. A lot of people would say that sin is when we do something bad or wrong. Did you know the word *sin* is actually an old Hebrew archers' term? When that skilled archer took an arrow from his quiver and shot at a target, what was he aiming for? The bull's-eye, right? When the archer hit it, he celebrated. When he missed it, he called it "sin." It didn't matter if the arrow was a millimeter away from the bull's-eye or whether the arrow missed the target altogether. Both were "sin" or "missing the intended target."

God made you and everything about you. He knows what the "bull's-eye" is for everything in your life—from how you talk to your parents to the effort you put into your homework. He has a "bull's-eye" for you that enables you to live exactly as you were designed to live. When you miss it, that's "sin." It doesn't matter if you miss big time—by robbing a bank—or just a tiny bit—by "borrowing" a quarter from someone's purse. Both are equally bad in God's eye.

Our focus verse for today, Romans 3:23, says that everyone has sinned and come short of God's "bull's-eye" plan for us. That's *everybody*. So everybody needs Jesus.

Today we're starting a five-part devo series on something called "The Romans Road." The Romans Road is a series of five verses in the book of Romans in the New Testament that clearly explains God's plan of salvation and our need for salvation. If you take the time to memorize these five Scripture verses over the next five days, you will always be prepared to share the Good News of Jesus Christ in a clear, truthful way.

There's no better place to start with a friend who doesn't know Jesus than Romans 3:23: "Everyone has sinned."

Bible Blast: Read Romans 6:19-23

The wages of sin is death, but the free gift of God is eternal life through Christ Jesus our Lord. ROMANS 6:23

There was a boy named Drew who had a great passion for money and did everything he could to earn more. One day he created a bill for his mom, charging her for everything he'd done for her recently:

Mom owes Drew . . .
For taking out the garbage. . . . $1.00
Feeding the dog $2.00
Setting the table $3.00
Cleaning the litter box $4.00
Total owed. $10.00

Drew's mom was shocked at the paper lying beside her morning coffee. She read it silently and tucked it in her pocket.

At lunch time, Drew found the note he had written and a ten-dollar bill beside his plate of macaroni and cheese. He smiled triumphantly and began thinking about how he would spend his money. As he daydreamed about a new computer game, his mom placed another piece of paper beside his lunch. This is what it said:

Drew owes Mom . . .
For hugging him when he's scared . . . Nothing
For nursing him through the flu . . . . . Nothing
For clothes when his wear out. . . . . . . Nothing
For hot meals and a warm bed. . . . . . . Nothing
Total owed. Nothing

Drew got the point. He gave the ten dollars back to his mom with a big hug.

God's love for us is free. It's a gift that costs us nothing, as we learned in Romans 6:23. All we have to do is ask for it. Those who receive this free gift of salvation through Jesus Christ will spend eternity with him in heaven.

Girl Gab: Practice yesterday's verse, Romans 3:23, and memorize today's verse, Romans 6:23. Take time to pray for someone you know who has not accepted God's free gift of eternal life with him.

Bible Blast: Read Romans 5:6-8

God showed his great love for us by sending Christ to die for us while we were still sinners. ROMANS 5:8

Girl Gab: Mom, it's a good time to focus on the fact that Jesus came back to life and still lives! Daughter, how does it make you feel to know that Jesus died for you? How does it make you feel that he's alive? Tell Jesus "thank you" for giving himself as a sacrifice for you.

Imagine you're a little Hebrew girl growing up about 1440 BC. You laugh and play and help Mom cook a lot. One of the things you love is the family lamb. Lulu the lamb wanders around the house bleating for Mom to feed her, curls up at your dad's feet at night while he tells everyone about his day, and sleeps beside you at night. She's the sweetest lamb. Your dad reminds you that you won't have Lulu forever, and you know that because you remember the other lambs. One day Lulu will have to go to the Temple and be given to God as a sacrifice offering. It will be a really sad day because Lulu has become like a pet.

Why on earth would your dad let you grow so close to this little lamb if it was going to die? Well, one requirement for a lamb that God would find acceptable is it had to be spotless, without any blemishes—a pure spotless lamb (see Leviticus 4:32-35). In order for that to be possible, Hebrew families often brought a lamb out of the flock to protect it and keep it blemish free. Can you imagine how sad it would be to live affectionately with a pet that would soon be sacrificed? But Hebrew girls knew that forgiveness depended on a sacrifice of a pure lamb.

The need to sacrifice animals to the Lord changed when Jesus Christ showed up. You may run into people who ask, "Why did Jesus have to die? How does his death take away my sin?" In John 1:29, John the Baptist saw Jesus coming toward him and he said, "Behold, the Lamb of God, who takes away the sin of the world!" (NIV). When God sent his Son to die for us, Jesus became the final sacrifice for all sins. He became the pure, spotless Lamb who was killed because of our sin.

If you think it was hard for that little Hebrew girl to say good-bye to Lulu the lamb, just imagine how hard it was for God to sacrifice his one and only Son.

Bible Blast: Read Romans 10:9-13

If you confess with your mouth that Jesus is Lord and believe in your heart that God raised him from the dead, you will be saved.
ROMANS 10:9

Nancy was only ten years old when her dad died. Since her mom was very sick and lived in a hospital, Nancy had to go live with her aunt. Her aunt wasn't kind to her and made her work very hard. One day her aunt yelled at her because she didn't think that Nancy had done a good job of making the bed. She angrily ripped the bedspread off the bed and threw it at Nancy, telling her to do it right.

This was Nancy's breaking point. Tears came to her eyes as she reached for the blanket. At that moment, she remembered visiting church as a little girl, and she wondered if maybe God was real. So she simply said, "Please God, help me." Then she lifted the blanket up as high as her short arms would stretch. She felt as if a gust of wind came up under the blanket and lifted it higher. It then slowly settled onto the bed in the most perfect, smoothed-out manner possible. Nancy smiled, and she decided that day that she believed in God. Even though things didn't get easier, she always knew that God was with her. And she eventually was able to confess with her mouth that Jesus was her Lord.

There are miraculous stories all over our globe about children having dramatic conversations with God. These are conversations that lead them to the important act of confessing that Jesus is Lord and that God raised him from the dead.

You don't have to be very old to confess with your mouth that Jesus is Lord. Janet gave her life to Jesus when she was in seventh grade. Before that, she thought that since her dad was a pastor, she was automatically saved too. When she realized that she needed her own relationship with Jesus, she confessed her sins to God and began her new life with him. It's important to understand that you have sinned and that Jesus died for you, but you don't have to have it all figured out.

Do you believe that Jesus is Lord?

Girl Gab: Mom, tell your daughter about the circumstances and environment when you first confessed Jesus as Lord. Daughter, do the same. If either of you hasn't done this, why not do it today?

The Romans Road: Part 5 of 5

Bible Blast: Read Romans 5:1-5

Since we have been made right in God's sight by faith, we have peace with God because of what Jesus Christ our Lord has done for us. ROMANS 5:1

About eight hundred tornadoes touch down in the United States every year. Twisters are extremely dangerous, and you definitely need to take cover if one is headed your way. But did you ever learn about the eye that's in the center of a tornado?

The eye is a place in the middle of a circular storm that is relatively peaceful. A couple of people have experienced actually standing in the eye of a tornado. One of these people was Will Keller, from Greensburg, Kansas. In 1928, a tornado was coming toward his house, so he put his family in the storm shelter while he stayed outside to observe the violent storm. (I'm not sure that was a great idea.) Somehow he managed to hold his ground as the twister surrounded him. He said when he was in the center of it, he noticed that everything was really still. Isn't it magnificent that something so terrible and destructive could have a place of total stillness right in the middle of it?

That still, safe center of the storm is a lot like God's peace. His peace doesn't promise there will be no storms or hard times in our lives. But it does promise strength during any circumstance because he loves us and we have the promise of heaven. Philippians 4:7 tells us that God's peace is still there when we don't understand what's going on in our lives. It also says that his peace guards our hearts and our minds in Christ Jesus.

A girl who puts her faith in Jesus gets to share in this amazing peace with God. Whatever happens in her life, whether she gets an A on a test or fails a quiz, she can be confident that God is with her. She has peace knowing God has forgiven her, and she has peace knowing he'll never leave her, no matter what.

Girl Gab: Mom, talk about a time when you were in the "eye" of a "storm" in your life—when you knew that God's peace was protecting you and giving you calmness, even though circumstances were difficult. Daughter, is there anything in your life right now that is making you feel fearful? Pray that God would give you his peace.

Amazing Animals: Peanut the Pony

Bible Blast: Read Proverbs 12:8-14

The godly care for their animals, but the wicked are always cruel.
PROVERBS 12:10

When Peanut the pony was young, the family who owned him adored him. The children would hitch their sleds to him on snowy days. Peanut's small size helped them not be afraid as they learned to ride.

But as Peanut eventually grew older, he became more difficult to take care of and wasn't a lot of fun. The family had to buy special cream to treat the rashes on Peanut's skin. His food needed to be specially prepared so he could digest it. On top of everything else, he required expensive daily medications.

Peanut had become an annoyance to everybody until the day he met Matthew.

Matthew was an elderly man who had come to live with his daughter down the lane from Peanut's farm. During one of his strolls Matthew discovered Peanut standing by the fence, with his head reaching up as high as he could to say hi. It soon became a daily ritual for Matthew to bring Peanut a bunch of carrots and have conversations with the tiny horse. Peanut's owner noticed the developing relationship and gave Matthew permission to take Peanut along on his walks. Every single day without fail, Matthew would come by to find Peanut waiting by the fence, looking for his dear friend to go for a walk. It appeared as though Matthew and Peanut shared many meaningful conversations.

One day Matthew didn't come. The kind man had died in his sleep. For several days, Peanut stood waiting by the fence, looking for his best friend, Matthew. Then Peanut just lay down in the grass and didn't get up again.

God's Word tells us to be concerned with the welfare of our animals. Peanut's family was faithful to take care of their little horse, and Peanut was a great blessing to an old man.

Girl Gab: Do something nice for the furry—or feathered—creatures in your house today. Take your dog for an extra long walk, teach your bird to talk, or play with your hamsters! If you don't have any pets, walk the neighbor's dog.

Betty and Bogie

Bible Blast: Read 1 John 1:5-10

If we confess our sins to him, he is faithful and just to forgive us our sins and to cleanse us from all wickedness. 1 JOHN 1:9

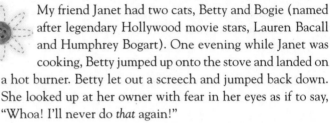

My friend Janet had two cats, Betty and Bogie (named after legendary Hollywood movie stars, Lauren Bacall and Humphrey Bogart). One evening while Janet was cooking, Betty jumped up onto the stove and landed on a hot burner. Betty let out a screech and jumped back down. She looked up at her owner with fear in her eyes as if to say, "Whoa! I'll never do *that* again!"

But just a couple of minutes later, Betty jumped right back up onto the hot burner, screeched, and hopped off again. Betty the cat was not a good example of what true confession is.

Confession is made up of two parts: admitting your sin and turning away from it. When you're confessing your sin to God, you're telling him that you agree with his view of sin and that you don't want it to separate you from him. The closer you get to Jesus, the more you'll see that sin stands out glaringly. It doesn't fit into the life of a believer—kind of like a round peg in a square hole.

In order for confession really to change your life, you have to turn from your sin—what is often called repentance. Janet thought Betty had learned her lesson after getting burned the first time. But Betty didn't get the message, so she tried it again. Confession isn't like taking a shower. You don't confess your sins to God to clean off so you can just go get dirty again. Confession is meant to include a change in your behavior.

The Bible shares some neat stories about people who are good examples of true confession. Zacchaeus the tax collector gave back four times the amount of money he'd cheated taxpayers out of (see Luke 19:1-9). The apostle Paul went from persecuting Christians to preaching about the Good News. The change that comes from true confession is truly amazing.

Girl Gab: As you read today's devotional, did anything come into your mind that you need to confess? If so, make sure you take care of that today, and don't forget to turn from that sin so it doesn't become a habit.

Meditation Moment: Genesis 1

God said, "Let us make human beings in our image, to be like us. They will reign over the fish in the sea, the birds in the sky, the livestock, all the wild animals on the earth, and the small animals that scurry along the ground." So God created human beings in his own image. In the image of God he created them; male and female he created them. GENESIS 1:26-27

The big bang theory says that the universe began billions of years ago. The scientists who believe this say the universe we live in had just a few tiny atoms that bumped into each other and blew up into our whole complicated universe. Thus the name "Big Bang."

Just because a scientist or a teacher says something doesn't make it true. (Even if it were true, where did those first few atoms come from? Science can't explain that.)

God created the universe possibly as recently as 6,000 years ago. When we believe that God created the world and us, we can know that we didn't happen by accident. God made us on purpose and in his image. He does everything perfectly, and that includes his creation of humans.

Remember that as you meditate on Genesis 1:26-27. Make sure you pray before you go over the verses, and then be still and wait for God to reveal what he wants you to know today. Once you have a picture, thought, or idea in your mind, go ahead and write it down here or in a journal.

Girl Gab: Talk to each other about what your response should be when someone tries to teach you something that doesn't agree with the fact that God created the world.

Race against Evil

Bible Blast: Read Romans 12:17-21

Don't let evil conquer you, but conquer evil by doing good.
ROMANS 12:21

Girl Gab: Mom, tell your daughter about a time when you were her age and someone was mean to you. Daughter, tell your mom about someone who isn't very nice to you, and pray together that you'll respond to that person's evil by doing good.

Do you know anything about Adolf Hitler? He was an evil ruler in Germany in the early 1900s. He hated people of different races and religions. He wanted to prove to the world that people of other races were inferior—or not as good as—people like him. To prove his point, he hosted the 1936 Olympics in Berlin. He was hoping that his "perfect" athletes would win all the medals, leaving athletes of other colors and religions in their dust.

But there was Jesse Owens. This African-American man from Alabama proved Hitler wrong. He ended up winning four gold medals right in front of Hitler's eyes in the 100-meter dash, long jump, 200-meter dash, and 400-meter relay, setting three records and tying one! Hitler refused to shake Jesse Owens's hand in congratulations for his amazing accomplishments, but no one was surprised.

As a dark-skinned man, Jesse would probably have felt intimidated spending time in Nazi Germany, knowing Hitler was trying to eliminate all people like Jesse. But instead of giving in to fear, he gave his very best at the Olympics. Many people feel that Jesse Owens did his part to help overcome Hitler's evil by winning those four gold medals.

When someone is mean to you or says hurtful things about you, it's easy to want to "get even" by doing something mean back to her. Anyone can pursue revenge. God says getting even is not the way to handle it. He says we're supposed to conquer evil by doing good. If a bully at school knows that when he's rude to you you'll start yelling at him, he'll keep on bullying you. He's trying to get you upset and make you respond in anger; that makes him happy. But if you hold your tongue and don't respond to him, there's a good chance he'll get bored with picking on you and move on.

When you're upset, don't do what feels natural in that moment. Instead, take a moment, and ask God how you should respond.

The Book with the Gold Letters

Bible Blast: Read Psalm 119:9-11

I have hidden your word in my heart, that I might not sin against you. PSALM 119:11

Carla was excited on her tenth birthday
To open the gifts stacked beside the cake.
Mom handed her a gift, and Carla took the paper off.
It was a Book with gold letters and pages so soft.
"Tell me about it," she said as she looked at her dad.
"This is one of the most precious things that we have.
In good times and bad times give it a look.
This Book will keep you from sin.
Sin will keep you from this Book."
Carla put the Bible on the table beside her bed.
The next day before school she picked it up and read
That love is patient and kind no matter what.
She prayed and asked God to help her be like that.
In gym class when Anne wanted Carla to make fun
Of another girl who couldn't really run
Carla said, "No, because that isn't kind,"
And went to run with the girl who had fallen behind.
After school Carla's brother was watching TV,
But Carla wanted her show, so she disagreed.
The argument turned into more and more
Til it ended when Carla shoved him onto the floor.
She sat in her room with a bad attitude.
"Should I read the Bible? Not in the mood."
When her dad came home she looked in his eyes
And spoke her opinion, trying hard not to cry:
"Today that Book kept me from sin, like you said,
But sin also kept me from that Book," and she hung
    her head.
Her dad hugged her and whispered, "I know how
    you feel.
I've had days like that, too, but here's the sweet deal;
Keep reading this Book and you'll know from the start
God's truth will change your big ten-year-old heart."

Girl Gab: Do you think my poetry is silly? Why don't you try to write a short four-line poem about today's focus verse, Psalm 119:11. Put it somewhere that you can see it every day.

6 May

Girl Gab: Mom, imagine with your daughter what it would have been like to see Jesus after he rose from the grave. Take some time to thank God that he is eternal.

Language Lab: What Is the "Resurrection"?

Bible Blast: Read John 11:17-27

Jesus told her, "I am the resurrection and the life. Anyone who believes in me will live, even after dying." JOHN 11:25

After Jesus was crucified a man named Joseph (not the same Joseph who was Jesus' earthly dad) took Jesus' body and buried him in a tomb. The tomb was sealed with a large stone, and guards were placed by it so no one would be able to steal Jesus' body.

Well, that didn't stop Jesus from coming back from the dead three days later. An angel came, rolled the stone away, and sat on it. The guards were so freaked out they started shaking and fell over, looking as if they were dead. Jesus was alive again and on the move. When Mary Magdalene and another lady named Mary (not Jesus' mom) went to the tomb, the angel said, "He isn't here! He is risen from the dead, just as he said would happen" (Matthew 28:6). Jesus then appeared to those two women on their way back to the house where the disciples were. He told them to tell the others that he was no longer dead but alive. Later he also came to visit the disciples.

To be "resurrected" means to be raised up, or brought back to life. The "resurrection" is a term that refers to that moment when Jesus overcame death, stood up, and walked again. If Christ didn't rise again after being killed, our faith wouldn't mean anything. If he wasn't resurrected, then there would be no promise for us of life with him after death. But he did rise again, and so will we. Check out 1 Corinthians 15:23: "There is an order to this resurrection: Christ was raised as the first of the harvest; then all who belong to Christ will be raised when he comes back."

Christ's resurrection is one of the very major things that set him apart from any and every other god in this world. He truly lives forever, and because of that, so will we if we love him with all our heart, soul, mind, and strength.

Would You Know What to Say?

Bible Blast: Read Acts 4:1-14

In your hearts set apart Christ as Lord. Always be prepared to give an answer to everyone who asks you to give the reason for the hope that you have. But do this with gentleness and respect.
1 PETER 3:15 (NIV)

Girl Gab: Okay, Mom and Daughter, it's time to gab! Talk about a time when you told someone about Jesus and what he means to you. Were you afraid? What was difficult about it?

Lexi was twelve years old when I dropped her off at pottery class. I wasn't sure if I should leave her. When we arrived, there was a gallery of skeletons and scenes of death portraying very ungodly things. I wanted to confront the pottery teacher and ask how he could justify displaying this kind of stuff in an art studio where children come to learn. I was so angry, but I felt God clearly telling me to leave Lexi. I also felt God telling me to pray for her while she was in class. I don't think I've ever prayed so hard!

"Mom, you won't believe what happened!" beamed Lexi when I picked her up. "You know my teacher . . . well, he's an ag . . . oh, what's that called when you don't know and don't care if there is a God?"

"Agnostic." I said, wondering where this was going.

"Okay, so when he said he was agnostic, one of the older students said she didn't believe God existed at all. So they both talked about heaven and hell not being real.

"Anyway, I saw the new girl looking really scared during all of this, and I don't know where it came from but I just said, 'Well, I'm a Christian and I'm going to heaven. High five!' The new girl just smiled. And then we *all* had this really good talk about God."

I was so proud of Lexi that day. She knew she was risking a lot. She wasn't sure the other students would like her if she said what was on her heart. In fact, they respected her for it. She thought her teacher would be angry, but he wasn't. It reminded me of Peter's words that we should "always be prepared to give an answer to everyone who asks you to give the reason for the hope that you have." He was basically saying, "Be ready to talk about Jesus all the time to everyone, no matter what the risk."

Love Your Hubbie

Bible Blast: Read Proverbs 31:10-12

She brings him good, not harm, all the days of her life.
PROVERBS 31:12

Girl Gab:

Daughter, talk with your mom about your dreams for when you grow up. Make sure she shares some of her childhood dreams too! Pray for your future husband, if you feel led to do so.

Did you know that you can start becoming a great wife right now? Read today's focus verse out loud one more time. Did you notice the words "all the days of her life"?

That's right. God wants you to do good for your husband today, even if he is a husband in the future.

That's what Delores Cummings of Lindale, Texas, did. (Shout out to all my Texas friends!) She was only a girl herself when she prayed a really important prayer for her husband. Church bells rang, reminding everyone in town to pray for the young soldiers who were trapped in the Battle of the Bulge. Delores remembers feeling something in her spirit say, "Your future husband is in that battle—pray." So she did.

Then she pretty much forgot about the prayer.

When she was older, she met a guy named Robert. They began to date and were eventually married. It would be years before he recounted to her a tragic scene from his past. He had in fact been trapped in the Battle of the Bulge and remembered lying wounded, face down in a beet field. He heard the German soldiers coming through and shoving their sharp bayonets into his wounded friends to kill them, but for some reason they just stepped over Robert's body. Delores remembered her prayer and thanked God for answering it.

It might seem like a long time until you meet your husband, and it probably should. All the boy craziness that surrounds you is just that—crazy. One way that you can do your future husband good is to avoid the boy-crazy mentality. You can be a girl who chooses to dream of a pure and romantic future. Wait faithfully for the right time to meet him, and ask God for strength to do that. (It is possible that God will ask you to be single, but most girls will marry.)

Start doing your husband good *today*!

"Don't Talk About Jesus"

Bible Blast: Read Matthew 10:26-33

Everyone who acknowledges me publicly here on earth, I will also acknowledge before my Father in heaven. MATTHEW 10:32

One of the most courageous young women I've ever heard about was a seven-year-old named Sallie who lived in Los Altos, California. She loved Jesus so much that she was often found praying for a classmate or encouraging her with Bible verses. Sallie's teacher didn't like that. She told her about "separation of church and state," which the teacher said meant that Sallie could only talk about Jesus at church, not at school. Sallie's mom explained that the teacher didn't understand what "separation of church and state" really meant. By law, Sallie as a student was definitely allowed to talk about Jesus. So Sallie kept talking.

Pretty soon, Sallie's principal walked by while she was telling a friend about Vacation Bible School. "Don't talk about Jesus so much," he told her. But Sallie kept talking.

Soon she was assigned to counseling because her school teacher and principal felt she didn't embrace other people's beliefs. And you can guess that Sallie kept talking about Jesus.

Eventually Sallie experienced so much persecution that her parents enrolled her in a private school, where she could talk about Jesus all she wanted. That made Sallie very happy.

If you go to a public school, you are allowed to talk about Jesus to your classmates. While you need to be respectful and kind when your teachers are not comfortable with it, you do have a legal right to talk about him.

Jesus said, "Everyone who acknowledges me publicly here on earth, I will also acknowledge before my Father in heaven." Sallie never stopped talking about Jesus. She kept telling others about him, no matter who told her she should do differently.

I just can't wait to hear Jesus call out her name in heaven one day and tell her how proud he is of her!

Girl Gab: Mom, talk to your daughter about "separation of church and state" and help her to understand that though teachers may have restrictions about how much they talk about their faith, a student has the full right to talk about hers. Daughter, do you ever feel like anyone at school wants you to stop talking about Jesus?

Kickin' Kraft:

Poppin' Calendar!

(Check out
p. 371 for a great
mother-daughter
craft that helps
reinforce today's
devo!)

Kickin' Kraft: Bubble Wrap

Bible Blast: Read Genesis 50:14-21

You intended to harm me, but God intended it all for good. He brought me to this position so I could save the lives of many people. GENESIS 50:20

Getting a package in the mail is a total blast—especially when whatever is in the box is surrounded with *bubble wrap!* It's a wonderful feeling to get a sheet of unused bubble wrap so you can just start pop, pop, popping away at those little bubbles.

Did you know when Marc Chavannes and Al Fielding invented bubble wrap, they weren't trying to make packaging materials? It's true. They were trying to invent a plastic wallpaper so it would be easy to clean. The wallpaper idea didn't take off, but the idea of using this bubbly paper as a cushion for packing fragile things sure did! And now we can have the fun of making joyful popping sounds with bubble wrap. Isn't it funny how what Marc and Al meant for wallpaper ended up being meant for packing materials?

The background to today's Bible Blast is that Joseph's brothers had done everything they could to get rid of him, including selling him as a slave. Through a series of events and Joseph's trust in the Lord, he actually became Pharaoh's right-hand man! So when Joseph's brothers came to him, expecting him to be really, really mad, they were of course shocked to hear his response to their groveling: "You intended to harm me, but God intended it all for good."

Have you ever heard the phrase "God works in mysterious ways"? In Joseph's case that's totally true. God took a situation that was meant for evil and changed its purpose to bring good.

The Ten Commandments: No Other God

Bible Blast: Read Exodus 20:1-17

You must not have any other god but me. EXODUS 20:3

God had just set the people of Israel free from a life of slavery in Egypt. At the beginning of Israel's freedom, God gave the Israelites rules for how he expected them to act toward him and toward one another. Probably the most famous part of those rules is what we call the "Ten Commandments." In Exodus 20, God gave the Israelites these very specific instructions that covered all the basics of how they should live now that he was their King.

The first commandment God listed was "You must not have any other god but me." You may be thinking, *Of course! He had just set them free from all that terrible stuff in Egypt, so how could they possibly put any other god in front of him?*

Egypt was a land where people worshiped many different idols and gods. The Israelites had spent their lives in that land and were naturally used to the idea of people worshiping lots of gods so they could receive as many blessings as possible. Worshiping God may have been easy for them, but setting him apart as their one and only God may have been a new idea. If you continue to read the book of Exodus, you'll see the Israelites often turned to other idols when they didn't feel the almighty God was doing enough for them.

One definition of *god* is "something that is so important that it takes over somebody's life." You may not have any actual idols or statues that you worship, but maybe there are things in your life you think are more important than your Creator.

Worshiping only the one, true God is really tough because everywhere we go in the world, we're encouraged to have other gods. A person has won a contest and is now going to be an amazing rock star. The sequel to a movie is in theaters, and you can't go anywhere without seeing the characters' faces on T-shirts, books, mugs, posters, and magazines. Doesn't it seem like we're being told to worship everything but the one, true God?

Girl Gab: Mom, tell your daughter about some of the things you used to totally obsess about when you were younger (e.g., movie stars, music, books). Daughter, talk about things girls your age are tempted to worship other than God. Pray together that God would give you hearts that are undivided—completely committed to your King.

12 May

The Ten Commandments: Don't Worship Creation

Bible Blast: Read Romans 1:21-23

You must not make for yourself an idol of any kind or an image of anything in the heavens or on the earth or in the sea. You must not bow down to them or worship them, for I, the LORD your God, am a jealous God who will not tolerate your affection for any other gods. EXODUS 20:4-5

Girl Gab: Here's a question for you two to talk about: Is it possible to be active in protecting your environment and animals without worshiping them? Take time to pray for a friend who seems to be tempted to worship the creation instead of the Creator.

In my local bookstore, I can find an entire wall filled with books about worshiping stars, nature, animals, and angels. Every time I sit near there, I'm always amazed at how many people stop and look at them.

Have you ever seen those toys for little kids that have holes cut out in circle, square, and triangle shapes? They get really frustrated trying to cram a square into a circle-shaped hole. Usually they'll try to jam it in and finally give up.

When people study how the stars can tell their future, aren't they just trying to cram a star shape into a God-shaped hole in their hearts? Some people think the way to God is to worship the things he's created. Many attempt this with poetry, dance, and meditation. Some try to capture the earth's energy with crystals. Others devote their entire lives to saving animals.

In Romans 1:22-23, Paul wrote about this: "Claiming to be wise, they instead became utter fools. And instead of worshiping the glorious, ever-living God, they worshiped idols made to look like mere people and birds and animals and reptiles." Later on in verse 25, he said, "So they worshiped and served the things God created instead of the Creator himself, who is worthy of eternal praise!"

Let's say you went to a friend's house and her mom served the most incredible apple pie. You wouldn't say to the pie, "Oh, apple pie, you were so tasty! Thank you! How did you do it?" No, you would go to the person who *made* that pie and tell her how great it was. The pie wouldn't be able to tell you anything. You would have to talk to its creator.

Instead of worshiping the things God made, worship him.

The Ten Commandments: Don't Disrespect the Name of God

Bible Blast: Read Philippians 2:9-11

You must not misuse the name of the LORD your God. The LORD will not let you go unpunished if you misuse his name.
EXODUS 20:7

When our daughter was born, Bob and I really wanted to name her "Lexis." The problem was that right about that time, the Lexus automobile was becoming very popular. Both sets of grandparents absolutely refused to have a granddaughter "named after a car." We finally gave in and named her "Alexis," but we call her Lexi.

Names are so important. When we meet someone, "What's your name?" is the first thing we ask. When a woman gets married, she often takes her husband's last name as her own. When a couple adopts a child, they're thrilled to give him or her their last name to show the world that this child is part of their family.

God's name is the most powerful name. The name of Jesus will one day cause everyone to confess that he is Lord. Philippians 2:9-11 says, "God elevated him to the place of highest honor and gave him the name above all other names, that at the name of Jesus every knee should bow, in heaven and on earth and under the earth, and every tongue confess that Jesus Christ is Lord, to the glory of God the Father." Jesus has a lot more names. But when Christ's name is spoken at one point in the future, *every knee will bow!*

When God tells us not to misuse his name, he's saying to remember the power of who he is. When you say his name, remember who it is you're talking about. It's very common for someone to say "God" or "Jesus" when they're surprised, happy, sad, or scared. Even those who say they don't believe in God will easily speak his name in regular conversation or from a poorly chosen habit.

I get really upset when I hear someone use *Jesus* as a swear word, but I know they do it because they don't know him. To a follower of Jesus Christ, his name is life, truth, love, strength, courage, and freedom.

Girl Gab: If you could rename yourself, what are some of the names you would choose? Have fun with it, and get creative! What about names like "Love," "Compassion," or "Fun"? What name would you choose for your mom or dad?

14 May

Girl Gab: Mom, could you consider calling for a family Sabbath on an upcoming Sunday? Just see how it goes. You might end up liking it! Daughter, support your mom as you try to convince the rest of the family to give it a try!

The Ten Commandments: Rest! Rest! Rest!

Bible Blast: Read Hebrews 4:6-11

Remember to observe the Sabbath day by keeping it holy. You have six days each week for your ordinary work, but the seventh day is a Sabbath day of rest dedicated to the LORD your God.
EXODUS 20:8-10

The Gresh family observes what we call Sabbath Sunday. From the time we get home from church until 5:00 p.m., we turn off the TV, stay home, and rest. We can—and often do—play games. Sometimes we pass out in our bedrooms. Other times we just talk. But we always unplug and rest.

At first, my kids didn't like it a lot. But they've come to think Sabbath Sunday is pretty fantastic. In fact, sometimes their friends come over to play games with us.

If you read the story of Creation, you'll find that God worked on creating the earth and all the living creatures for six days. Genesis 2:2-3 says, "On the seventh day God had finished his work of creation, so he rested from all his work. And God blessed the seventh day and declared it holy, because it was the day when he rested from all his work of creation." Whenever you see the word *holy* in the Bible, God is talking about something being "set apart." He set apart the seventh, or Sabbath, day as a day of rest.

But how do girls your age obey this commandment? It's all about creating good habits now so that when you're older, you will be a person who sees the value of rest and worship. You could make sure you do all of your homework on Friday night or Saturday so that you can rest on Sunday. Or you could ask your parents to change your chore schedule so you don't have to do any major work on Sundays.

Our bodies and minds need time to rest and get refueled. Learning the importance of rest is an incredible lesson, and if you make it important now, you'll be a healthier, wiser adult someday.

The Ten Commandments: Honor Your Parents

Bible Blast: Read Ephesians 6:1-4

Honor your father and mother. Then you will live a long, full life in the land the LORD your God is giving you. EXODUS 20:12

Janet has a *ginormous* collection of shoes. Most of the time all those fancy pieces of footwear end up in a big messy pile of sneakers, sandals, boots, and high heels in the bottom of her closet. Once in a while her nine-year-old daughter, Lucy, will take the time to organize her mom's shoes, pairing them up and placing them in neat rows side by side. Janet doesn't ask; Lucy just does it. It's one way Lucy shows her mom that she loves her.

It's great to be creative in expressing our love to our parents. Even though I'm older and have my own children now, I still enjoy showing love to my mom and dad. One of the most powerful ways we can show our parents how much we love and respect them is shown in John 14:15. In this part of the Bible, Jesus is speaking to his disciples. He said, "If you love me, obey my commandments."

Try very hard to imagine yourself as a parent. Let's say you've told your four-year-old daughter over and over again, "Do not throw your silverware when you're done eating." But every time she finishes her mac and cheese, she picks up her fork and launches it across the table until it finally lands in the dog's water dish. Do you think you would feel loved or honored by your daughter's disobedience? I know I wouldn't. When my children disobey me, I feel sad.

According to Jesus, there's a strong connection between "love" and "obedience." If you love people in authority over you, and they're asking you to do something that doesn't go against God's Word, you obey them. This doesn't just apply to your parents. Your schoolteachers, pastor, grandparents, and Sunday school instructors will know that you love them if you obey and respect them.

Since Jesus said we show love to him by obeying his commandments, when we obey this fifth commandment, we're not only honoring our parents; we're honoring God.

Girl Gab: Mom, share a story of when you didn't obey your parents and what the consequences were. Daughter, think of a creative way to show your mom love and respect today!

The Ten Commandments: Don't Murder

Bible Blast: Read Matthew 5:21-26

You must not murder. EXODUS 20:13

It's easy to look at today's focus verse and say, "That's a no-brainer. Of course murdering people is wrong. I'm definitely not going to kill anybody, so I can just skip to the next commandment." The odds are, you won't kill anybody—at least not physically.

Let's look at another verse that makes this "murder commandment" harder to skip on past without applying to our own lives. Read Matthew 5:21-22: "You have heard that our ancestors were told, 'You must not murder. If you commit murder, you are subject to judgment.' But I say, if you are even angry with someone, you are subject to judgment! If you call someone an idiot, you are in danger of being brought before the court." Ouch. Double ouch.

I can remember times when people have called me names and said mean things about me. Some of those names were used over twenty years ago, but it still hurts when I think about them. When I hear those words, I don't feel alive and healthy. I feel beaten down and confused. I can also remember times when I've hurt others with my words.

Have you ever done that? Have you ever called someone an idiot? Or have you ever said something like, "I'm gonna *kill* her!" or "I wish he would just die!" These are not words of life and blessing. And saying, "I didn't really mean it" or "I was just kidding" doesn't take away the pain the other person is feeling. According to the Bible, the anger in your hurtful words is considered the same as murder!

You see, not murdering people is important, but it isn't enough. We need to go even further than that. The Christian girl needs to express kindness and love to others, not anger and hatred. Probably the most practical way of doing this is by watching your words. Saying nothing is much safer than blasting everyone around you with hurtful words. As the saying goes, "If you don't have anything nice to say, don't say anything at all."

The Ten Commandments: Be Faithful

Bible Blast: Read Ecclesiastes 4:9-12

You must not commit adultery. EXODUS 20:14

I am crazy in love with a man named Bob Gresh. I love him for a lot of reasons, but one is that he makes me laugh when I feel like crying. Once when I was about to go on stage at a big speaking event, I thought I might just break down and cry. My hosts got me to the church late, the sound guy was mad at me, and my PowerPoint wasn't working. I texted Bob to pray for me. Do you know what he texted back? "I'm praying for you, and it will be okay. Jesus didn't use PowerPoint when he spoke—except at the Sermon on the Mount. I think he may have used it then!" That really made me laugh—just in time!

I plan to be married to this man until I'm old and gray and wrinkly. And he is planning to love me even when I'm old and gray and wrinkly! That's what this commandment is all about—being faithful for your entire life to just one man (or one woman, if you're a man).

The world probably isn't going to do a great job of teaching you about the importance of being faithful in relationships. But God's Word tells us differently. Did you notice what it says in verse 12 of Ecclesiastes 4? These relationships are supposed to be a "cord of three strands" (NIV). That's right! You, another person, and God are the three strands. The strongest marriage (or friendship) has God in the middle.

As you grow up, you may see lots of people giving up on relationships. They do it for lots of different reasons: fear, selfishness, sin, sickness, or weakness. Sometimes one person can try so hard to be faithful, but there is nothing he or she can do to make a relationship work. Bad things just happen in this sinful world. You need to know that God doesn't ever fail in relationships. No matter what goes on around you, always remember that God stays committed to you. He's your perfect heavenly Father who loves you so much that he sent his Son, Jesus, to die for you so that you could spend forever with him in heaven.

Girl Gab: Daughter, what's one thing you can do to remain faithful to your family? Mom, talk to your daughter about what this commandment means to you and the path you've walked in your life.

The Ten Commandments: Don't Steal

Bible Blast: Read Luke 6:28-30

You must not steal. EXODUS 20:15

How many ways can we say this commandment?

"Don't rob people."

"Don't take something that isn't yours."

"If the sign says *Take One*, don't take two."

This is an idea we begin teaching children at a very young age. If one child is playing with a truck and the other one takes it out of his hands, we say, "Now, Jimmy, you need to *ask* for the truck if you want to play with it. You can't just take it from Billy. Say, 'May I have it, please?'"

How do we deal with it when another person takes something from us without our permission? The Bible has the answer: "Bless those who curse you. Pray for those who hurt you. If someone slaps you on one cheek, offer the other cheek also. If someone demands your coat, offer your shirt also. Give to anyone who asks; and when things are taken away from you, don't try to get them back" (Luke 6:28-30).

Maybe you're thinking, *What?! So when someone steals from me, I'm just supposed to forget about it?* Actually, no. Read the first part of that again: "Bless those who curse you. Pray for those who hurt you." That could be pretty hard to do. But the prayer of blessing is an act of love. You're choosing to love someone who may not like you at all.

What if a big bully came up to you and said, "Give me your coat, or I'm gonna beat you up!" and you responded with, "Okay! And please take my hat, too! And before you walk away, let me pray for you." The look on that bully's face would be priceless! Maybe he would even change his mind about stealing from you.

God's motivation is always love. When Jesus was on the cross dying, he said, "Father, forgive them. They don't know what they're doing." Those people were literally killing him, and yet he was overwhelmed with love and compassion! If you have Jesus in your heart, you have everything you need to be loving toward someone who hurts you.

The Ten Commandments: Speak the Truth

Bible Blast: Read John 14:5-14

You must not testify falsely against your neighbor. EXODUS 20:16

Do you have chores you're responsible for? Is one of those chores weeding the garden? It can be so annoying because you pull a weed out of the dirt one day and it's gone, but then you go back just a couple of days later and it's back again! The only way you can get the weed to stop growing is if you dig down deep enough to get all the roots out of the ground. That's what happens when you tell a lie. It just keeps growing until you fess up and admit that you lied. Have you ever felt a fib grow?

Today's commandment tells us one big important instruction: Don't lie. "Falsely testifying against a neighbor" means that if you're in a courtroom and have to tell your view of a crime, don't lie about who did it.

In John 14:6 Jesus describes himself as "the way, the truth, and the life." He is the truth. When we choose not to speak the truth, we're choosing not to be like Jesus. And it's even crazier than that. Look at John 8:44 where Jesus talks about who the devil is, saying, "He has always hated the truth, because there is no truth in him. When he lies, it is consistent with his character; for he is a liar and the father of lies." Did you catch that? The devil is the father of lies! So when you choose to lie, you're just doing what the devil does all the time. I don't want to speak the devil's language, do you? No way! He's not my father. The King of all kings is my heavenly Father, and I want to speak like he does. I want to speak truth.

If you have a habit of lying, God will help you break it. Be honest with him, and tell him you have a problem. Ask him to show you when you're lying, because you might not realize when you do it. Once you see the lies you're speaking, ask God to help you hate lies and love truth.

Girl Gab: Cut two pieces of yarn or string about eight inches long. Have your mom put one in her pocket, and then you can put the other string in your pocket. Every time you lie today, take the string out of your pocket and tie a knot in it. Your mom can do it too. If at the end of the day you have a pocket full of knots, you may have a problem with lying. Ask God for his help.

Girl Gab: When
you "covet"
something, you
want what someone
else has so badly
that you obsess
about it, thinking
about it all the time.
Are there things
you covet that your
friends have? Ask
God to help you be
thankful and content
with what you have
today.

The Ten Commandments: Don't Be Envious

Bible Blast: Read Proverbs 14:30

You must not covet your neighbor's house. You must not covet your neighbor's wife, male or female servant, ox or donkey, or anything else that belongs to your neighbor. EXODUS 20:17

William was a poor stonecutter. He worked very hard, cutting giant mountain rocks into smaller stones, but he was happy. One day William went to a rich man's house and couldn't believe the things he saw!

That night, William said, "I wish I were rich so I could have a castle, a fluffy bed, and curtains of gold fabric!" The next morning he woke up in a fluffy white bed surrounded by gold curtains, and his little shack had turned into a castle!

One day he saw a prince in a beautiful carriage. William became unhappy and wished, "If only I were a prince!" The next morning he woke up as a prince and found himself in a beautiful carriage.

He enjoyed himself until he realized the carriage wasn't able to block the heat of the sun. "The sun is more power-ful than I am! If only I were the sun!" So the next morning William woke up in the sky as the bright golden sun. He was pleased until a cloud stopped right in front of him.

William was upset. "If only I were a cloud!" The next morning, William was a big cloud that began dropping rain day after day. Rivers overflowed, and towns were flooded. The only things unaffected by the rain were the big rocks on the side of the mountain. So William said, "Oh, if only I could be a giant rock!" The next day, he was quite content to be a strong rock and took a rest. His slumber was interrupted by a tap, tap, tapping. A stonecutter was chipping away at the rock. William felt weak. "That man has more power than I do! If only I could be that man!"

The next morning, William woke in the old straw bed of his old little shack. He went out right away and began work-ing on the big rocks on the moutainside—finally happy as himself.

Amazing Animals: The Giraffe

Bible Blast: Read Genesis 1:1-25

God made all sorts of wild animals, livestock, and small animals, each able to produce offspring of the same kind. And God saw that it was good. GENESIS 1:25

When my family went on safari in Kruger National Park, we were told that we got to go on two "game drives"—or adventures to spot animals—each day. We got up at the crack of dawn to go on our first drive, and—oh!—what animals we saw! Our first sight was a big, furry-headed male lion. We were only ten feet away from him in our open-topped Land Rover. Next, we drove up right beside some elephants munching tall African grass. There were impalas, zebras, warthogs, rhinos, and more. God's creativity was all around us. And our capable game ranger told us all about each animal. As he did, I could not help but be certain that God created these wonders. It was most apparent when the game ranger told us about the giraffe.

"Giraffes are the tallest animals on the planet," said the ranger, as we watched them grazing nearby. "A giraffe's heart weighs about twenty-four pounds and is two feet in length. That makes it bigger than two basketballs and as heavy as a small suitcase. It has to be that big to pump hard enough to get blood all the way up to that tiny little head. It's pumping so hard that without special walls in the giraffe's blood vessels, the arteries and veins would explode!"

"Wow," we said.

"There's one really big challenge for a heart like that," said the ranger. "If it kept pumping like that when the giraffe lowered its head to drink water, the poor animal would literally blow its mind. So God created these creatures with a special valve to slow things down. This actually saves their lives."

God created the giraffe so carefully. Only an intelligent God could account for the miraculous, well-thought plan of a giraffe's specialty heart-and-blood system.

Everywhere we look in nature, we can be reminded that God created what we see. That day on the safari in Africa, a giraffe reminded me.

Girl Gab: Daughter, pick one of your favorite strange animals—like a zebra, giraffe, aardvark, or platypus. Ask your mom to help you look the animal up online and find something cool to thank God about as you study how it was created.

Cash Isn't King

Bible Blast: Read Luke 12:15-21

Trust in your money and down you go! But the godly flourish like leaves in spring. PROVERBS 11:28

Margaret Layne of England died when she was eighty-nine years old. At the time of her death she owned (the equivalent of) a $564,000 house and a $161,000 trust fund. Who do you think she left her small fortune to in her will? Tinker, a stray cat that Margaret had befriended. Her neighbors were instructed to make sure Tinker had the run of the house and was well taken care of. Lucy and Stardust, two other kitties, have decided to move in with Tinker, and who could blame them? A three-bedroom house provides a lot of play space and sunny patches, perfect for three spoiled felines.

I doubt that Tinker has any idea of the gift he's received because money doesn't mean anything to a cat. Maybe we could learn something from that British kitty. Don't you think most people put way too much trust in the money they make? Some people really believe if they have a lot of money, nothing can harm them. They surround themselves with more and more stuff, and that's where their security is. Having a lot of money makes them feel safe.

Money is a necessary thing. It's important to work hard and make sure your needs are provided for. Money is not evil or bad. *Loving* and *trusting* money is the danger. The Bible talks about this problem. "The love of money is the root of all kinds of evil. And some people, craving money, have wandered from the true faith and pierced themselves with many sorrows" (1 Timothy 6:10).

The love of money will tempt people away from their faith in God. Many popular movies have main characters whose goal in life is simply to get more and more money. When money becomes a person's passion, she becomes willing to do anything to get it, and she is never satisfied for long. She always wants more.

Don't fall into the trap of obsessing about money. Money is paper. It can't save you. It doesn't last forever.

Speak Up!

Bible Blast: Read Matthew 18:5-6

Speak up for those who cannot speak for themselves; ensure justice for those being crushed. Yes, speak up for the poor and helpless, and see that they get justice. PROVERBS 31:8-9

Grace had a great sense of humor, and she loved talking to her friends. She was always making her friends laugh and getting into trouble for being so chatty in class. But as much as she talked, she had a big secret, and she didn't talk about that to anyone.

Grace was having some really big problems in her family. Someone was hurting her a lot, and she was afraid to tell anyone. One day her friend Selah came over to play. While Selah was there, Grace told her how she was being hurt. Selah gave Grace a big hug and said a prayer for her right there.

After dinner that night, Selah shared with her mom what Grace told her earlier that day. Her mom listened carefully, and they talked about what they should do. Selah's mom knew Grace's mom, so she called her up and asked to go out for coffee the next day. Very carefully and with a lot of prayer, she shared what Grace told Selah. At first Grace's mom was angry and upset, but as they talked, she calmed down and realized she needed to talk to her daughter.

Grace was so relieved finally to be able to tell her mom about her painful secret. She felt as if a huge weight was lifted off her shoulders. Her mom prayed with her and began to take steps to protect her daughter from any more hurt.

Hard things happen. Sometimes kids feel that they shouldn't talk about things that hurt them, but if they don't tell someone, they may never get the help they need. Grace felt trapped and couldn't find a way to tell a grown-up about what was hurting her. Selah was a true friend by speaking up to her own mom. Some secrets are too harmful to keep.

Speak up for those who feel they have to be silent. It may be difficult to do, but it's a big way of showing love for your friends.

Girl Gab: Have a talk with your mom today. Are you one of those girls who feels like you're not allowed to talk about something that's hurting you? Or do you know one of those girls? You can trust your mom. Let this be a day of breaking the silence.

24 May

Girl Gab: Kneel down with your mom today and ask God to plant all the knowledge you have about him deep into your heart.

Language Lab: What Is a "Pharisee"?

Bible Blast: Read Galatians 5:13-15

I warn you—unless your righteousness is better than the righteousness of the teachers of religious law and the Pharisees, you will never enter the Kingdom of Heaven! MATTHEW 5:20

Do you know the old kids' song "I Just Wanna Be a Sheep"?

I don't wanna be a Pharisee!
I don't wanna be a Pharisee!
'Cuz they just weren't fair, ya see! . . .
I don't wanna be a Pharisee!

Well, as silly as the song may seem to you, fairness definitely wasn't high on the Pharisees' list of things to do.

Pharisees were a group of Jewish people who wanted to be totally separate from the sin in the world. They did this by following lots of carefully written laws and rules. Following the rules wasn't necessarily a bad thing, but the Pharisees had one big problem: a lack of love. They followed God with their heads, but their hearts didn't get God's message that his rules were made to help them love people.

The Pharisees didn't believe that Jesus was God, either. At one point, they even said he must worship the devil because of the power he had (see Matthew 12:23-25).

In Matthew 23:3-5, Jesus talks about some specific ways the Pharisees hurt him: "They don't practice what they teach. They crush people with unbearable religious demands and never lift a finger to ease the burden. Everything they do is for show."

A lot of people use the words *Pharisee* and *hypocrite* interchangeably. A hypocrite is someone who says one thing but does another, which is just what the Pharisees did. The Pharisees really missed the point.

So when it comes down to it, that old kids' song was right. I really *don't* want to be a Pharisee.

More Than Words

Bible Blast: Read Matthew 17:14-23

If you had faith even as small as a mustard seed, you could say to this mountain, "Move from here to there," and it would move. Nothing would be impossible. MATTHEW 17:20

When I was twelve, my dad had a world-famous German shepherd named Bup. Well, Bup was famous in the dog world at least. He was one of the highest performing dogs in the American Kennel Club and the Canadian Kennel Club. As a tracking dog and obedience competitor, he had so many blue ribbons and trophies that we had a whole room dedicated to them. Bup was also a hero. Once there was a terrible flood in Johnstown, Pennsylvania, and since Bup was trained to track, my dad took him there to help with the rescue efforts. Bup was a great dog.

But then Bup got sick. He had cancer, and we were so sad. The vet said he would live only a few weeks.

I decided to pray. I knew God cared about my family and even our dog, so I taped a mustard seed to a picture of Bup and asked God to help my faith be at least that big. I knew that God said that if we have faith as big as a mustard seed, we could move mountains. Do you know what? Bup's cancer went into remission—that is, the cancer cells stopped growing. God did give us many more months with him. Those few months seemed a long time to me, and I believed God had answered my prayers. I got to tell a lot of people about faith in God by showing them my picture of Bup.

Sometimes it is hard to believe that God can do big things. It was hard for a crowd of people to believe that a boy who was possessed by a demon could be healed. Jesus told his disciples that if they only had faith the size of a mustard seed they could have healed the boy with their own prayers. Instead, he had to heal the boy.

Jesus wants you and me to have faith for the things that matter to us and to pray in faith. I hope you have at least one experience as wonderful as the time that my family and I enjoyed with Bup the Pup!

Girl Gab: Mom, pull out a mustard seed for your daughter to see just how small it is. You probably have one among the spices in your kitchen. Daughter, is there something you need faith to believe? Why not tape a mustard seed to it or to a picture of it to remind you to pray?

26 May

Girl Gab: Mom and Daughter, are you feeling artsy? Why don't you take time to draw a picture of what "bloom where you're planted" looks like? It may be a plant with lots of flowers on it in the middle of a hot desert. If you're not into drawing, then write a little poem or story about it today. Share your creations with each other at the end of the day.

Daniel: Bloom!

Bible Blast: Read Daniel 1

Daniel was determined not to defile himself by eating the food and wine given to them by the king. He asked the chief of staff for permission not to eat these unacceptable foods. DANIEL 1:8

Today's Bible Blast tells the story of Daniel, Shadrach, Meshach, and Abednego in Babylon with King Nebuchadnezzar. (Let's call him "Nebby" for short.)

Nebby's royal food was definitely going to be about a thousand times better than what they ate regularly. Nebby wanted them to eat those special meals because he thought the food would make them strong and healthy.

When Daniel and his buddies asked to be given veggies and water instead, it was because Nebby's food would defile them—make them dirty or unclean. Why would the king's food defile Daniel and his friends? There are three possible reasons:

1) In Leviticus 11, you'll find a list of foods Jewish people were not allowed to eat. If the king's meals had these forbidden foods, Daniel and his buddies would have been disobeying God by eating them.

2) King Nebby did not worship God. Sharing Nebby's food in that time may have been a way of accepting the king's worship of other gods.

3) Daniel knew that true strength didn't come from eating royal food. God was his strength.

At the end of the ten-day trial period, Daniel, Shadrach, Meshach, and Abednego were healthier than any of the men eating the king's food. God proved he was the true King.

Daniel was in a tough spot. He had been captured and taken to a foreign land to serve a king who worshiped other gods. Have you ever heard the phrase "Bloom where you're planted"? That means no matter where you are, you need to grow and bring life, even if it's not exactly a greenhouse environment. Daniel did this by obeying God even when others around him didn't. God blessed his obedience over and over again.

Daniel: Holiness!

Bible Blast: Look over Daniel 1 again.

Don't copy the behavior and customs of this world, but let God transform you into a new person by changing the way you think. Then you will learn to know God's will for you, which is good and pleasing and perfect. ROMANS 12:2

Daniel chose to bloom in his love for God no matter what situation he was in. Today let's talk about a word that maybe you've heard before: *holiness*.

In the Bible *holy* means "set apart, pure." Daniel's story is a great example of holiness. His *choices* are what set him apart from those who didn't worship God. If he had chosen just to do what everybody else was doing, he wouldn't have been set apart, and God wouldn't have received the glory for strengthening him.

Romans 12:2 says, "Don't copy the behavior and customs of this world, but let God transform you into a new person by changing the way you think. Then you will learn to know God's will for you, which is good and pleasing and perfect."

From Daniel's life we learn that a big part of living a holy life is making choices that honor God above everything else. As Romans 12 teaches us, we can't just do whatever the world is doing. We need to let God entirely change the way we think. Do you feel like you just do whatever everyone else is doing?

Look at the following areas of your life. Pick one that you want to be more "set apart" in and put a check by it.

___what you listen to

___what you watch

___what you read

___what you say

___how you dress

___how you treat your family

___how you treat your friends

___how you eat

___how you take care of your body

___how you spend your free time

Girl Gab: Mom, encourage your daughter in areas where you see her being "set apart" from the rest of the world. Daughter, together with your mom, think of one specific thing you can do to help you start making better choices in that area you checked today.

Kickin' Kraft:
Slick Bath Salts!

(Check out
p. 371 for a great
mother-daughter
craft that helps
reinforce today's
devo!)

Kickin' Kraft: Pour on the Salt

Bible Blast: Read Matthew 5:13-16

You are the salt of the earth. But what good is salt if it has lost its flavor? Can you make it salty again? It will be thrown out and trampled underfoot as worthless. MATTHEW 5:13

If you take a trip to the grocery store, you'll see lots of packages that say things like "Less Salt," "No Salt Added," and "Low Sodium" because people who want a healthy heart are cutting back on how much salt they consume. As much as I sometimes want to eat the chips with tons of salt all over them, I know it is a good idea to watch the amount of sodium my body takes in.

As much as the nutrition experts are telling us to cut back on salt, God is saying, "More salt! More salt!" Jesus told his disciples that they were salt. (I wonder if they were tempted to lick the backs of their hands and see if they tasted salty!) How can a person be salt?

Jesus said we are the salt of the earth, so let's look into what salt is good for.

1) Salt brings out the flavor of food, making it taste better. A Christian's positive influence in the world helps others see the true flavor of God's love. She helps others get a taste of the truth of Jesus.

2) Salt tenderizes. When I have a relationship with those who don't know Christ and I love them, that makes their hearts more tender to receive God's truth.

3) Salt preserves. Part of our job as Christians is to help God's Word get really planted into others' lives. If people hear the truth but don't have anyone to help them really understand and live it, the truth can get stale in their lives.

Get out there and spread the salt around so you don't lose your saltiness. Salt doesn't do any good if it just sits in the shaker.

Gazes and Glances

Bible Blast: Read Colossians 3:1-4

Think about the things of heaven, not the things of earth.
COLOSSIANS 3:2

Do you know the difference between gazing and glancing? "Gazing" is when you look for a long time at something with a steady stare. "Glancing" is looking over something quickly without really studying it.

What's the last thing you remember gazing at? A beautiful sunset? A photo of your favorite celeb? The perfect hoodie? Staring at an object isn't necessarily a problem. The problem is that "gazing" has a partner, and its name is "obsessing." It's happened to me. I've seen something in a store that I want to buy but know I shouldn't, and I think about it for the rest of the day! Have you ever done that?

When the Bible tells us to think about heavenly things, not earthly things, it's not saying that you can't even look at the world around you. It's a matter of what you're gazing at. It's easy to find ourselves gazing at things in the world when we should just be glancing at them. Along with that, we often glance at the things of God when we totally should be gazing at them.

David understood this battle for our attention, and he wrote about it in Psalm 27:4. "One thing I ask of the LORD, this is what I seek: that I may dwell in the house of the LORD all the days of my life, to gaze upon the beauty of the LORD and to seek him in his temple" (NIV).

When David wrote those words, he was in serious trouble because he had enemies who were trying to kill him. If I had people chasing me like that, it would be hard to think about or look at anything else. Many of David's psalms have to do with trying to keep his focus on God and eternity instead of on the things that scared him. He knew if he could set his gaze on God, he wouldn't be frozen by fear.

When we gaze at the things we should be glancing at, it's easy to get discouraged. But when we choose to stare deeply into the Lord, his Word, and his creation, discouragement and fear won't be able to have control over us.

Girl Gab: Have a staring contest with your mom. Sit across from each other, count to three, and say, "Go!" Stare into each other's eyes until one of you blinks. Whoever blinks first gets to say something encouraging to the winner. While you're at it, have the winner say something encouraging to the blinker, too! Pray for each other's day.

Girl Gab:

Definitely share what God has shown you with your mom. Let God's love be the reason you do everything today.

Meditation Moment: 1 John 4

Dear friends, let us continue to love one another, for love comes from God. Anyone who loves is a child of God and knows God. But anyone who does not love does not know God, for God is love. 1 JOHN 4:7-8

God's love doesn't mean that he just gives you everything you want. Since he knows everything about you and what's best for you, he loves you by giving you what you need.

We need to grab onto God's love so we can truly love others. As you meditate on these verses today, ask God to help you understand his love more and more so you can give that love to others.

Take a moment to pray that God would open your heart and mind to the truth of 1 John 4:7-8. Read the verses over a few times. Wait a couple of minutes and see if God speaks to you through a thought, idea, or picture. Use the space below or grab a journal to record what God teaches you today.

You Will Get Wet on This Ride

Bible Blast: Read Isaiah 48:16-18

Oh, that you had listened to my commands! Then you would have had peace flowing like a gentle river and righteousness rolling over you like waves in the sea. ISAIAH 48:18

The Nile River in Africa is said to be the longest river in the world. It's over 4,100 miles long. To give you an idea of how long that is, it's 2,848 miles from Albany, New York, to Sacramento, California.

Everything the Bible says means something, so when God says, "peace flowing like a river," he isn't saying it just because rivers are pretty. There's more to it. Let's figure it out. What do you think about when you think of a river? Take a moment to reflect.

Okay, here's my list and what it teaches me about peace:

1) River water is always moving. Peace is active and moving in our lives.

2) River water is powerful. Peace is strong and powerful, not a weak way of living.

3) River water makes a cool sound. Just because someone's quiet, it doesn't necessarily mean she has peace.

4) Animals live in rivers. Peace gives life to others. It doesn't take life and energy away.

5) I can float on river water. Peace helps people get from one place to another by letting them know God is in control.

I've always thought of peace as being "still, quiet, calm," but that's the opposite of a river, isn't it? God's peace doesn't have anything to do with circumstances. It's an inner confidence and assurance that God is perfect in love and that we will spend eternity in heaven with him. When peace flows in my life, sometimes it comes out as quiet hours spent with Jesus, and other times it shows up as loudly praising him with my whole heart. I can be in the middle of the noisiest place in the world and still have peace like a river flowing in my heart.

Girl Gab: Mom, lead your daughter through the second part of today's focus verse. Together make a list of five things that describe the sea and talk about how righteousness (living according to what God says is right) is like the sea. Commit your heart to obeying God's commands.

To Know Him Is to Love Him

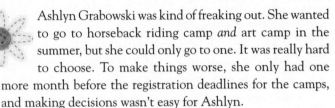

Bible Blast: Read John 10:22-30

My sheep listen to my voice; I know them, and they follow me.
JOHN 10:27

Girl Gab: Mom, ask your daughter, "How is your relationship with God the same as your other relationships? How is it different?" Ask God to help you be consistent about spending time with him.

Ashlyn Grabowski was kind of freaking out. She wanted to go to horseback riding camp *and* art camp in the summer, but she could only go to one. It was really hard to choose. To make things worse, she only had one more month before the registration deadlines for the camps, and making decisions wasn't easy for Ashlyn.

"I don't know what to do!" she pouted to her mom. "I want to go to *both* camps!"

Mrs. Grabowski stopped stirring her soup and turned to her daughter. "Ashlyn, have you prayed about it?"

Ashlyn let out a heavy sigh and said, "Well, no. I'm not sure I would know if he was speaking to me or not. Like, how do you know when God wants you to do something?"

Her mom smiled and said, "Let me ask you something. If I gave you money and said, 'Go to the store and buy me a purse,' what kind of purse would you buy for me?"

Ashlyn thought for a second and said, "That's easy. I know you like to have a bright-colored bag, so I would get red or yellow. And since you like to carry a lot of stuff, I would make sure it was pretty big, not one of those little purses."

"That's exactly right, Ashlyn. But how did you know?"

"I guess it's because I've shopped with you a lot, and I know you pretty well because we hang out," she answered.

Mrs. Grabowski handed her a glass of lemonade. "That's how it is with God. The more you get to know him and love him, the more you understand what he wants from you, and his voice becomes much more familiar to you. Take some time to 'hang out' with God, and his will won't be such a mystery."

Ashlyn looked hopeful. "That makes a lot of sense. I can definitely hang out with him more than I do. Do you think he'll tell me which camp to go to?"

Her mom gave her a squeeze. "He might. Or he might just leave the decision up to you. Either way, you can't go wrong by getting to know him better. That's always good."

Language Lab: What Is a "Testimony"?

Bible Blast: Read John 3:1-15

I assure you, we tell you what we know and have seen, and yet you won't believe our testimony. JOHN 3:11

The courtroom is tense. The judge is tapping his fingers on his desk in deep thought. An attorney calls an older lady to the witness stand. The witness raises her right hand and swears to tell "the truth, the whole truth, and nothing but the truth, so help me, God."

Once she is seated, she leans toward the microphone and begins to tell everything she saw when she just happened to be on site during a crime. She gives vivid details of what she heard and experienced, helping the others to see the scene in their minds.

She gives her testimony.

Jesus actually gives the definition of a testimony in today's focus verse. When someone gives a testimony, she tells others what she knows and what she has seen. In a courtroom situation, a person's testimony has the power to send someone to jail or set him free. That's a lot of power, isn't it? In God's Kingdom, a person's testimony has the power to overcome the devil (see Revelation 12:11). That's even more power!

When a person speaks about what she's seen God do, it chases away darkness and confusion. It also causes people who don't know Christ to think about his power and his ability to save them.

When we "share a testimony," it doesn't have to be about the day we asked Jesus into our hearts. Testimonies can be about anything God has done for us. If you tell a friend how God protected you from a really mean dog, that's a testimony. If your mom tells your aunt that when she couldn't find her keys, she prayed and God showed her where they were, that's a testimony. If you've been having bad dreams and you ask God to take them away and replace them with good dreams, and he does, tell someone about it. Share that testimony.

You never have to be afraid to testify to your friends about Jesus. Just tell them what he's done for you. If you talk about what you've seen God do, he'll take care of the rest.

Girl Gab: Mom, tell your daughter a testimony of what you've seen God do. Now, Daughter, do the same thing for your mom. Is there someone you want to share that story with today? Ask God for the opportunity to talk to that person and ask him to prepare her heart to see the truth of God in your testimony.

3 June

Girl Gab: Grab your mom, and talk to her about what you learned today. Be amazed together at the things God has created— including you!

Meditation Moment: Job 39

Have you given the horse its strength or clothed its neck with a flowing mane? Did you give it the ability to leap like a locust? Its majestic snorting is terrifying! It paws the earth and rejoices in its strength when it charges out to battle. JOB 39:19-21

Have you ever felt as if you were living in a fairy tale? Like, when you look at the world around you, are you totally amazed at all the things God created?

The trees.

The flowers.

The ocean.

The birds.

The sun.

The planets.

The stars.

Our earth is incredible, and God made every bit of it. Today you're going to meditate on Job 39:19-21. This passage contains God's words spoken to Job about one of his fabulous creations: the horse.

First pray and ask God to teach you. Read the verses a few times and then just wait on God. When you feel like he's shown you something or taught you something through these verses, go ahead and write it down.

Good Practice

Bible Blast: Read Mark 7:1-8

These people honor me with their lips, but their hearts are far from me. MARK 7:6

Greta, Molly, and Kelli are sitting together at lunch. Molly and Kelli are excitedly talking about their plans for a sleepover Friday night. Kelli leaves the table to get another straw because hers has a hole in it. As soon as she leaves, Molly leans over to Greta and says, "I can't stand her! She laughs at everything even when it's not funny. I can't believe I have to spend the night at her house this weekend!" When Kelli comes back, Molly smiles big and begins chatting away again about the sleepover.

Molly is honoring Kelli with her lips (when she is right there in front of her), but her heart is far from her.

In today's focus verse, Jesus describes that very thing. Some of the church leaders were speaking all sorts of things that honored and glorified God, but their hearts didn't follow what their mouths were saying. They were being fake, and Jesus didn't like it—at all. Those leaders didn't realize that God doesn't focus on the outside of someone. He looks at the heart (see 1 Samuel 16:7).

That kind of hypocrisy reminds me of some of the things I experienced when I was a tween. "Mean girl" moments were all around. Some girls said terrible things right to my face, and others said them in a loud whisper. Still others tried to hide their whispers but weren't very successful at keeping what they said from me. I'm particularly saddened by some of the memories, the ones when I was the mean girl, saying terrible things about someone else. Have you experienced some of this?

How you treat other people really matters. If you find it really easy to be dishonest and two-faced with girls in your school, then it could be just as easy to be that way in your relationship with God. Like, it might not bother you to tell someone at church that lying is wrong, even though you often stretch the truth when you're at school.

It's important that our actions match up with our words. It shows God and others that we really love them.

Girl Gab:
Daughter, talk to your mom about situations you've encountered like the one with Greta, Molly, and Kelli in today's devo. Mom, do you remember anything like that when you were a tween? Tell your daughter about it. Ask God to connect your heart with the words you speak.

5 June

Kickin' Kraft:
Punky Pins!

(Check out
p. 372 for a great
mother-daughter
craft that helps
reinforce today's
devo!)

Kickin' Kraft: Solomon's Safety Pin

Bible Blast: Read Ecclesiastes 2:18-22

Some people work wisely with knowledge and skill, then must leave the fruit of their efforts to someone who hasn't worked for it. This, too, is meaningless, a great tragedy. ECCLESIASTES 2:21

When someone needs a safety pin, it's usually an emergency! For example, a woman may be getting ready to give a speech in front of thousands of people and just before she walks out onto the stage, the button on her skirt pops off. She grabs her skirt just before it falls to the floor and frantically says, "Does anybody have a safety pin? I *need* a safety pin *now!*"

Ironically, the safety pin was *created* in an emergency situation. Walter Hunt came up with it in just a few hours. He created it to pay off a fifteen-dollar debt to another guy. That guy ended up giving Walter four hundred dollars for the safety pin and the rights to re-create it. Of course, he went on to make millions with the invention while poor Walter could only watch and weep at what might have been.

King Solomon (who wrote the book of Ecclesiastes) understood what it meant to work hard and create something, only to leave it in someone else's care. Solomon had worked hard for seven years of his reign to build God's Temple, and he was wealthier than any other king had ever been or ever would be (see 2 Chronicles 1:12). Eventually he realized that all he had worked for would just be left to someone else to take care of after he was gone.

The book of Ecclesiastes is full of Solomon's thoughts about how pointless it is to strive after money, things, positions, or anything temporary. At the conclusion of the book he says, "Here now is my final conclusion: Fear God and obey his commands, for this is everyone's duty" (Ecclesiastes 12:13).

The wealthiest man to ever walk the face of the earth understood that honoring and obeying God was worth more than any amount of riches.

Hello, Dolly!

Bible Blast: Read John 14:23-24

Commit your actions to the LORD, and your plans will succeed.
PROVERBS 16:3

I will never forget the feeling that I had when I was sitting watching a church musical, the lights went dark, and a bright spotlight shone on one single face in the children's chorus: my Lexi. She was about your age, and she had kept her solo a secret from me. The sweetest sound in the entire world began to fill the sanctuary, and I heard the words, "All is well." It was a lullaby from the heart of Mary on the night that Jesus was born, and it sounded heavenly. What? Could this be my Lexi? She sounded like an angel!

She's been singing ever since, and has about ten musicals under her belt. In fact, as I write this, I am sitting in the waiting room of tryouts for our community theater. Just a moment ago, Lexi was called back to sing a solo, read her lines, and learn a short chorus dance. I immediately began to pray, and I didn't know what to pray, but then I looked up at the verse that my friend Janet had selected for today and my problem was solved. (How perfect God was to supply this verse!)

So I sat there committing the actions of Lexi Gresh to the Lord and knowing that no matter what happened, she would be a success in God's eyes. What a peace this gave me. You see, in a few minutes she could come out and be called back for a second tryout. Or she could come out and be sent home. Either way, when we commit our plans to the Lord, we can know that he is moving us toward success. You see, God sees Lexi's life far beyond tryouts for *Hello, Dolly!* He sees everything that he wants for her this summer, and there might be something greater than *Hello, Dolly!* in his plans.

A Christian can have a different perspective on success, and that can offer you peace in auditions, sports tryouts, academic tests, and all of life. The next time you feel a little nervous about the outcome of something, remember to "commit your actions to the LORD." Then move forward, giving your best effort possible, knowing that your plans will be successful through the eyes of the One who sees your whole life plan.

Girl Gab: Mom, tell your daughter about a time that you felt nervous for her. Did you pray? cry? talk nervously? Daughter, tell your mom about something in your life that you'd like to "commit" to the Lord because you feel a little nervous or fearful. Then, pray together about that, knowing that God will help you to succeed in his eyes.

7 June

Amazing Animals: Loving Enemies

Bible Blast: Read Matthew 5:43-48

If you are kind only to your friends, how are you different from anyone else? Even pagans do that. MATTHEW 5:47

Girl Gab: Who do you need to show love to today? Is there a type of person you have a hard time loving? Ask God to help you love all kinds of people, no matter who they are, what they look like, or where they come from.

A camera crew had been watching and filming the life of Legadema, a young leopard in Botswana, Africa. On one particular day, they filmed her as she stealthily attacked and killed an adult baboon for dinner. Baboons are enemies of leopards and one of their main food sources, so this wasn't an unusual sight for the cameramen. But what happened next was extraordinary.

After an animal makes a kill, it's common for hyenas to gather around hoping for some leftovers, and that's exactly what happened when Legadema got the baboon. In order to keep her meal from the scavengers, she took it up into a tree. Suddenly a tiny sound came from the grass below. Legadema looked down and saw a tiny baby baboon, now an orphan. Legadema shocked them all when she walked over to it, sniffed it, and lay down beside it.

When Legadema noticed the hyenas' interest in the baby baboon, she picked it up by the scruff of its neck and carried it up the tree, out of harm's way. The observers watched in wonder as Legadema mothered the orphan all through the night. If it fell out of the tree, she jumped down and carried it back up to safety. She lay beside the baby to keep it warm.

We could learn a thing or two from Legadema.

Do you ever find yourself not wanting to talk to someone because she's different from you? Did you ever have a person hurt you or your family to the point that you instantly dislike anyone who reminds you, even a little, of the person who hurt you? It may be something as trivial as the same skin color as that person who hurt you.

God doesn't want us to play favorites with people. As it says in today's Bible Blast, if you're mean to your enemies, how does that set you apart from anyone else in the world? All people naturally want to be unkind to those who hurt them, but it takes a special, strong person to show love toward someone who doesn't return the favor.

Do You Look for It?

Bible Blast: Read James 1:16-18

Every good and perfect gift is from above, coming down from the Father of the heavenly lights, who does not change like shifting shadows. JAMES 1:17 (NIV)

My friend Janet went for an early morning walk with her golden retriever, Blue, in a field where they often walk. She spends this time talking to God as if he's walking right beside her. In the middle of her walk, she said, "Lord, how come I've never seen any animals as I walk through this field?" She felt like God answered, "Have you ever asked me?" So she timidly said, "Lord, I would like to see an animal—as long as it wouldn't hurt me or Blue."

As she rounded the last corner on her way home, she said, "I guess if God's going to show me an animal on this walk, now's my last chance since I'm getting closer to the road. I don't see anything in front of me, so I'll turn around and see if there's anything behind me." She slowly turned around. Standing just twenty yards away from her was a white-tailed deer and her fawn looking right at her.

She was so amazed that all she could say was, "Yes, Lord. Yes, Lord. Yes, Lord!" over and over again. She had stuffed her camera in her pocket before she left that morning, so she took a couple of pictures of the beautiful doe and her baby. After several minutes, the fawn walked over to its mama, and they bounded off across the field.

Every good thing is from God, just as our focus verse says. That experience with those deer didn't necessarily change Janet's life, but she knew it was a gift from God. She asked God for something, and she believed he would answer it. Imagine if she had never turned around! She would have missed the blessing entirely! She had faith that God heard her prayer, and she knew how much God loves to bless his children.

That challenges me to remember all the good things God has brought into my life. Even on totally bad days, I always have many things to be thankful for. God has given me so many good gifts, and he loves it when I take the time to thank him for them!

Girl Gab: When you ask God for something, do you look for his answer? Do you expect him to hear you and help you? Make plans to go for a walk together. Look for all of God's gifts along the way. Whether you live in the city or the country, you can find blessings from God all over the place. At the end of your walk, talk about the amazing things you saw and what they taught you about God.

9 June

Revelation Letters: Ephesus

Bible Blast: Read Revelation 2:1-7

I have this complaint against you. You don't love me or each other as you did at first! REVELATION 2:4

Girl Gab: Take a moment to evaluate how well you show love to people around you. Specifically, do you tend to love others more than you pick on others' behavior? It's easy to look at a teenaged girl and see that maybe she is dressed immodestly, but it is a lot harder to overlook that and love her. Pick one person who you have judged more than you have loved. Decide on a specific expression of love for that person that you can put into action together this week.

The second and third chapters of the book of Revelation are made up of letters Jesus has written to seven specific churches: Ephesus, Smyrna, Pergamum, Thyatira, Sardis, Philadelphia, and Laodicea. These letters contain encouragements and challenges for the people of those churches, but there is a lot we can learn from them too. These next seven days, we'll go through those letters together!

We'll begin with the letter to the church in Ephesus. If that word makes you think about the book of Ephesians, you're on the right track. Paul wrote the book of Ephesians to the church of Ephesus, so there are at least two letters in the Bible written specifically for the people who lived in Ephesus.

In the Revelation letter, Jesus tells the believers in Ephesus that they are great at rejecting evil things and evil people. They know how to tell the difference between the truth and lies. They are faithful and work really hard, *but* their love for him and for each other has fizzled out. This was a big deal because in Ephesians 1:15-16, Paul pointed out that the church of Ephesus was known for its great love for others. He said, "Ever since I first heard of your strong faith in the Lord Jesus and your love for God's people everywhere, I have not stopped thanking God for you." Somewhere along the way the Ephesians got weak in their love for others and the Lord.

When someone first becomes a Christian, she might be really excited about God and want the whole world to know about salvation through Jesus Christ. Her "first love" for God and people is a bright flame. As time goes on and other distractions come along, it can be easy to focus more on *doing* than on *loving*. That flame of first love turns into a tiny ember.

In your walk with God, if you have times where things feel complicated or really busy, remember to get back to the basics of your faith found in Matthew 22:37, 39: "Love the LORD your God with all your heart, all your soul, and all your mind" and "Love your neighbor as yourself."

Revelation Letters: Smyrna

Bible Blast: Read Revelation 2:8-11

I know about your suffering and your poverty—but you are rich!
REVELATION 2:9

Smyrna was about twenty-five miles north of Ephesus, the church we learned about yesterday. If you read Revelation 2:8-11, which is the letter to the believers at Smyrna, you may have thought, *Wow! Those people must have had a rough life!* And you'd have been right. The church of Smyrna truly suffered for their faith.

There were two groups of people in Smyrna that made it really hard to live for Christ. One group was the Jews who were very much against Christianity. They didn't believe that Jesus was God or the Savior. They thought Jesus was wrong to say that he was God. The other group that made it hard for Christians in Smyrna included a group of people who wanted to worship their ruler (the emperor). According to today's Bible Blast, some of the Christians in this city were being thrown into prison and even killed for their faith in Jesus.

And yet, our key verse today says that they were rich! Now, why do you think they were considered rich? I wouldn't say the word *rich* is usually defined as "in prison and murdered." It must be that God was talking about a different kind of wealth. When he said that if the church of Smyrna remained "faithful even when facing death" he would give them the crown of life, he was talking about eternity in heaven. He was reminding them that nothing could take away their eternal reward as followers of Christ, and that made them rich!

It was very meaningful that the kind of "riches" God talked of in heaven included a crown. You see, Smyrna was well known for its sports, and a crown made of leaves was often given to the winners of athletic events. So the people of Smyrna understood that the "crown of life" Jesus promised meant their real victory was heaven forever.

Matthew 6:21 says that where our treasure is, there our hearts will also be. In other words, if we build up treasures in heaven, we will yearn for heaven. I think God wants us to yearn for heaven, just like the believers in Smyrna did.

Girl Gab: Mom, explain what it means when a person is a martyr for faith in Christ. Daughter, did you know that Christians are still being martyred all over the world even today? Spend some time talking about how wealthy you are in Jesus Christ. What about eternal life excites you? Is there anything about it that kind of scares you? Pray that you will be able to stand strong in your commitment to God no matter what.

11 June

Revelation Letters: Pergamum

Bible Blast: Read Revelation 2:12-17

He showed you these things so you would know that the LORD is God and there is no other. DEUTERONOMY 4:35

Girl Gab: Have you ever been tempted to think that an object has special powers? Talk about this with your mom. If so, confess this to God and ask him to forgive you. Tell him that you know he has all the power you'll ever need.

Pergamum was a city built on top of a high hill. It was known for two things: its ginormous library and its idols. Many people came to Pergamum to worship its idols or "other gods."

One of the prominent idols people worshiped in Pergamum was in the shape of a serpent, and the local people believed it had the power to heal. That may sound ridiculous to you, but the idea of a serpent statue with healing power may actually go back to an episode recorded in Numbers 21. Many Israelites were bitten by poisonous vipers as a result of their bitter complaining against God and Moses. God told Moses to make a serpent out of bronze and hang the bronze figure up on a pole. Someone who was bitten by a poisonous snake could look at the bronze serpent and be healed.

Second Kings 18 tells how King Hezekiah got rid of all the idols that were in the kingdom. Second Kings 18:4 says, "He broke up the bronze serpent that Moses had made, because the people of Israel had been offering sacrifices to it." Did you catch that? The people were worshiping the snake Moses made. They didn't realize that *God's* power healed them, not the bronze snake. Maybe the people of Pergamum had heard about that bronze snake incident and decided it was a good idea to worship a bronze serpent again.

Jesus was not pleased that the Christians in Pergamum were tolerating the idol worship in their city. Tolerating doesn't mean they participated in their evil practices, but it does mean the believers didn't do anything to stop it. Since so many in Pergamum worshiped other gods, Christians may have felt it was too overwhelming to fight against the practice or tell people the truth of Christ. God wasn't pleased.

Doing nothing about evil, ungodly stuff going on around you isn't what God wants. You can stand up for holiness. Don't just turn your head and hope the bad stuff goes away. Pray hard against it, and if you get the chance, speak the truth in love.

Revelation Letters: Thyatira

Bible Blast: Read Revelation 2:18-29

I know all the things you do. I have seen your love, your faith, your service, and your patient endurance. And I can see your constant improvement in all these things. REVELATION 2:19

One of my best days of 2010 happened when I found out that my good friend Dr. James Dobson had recommended one of my books in his best-selling book *Bringing Up Girls*! He said that my original Secret Keeper Girl mother/daughter "date" resource is one of the best resources for a mom to use when raising her little girl. I am not ashamed to say that I screamed joyfully at the top of my lungs when I found out! Of course, I told my mom first.

It feels so good when someone notices your hard work. Let's say you've recently started piano lessons and you've finally mastered "Mary Had a Little Lamb." It would be great to hear your instructor say, "You've done so well!" instead of saying, "Big deal. I can't wait until you can play one of Beethoven's sonatas." Jesus told the believers in Thyatira that he noticed their "constant improvement" in their love, faith, service, and patient endurance. He didn't say, "What you're doing isn't good enough." Jesus is an encourager!

We are to try to be like God who is perfect (see Matthew 5:48), but we won't be entirely perfected until we're with him in heaven. Until then we are "to do what is right, to love mercy, and to walk humbly with . . . God" (Micah 6:8).

The Christians of Thyatira must have been so encouraged to hear positive words, because it sounds like an evil woman named Jezebel was all over their city spreading bad ideas, especially about not being faithful and true in marriage. Knowing that Jesus saw their spiritual growth may have been just what they needed to overcome discouragement about Jezebel's influence on the people in their city.

Did you know the word *encourage* literally means to "breathe courage" into another person? In this letter, I can see why Jesus breathed courage into the Thyatira church right away. They were feeling weak. Encouragement from Jesus has the power to help a tired person get up and keep on obeying.

Girl Gab: Take some time to "breathe courage" into each other today. You can encourage each other verbally right now or later after you've had time to think about it, or you could write it in a note. You could even play a song that would bring encouragement and strength.

13 June

Revelation Letters: Sardis

Bible Blast: Read Revelation 3:1-6

I know all the things you do, and that you have a reputation for being alive—but you are dead. REVELATION 3:1

Girl Gab: Write Matthew 23:25-26 on a piece of paper. Post it by your dishwasher or sink for a week. As you do dishes or load the dishwasher, make this a prayer for yourself, like this: "God, help me not just be concerned about what people see on the outside. Help me make sure the inside of me is clean and pure too. Amen."

Imagine you went to your grandma's house to hang out. While you're there, she asks you to make a cup of tea. You open the kitchen cabinet to get a mug, choosing the one you gave her for her birthday. It has "World's Greatest Grandma" written on it in gold cursive letters. When you set it on the counter, you gasp because the inside of that beautiful mug is disgusting! It's dirty and moldy and even has an old tea bag in it. "Grandma!" you shriek. "The inside of this mug is filthy! Don't you wash things before you put them away?" Your grandma says, "Of course I wash them, dear! But I just wash the outside. It's a lot less work, and the mugs still look pretty stacked and lined up in the cabinet."

That may sound ridiculous to you, but that's what Jesus' problem was with the church in Sardis. The believers looked great on the outside and appeared to be alive and well, but actually the people of the church were full of sin and filth.

In Matthew 23:25-26, Jesus challenged the Pharisees with the same problem. Pharisees were religious leaders who followed lots of laws but didn't know much about love and grace. Jesus said to them, "What sorrow awaits you teachers of religious law and you Pharisees. Hypocrites! For you are so careful to clean the outside of the cup and the dish, but inside you are filthy—full of greed and self-indulgence! You blind Pharisee! First wash the inside of the cup and the dish, and then the outside will become clean, too."

Don't judge churches or people on all the things they *do* for Jesus. A person can be really busy with church activities, yet still be almost dead in her faith in Jesus, just like the church of Sardis. In verse 3 of today's Bible Blast passage, Jesus told them to get back to what first brought them to Christ and grab onto it tightly. They also needed to repent.

Being busy with lots of churchy things isn't what gets you to heaven; Jesus paid that price. Being alive in your faith is all about loving Jesus with everything you've got.

Revelation Letters: Philadelphia

Bible Blast: Read Revelation 3:7-13

I know all the things you do, and I have opened a door for you that no one can close. You have little strength, yet you obeyed my word and did not deny me. REVELATION 3:8

Have you ever felt like you can't do anything great for God until you're an adult? Do you feel as if adults who live for Jesus have greater strength than you? According to today's focus verse, the amount of strength you have doesn't matter to Jesus. It's what you *do* with that strength.

Just because you're young, it doesn't mean you have an excuse to sit back and wait until you're older to live for God. 1 Timothy 4:12 says, "Don't let anyone look down on you because you are young, but set an example for the believers in speech, in life, in love, in faith and in purity" (NIV).

Let's break that verse down together. You can set an example in:

Your speech. Matthew 12:34 says that whatever is in your heart is revealed by the words you speak. If you have anger, jealousy, unforgiveness, and criticism in your heart, that's what will be coming out of your mouth. To set an example in the way you speak, make sure your heart is right before God.

Your life and your love. Ask yourself, "Why do I do what I do?" Romans 12:1 challenges us to "take your everyday, ordinary life—your sleeping, eating, going-to-work, and walking-around life—and place it before God as an offering" (*The Message*). If you do everything as worship to God, your life will naturally be an example for others.

Your faith. One thing I really admire about children is their faith seems so strong. They believe the impossible can happen so easily. Jesus admires their faith too. "I tell you the truth, anyone who doesn't receive the Kingdom of God like a child will never enter it" (Mark 10:15).

Your purity. You take the first step toward living a pure life in your thoughts. Philippians 4:8 reminds you to "fix your thoughts on what is true, and honorable, and right, and pure, and lovely, and admirable." If your mind is set on the pure things of God, your actions will follow.

Girl Gab: Pray today that others would be challenged by the example of your speech, life, love, faith, and purity.

Revelation Letters: Laodicea

Bible Blast: Read Revelation 3:14-22

I know all the things you do, that you are neither hot nor cold. I wish that you were one or the other! REVELATION 3:15

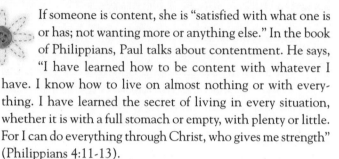

Girl Gab: Get three cups of water. Put ice in one. Microwave one until it's really hot. And make one neither hot nor cold, but lukewarm. Which one appeals to you the most today? If it's a warm summer day, you may not want a hot drink! So have a cold drink of water with your mom and talk about contentment.

If someone is content, she is "satisfied with what one is or has; not wanting more or anything else." In the book of Philippians, Paul talks about contentment. He says, "I have learned how to be content with whatever I have. I know how to live on almost nothing or with everything. I have learned the secret of living in every situation, whether it is with a full stomach or empty, with plenty or little. For I can do everything through Christ, who gives me strength" (Philippians 4:11-13).

Godly contentment is being satisfied no matter what your circumstances. It's not always wanting more stuff or a different life. It's living for Christ in all situations. According to Paul, the main secret to contentment is relying on Christ's strength, knowing you can't do it without him.

There is a bad kind of contentment. It's being satisfied to stay the same, without striving to become more like Jesus. If that applies to you, then you've asked Jesus into your heart but that's all you really want to do. You're not hot or cold. You're lukewarm in your relationship with him.

Personally, if I have a drink I either want it to be ice cold or piping hot. If I forget and leave my hot tea on the counter and take a sip of it a half hour later, it's not satisfying at all. I immediately stick the cup in the microwave and "nuke" it until it's nice and steamy again.

The unbelievers in our world have a hard time finding refreshment in the life of a lukewarm Christian. They might see the truth in her life but wonder why she doesn't really live it. Her lukewarm life is not very inspiring.

Every moment of the day, we're choosing who or what we're going to serve. Don't be content just to float through life with Jesus in your heart. Decide today that you will be totally on fire for your King!

Kickin' Kraft: Surfer Girl

Bible Blast: Read Jeremiah 29:11-13

I thank Christ Jesus our Lord, who has given me strength to do his work. He considered me trustworthy and appointed me to serve him. 1 TIMOTHY 1:12

Bethany Hamilton was practically born surfing. Living in Hawaii, her mom and dad started putting her on a surfboard when she was just learning to walk. When Bethany was eight years old, she entered her first surfing competition and won! By the time she was thirteen, her surfing talent became well known among other surfers. Everyone was convinced she would become a professional surfer—until October 31, 2003.

Bethany was surfing with her brother, her BFF, and her BFF's dad off Kauai's North Shore when she was attacked by a fourteen-foot-long tiger shark. Her surfing companions went into action to stop the bleeding as much as possible and got her back to shore as fast as they could. She lost more than 60 percent of her blood and had to undergo several surgeries. It was a miracle that the tiger shark did not take Bethany's life— but it did take her entire left arm.

People were amazed at Bethany's positive attitude throughout the whole ordeal. They discovered that surfing wasn't the only thing her parents had taught her. They had also taught her about Jesus Christ. When Bethany was just five years old, she gave her life to Jesus. That's where her peace came from in the midst of a life-changing shark attack.

Her positive attitude wasn't the only amazing thing about Bethany. About a month after the shark attack, she was back up on a surfboard. She still wanted to become a professional surfer and had the courage to keep trying even though she only had one arm. Bethany worked hard and eventually won first place in the Explorer Women's division of the 2005 National Scholastic Surfing Association National Championships! And that's just the beginning of her achievements as a one-armed surfer. She's gone on to place in many other surfing competitions, and she's done it all without receiving any special treatment for her "handicap."

Kickin' Kraft: Boomin' Beach Bag!

(Check out p. 372 for a great mother-daughter craft that helps reinforce today's devo!)

17 June

The People's Pedestal

Bible Blast: Read 1 Corinthians 12:12-20
The human body has many parts, but the many parts make up one whole body. So it is with the body of Christ.
1 CORINTHIANS 12:12

Girl Gab: Here's a trivia question: Daughter, do you know why the Statue of Liberty is green? If you don't know, make sure you find out today and quiz other people! If there's someone who's a Christian who you don't really like, pray that God would show you what her job might be in the body of Christ. Then pray that God would bless her efforts and abilities.

The country of France gave the Statue of Liberty to the United States as a gift. France and America had fought side by side during the American Revolution. The French wanted to give us a gift to symbolize our passion for freedom and their friendship with us. So a sculptor named Frédéric-Auguste Bartholdi began designing the 151-foot-tall statue in the late 1860s with the help of Alexandre Gustave Eiffel (who later designed the Eiffel Tower in Paris).

In order to pay for the gift, the French people conducted fund-raisers and lotteries to cover the cost of the actual statue and told the Americans they were responsible for paying for the pedestal she stood on. Well, for different reasons, the government didn't approve the money needed for the pedestal, which was close to $250,000. Eventually, the American people started raising money for it, mainly led by John Pulitzer of *The World* paper. He told the people if they donated any amount toward the Statue of Liberty's pedestal he would print their name in his paper. Money started coming in, in all different amounts. There are even reports of kindergarteners in Iowa sending $1.35 toward the cause.

When the Statue of Liberty was finally dedicated on October 28, 1886, it was of great significance to both the French and the American people. The statue and the pedestal were paid for with the nickels and dimes of the individual people, both rich and poor, living in France and America. It had become a project that included everybody.

God created us to work together as one body—the body of Christ. Just like you read at the beginning of your devo today, we're all different parts of the body with important roles. All the parts are meant to work together to glorify God.

The next time you visit Lady Liberty or see a picture of her, be reminded that if we work together, God can do extraordinary things through us!

Lucy's Question

Bible Blast: Read Psalm 5:1-4

O LORD, hear me as I pray; pay attention to my groaning.
PSALM 5:1

Lucy had a zillion math problems to do for homework one night. She began her work at the kitchen table and got frustrated quickly.

"What's wrong, honey?" her mom asked.

"I have all this work to do, and our teacher said our homework's only supposed to take us thirty minutes, but tonight it's definitely gonna take longer than that. I can't focus, either, " Lucy answered as her shoulders sagged.

"I'm really sorry, but sometimes that happens. Just start at the beginning and keep on going until it's done. Why don't you go work on them at the desk in your room where it's quieter and less distracting?" asked her mom.

Lucy said, "Okay, but I'm not sure it's gonna help."

As she walked toward her room, her mom stopped her and said, "Lucy, have you prayed and asked God to help you focus on your work?"

"No," she answered. "But I guess I will."

About fifteen minutes later, Lucy cheerfully came out of her room because she had finished her math. Her mom gave her a hug and encouraged her. "Lucy, I'm so proud of you! Even though you didn't want to do that work, you did it—and with a good attitude! That's so great!"

"Thanks, Mom," she said. "But how do you know if God is helping you?"

"Did you pray and ask him to help you?"

"Yeah," Lucy said.

"Did you get it done and was it easier to focus?"

"Yeah," Lucy said again.

Her mom said, "So wouldn't you say God helped you?"

"Yeah, I guess he did," Lucy answered.

"Sometimes God helps us in ways we can see and touch, and sometimes he helps us in ways we can feel. God heard your prayers, and he gave you the ability to focus, just like you asked," her mom said warmly, and this made Lucy feel good.

Girl Gab: Did you know you can ask God for help with absolutely anything? Take time to pray now about something you need his help with.

Bible Blast: Read Psalm 127:3-5

Children born to a young man are like arrows in a warrior's hands. PSALM 127:4

Girl Gab:

Mom, I'm going to ask you to do something kind of different. I want you first of all to tell your daughter what a gift she is to you. Then take her hands in yours, look her in the eyes, and say (inserting her name), "_____, you are my arrow, and I want you to go into the world and share Jesus Christ." Daughter, if your mom cries while she does this, it's because she's filled with love for you.

When I say, "Wanna go for a walk?" to my dog, Stormie, she begins to quiver with excitement. Walking is one of her favorite things to do. Sometimes she hears us mention the word *walk* just in conversation with each other, and she starts quivering. It's hilarious! To avoid traumatizing her, we have resorted to spelling the word—W-A-L-K—when we're using it in any circumstance other than the moment before we take her for a walk.

Did you know that *quiver* is an archery term, too? A quiver is the case that holds an archer's arrows. In all the Robin Hood movies, Robin holds up his bow and grabs arrows one by one from the quiver on his back to shoot.

According to Psalm 127, you're in a quiver, but not literally, of course. That would be uncomfortable! When someone is given the gift of a child, it's like he's been given an arrow. How can children be "like arrows in a warrior's hands"?

Ever since our first son, Robby, was born, Bob and I have been teaching him the ways of the Lord. The same thing goes for our daughter, Lexi. And when we adopted Autumn, we immediately started filling her in on our faith and the truth of God's Word. When parents do this with their children, they are turning them into effective weapons to be shot out into the world.

So when Lexi goes out with friends who aren't believers, I feel as if I'm putting her into my bow, aiming her at those who don't know Christ, and releasing her to make an impact for Christ. She's one of my precious, strong arrows. If I just kept my kids in my "quiver" and never let them affect the world around them, they wouldn't get to experience the blessing of leading others to Jesus Christ.

You are an arrow, and you are such a gift from God! When your parents teach you about how God wants you to live or correct you for doing something wrong, try to see it as a blessing. They're turning you into a super-sharp arrow!

Running with Love

Bible Blast: Read John 15:12-13

If one falls down, his friend can help him up. But pity the man who falls and has no one to help him up! ECCLESIASTES 4:10 (NIV)

Derek Redmond was a fast runner. He hoped to make his dreams come true and win a medal in the 400-meter race at the 1988 Olympics in Seoul, Korea, but just minutes before his race he had to back out because of an injury. He had to undergo five surgeries to heal it.

So when an opportunity came for Derek to participate in the 1992 Olympics in Barcelona, he was pumped and ready to show the world just how fast he was. His dad, Jim, who is also Derek's very best friend, went with him, just as he always had done for all his son's races. When it came time for the 1992 Olympics, they agreed that, no matter what happened, Derek would finish his race.

On the day of the race that would qualify Derek for the finals, excitement was high in the Olympic stadium. Derek had a really strong start to the race. His dad watched from the stands, knowing his son was going to qualify and have a shot at a medal.

Derek was not far from the finish line when he heard a "pop" from his right hamstring muscle. He fell to the ground, and medical teams ran to help him. They wanted to put Derek on a stretcher to get him off the track, but before they could get to him, he stood and began slowly limping his way to the finish line. The crowd went wild cheering for Derek.

When Jim saw his son fall, he started making his way down through the stands, doing whatever he could to get to Derek. He got past security guards to reach his son. He put his arm around Derek's waist and said, "We'll finish this."

Father and son slowly made their way to the goal. When they got a couple of steps away from the finish, Jim let go of Derek and let him cross the line by himself. Then he held his son as they both cried on each other's shoulders.

Later, Jim said, "I'm the proudest father alive. I'm prouder of him than I would have been if he had won the gold medal. It took a lot of guts for him to do what he did."

Girl Gab: Do something special for your dad today or for someone who's like a father to you. Take time now to pray for him.

21 June

Girl Gab: Talk to your mom about today's Meditation Moment. What kind of season do you both feel that you're in right now?

Meditation Moment: Ecclesiastes 3

For everything there is a season, a time for every activity under heaven. A time to be born and a time to die. A time to plant and a time to harvest. ECCLESIASTES 3:1-2

It's so good to have different seasons.

The colder weather of winter is nice for snuggling up in a cozy hoodie and fuzzy slippers.

Spring's flowers and new green grass are so beautiful and inspiring.

Summer's great to get a break from school and hit the pool.

The red, gold, and orange leaves of autumn are so rich and wonderful to photograph.

Our lives have different seasons too. There are times of great joy and laughter and times of sadness and tears. There are times when we feel surrounded by friends and times when we feel alone.

As you meditate on today's verses, remember that no matter what the season is, God is always with you. Pray first, then read the verses a few times. Take a minute to be quiet and let God speak to you. When you feel like he's shown you a picture, thought, or idea, write it down.

Getting What We Don't Deserve

Bible Blast: Read Matthew 27:15-22

He canceled the record of the charges against us and took it away by nailing it to the cross. COLOSSIANS 2:14

When looking at the story of Jesus' crucifixion, it can be easy to overlook one very important person, Barabbas. You read his story in the Bible Blast today.

Do you want to know why Barabbas was in prison? You can find the answer in Mark 15:7. Basically, Barabbas had rebelled against the Roman government and had murdered someone. When the crowd chose to have Barabbas released and Jesus crucified, they were setting a murderer free and having an innocent man killed.

It's impossible for us to know exactly what Barabbas thought about the whole thing. We can assume he was excited to be set free that day, but how did he feel about Jesus Christ, a man who had never hurt anyone, being executed in his place?

It was common for the people to watch when criminals were crucified. There's a good chance Barabbas saw the entire thing. When Jesus spoke to the criminal hanging on a cross beside him, saying, "I assure you, today you will be with me in paradise," was Barabbas thinking, *Can my sins be forgiven too?* When they put the nails in Jesus' hands and feet, Barabbas would have known that the man on the cross should have been him. When they pierced Jesus' side with a spear, maybe Barabbas laid his hand on his own side.

Jesus took all of our sin upon himself when he died on the cross (see 2 Corinthians 5:21). When he was nailed to the cross, so was our sin. For Barabbas, that was what happened, just as today's focus verse describes. I wonder what Barabbas did after he was released.

When people choose to give their lives to Jesus, they need to understand that Jesus broke the power of sin and death when he died on the cross and rose again. When a person lives her life knowing she's been forgiven and set free, she will impact the world around her in great ways.

Girl Gab: Are you friends with someone who doesn't know Jesus nailed that person's sins to the cross so he or she can be forgiven? Pray this prayer for him or her today: "Dear Jesus, thank you for dying on the cross for my friend, _____. Please help him/her to understand that you took all the sin on your shoulders so that he/she could be forgiven and set free. Let him/her believe in you, live for you, and do great things because of you. In your name, amen."

One Hare-y Situation

Bible Blast: Read James 1:12-15

Temptation comes from our own desires, which entice us and drag us away. JAMES 1:14

Girl Gab: You can actually find photos of the large groups of rabbits in Australia and the severe damage they've done. Get your mom, and check it out online! Ask God to help you not to let sin into your life knowing you can't control it.

Thomas Austin left England and moved to Australia. Before his move, he was really into hunting, and Australia didn't have opportunities for the sport that he was used to. To solve the problem, he had twenty-four rabbits and some other animals sent from England so he could release them onto his property.

If you know anything about rabbits, you probably know that they produce baby rabbits very, very quickly. From the time a mama rabbit gets pregnant, it only takes about thirty days before the babies are born. A female rabbit can have up to fourteen babies at a time. So if a mama bunny is able to have a litter of babies once every month, and those babies can start having babies when they're just a few months old, rabbits could take over the world!

Well, not really, but they sure began to take over Thomas Austin's property in Australia. The twenty-four rabbits he had released multiplied so quickly that within ten years, people caught *two million* rabbits and still didn't affect the population of those little guys. By 1950, there were about 600 *million rabbits* overtaking the area!

The rabbits have done serious damage to the land because of all their eating, especially to farmers' crops. When Thomas Austin was asked about this, he said, "The introduction of a few rabbits could do little harm and might provide a touch of home, in addition to a spot of hunting."

A lot of people feel the same way about sin. They think if they just let one little area of sin into their lives, they'll be able to control it, but that isn't the case. Just like verse 15 of the Bible Blast says, "These desires give birth to sinful actions. And when sin is allowed to grow, it gives birth to death."

Giving into "little" sins leads to getting wrapped up in "bigger" sin.

You may think, *It's just a few rabbits*, but those rabbits can lead to "destruction."

Sweet from Sour

Bible Blast: Read Psalm 42:1-5

Why am I discouraged? Why is my heart so sad? I will put my hope in God! PSALM 42:5

Years ago, my husband and I started a community-wide event called Lemon-AID! It was a huge county-wide lemonade sale hosted by kids in their own backyards. Our purpose? To fight child abuse, which means children being harmed by adults. We sold thousands and thousands of gallons of lemonade and made thousands of dollars, just by letting kids help other kids! That event reminds me of this famous quote: "When life hands you lemons, make lemonade."

What do you think that means?

Most people would say that because it's so sour, a lemon isn't good for much unless you do something with it. So you could interpret this quote as meaning, when something happens in life that seems really bad, see what good you can bring out of it.

That's exactly what George Eyser did. He was born in the late 1800s, and when he was a boy, his left leg was run over by a train. The doctors had to amputate most of his leg, leaving him with an artificial leg made out of wood. (There's the lemon.) Nowadays, artificial limbs are much more high-tech and realistic than the one George had.

George liked sports, so he began to train as a gymnast for the 1904 Olympics in St. Louis in spite of his wooden leg. He amazed everyone when he won six medals in one day! Three of the medals were gold, two were silver, and one was bronze. (There's the lemonade.)

It would have been very easy for George to look down where his leg used to be and just be discouraged 24/7. Instead, he decided to do what he would have done if he had both legs: compete in sports. It turns out he was really good!

If you get handed a lemon in life, tell God how you feel about it and then ask him how you can use it for something good. Don't just give up and stay discouraged. God has a plan for everything.

Girl Gab: Make some Luscious Lemonade together while you talk about bad things that God can use for good! You can find the recipe in the Wacky Appendix.

Amazing Animals: The Dana Octopus Squid

Bible Blast: Read Psalm 139:7-12

When you go through deep waters, I will be with you. When you go through rivers of difficulty, you will not drown. When you walk through the fire of oppression, you will not be burned up; the flames will not consume you. ISAIAH 43:2

Some wild creatures live in the deep parts of the ocean, and the Dana Octopus Squid is no exception. It's one of the largest species of squid, growing up to 135 pounds.

Up until 2005, no one had been able to catch one of these funky guys on film. And do you know how deep into the ocean they had to go to find one? More three thousand feet down! The Dana Octopus Squid doesn't have the two tentacles that other squid have to catch their prey, so it has to rely on an entirely unique hunting skill: lights.

The Dana Octopus Squid has things called "photophores" on the ends of its arms that emit bright light. Scientists think the squid flashes the bright light (remember, it's pitch-black dark that deep in the ocean, so animals' eyes aren't used to light) in its prey's face, which stuns the soon-to-be-food. The squid grabs it and—well, you know.

Once again, God's creativity is mind-blowing. Only he would know to give a squid flashlights!

When people are in the midst of a difficult time, sometimes they'll say, "We're going through some deep waters." It's true that hard times happen to everyone. But today's focus verse reminds us that although we'll go through the deep waters, we won't be overcome by them because God is in the waters with us. And guess what? He's got something a lot better than flashlights on the ends of his arms to help us. He has undying love for me, for you, for everyone.

When we're going through the deep waters, God is right there saying, "It's okay. We'll get through this. Just trust me, and you will not drown or be burned. Keep your eyes on me. I love you." No human can promise he'll always be there for us, but our heavenly Father can. He is our Forever God, and he's full of Forever Love.

A Word from the Wise

Bible Blast: Read Proverbs 31:25-26

A fool is quick-tempered, but a wise person stays calm when insulted. PROVERBS 12:16

Think of somebody you consider really wise. Now think of a character in a movie or book who is wise. What about that character tells you he or she has wisdom?

Wise people are amazing at giving advice. It's as if they have a flashlight they shine into a situation that makes everything clear. Wisdom is different from knowledge because it's an ability to use knowledge, experience, and the Holy Spirit to figure things out. Knowledge is simply knowing stuff, which is also good but not as good as wisdom.

According to the Bible, wise people are also good at silence. Those who I think are wise aren't usually the ones who are talking 24/7 and have an answer for everything. They stop and take time to think and pray and watch their words.

It's easy to get angry when someone hurts your feelings, isn't it? You want to defend yourself right away or say something back to make her feel bad too. But if you do that, you're just grabbing onto that person's sin and passing it on.

Proverbs 10:19 says that where there's a lot of talking, there's a lot of sin. Have you ever seen that happen? Chances are if a group of people is talking, talking, talking, something sinful is going to come out of their mouths at some point.

If someone insults you and you immediately lash out with angry words back at her, you'll just make the other person happy. She *wanted* to upset you. That's why she said it in the first place. Instead, try to respond with silence. Think about the wise thing to say right in that moment.

A verse I like to remember when I'm in a difficult situation is "Even fools are thought wise when they keep silent" (Proverbs 17:28). When I'm tempted to speak harsh words out of anger or frustration, I try to remember this verse and keep my words to myself.

Be like God as it describes him in Psalm 145:8: "The LORD is merciful and compassionate, slow to get angry and filled with unfailing love."

Girl Gab: Plan an evening for your family to have one hour of silence—when you can't talk at all (that includes texting!). See who has the hardest time with it, and talk about how it made you feel afterward. Next time, try two hours! Maybe you'll even decide to do it for a whole day! Ask God for wisdom in your words today.

27 June

Big Hill, Really Big Name

Bible Blast: Read Exodus 17:8-13

Moses' arms soon became so tired he could no longer hold them up. So Aaron and Hur found a stone for him to sit on. Then they stood on each side of Moses, holding up his hands. So his hands held steady until sunset. EXODUS 17:12

What would you say if I walked up to you and blurted out this word: "Taumatawhakatangihangakoauauotamateaturipukakapikimaungahoronukupokaiwhenuakitanatahu"?

Believe it or not, that's an actual word. It's the name of a thousand-foot-high hill in New Zealand. It's known as the longest name for a place in an English-speaking country. (The local people often just call it "Taumata.")

I bet you're wondering what this gigantic word means, aren't you? This really cracks me up. According to Wikipedia, it means "the summit where Tamatea, the man with the big knees, the climber of mountains, the land-swallower who traveled about, played his nose flute to his loved one." Crazy!

Sometimes important hills have big names, and sometimes they don't have any names, like the one Moses, Aaron, and Hur climbed in the story told in our Bible Blast today. What a cool picture of friendship. Moses knew he needed to keep his staff raised so Joshua and his army could beat the Amalekites, but after a while Moses' arms got tired. So his buddies held up his arms for him, and the Israelites won.

There will be times in your life when you run out of strength to do the right thing, and your BFFs will need to come and help you out. God never intended for us to do everything all on our own. He wants all believers to be connected and depend on each other, just like the parts of a body. "Just as our bodies have many parts and each part has a special function, so it is with Christ's body. We are many parts of one body, and we all belong to each other" (Romans 12:4-5).

If you never let people help you, it doesn't mean you're strong, at least not in God's dictionary. He's not waiting for you to prove that you can "do it all by yourself." He totally loves it when his children work together and help each other out.

Girl Gab: Mom, do you have a hard time asking for help? What about you, Daughter? Today pray that God would teach you what real strength is and help you see the importance of being part of the body of Christ.

Language Lab: What Is "Conviction"?

Bible Blast: Read Romans 14:22-23

If you have doubts about whether or not you should eat something, you are sinning if you go ahead and do it. For you are not following your convictions. If you do anything you believe is not right, you are sinning. ROMANS 14:23

One way you'll hear *conviction* used is when someone is found guilty of a crime. Once the judge or jury decides that a person is guilty, the guilty person is convicted and will get punished in one way or another for the crime.

The other use of the word means you have a strong belief about something. You don't have to be a Christian to have a conviction. Most people are convicted about what they think is right and wrong. However, the thing that makes a Christian's conviction different and more powerful is the Holy Spirit. The Spirit who lives inside of us convicts us about what we should or should not do, but then he gives us the strength we need to do something about that conviction.

Do you know what conviction feels like? Answer a few questions: Have you ever been watching a movie when a scene comes on that makes you very uncomfortable? What about that weird feeling you get when you hear someone talking about inappropriate things? Did you ever tell a "little" lie and feel terrible about it later? All of those things are examples of conviction. It's the Holy Spirit inside of you saying, "Hey, wait a minute! That's not right, and it doesn't honor God!"

When God convicts you, you need to ask him what you should do about it. Does he want you to pray about it? Should you say something? Is there something he wants you to do?

One thing that can be tough is when you're convicted about something, but your friend or family member isn't. Like maybe you're convicted that there's certain music you absolutely shouldn't listen to, but your BFF doesn't feel the same way. In situations like this, you need to ask God for wisdom. God's wisdom will let you know when to speak up and when to pray.

The closer you get to Jesus, the more you will notice the Holy Spirit convicting you.

Girl Gab: Mom, talk about conviction with your daughter to make sure she really gets it. Tell her about a time when you were convicted about something. Take some time to pray together, and ask God to help you listen and obey when he's convicting you about something.

Truth or Dare?

Bible Blast: Read Psalm 18:30-32

God's way is perfect. All the LORD's promises prove true. He is a shield for all who look to him for protection. PSALM 18:30

Girl Gab: Play Truth or Dare with your mom! When you're done, ask God to strengthen your faith.

Girls have been playing Truth or Dare at slumber parties for years and years. I even went to a slumber party with my grown-up girlfriends not so long ago, and we played it! If one of us didn't want to reveal a secret, we chose to take a dare instead.

It's not right to dare God, but sometimes we want to know he's really there. The Bible tells about one man who desperately needed proof of God's faithfulness; it was Gideon, whose story is found in the book of Judges.

God called on Gideon to be a warrior and rescue his people from a group called the Midianites. He told Gideon to tear down an altar and false god his own dad had set up to worship. Gideon obeyed and did just that.

When it was time for him to lead the people into battle, Gideon was full of God's Spirit (see Judges 6:34) but still nervous. He had never done anything like this before. So he asked God for a favor (see Judges 6:36-40).

Gideon put a wool fleece on the threshing floor (where people prepared wheat after the harvest). He said, "If you are truly going to use me to rescue Israel as you promised, prove it to me in this way." He asked God that the fleece would be wet from the dew in the morning, but the ground around it would be dry, which would be impossible without God's power. The next morning, God had done what Gideon asked.

Then Gideon used the same fleece and asked that God would make it dry and the ground around it wet with dew the following day. Sure enough, God answered Gideon and proved he was definitely going to use him to free Israel.

It's not right to test or dare God, but it's okay to ask him for help when your faith is shaky. If you're having trouble believing, just ask him to increase your faith, and he'll answer.

Bad Apples

Bible Blast: Read Matthew 16:5-12

Do not be misled: "Bad company corrupts good character."
1 CORINTHIANS 15:33 (NIV)

You know that phrase "One bad apple spoils the whole bunch"? It's true! If you have a bag of apples and one of them starts to ripen faster than the others, two things can happen that cause the rest of the apples to begin rotting. First, mold can grow on that apple, and then mold spreads onto the other apples, causing them to rot. Second, once an apple begins ripening, it gives off a gas that causes the other apples to start ripening very quickly.

What does this saying mean for real life?

If there's a group of girls who hang out all the time and one of those girls is a major gossip, it's going to be very hard for the others not to get into gossiping too. They should do what they can to avoid spending lots of time in that particular "bag of apples," or they will end up just like the gossiping girl.

Today's focus verse isn't saying you should never talk to people who sin. Certainly one of the biggest reasons we're on this earth is to share the gospel with those who don't know Christ. However, if we spend all or most of our time with sinners, it's going to be extremely difficult to honor Christ with our lives.

I have a quick activity I want you to do with your mom. Stand up on a chair, and have your mom stand on the floor beside you. Now grab one of your mom's hands and try to pull her up onto the chair with you. Did it work? Unless you're Supergirl, probably not! Now have her try to pull you down from the chair onto the floor. Did you end up on the floor? I bet you did! In a relationship, it's easier to get pulled down by someone else's sin than to pull that person up out of her sin.

It's way important that your best friends are God's girls. These are the people you share your deepest thoughts and feelings with. Don't you want them to love Jesus like you do?

Girl Gab: Mom and Daughter, is it possible for a girl who says she loves Jesus and has him in her life to be a "bad apple"? Who are some of the "bad apples" in your life? Pray for them (even if the bad apple might be you).

1 July

Concealer

Bible Blast: Read Romans 13:12

This is the message we heard from Jesus and now declare to you: God is light, and there is no darkness in him at all. 1 JOHN 1:5

Girl Gab: Mom, talk to your daughter about what's appropriate for cleaning her face at her age. Some girls may be just fine scrubbing their faces with a washcloth in the morning and at night. Others may find it's time to start using a gentle facial cleanser.

Pimples. Some people call them "zits." Whatever we call them, nobody likes to get them.

Maybe you haven't yet encountered any of those blemishes when you've looked in the mirror. As you get older, sometimes the oil in your skin can clog up your pores. This may create red bumps on the skin. The good news is that they only last a few days.

It's important to take good care of your skin by keeping it clean, drinking lots of water, and eating healthy foods. These practices can really help win the war on zits, but sometimes, no matter how clean your skin is, a pimple may still pop up. When this happens, lots of women and teenagers use a secret weapon. It's called "concealer." A woman purchases concealer in a color that closely matches her own skin tone. She'll take the concealer and apply it to her pimple and blend it in to the rest of her skin. Usually this works pretty well, and the blemish seems practically invisible.

"Living in the light" means we walk with God and don't ever hide in the darkness. That means we don't use some sort of spiritual "concealer" to cover up our sin.

If we cover up the bad stuff, we're trying to make the world believe we never do anything wrong. First John 1:8 says, "If we claim we have no sin, we are only fooling ourselves and not living in the truth." When a woman has a pimple on her face and covers it up with concealer, the zit is still there, even if no one can see it. In the same way, covering up our sin doesn't fool God.

God knows all about our sin, and he wants to do more than cover it up; he wants to take it away. All we have to do is honestly and completely confess our sins to him, and he will forgive us and cleanse us.

He'll take our sins away, and he won't even have to use concealer!

Say What You Mean, Mean What You Say

Bible Blast: Read Matthew 5:34-37

Just say a simple, "Yes, I will," or "No, I won't." Anything beyond this is from the evil one. MATTHEW 5:37

The animated movie *Alice in Wonderland* is such a wild adventure! Since the book was written in 1862, it's been extremely popular with all age groups. That's pretty funny considering it was never intended to be a book.

The author, Lewis Carroll (whose real name was Charles Dodgson) made up the story to entertain three bored sisters, one of whom was named Alice. The girls loved the nonsense story so much, they begged him to write it down. Lewis did just that and even illustrated it and gave it to Alice for Christmas. Others pressured him to have it published. When it was printed, it was instantly successful.

One of the most popular characters in the story is the White Rabbit. He's known for saying, "I'm late! I'm late! For a very important date!" while he frantically checks the time on his big pocket watch.

Luckily, the White Rabbit's bad habit of being late led to Alice's thrilling adventures. In real life, though, being late isn't a very respectful thing to do. Although there are times when things happen and we have no choice but to be late, in general it is courteous for you to be on time.

Today's focus verse reminds us that we need to keep our promises. If we say we're going to do something, we need to follow through and do it. If you tell your mom and dad you'll be ready by 9:30 to head out the door to church, you need to do everything you can to keep that promise and be ready. This is called "keeping your word."

When you keep you word, others know they can depend on you. If friends and family don't have to sit and wait for ten minutes while you finish getting ready to go somewhere with them, you're showing them that you think their time is valuable. That's a really practical way to show respect and love.

So change your song from "I'm late! I'm late!" to "I'm right on time! I'm totally right on time!"

Girl Gab: How does your family do in the area of being on time? Brainstorm some practical things you can do to be prompt. Some examples are laying out clothes the night before, not hitting the snooze button, and doing what's most important first.

Kickin' Kraft:

**"Quick"
Sand Stuff!**

(Check out p. 373 for a great mother-daughter craft that helps reinforce today's devo!)

Kickin' Kraft: Just Stop Struggling

Bible Blast: Read Psalm 40:1-5

He lifted me out of the pit of despair, out of the mud and the mire. He set my feet on solid ground and steadied me as I walked along. PSALM 40:2

Quicksand is not something most of us encounter on a regular basis. Made of a little bit of sand and a little bit of salt water, quicksand looks like solid ground but acts like liquid. It can be very dangerous if you don't know how to respond when you get close to it.

If I ever got stuck in quicksand, I'm pretty sure I would be tempted to freak out completely, floundering around in a panic. But the truth is, the more you struggle and move, the deeper the quicksand will take you. If you just remain calm, you will eventually float up to the top. Once you've floated up enough to have control of your arms and legs, you can very slowly and carefully crawl out of the miry muck. A friend could toss you a rope or stick to grab onto and help pull you out. This would take a lot of your energy and strength because the quicksand is very heavy, so afterward you might need to rest your legs before you could get up and start running around again.

When David wrote Psalm 40, he must have been going through some serious stuff! He said that the problems he was having were like being stuck in the mud and that God rescued him out of it, setting him back onto a place of safety. God even helped him walk as the strength in his legs returned.

If you find yourself going through hard times that make you feel "stuck," don't wiggle around and struggle, struggle, struggle to get out. Be still. Tell God how you feel about what's going on and ask him to pull you out. Be patient. Some valuable lessons can be learned when we're feeling stuck, and God's timing is always perfect.

No quicksand is too strong or deep for our God!

America the Beautiful

Bible Blast: Read Psalm 24

The earth is the LORD's, and everything in it. The world and all its people belong to him. For he laid the earth's foundation on the seas and built it on the ocean depths. PSALM 24:1-2

Katharine Lee Bates taught at a college in Massachusetts. In 1893, she and some other teachers went on a trip to Colorado. While they were there, the group took a trip to the top of Pike's Peak. (Pike's Peak is 14,115 feet high. That's over two and a half miles!) They took a wagon up most of the way but had to ride mules to get to the very top. When Katharine got to the top, the view was so awesome it inspired her to write the poem "America the Beautiful." Later on it was set to music and became one of America's favorite songs. Each verse describes the beauty of our country, and each chorus is a prayer for America. Read some of the lyrics of "America the Beautiful," and think about what Katharine might have been seeing on top of that mountain in Colorado.

> O beautiful for spacious skies,
> For amber waves of grain,
> For purple mountain majesties
> Above the fruited plain!
>
> America! America!
> God shed His grace on thee,
> And crown thy good with brotherhood
> From sea to shining sea!
>
> O beautiful for heroes prov'd
> In liberating strife,
> Who more than self their country loved,
> And mercy more than life.
>
> America! America!
> May God thy gold refine
> Till all success be nobleness,
> And ev'ry gain divine.

Girl Gab: Have you ever been inspired by nature? Look out the window of the room you're in right now. Do you see any of God's creation that makes you realize how amazing God is? Thank God for creating such a beautiful country.

Crisis Prayers

Bible Blast: Read Jeremiah 2:26-27

They turn their backs on me, but in times of trouble they cry out to me, "Come and save us!" JEREMIAH 2:27

I've heard stories about people who get into really sticky or life-threatening situations and frantically say, "God, if you get me out of this—if you save my life—I'll do whatever you ask! I'll never sin again! I'll become a missionary! Just get me out of this mess!" I guess some people do end up serving God after situations like that, but many don't.

Today's Bible Blast talks about such desperate people calling on God in a time of trouble. God was talking about the people of Israel because they worshiped all those other silly, powerless gods, yet when things got tough, they cried out to God to rescue them. That kind of life doesn't please God. He knows that when people pray these prayers of selfish desperation, it's not because they love him and want him to be their God. They just want him to do anything they wish.

What about you? Do you only pray when you need or want something? Do most of your prayers contain lists of all the things you want God to do for you? It's easy to get into that kind of habit, isn't it? We hardly notice that we're only talking to God when we need his help.

I had a friend like that once. She always called me when she needed me to help with her chores. If she needed help with homework, we were best friends. But her need was the extent of our friendship. As you can imagine, the relationship didn't last very long.

It's such a blessing when friends spend time with you just because they enjoy you and they want to know your thoughts, dreams, and ideas. And it blesses God when you just enjoy him or thank him. He enjoys you every moment of every day. He created you and loves to watch the amazing things you do.

Once you begin to express your love to Jesus, it can be habit forming. You'll find that you're thanking him and talking to him all the time. It will become as natural as breathing.

Pamper Yourself

Bible Blast: Read Song of Songs 6:8-10

Who is this, arising like the dawn, as fair as the moon, as bright as the sun, as majestic as an army with billowing banners?
SONG OF SONGS 6:10

Do you know the story of Esther? It goes something like this: King Xerxes (most people pronounce that first X as a Z) was pretty lousy. He was totally into himself and got really angry if he thought anyone made him look foolish. Unfortunately for his wife, Queen Vashti, she didn't obey him in front of a huge party he was having, and that didn't go over very well. So he was done with her and began hunting for a new queen who would listen to him better.

King Xerxes' people gathered a bunch of women from the city and brought them into the palace to be prepared to meet the king. Esther was one of those women. In order to be presented to the king, a girl first had to have some beauty treatments. You may be thinking the king's beauty team took one afternoon to do the girls' hair, nails, and makeup, put them in a new toga, and off they went to meet the king.

No. Not exactly.

Esther 2:12 says that before a girl was brought before the king, she had *six months* of beauty treatments with oils and *six months* of beauty treatments with perfumes and makeup! That's an entire year of beauty treatments before she could even be with the king! That's a serious "day at the spa"! It worked out well for Esther because she became queen and ended up saving all the Israelites from one of Xerxes' foolish decisions.

Aren't you glad you don't have to take that long to get ready for a day at school? But you know what? As you get older and your body starts to change, it does become important to start washing your hair and body regularly. As you grow, your hair may start to get a little more oily, and your body will produce more sweat. Both of those things can produce an unattractive odor if you don't wash up. God created your body, and his Spirit lives in you. Honor your Creator by taking care of yourself, all the while remembering that true beauty comes from having a real relationship with God.

Girl Gab: Mom, talk to your daughter about taking showers and baths and washing her hair. Does she need to clean her body more often? Is it time for her to start wearing underarm deodorant yet? Daughter, praise your heavenly Father today that you are growing up and becoming an amazing woman of God!

7 July

Girl Gab: First, look for a photo of a rhinoceros beetle on the Internet. If you had one as a pet, what would you name it? (Mom, you answer that question too!) Ask God to strengthen you both for everything you have to do today.

Amazing Animals: The Rhinoceros Beetle

Bible Blast: Read Isaiah 40:28-31

He gives power to the weak and strength to the powerless.
ISAIAH 40:29

If you have never seen a rhinoceros beetle in real life, you have to find a picture of one because they are one of the funkiest beetles around. The rhinoceros beetle gets its name from the big horn most of the males have on the top of their heads. I guess the beetles kind of look like rhinos.

If you ever see one of these bugs in person—and not just in a picture—it will probably make you scream at the top of your lungs. Some of them are more than two inches long, and their horns can be very intimidating. If you ever come across two fighting, don't worry. It's just two guys fighting over a cute "girl" rhinoceros beetle. But since you're not another rhino beetle competing for the cute girl, you don't have to worry. They are completely harmless to people.

Here's what I think is amazing about these beetles: They are without question the strongest creature alive! Even the biggest, strongest elephant isn't as strong as the rhinoceros beetle.

How can that be?

Let's compare the elephant to the rhino beetle. An elephant can carry about 25 percent of its weight. So if a female African elephant weighs 1,000 pounds, she can carry about 250 pounds. The rhinoceros beetle can carry up to 850 *times* its weight. That's like your mom carrying thirty-two cars on her back!

God doesn't just give strength to beetles. He gives strength to us, too. If you ever feel like you're not strong enough to do the right thing or to finish a project or to run one more lap in gym class, ask your heavenly Father for strength. Philippians 4:13 says very plainly that we can do anything with Christ's strength. His strength never runs out, and nothing will ever beat it. If Jesus is in your heart, then his strength is something you can always depend on.

Potty Mouth

Bible Blast: Read Isaiah 6:1-8

He touched my lips with it and said, "See, this coal has touched your lips. Now your guilt is removed, and your sins are forgiven." ISAIAH 6:7

Lily sat at the lunch table with her friends and suddenly got very uncomfortable with where the conversation was going. Before she knew it, she was in a conversation with her new friends who were using really foul language.

"Guys, what's with the cussing?" she said, hoping they would agree with her and watch their language.

One of the girls replied, "Lily, we are going to cuss. If you don't like it, then you can sit somewhere else."

Poor Lily. She knew that swearing wasn't honoring God, but when she took a stand, she got rejected—big time. But Lily did the right thing when she didn't join in.

Isaiah had a problem with his language; you can read about it in today's Bible Blast. He describes a vision he had of God on his throne. He's surrounded by angels worshiping God in song and can even see the glory of God, which was like a bright light. In the midst of all of that heavenly beauty, Isaiah says, "It's all over! I am doomed, for I am a sinful man. I have filthy lips, and I live among a people with filthy lips."

The first thing Isaiah feels is conviction about the things he says that don't honor God and the people he hangs out with who have the same problem: filthy lips. Maybe a modern-day translation might say, "I live among people with potty mouths!"

After Isaiah realized his problem, one of the angels, called a "seraphim," flew over to him, touched his lips with a burning coal, and told him his sins were forgiven.

Do you hang out with people who have potty mouths? Is it hard for you to keep your language clean? If you can give God control over your words now as a tween, it will be much easier for you to not have a potty mouth when you're older.

You *can* have clean words come out of your mouth every time you speak. God will help you.

Girl Gab: Confess your "word sins" to God right now. Ask him to make your words clean and holy for his work and his glory.

Girl Gab: Talk this verse over with your mom. If she meditated on it, too, have her tell you what God spoke to her about. Pray that you would be willing to go wherever God wants you to go in your life.

Meditation Moment: Isaiah 6

Then I heard the Lord asking, "Whom should I send as a messenger to this people? Who will go for us?" I said, "Here I am. Send me." ISAIAH 6:8

Yesterday you learned about how Isaiah responded when he was face to face with God's glory and perfection. Today you're going to meditate on his response when God asked him a very important question: "Who will go?" God needed someone to go be a representative for him. The Lord said, "Who will go for *us*?" because he was referring to God the Father, God the Son, and God the Holy Spirit.

Something I want you to remember as you meditate on this verse today is that right before God asked this life-changing question of "Who will go?" Isaiah had just experienced God's forgiveness for his "potty mouth." He knew he had been completely forgiven. He didn't answer this question with, "Well, Lord, I know you forgave me and everything, but my lips might still be dirty, so you had better find someone else for the job." Instead, Isaiah said, "Here I am. Send me."

When we confess our sins and God forgives us, that's it. It's a done deal. It's the final answer. You don't have to wonder if you are ready to serve him. You are!

You know the meditation drill by now. Stop and pray, asking God to speak to you through this Scripture today. Read over it a few times and then silently wait for God to speak to you. Write down whatever comes into your mind about Isaiah 6:8, whether it's an idea, thought, picture, or memory.

Self-Talk

Bible Blast: Read Genesis 1:26-31

God looked over all he had made, and he saw that it was very good! GENESIS 1:31

I asked my friend Kim, "What's something your daughter struggles with?"

She answered, "Self-talk."

I was curious. "What's 'self-talk'?"

Kim told me that's the label she uses for the overwhelming number of sentences her daughter says that begin with the word "I."

I totally get that.

Self-talk can be spoken out loud or just inside your head, and it is often negative. If you write in a journal, there's a good chance it's made up of a lot of words about yourself.

Here are some examples of negative self-talk:

"I'm so stupid."

"I'm ugly."

It's almost a popular thing for girls and women to say really terrible things about themselves like the sentences you just read, but here's the cold, hard truth about negative self-talk: When God created you, he said, "Very good. Exactly as I need her to be." When you say degrading things about yourself, you're telling God it *wasn't* "very good" when he created you.

If you say something negative about yourself long enough, you'll eventually believe the words you're saying, and that's how you'll live. Isn't that sad to think about?

On the other hand, we don't need to go around telling everyone how utterly amazing we are. First Corinthians 1:31 says if we're going to brag about something, brag about God and what *he's* done.

Self-talk needs to support the fact that God created you just like you are for a purpose. When you say something about yourself, either silently or out loud, ask yourself, "Is this something God would say about me?" If it isn't, ask God to show you how he feels about you and start using that for your self-talk.

Girl Gab: Do you sometimes hear each other's self-talk? Do you hear mostly negative or positive things? Ask the Lord for his help in turning your self-talk into godly truth.

You Can't Hide Forever

Bible Blast: Read 2 Timothy 2:19-21

People may be pure in their own eyes, but the LORD examines their motives. PROVERBS 16:2

Nadia let out a huge sigh as she looked down at the reading assignment sheet Ms. Malcolm had just handed her.

Along with the assignment sheet, Ms. Malcolm gave the students a paper to write down what book they read and how many pages it had in it. Nadia took the papers home and kept them tucked away in her folder. Before she knew it, she was out of time and hadn't actually done the reading.

The day the assignment was due, Nadia took the sheet out and wrote down the name of a big book she had never read but that would meet the three hundred–page requirement for an A. That's right: Nadia lied. But she made herself feel better about it by saying, "Well, I do want to read that book someday, so it's not like I'm really lying."

A couple of days later, Nadia's mom looked through her folder to find the school lunch menu, and she found the reading assignment paper Nadia had lied on. She knew her daughter had never read that book.

Nadia felt terrible because her sin "found her out." Is that a phrase you've heard before? It's in Numbers 32:23, and it means that your sin won't remain hidden forever. Eventually, your sin will be revealed. Nadia thought if enough time passed, her lie would just "go away." However, God needed her sin to be exposed so she could learn a lesson and make it right.

Nadia's mom had her write an apology to Ms. Malcolm, explaining what she had done and asking forgiveness for cheating. Ms. Malcolm was blessed by Nadia's apology, although, of course, she couldn't let Nadia keep the A.

Sometimes our sin gets revealed through another person, and sometimes God does it by having his Holy Spirit make us feel really uncomfortable with what we've done. However it will be exposed in the end, hiding sin in the meantime won't help you grow. You learn the true meaning of God's healing and forgiveness when you confess your sin and turn away from sinning again.

Language Lab: What Are "the Gospels"?

Bible Blast: Read Galatians 1:11-12

Preaching the Good News is not something I can boast about. I am compelled by God to do it. How terrible for me if I didn't preach the Good News! 1 CORINTHIANS 9:16

 Before we talk about "the Gospels" (plural), let's define "the gospel" (singular). The gospel is referred to as the "Good News" in today's Bible Blast verse. It is the story of Christ's love for us. It's talking about the basics of our faith: the death, burial, and resurrection of Christ, and our salvation in him. The Gospels (plural) are the first four books of the New Testament in your Bible. Those books are called *Matthew, Mark, Luke,* and *John* because they were written by Matthew, Mark, Luke, and John. (That makes it easy, doesn't it?) They are called "the Gospels" because they tell the story of Christ and how his actions can change the lives of people.

Each of these four authors walked with Jesus Christ when he was on the earth. They ate with him, traveled with him, listened to him speak, watched him die on the cross, and witnessed his resurrection. They knew Jesus personally, and each of them wrote a book about their experiences with him.

Each of the Gospels tells the same story of Jesus, but from four different people's views. That doesn't mean that one Gospel is more "correct" than another. It just means that all four men weren't always in the same place at the same time, and they saw and noticed different things. For instance, when John writes about the Last Supper the disciples had with Jesus, he mentions that he lay back on Jesus' chest. That's something special John remembered from that experience. The other disciples may not have noticed or cared much about what John did that night, so they talked about other things that happened during the meal. The fact that leaning against Jesus had an impact on John is a big part of his understanding of the gospel. It made Jesus, the Son of God, personal to John.

You get to share the gospel too. You might never write a book like Matthew, Mark, Luke, and John, but you can tell people about how Jesus' death, burial, and resurrection affects your life. The Good News is yours, too.

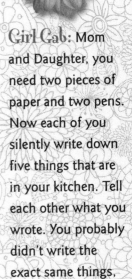

Girl Gab: Mom and Daughter, you need two pieces of paper and two pens. Now each of you silently write down five things that are in your kitchen. Tell each other what you wrote. You probably didn't write the exact same things, but both lists are true, aren't they? That's how writing the Gospels was for Matthew, Mark, Luke, and John.

Black Cats and Ladders

Bible Blast: Read Galatians 4:7-9

Now that you know God (or should I say, now that God knows you), why do you want to go back again and become slaves once more to the weak and useless spiritual principles of this world?
GALATIANS 4:9

Girl Gab: Chat together about superstition. Mom, did any of the things in today's devo get your attention? What about you, Daughter? Take time now to give God glory for the good in your lives.

Imagine with me: You have a really big test at school one day. Before school you pray, "Lord, please help me do well on this test!" On the way to school, you see a white horse running through a field. You get an A+ on your test that day. Now every time you see a white horse running, you know it means you're going to do well on a test.

Right?

Big, fat *wrong!*

Do you know what that is? Superstition.

Superstition means you believe if a certain thing happens it has the power to make something else happen. Like, some people believe if you break a mirror you'll have bad luck. That's not godly. That's called superstition.

Superstition shows up in many ways. Some people stay away from certain animals, numbers, dates of the year, or colors because they think something bad will happen. Sometimes people try to make their relationship with God into a superstition by saying, "God has really blessed our family these past several months. He must be preparing us for something bad around the corner."

Superstition is sin because it acknowledges other things or situations as having more power over your life than the Lord. Living a superstitious life also brings a lot of fear. If people are constantly trying to avoid certain things because they don't want to have something bad happen, it will make them very nervous to do anything out of fear that they might "get it wrong."

Get into a habit of not even joking about superstitious things. Don't have a "lucky number." Pet a black cat. And most importantly, praise Jesus every time something good happens—and praise his name even when something bad happens. God is totally in control!

Safety First

Bible Blast: Read Psalm 5:11-12

The LORD is my light and my salvation—so why should I be afraid? The LORD is my fortress, protecting me from danger, so why should I tremble? PSALM 27:1

When I was a kid we lived next to a dairy farm. The dairy farmers milked hundreds of cows every night, and all that activity produced a lot of strange noises.

I remember this because those noises produced some scary nights for me. Have you ever heard a noise at night and gotten scared because your imagination ran wild?

I used to dream the same nightmare over and over while living next to that dairy farm. It still gives me a creepy feeling so I'm not even going to tell you what it was, but it made me afraid that something was going to happen to my family. My dad would come in and check on me, and I would crawl up onto his lap because I was so afraid.

I don't have that nightmare anymore. In fact, I can honestly say that while I used to be afraid of the dark (even as an adult), I'm very confident and unafraid at night these days. How did I stop being afraid? I used Bible verses to remind me that God protects me.

The book of Psalms is full of verses proclaiming the truth that God is our protection, refuge, help, guard, and rescuer. He sees us and loves us, and he's all-powerful. We need to believe the truth of God's Word instead of believing that a strange noise or creepy feeling means danger is near.

I believe one way we can eliminate a lot of scary feelings and thoughts is by being really careful about what we watch and read. It may feel kind of thrilling and fun to watch a scary movie, but if it puts untrue, dark thoughts into your head, it's not honoring God (or helping you sleep!). And if you're into a great book, I know it's hard to skip over pages if a creepy part comes up, but it will help keep your mind pure.

As God's child, you have no reason to be afraid. It's true that sometimes people experience bad things, but you can always know that God has a big plan for everything that happens.

Girl Gab: Write today's focus verse big on a sheet of paper and hang it up by your bed where you can see it if you get afraid. When your mind starts wandering to creepy things, read this verse out loud and know that God is your Protector!

Who Have You Been Talkin' To?

Bible Blast: Read Exodus 34:28-35

His face had become radiant because he had spoken to the LORD.
EXODUS 34:29

Girl Gab: Grab a flashlight. Find a dark place in your house and see who can make the best shadow puppets, you or your mom. Keep the lights out and the flashlight on as you pray that God's glory would shine through your lives, just like it did with Moses' life.

When I began to fall in love with my husband way back when, it was amazing. I felt like I was walking on air when I was with him. When we were together, it was like we were the only ones in the room because nothing else mattered but how we felt about each other. We laughed together, and I had a goofy smile on my face most of the time. If I had recently been talking to Bob Gresh, my entire appearance changed.

Speaking with happy people we love changes how we look—unless you're Eeyore, that sad little donkey who is a friend of Winnie the Pooh. Eeyore looked sad no matter who he hung out with. I'm not sure what his gloomy problem was. But this devo isn't about Eeyore and Winnie the Pooh. It's about you and God!

I hope that after you read today's Bible Blast about Moses, you were amazed. After spending time with God, Moses' face literally glowed. It actually gave off light! They could have stuck Moses in the corner of their tent and played board games all night long! His face shone so much that he covered it with a veil when he wasn't meeting with God because he was afraid that the brilliant light from his face would frighten people. We're talkin' seriously bright! The people were weirded-out by Moses' shining face. When he put the veil over it, they felt more secure about being with him.

There are two things I want you to take from the story of Moses' radiant face. One is that you should spend most of your time with people who cause you to shine—people who give you life and encouragement, not yuckiness and criticism.

The second thing is that when we spend time with God, we change. We act differently, speak differently, think differently. We even look different. God's glory begins to shine through our lives, and people wonder what makes us so different. Some people might be freaked out at first, but eventually they will see God's love, and they'll want to shine too.

Like Putty in His Hands

Bible Blast: Read Romans 9:20-24

O LORD, you are our Father. We are the clay, and you are the potter. We all are formed by your hand. ISAIAH 64:8

Working with clay is a blast. You can form it into just about any shape you can imagine. I just love the feeling of wet, slippery clay under my hands when I'm using a pottery wheel. When I was your age, I made my mom a lot of things out of clay—pots, cups, frogs.

Even if you're not really great at sculpting, clay still feels really good in your hands as you move it and shape it. It's fun to use little tools to create different designs. And if you don't like what you've created, you can ball it up and start over again.

After you've made your shape, you need to put it in a kiln to "cook" it. This makes the clay hard. Then there's the colorful step of painting your sculpture! The glaze used to color clay is weird because it doesn't really look like the color it's going to be when you're painting it on. But after you fire it in the kiln again, the colors come shining through!

When the shaping, baking, painting or glazing, and re-baking is all done, you have your very own masterpiece!

Doesn't it feel good to create something?

Our heavenly Father created you in the same way. In your birth mom's belly, he began molding and shaping your body to be just what he wanted it to be from the top of your beautiful head to the bottoms of your cute feet. He even "painted" your sparkling eyes, gorgeous hair, and stunning skin just the way he wanted.

The day you were born, he said, "My masterpiece."

You are more priceless than a clay sculpture.

You are more gorgeous than any vase ever made.

You are more important than anybody's water pitcher.

You are not replaceable.

Just like today's focus verse says, you were formed by God's hand! So when you look in the mirror, you can know absolutely that you are a priceless masterpiece created by your heavenly Father.

Girl Gab: If you can get your hands on some clay, Play-Doh, bread dough, cookie dough, or anything moldable, both of you sculpt your favorite animal. As you sculpt, talk about why it's your favorite. Pray today's focus verse like this: "Father, I know that you are the Potter and I am the clay. I am the work of your hands. Thank you. Amen."

Compassion Passion

Bible Blast: Read 1 John 3:16-18

The LORD gives righteousness and justice to all who are treated unfairly. PSALM 103:6

Girl Gab: Is there someone you know who would appreciate a cheerful smile and a plate of cookies? Make plans with your mom to make those cookies and deliver them with an encouraging note. When you give that person the treat, pray for him or her. If you can't think of anyone, ask God to show you who needs you right now.

Agnesë Gonxhe Bojaxhiu was born into a wealthy family in Macedonia. I guess she could have spent her entire life enjoying her riches, but she didn't. When she was yet a teenager, she left home to become a missionary. After a short time with the Sisters of Loreto, she was riding on a train when she received what she named "the call within a call." God was asking her to spend her life loving the poorest of the poor *while living among them.*

She became a citizen of India and began the Missionaries of Charity in 1950. She and the other missionaries would own only two Indian saris (or dresses). The day they wore one, they would wash the other. They lived simply with no possessions, and they poured themselves daily into the care of "the hungry, the naked, the homeless, the crippled, the blind, the lepers, all those people who feel unwanted, unloved, uncared for throughout society, people that have become a burden to the society and are shunned by everyone."

She became known as Mother Teresa, and her little missions group grew from thirteen people to more than 4,500 members in help centers of various kinds in 133 countries. When she died in 1997, tens of thousands of people lined the streets as the funeral procession went by. The work goes on without her today. She wasn't wealthy or even a movie star. She was famous for one thing: loving people, especially the poor and sick.

Maybe God will use you to start hundreds of help centers all over the world. But until then, begin to notice those in need around you now. You might be in a situation where you don't feel like you have much to give, but there is always someone you can help.

You won't just be giving to a person. You'll be giving to God.

Together Forever

Bible Blast: Read John 14:1-6

In my Father's house are many rooms; if it were not so, I would have told you. JOHN 14:2 (NIV)

Do you want to eat dinner in the bathroom tonight?

Well, maybe not! But there is actually a restaurant in Jakarta, Indonesia, where you could enjoy a gourmet dinner in a bathroom. The restaurant is called The Apartment, and the designer of it wanted to create an atmosphere that was really different where diners could feel very comfortable. The Apartment has several rooms to choose from, such as the kitchen, library, bedroom, and, of course, the bathroom. Your waiter takes you to the room of your choice, and you're led into a beautifully decorated room that looks just like something you would find in a really nice apartment or home. In the bedroom, you could eat while sitting on a bed. In the bathroom, you'll find a large bathtub and showerhead.

God has created a place with lots of cool rooms too. In fact, most people would say it's "heavenly"! Before Jesus was betrayed and crucified, he encouraged his disciples by letting them know there's a place in heaven reserved for them. He described it as a house with many rooms. Then he told them he was going there to prepare a place for them. And here's the best part: Jesus made sure the disciples knew that, when they went to heaven, they would be with him forever.

The disciples loved Jesus very much, and he loved them even more. They had walked together, talked together, and experienced so many incredible things together. The thought of losing Jesus must have been horrible for his friends. When they saw him on the cross in such agony, maybe those words he had spoken in verse 3, "I will come and get you, so that you will always be with me where I am," brought them comfort.

Isn't that the coolest thing ever to know Jesus is preparing a place for those who love him in heaven? Wow!

I don't know what the rooms in our heavenly Father's house look like. I'm not sure if there will be a pantry, kitchen, or bathroom. But I do know that once we're there, we won't ever want to be anywhere else.

Girl Gab: Make plans to eat dinner in a room other than the dining room sometime this week. If your family's really adventurous, try the bathroom or the garage! While you eat, talk about what you think your room will look like in heaven.

Amazing Animals: AJ and Boo Boo

Bible Blast: Read Psalm 18:16-19

The godly people in the land are my true heroes! I take pleasure in them! PSALM 16:3

Girl Gab: Mom, tell your daughter about one of your childhood heroes. Pray with your daughter that God would bring incredible godly role models into her life.

A.J. and Boo Boo were best buddies, in spite of their very obvious size difference. A.J. was an older, very large golden retriever. Boo Boo was a tiny, fluffy, white Maltese. Those two dogs ran all over their farm exploring and playing together.

Living next to the farm were a couple of dogs that were sometimes kind of mean. It wasn't a problem, though, because those dogs were fenced in and not allowed to run free.

One day, horrible sounds of yelping, growling, and barking came from the backyard. When the dogs' owner ran out to see what was going on, she saw one of the neighbor's dogs had gotten out. He had Boo Boo in his mouth and was shaking him hard back and forth like a little toy. The owner didn't know what to do and began calling for help. Just then, something amazing happened.

A.J., who was very upset at what was going on, hauled her plump body over to the dog that was attacking Boo Boo. Using the only weapon she had, A.J. put her paws on the vicious dog and . . . lay down. The dog was so trapped by A.J.'s size and weight that it had no choice but to release Boo Boo from its mouth. A.J. remained on top of that dog until Boo Boo was taken to safety. Boo Boo had to go to the veterinarian and receive surgery and some stitches, but he was fine once he healed up.

Boo Boo's best friend saved his life that day. It seemed as if the two dogs had a closer bond than ever after that experience. It was almost as if Boo Boo was telling all the other animals on the farm, "A.J.'s my hero! A.J.'s my hero!"

It might be easy to define a hero as someone who risks everything to help another, like A.J. did for Boo Boo. That's definitely an awesome thing, but our heroes need to be more than that. Our heroes should be men and women who love God with all their heart, soul, mind, and strength. True heroes inspire us to be more like Christ.

Don't Stop Talking

Bible Blast: Read Deuteronomy 11:18-21

Teach them to your children. Talk about them when you are at home and when you are on the road, when you are going to bed and when you are getting up. Write them on the doorposts of your house. DEUTERONOMY 11:19-20

If you have a ton of money to spend, buying a door can be like purchasing a piece of art. There's a company in Romania that makes personalized doors out of leather and more than thirty thousand beautiful crystals. They claim to be the world's most expensive doors. You can grab one for around $34,000! (I think I'll just stick to my very plain, functional door, thank you very much.)

Moses had a great idea for increasing the beauty of the entrance to a house. He suggested writing God's truth on the doorposts of the Israelites' homes. Our family hasn't written God's truth on our doorposts, but we did have an artist friend of ours write Scriptures and quotes all over the walls of our basement family room. Every time we look at it, we are reminded of God's truth.

The idea behind what Moses said in Deuteronomy 11 was that the words God speaks are important. In fact, they're the most important words anyone will ever hear or read. Those words need to be read, talked about, and memorized. Your mom is *doing* Deuteronomy 11:19 with you by having these devos with you. (Go, Mom!)

One of my favorite things in the whole world is when my family talks about the Bible and what God's doing in our lives. It doesn't happen every day, but when it does I'm a blessed wife and mom because I'm crazy about hearing stories of God's faithfulness and love.

God really wants us to speak his truth any chance we get, from the time we wake up until the time our sleepy heads hit the pillow. He wants you to bring up the Bible in conversation over the dinner table, on trips, or when you're grocery shopping with your mom or dad. It may feel uncomfortable at first, but soon your family will begin to enjoy talking about something deeper than just what's on TV.

Girl Gab: Talk to your mom about a favorite Bible verse that you have. How can you put it on the doorframe of your bedroom? Maybe you could make a cool poster and hang it where you'll see it each morning. Ask your mom for permission.

21 July

Girl Gab: You can check out that vintage Porky Pig cartoon online with your mom. The episode is called "Swooner Crooner." Today let excitement fill your heart as you think about your heavenly Father singing sweet words of joy and love over your life.

The Savior Sings a Serenade

Bible Blast: Read Psalm 63:3-8

The LORD your God is living among you. He is a mighty savior. He will take delight in you with gladness. With his love, he will calm all your fears. He will rejoice over you with joyful songs. ZEPHANIAH 3:17

Back in the 1940s and 1950s, "crooners" were very popular. Crooners were men who sang slow, smooth love songs. Their voices were beautiful and could make a girl's heart skip a beat. Some of the most famous crooners were Dean Martin, Bing Crosby, and Frank Sinatra. (Have you even heard of any of those guys?)

One hilarious picture of the power of a crooner's song is in a Porky Pig cartoon. In the cartoon Porky owns an egg business. He has a bunch of hens, which lay eggs every day for him to pack up and sell. But then Frankie (as in Frank Sinatra) the rooster comes along and begins crooning romantic songs outside of the henhouse. Well, the hens immediately leave their nests to listen to him sing. Then, one by one, the ladies faint because they are overwhelmed by the coolness of the feathered crooner.

Porky needs his hens to lay eggs again, so he holds auditions for another singing rooster and eventually hires Bing (as in Bing Crosby). When Bing starts singing, the hens wake up and start laying eggs again. As both Frankie and Bing sing, the hens lay thousands and thousands of eggs until Porky Pig is sitting surrounded by mountains of them.

Ah, the power of a beautiful song!

The most incredible song ever sung is the one mentioned in our focus verse today. When I see the words "He will rejoice over you with joyful songs," my heart flutters and my cheeks might even blush a little. My mighty Savior *sings* over *me*?

Yes! And he sings over you, too. God loves you completely, and that love compels him to sing over you. He's your biggest fan.

Meditation Moment: Psalm 4

In peace I will lie down and sleep, for you alone, O LORD, will keep me safe. PSALM 4:8

As a growing girl, you need to get your sleep. Most doctors would say that tweens should get between nine and eleven hours of sleep every night. Getting a good amount of sleep will help you be more attentive and have more energy. Your mind and body need the rest to get ready for the next day.

If you have trouble sleeping, here are some things you can try:

Do something relaxing before it's time to go to bed, like taking a hot bath, reading a relaxing book, writing in a journal, or listening to soft music.

Don't eat sugary stuff or have caffeine after dinner.

Don't get too involved in tons of activities. Doing too much can get you too stimulated, making it difficult to get your mind and body to slow down and go to sleep.

Sleep is the main topic of today's Meditation Moment verse. Before you begin to meditate on it, pray that God would speak to you through it. Read over it a few times and wait for God to show you a truth about Psalm 4:8. Once you feel like he's spoken to you through an idea, thought, picture, or some other way, write it down.

You know what? Meditating on Scripture is another great way to get ready for bed.

Girl Gab: Show your mom what you've learned. Talk to her about how you sleep. Do you need to make any changes to help you get the rest you need? Have your mom pray that you would be blessed with peace while you sleep.

SOS

Bible Blast: Read Matthew 14:22-31

But Jesus spoke to them at once. "Don't be afraid," he said. "Take courage. I am here!" MATTHEW 14:27

Girl Gab:

Write a note of encouragement to your mom in Morse code. The chart is printed below.

A . _
B _ . . .
C _ . _ .
D _ . .
E .
F . . _ .
G _ _ .
H . . . .
I . .
J . _ _ _
K _ . _
L . _ . .
M _ _

N _ .
O _ _ _
P . _ _ .
Q _ _ . _
R . _ .
S . . .
T _
U . . _
V . . . _
W . _ _
X _ . . _
Y _ . _ _
Z _ _ . .

. . . _ _ _ . . .

Do those dots and dashes mean anything to you? If you've grown up in a sailing family, you might recognize that as Morse code for "SOS." Morse code is a method of communicating using rhythm. You just tap out letters and numbers until you have a message. You can do it on a wall to talk to someone on the other side, or you can use electronic equipment to send a message across the world in code.

SOS, the message above, is a message people send out when they are in trouble and need help. Some have said that it stands for Save Our Souls, but it actually doesn't stand for anything at all. Three dots, three dashes, and three dots just seemed to the original telegraphers as an unmistakable way to communicate, "Help!"

Peter sent out a major SOS when he was walking on the water toward Jesus. Jesus told him before he even stepped out onto the sea that he didn't need to be afraid because "I am here!" Peter did well for a bit, but then he got terrified. The water started working its way up his legs, and he called out to Jesus, "SOS! SOS!"

I really love that God's Word says Jesus "immediately" reached out and rescued Peter. I can just picture Jesus holding onto him, saying, "I'm right here, and I love you more than you'll ever know."

God wants to rescue you, too! Talk to the Lord every day about anything and everything. Let your faith grow and grow so that in times of trouble, you can be sure that he hears your SOS.

My Best Friend

Bible Blast: Read John 15:9-15

There is no greater love than to lay down one's life for one's friends. JOHN 15:13

What do you look for in a best friend? Here's my list:

- We have things in common, including loving Jesus.
- We can laugh and cry together.
- I know she's trustworthy.
- She prays for me.
- She gets me.

Even though I have a couple of girlfriends who fulfill every item on that list, I have another very, very best friend. Jesus! Oh, he's your best friend too? Cool! I think most people want a BFF who they can trust and who is "there" for them. Jesus certainly can be trusted, and he is always there! Since Jesus is God, he's "omnipresent," meaning he can be everywhere all the time. He can meet with all of us at the exact same time. That's why he can be everyone's very best friend.

Since Jesus himself isn't standing in front of you, you have to look for him in touchable ways. When your friend writes you an encouraging note, that's Jesus sending you love! When your mom nurses you back to health when you're sick, that's Jesus faithfully caring for you! When a beautiful landscape makes you stop and stare, that's Jesus blessing your day! Jesus is in creation. He uses many different things to express his friendship and love for you. You just have to learn to recognize what he's doing and how he's speaking.

Girl Gab: Make your own BFF list. Thank Jesus for being your friend.

25 July

Perfect?

Bible Blast: Read Genesis 3:1-7

Look beneath the surface so you can judge correctly. JOHN 7:24

Perfect.

What does that word even mean? Most people define it as "without faults, flaws, or problems." Sadly, way too many of us girls think that we have to be "perfect" to be beautiful. Since all of us have flaws, this makes beauty an unattainable goal.

Fashion magazines are probably the biggest liars when it comes to what's "perfect" or "beautiful." The girls on the covers always appear to have shiny hair, flawless skin, big sparkling eyes, long dark eyelashes, tiny tummies, and super thin legs. But did you know none of that is real?

You see, after a photographer takes a model's picture for a magazine cover, that picture gets sent to a graphic designer. The graphic designer's job is to load that photo onto a computer and make that woman look as perfect as possible. Using computer art tools, he removes any dark spots or pimples from her skin. He makes her hair look full. He increases the size of her eyes and plumps up her lips. Then as he goes down her body, he lengthens her neck, makes her chest bigger, and makes her waist smaller. He even cuts off the sides of her thighs so they appear thinner. By the time the graphic designer is done with the photo, the model may look very different than she does in real life. The models don't ever look as flawless in real life as they do on those magazine covers!

Many women love the idea of trying to look perfect, and they spend a lot of money in the attempt. One woman even spent tens of thousands of dollars on more than a hundred surgeries to make her body look as perfect as possible.

If you find yourself beginning to obsess about how you look and you spend more time looking in the mirror than spending time with God, you need a "Perfection Extraction"! Ask God to remove your obsession with looking perfect and replace it with an obsession for pursuing your perfect God. If you make him your number one thing, he'll become more important to you than your appearance.

Girl Gab: Mom, today try to set aside a little more time than usual to talk about this devo with your daughter. Daughter, tell your mom how you feel about the way you look. Mom, even if your daughter doesn't seem to struggle in this area, grab onto her and ask God always to help her win the battle against the "perfection" being portrayed in the media.

Girls Rule—Boys Drool?

Bible Blast: Read Genesis 2:21-24

This explains why a man leaves his father and mother and is joined to his wife, and the two are united into one. GENESIS 2:24

You can go into clothing stores all over the place and find T-shirts designed for girls your age that have lots of things to say about boys.

- "Girls Rule. Boys Drool."
- "Boys Smell."
- "Girls Are Better Than Boys."

Adult women really want young women to feel strong and powerful. They don't want their daughters to feel weak and useless. One approach to achieving this is to encourage girls and help them believe they can do anything. Another approach is to tear down boys, trying to make them feel weak and small. Those T-shirt slogans tear down boys.

I understand that you might still be at a stage where you really don't care for boys. I also understand that sometimes boys really do smell after they've been running around like crazy. However, I also understand that boys were created by God, just like you.

Many of you will fall in love and get married some day. You want your future husband to be a protector, leader, and friend. Those boys that you see running around at school and youth group are going to be men who become husbands. What happens in their lives now helps to determine what kind of men they will become later.

When you make fun of boys or call them "dumb" and other names, it can cause a lot of pain. And boys don't like to appear like they have feelings, so they hide it. You may never even know a boy is being hurt by your words.

The next time you see a boy doing something weird or annoying, instead of telling him he's weird and annoying, don't say anything at all. Ask God to help you see that boy as a wonderful creation of God. Once you begin to see those "icky" boys differently, your opinion of them just might change.

Girl Gab: Mom, tell your daughter about a boy who annoyed you when you were younger. Daughter, tell your mom about a boy who is hard for you to deal with. Pray for both of those boys now.

Girl Gab: Mom and Daughter, do you each have someone in your mind you know you need to forgive? Start by praying this simple prayer: "Dear heavenly Father, I choose to forgive (name) for hurting me by (what he or she did). Help me not be bitter anymore. In Jesus' name, amen."

Bible Blast: Read Matthew 18:21-22

Get rid of all bitterness, rage, anger, harsh words, and slander, as well as all types of evil behavior. Instead, be kind to each other, tenderhearted, forgiving one another, just as God through Christ has forgiven you. EPHESIANS 4:31-32

When you hear the word *bitter*, you might automatically think about food. Bitter foods have a sharp, mostly unpleasant taste. Coffee, olives, orange peel, and unsweetened chocolate would all be considered bitter.

The kind of bitterness we're talking about today isn't about food. It's an emotional state of being frozen in unforgiveness. It's what happens when we choose to be eternally angry rather than to let go of offenses. Maybe you're still "bitter" from the time your friend hurt your feelings in first grade. It's time to let that go!

As you read in the Bible Blast, Jesus commands us to forgive those who hurt us. Did you notice how many times? Seventy times seven times. Does that mean you should only forgive someone 490 times and not once more?

Jesus was telling Peter that showing God's grace to others is not about counting how often you forgive. Forgiveness needs to be a habit and a way of life.

But what if someone does something super bad? Do you have to forgive even that person? Yes. Jesus doesn't say, "Forgive people most of the time. If someone hurts you really, really badly then you should never forgive her because she doesn't deserve it." Colossians 3:13 says, "Forgive *anyone* who offends you" (emphasis added).

The only way to get rid of bitterness is by choosing to forgive, and that's not always easy to do. But remember, when you forgive someone, it doesn't mean that you're saying what that person did was okay. Forgiveness just means that you're not going to let that hurt control you anymore, and you don't expect the ones who hurt you to do anything to earn your forgiveness.

Choose to forgive someone today!

Defogger

Bible Blast: Read James 4:13-16

How do you know what your life will be like tomorrow? Your life is like the morning fog—it's here a little while, then it's gone.
JAMES 4:14

George Müller lived in England in the 1800s. He went all over the place telling people about Jesus Christ, and he started a bunch of orphanages.

Once George had an appointment in Quebec. Back then, people traveled mainly by boat and not by airplane. On the way to Quebec, the ship encountered a very thick fog. The captain of the boat had no choice but to sit and wait until the fog lifted. He waited and waited and waited.

It was on a Wednesday that George Müller tapped the captain on the shoulder and said, "Captain, I have come to tell you that I must be in Quebec on Saturday afternoon." The captain told him it would be impossible because of the fog.

George said, "Let's go downstairs and pray."

The captain said, "Don't you see how heavy this fog is?"

George looked at him and said, "My eye is not on the density of the fog, but on the living God, who controls every circumstance of my life."

The captain reluctantly followed him downstairs, thinking he was crazy. George prayed a super-simple prayer asking God to lift the fog within five minutes so that he could get to Quebec on time. You can just imagine how foolish the captain thought George was being. In fact, George sensed the captain's lack of faith and told him that he himself didn't need to pray since God had already answered. He then told the captain to open the door and look outside because the fog was gone. Sure enough, the fog had completely lifted! George Müller was in Quebec that Saturday, just as he needed to be.

Following Christ means you see things differently from the way other people do. You don't just see what's in front of you, but you focus more on the eternal things of God. What obstacles are you facing right now? Ask God to give you eyes to see his power and love in that situation and begin to pray in faith for him to move them.

Girl Gab: Is there a situation in your life that you're focusing on even though you know you should be turning your attention and prayers to God and his powerful love? Pray that God would "lift that fog" today.

Kickin' Kraft:

Campin' Cookie Dough Sticks!

(Check out p. 373 for a great mother-daughter craft that helps reinforce today's devo!)

Kickin' Kraft: Cookie Monsters!

Bible Blast: Read Psalm 19:9-11

How sweet your words taste to me; they are sweeter than honey.
PSALM 119:103

The camp cook shook his head in disbelief. "I don't get it. I just don't get it!"

"What don't you get?" one of the other cafeteria workers asked.

"I don't understand how every time I go to bake cookies for the campers, the frozen cookie dough container seems to be emptier and emptier. How can that happen?"

Through a little research and some secret detective work, the camp chefs discovered that campers were sneaking into the kitchen, opening the freezer, and stealing frozen cookie dough for a snack!

One night, the cook finally had had enough. He said, "If they want cookie dough, let's give it to them." They took balls of the dough and stuck them on the ends of popsicle sticks. When they passed them out to the campers, everyone went wild. It was just what they wanted, and they didn't even have to sneak around to get it!

My friend Melissa, who works at a Christian camp, told me about that true mystery. Cookie dough is amazing stuff, isn't it? It feels so good in your mouth as it slowly dissolves into perfect sweetness. Yum!

God's words are sweet too! Does that sound weird to you? Every word God speaks is true. God's words will never hurt you. The more you read and study his words, the more you will begin to want them, just like a fabulous sweet treat.

Dive into his Word! Read the Bible and "chew" on it. Soon you'll crave it!

The Airport Singer

Bible Blast: Read Luke 14:7-11

Those who exalt themselves will be humbled, and those who humble themselves will be exalted. LUKE 14:11

Looking for a new vacation spot?

The Cook Islands are located south of Hawaii and experience warm, sunny weather all year round. One of the islands, Rarotonga, is becoming more popular for tourists. Rarotonga is only twenty miles around the whole island! In spite of Rarotonga's size, it does have an international airport with a runway right along the water. When you step off your plane and into the airport, you'll hear singing.

There's a man who plays a ukulele and sings songs for every arriving flight at the Rarotonga airport. After such long journeys, passengers find the man's song quite welcoming.

This may not seem terribly unusual until you know one more piece of information. Many of the flights arrive at the airport in the middle of the night. Even if your plane lands at 2:30 a.m., that man will be warmly greeting you with a song.

He's not famously known for his singing. Most people probably don't stop to ask him for his name or autograph. When his music fills the airport in the middle of the night, he's not getting a standing ovation. He's just doing something he really enjoys, no matter who the audience is.

Humility is something Jesus spoke about often. In Luke 14, he urged the people not to assume that they would be honored by others: "Don't take a seat of honor at the head of the table, because you might be asked to move." It certainly would be better just to sit somewhere unnoticed and have someone else move you to a more honored seat, wouldn't it?

You may be hearing a lot of messages in the world around you about "making it big." If God chooses to make somebody's name famous, that's a great blessing and a big responsibility, but you should never make becoming famous your goal. Make Jesus' name famous above all else everywhere you go, no matter what you do. Let him be the one to move you to a seat of honor, if that's what he wants to do. Otherwise, be content to sit on the floor and enjoy using your gifts for God's glory.

Girl Gab: A man named Charles Wesley said, "Keep us little and unknown, prized and loved by God alone." Make that your prayer and your mom's prayer today.

31 July

God's Definition of *Harmony*

Bible Blast: Read 1 Peter 3:8-12

Live in harmony with one another; be sympathetic, love as brothers, be compassionate and humble. 1 PETER 3:8 (NIV)

Girl Gab: Mom, talk to your daughter about the importance of God's harmony in relationships. Daughter, pray for a "future brother or sister in Christ" that you know. Ask God to help him or her see that he or she needs Jesus.

It seems as though a lot is being said about "living in harmony" with other people and "becoming one" with the earth and animals these days. Although these ideas and songs make us feel warm and fuzzy inside, sometimes they are nice words that compromise God's truth.

God's definition of harmony is very different from the world's. The world's definition of harmony is that we can all believe whatever we want, do whatever we want, and all be equally right. The world wants us to blend God's truth with the doctrines of Buddha, Mohammed, and other religious leaders. That is the world's idea of harmony.

God says something quite different. When you look at today's focus verse and see that word, it's literally saying, "be like-minded, have the same mind." Now obviously, we can't all share a brain. Being like-minded means that our thoughts are united. In other words, harmony comes from believing the same thing and living according to God's standard of truth.

What's the standard for what our minds should be like? First Corinthians 2:16 says that those who follow the Lord have "the mind of Christ." The mind of Christ is 100 percent truth, and those who don't love him can't understand that truth (see 1 Corinthians 2:14). Living in harmony means having the mind of Christ, and those who don't know Jesus can't be like-minded with those who do know him. So if someone doesn't know Christ, you can't live in "perfect harmony" with him or her.

That doesn't mean we should be mean or rude to those who don't know Christ. Jesus preached often about the importance of loving others no matter who they are. You can love other people but not love what they do.

When you know people who don't love Jesus, try to look at them as friends who could one day become your brothers or sisters in Christ. Once that happens, you'll be in true harmony.

Olympic Fever!

Bible Blast: Read Proverbs 3:5-6

Some nations boast of their chariots and horses, but we boast in the name of the LORD our God. PSALM 20:7

I love the Olympics! They give us a chance to watch the "ending" to great athletic stories. God was teaching me something as I watched the pairs figure skating competition in the 2010 Winter Olympics.

When former figure skater Yao Bin decided to become a coach, he set the goal of winning gold at the Olympic level for China. To do this, he would not only have to improve the Chinese skating program drastically, but he would also have to defeat the powerhouse of the Russian skaters.

Russia approached the 2010 Olympics with their hopes set on a Russian male paired with a young girl from Japan whose dream was to win a gold medal. Because she was one of the world's best, Russia gladly welcomed her to the team. This Japanese girl eventually changed her citizenship from Japan to Russia so she could compete.

Yao Bin set his hopes on the team of Shen Xue and Zhao Hongbo. These two skaters were so old that they might as well have been in wheelchairs when it came to skating. He was thirty-eight. She was thirty-one. They had retired from skating but came back to compete.

Would this even be a contest? The world's winning-est team powered up by a Japanese world champion versus two retired, never-winning-gold Chinese teammates?

On February 15, 2010, Yao Bin cried great tears of joy when the team of Shen and Zhao took the gold, followed by his other Chinese team, who took silver!

Russia placed fourth.

I don't claim to know the faith of any of the competitors, but this story shows us what it looks like to trust in man-made chariots. Look back at today's focus verse. I think that manipulating our lives at any cost is like trusting in chariots. And it often doesn't pay. It didn't pay for Russia and their Japanese skater. Instead, we can put our trust in God, knowing that he will work everything out for our good.

Girl Gab: How do you need to let go of things to trust in God today? Have you been trying to change who you really are so that you'll be successful at something? Confess this to your mom and to God. Ask him to increase your trust in him.

Attention, Everyone!

Bible Blast: Read Psalm 7:13-15

The wicked conceive evil; they are pregnant with trouble and give birth to lies. PSALM 7:14

You've probably heard this story, but here goes.

There once was a boy who was in charge of watching a herd of sheep as they grazed on the hill. Since there wasn't very much to do, he got bored. In order to entertain himself, he yelled, "Wolf! Wolf! There's a wolf!"

Immediately other shepherds who were grazing their sheep at the bottom of the hill came running up to the boy to help him get rid of the sheep-stealing wolf. When they saw the boy, he was holding onto his stomach laughing. "There's no wolf! Ha, ha! I was kidding!"

The other shepherds sternly said, "Never call 'Wolf!' when there is no wolf!" and they went back to their sheep.

A little while later, the boy cried wolf again. The shepherds came running up the hill to help him, and again they just found the boy laughing at them. One of the shepherds grabbed the boy by his shoulders, looked him right in the eyes, and said, "*Do not* cry 'Wolf!' when there is no wolf!"

Not long after that, the boy saw an actual wolf prowling near his sheep. He got very afraid and yelled, "*Wolf! Wolf!*" But the shepherds thought he was playing again, so they didn't run up to help him.

When it was time to take the sheep back to their barns, the shepherds went up to check on the boy and his herd. They found him sitting on a rock, crying, "There really was a wolf, and he chased all my sheep away! I'm so sorry for tricking you! It's my fault that my sheep are gone!"

Some people will do anything to get attention. They might even lie. They sound a lot like the boy who cried "Wolf!" in the old story.

Our focus verse says that evil ideas give birth to lies. It's never okay to lie, even if you're bored and lonely from "watching sheep." In the story, the boy fell into his own trap. You can be sure that God protects those who tell the truth but lets liars fall into their own pit.

Meditation Moment: James 1:2

Dear brothers and sisters, whenever trouble comes your way, let it be an opportunity for joy. JAMES 1:2

Let's look really hard at this verse before you begin to meditate today. You see those words "let it be"? Well, in the original language of the New Testament—Greek—that would have read, "Count up the ways." What might be a better way to understand this verse is to put it into today's words: "Hey, guys and girls, whenever you have troubles, count up the ways you can be joyful about it."

Finding ways to be joyful isn't always easy to do. You might have a family member who is really sick. Your mom and dad might be having a hard time with money. Maybe you don't feel like you have any close friends. These are real troubles, and God cares about them. Still he wants you to "count up the ways" that these troubles can produce joy. For example, maybe one reason you don't have a lot of friends is so you can grow for a while in your friendship with God. Or maybe God is giving you time to appreciate your friendship with your mom.

Today I want you to meditate on a trouble you've been having and write a list of all the things God wants you to "count up" as joy. As always, pray before you begin meditating on this Scripture today. After you've gone over it a few times, just sit and wait quietly for God to speak to your heart. If you feel that God has given you a thought, picture, or idea, go ahead and jot it down.

Girl Gab: Talk this verse over with your mom. Pray together that God would give you the strength to live and think differently from the rest of the world.

The Duck

Bible Blast: Read Romans 8:13-17

Letting your sinful nature control your mind leads to death. But letting the Spirit control your mind leads to life and peace.
ROMANS 8:6

Jerry had a buddy that just happened to be a big white duck. He never really named it. He just referred to it as "The Duck." It followed Jerry all around the yard while he did his different tasks of mowing the grass, working in the garden, or whatever.

One day the Duck was watching Jerry while he filled the lawn mower with gasoline. He accidentally spilled some fuel onto the bird. The Duck was obviously in pain from the gas, so Jerry grabbed it and ran into the house to get the gasoline washed off. He put the Duck in the kitchen sink and used a gentle dish liquid to clean off the fuel and provide relief for his feathered friend. It seemed to work very well.

Jerry was glad to see the Duck feeling better, so to give it a chance to get really rinsed off, he placed it in the swimming pool. Do you know what happened? Jerry had to rescue the Duck because it began to sink!

Do you know why?

God gave ducks an oil that covers their feathers and makes them waterproof. If the oil is taken away (by something like dish soap), the feathers become soaked with water, and the bird will sink. So while Jerry was removing the harmful gasoline from the Duck, he was also removing the necessary oils that enabled it to float.

The Holy Spirit inside of us provides many things. One of those things is protection from living a sinful life. The Spirit warns us when we're being tempted and gives us the strength we need to "stay floating" and not give in to that temptation. But if you ignore the Spirit's work in your life too often, eventually it will become very hard for you to hear him at all, and you'll find yourself sinking down into things you know you shouldn't do.

God's Holy Spirit is there to help you and strengthen you. Go ahead and listen to him!

A Shoe? Really?

Bible Blast: Read Psalm 127:1-2

Unless the LORD builds a house, the work of the builders is wasted. PSALM 127:1

In 1948 an über-rich shoe-business dude name Mahlon Haines built a shoe-shaped house in York County, Pennsylvania. It has three bedrooms, two bathrooms, a kitchen, and a living room! It's forty-eight feet long and twenty-five feet high. Mr. Haines (also known as "The Colonel") built the shoe as a guesthouse. He invited an elderly couple to stay in his big shoe for a weekend, and he pampered them with a maid, a cook, a chauffeur, and a car. He also gave the couple brand-new clothes from local stores.

Later the shoe was turned into an ice cream shop, and now it's a museum displaying interesting things from the Colonel's life. Maybe you can check it out on a family road trip someday. It's called the Haines Shoe House.

Building any kind of thing in life—shoe shaped or otherwise—is pointless if you do it without the Lord. In fact, doing anything without God is useless or wasted, like our focus verse Psalm 127:1 says.

God builds things for eternal purposes. He doesn't do something just because he "feels like it" or gets bored or has some extra cash lying around. Everything God does has great purpose to it, and he wants us to live our lives with that same sense of purpose.

You may not build buildings yet, but you build relationships, dreams, goals, projects, and ideas. God wants to be the One who really builds those things. If you let him, the things you create will have deeper meaning to them.

Letting the Lord "build your house" means you need to ask constantly for his will to be done in everything you decide to do in life. Ask him to guide you and show you what to do and how to do it. He will hear your prayers and build something life changing with you.

So if your dream is to live in a shoe, make sure you ask God about that. He may have a different plan—like, maybe he wants you to live in a hat!

Girl Gab: Look at photos of the Haines Shoe House online or in a book at the library. If you could make your house into any shape, what would it be? What shape would your mom choose? Commit all your "building plans" for today to the Lord.

Forever Is a Long Time

Bible Blast: Read Psalm 136

Give thanks to the God of heaven. His faithful love endures forever. PSALM 136:26

Girl Gab: Make up your own psalm like Psalm 136 together. Just have fun saying things out loud that God has done in your life, like "He gave our family the money to go on a great camping trip." After each statement, say, "His love endures forever." See how long a psalm you can write!

Most likely, someday the man you love will bow down on one knee, hold out a diamond engagement ring, and say, "Will you marry me?" If you say yes, he will take that ring and place it on the ring finger of your left hand. People say wedding rings are placed on that particular finger because it has a direct connection to the heart by a long-reaching vein.

We use diamonds in rings because "diamonds are forever." While it is possible to destroy a diamond, it's pretty difficult. They're the hardest gemstones on the planet. That's why people can pass their diamonds on in a family for generations. Diamonds are a symbol of pure love for eternity.

Psalm 136 is a beautiful love song written for God. The pattern of the psalm is to state a truth about God and then follow it with a diamond of a statement: "His faithful love endures forever." Isn't that what a man is saying when he proposes to his true love? "My love is true, and I'll love you forever."

No matter what happens, God's love doesn't change or disappear. The day you gave your heart to Jesus, he gave you that diamond promise of his love.

It doesn't take long to figure out that lots of things don't last forever. In spite of that, girls still obsess over things like boys, clothes, music, celebrities, food, and stuff, as if those things are never going to go away. Those things are all like "fake diamonds." They *look* pretty and *feel* like the real thing, but over time they fade away or get crushed.

God's love is the real deal. His love lasts forever. It doesn't make sense to obsess over something that's temporary, does it? God's eternal love is the only thing worth obsessing over. It won't go away, and it won't ever cause us harm.

The next time you get hurt by a relationship gone bad or you lose something you totally love, remind yourself that "God's love is faithful, and it lasts forever."

Kickin' Kraft: Presto Change-O!

Bible Blast: Read Isaiah 61:1-3

To all who mourn in Israel, he will give a crown of beauty for ashes. ISAIAH 61:3

God is *big* into recycling. Did you know that?

I'm not talking about a special bin for plastic and glass containers! God recycles yucky stuff in our lives and turns them into something beautiful. He can take any bad thing in your life and transform it into something that brings glory to him and encourages others.

J. R. Celski is a short-track speed skater (on ice). Five months before the Olympics, he crashed during the trials. When he crashed, his ice skate impaled his left thigh. Not to be gross, but the skate was in there deep enough that when they took the skate out, they could see his bone. (That's the last of the gross things. I promise.)

When J.R. realized what had happened, his dream of winning an Olympic medal vanished—or so he thought. After having surgery and spending six weeks on crutches, J.R. got right back into training. He trained hard for three and a half months, thinking he had no chance. But not only did he make it to the Olympics; he ended up winning a bronze medal!

J.R.'s accident was terrible and potentially life threatening since the cut in his leg was only one inch from a major artery. But J.R.'s determination and desire didn't allow him to give up on his dream. He went for it and achieved a place in Olympic history! Before the accident, he was a nice kid with a dream. But after the accident, he became a nice kid whose story has inspired millions all over the world not to give up even when things look really bad.

That's the kind of thing God does. He takes the stuff the devil means for evil and destruction and turns it into something good and inspiring.

Kickin' Kraft:
Groovy Garbage Can!

(Check out p. 374 for a great mother-daughter craft that helps reinforce today's devo!)

The M Word

Bible Blast: Read 1 Peter 3:3-4

Let your wife be a fountain of blessing for you. Rejoice in the wife of your youth. . . . May you always be captivated by her love. PROVERBS 5:18-19

School will be starting soon. That means one thing: *back-to-school shopping*! Since you're growing so fast right now, you might need to replace something in your wardrobe by the time school rolls around because it just doesn't fit you anymore.

How do you approach school shopping? Do you just buy whatever the stores say is cool? Do you and your mom end up being totally stressed out by the end of it? One way to reduce that stress is to find out what God says about "modesty" before you hit the thrift store or the mall. What do you think of when you hear the word "modesty"? Maybe you think it means to dress in a way that doesn't show off too much of your body. And you're right. That is basically what it means. But let's go deeper.

Today's focus verse may have made you giggle a little bit. It's sooo mushy-gushy lovey-dovey! When it says, "Rejoice in *the* wife of your youth," it's a reflection of God's desire that a man should be totally captivated by only one woman's beauty—his wife's. In the same way, your beauty is meant to captivate only one man someday, and that's your husband.

When girls and women dress in clothes that show off their tummies, breasts, legs, and other parts of their bodies, they're not saving the deepest secrets of their beauty for that one man. They're showing that beauty to just anybody who sees them. Not cool!

It's tough to dress modestly right now because all the magazines, TV programs, movies, and store ads tell us that if you want to look cool, you have to show off your body. That's a *total* lie! The girls and women I know who have the coolest personal style are the ones who choose not to show off their bodies.

Choosing to hide the deepest secrets of your beauty gives you an opportunity to set yourself apart and develop an awesome style all your own. Now take that info, grab your purse, and go shopping!

Language Lab:
What Does "Blasphemy" Mean?

Bible Blast: Read John 10:36-38

I tell you, every sin and blasphemy can be forgiven—except blasphemy against the Holy Spirit, which will never be forgiven.
MATTHEW 12:31

Blasphemy. Now there's a word you don't use every day!

Blasphemy is basically the worst kind of false thing you can say about God or the Bible. It's not something someone can do "by accident." It's a very "on purpose" word-bashing against our faith. You see it a lot in the Gospels (Matthew, Mark, Luke, and John) when the religious leaders accused Jesus of saying false things about God.

The religious leaders in Jesus' time didn't like Jesus. They thought he was a guy lots of people liked who was speaking lies about God when he said he was God's Son, and that was blasphemy.

The weird thing is, since they didn't believe he was God, they were the ones saying blasphemous things all the time. In Matthew 12, the Pharisees actually said Jesus could do miracles because he got his power from the devil! That is some serious blasphemy, and Jesus told them so.

Jesus said that blasphemy against the Holy Spirit won't be forgiven. Huh?

A person who lives a life of constantly and intentionally speaking against the Holy Spirit and denies the work of Jesus Christ won't be forgiven because he or she will never ask for God's forgiveness. A blasphemous person has removed himself or herself from the Holy Spirit's influence—and the Holy Spirit is the only one who can lead someone to salvation.

You may not be at risk for blasphemy of the Holy Spirit, but you could very easily "blaspheme" another person. Although it may not be exactly the same as blasphemy, lying about other kids to make them feel bad is not something Jesus would want you to do. It may be tempting to say untrue things about a person behind her back, and yes, God forgives you, but what does he *really* want you to do in those situations?

Girl Gab: Grab a piece of paper. Think about someone you're tempted to say bad things about. Write down five positive things about that person. (You might need your mom's help with that.) As you go down the list, thank God for each of those things.

10 August

Strong Tower

Bible Blast: Read 2 Samuel 22:1-4

The name of the LORD is a strong tower; the righteous run into it and are safe. PROVERBS 18:10 (NIV)

Girl Gab: List a few ways that you can "stay in God's tower" when you need to be safe. Mom, you go first. Try to come up with at least five together.

The CN Tower is the world's tallest tower. Located in Toronto, Canada, it is 1,815 feet high. (The world's tallest *building* is in Dubai.) Anyway, back to the tower.

Since the average American house is about eighteen feet tall to the eaves, you'd have to stack most houses one hundred high to have a building as tall as the CN Tower.

A few years ago, my husband, Bob, and I had an extra day to spend in Toronto, and we made sure to visit the observation deck of the CN Tower. When you're up there, you are so high that you can see one hundred miles—all the way to Niagara Falls and into New York state on a clear day! We were not there on a clear day. In fact, we went at night in the middle of a storm that turned ugly. By the time we got to the observation deck, the officials were closing it because of high winds, thunder, and lightning. I felt a little bit afraid, but I was assured by one of the tour guides that we were incredibly safe. In fact, she told us we were safer in the tower than on the ground because of the lightning.

"The tower gets hit by lightning about seventy-five times a year," she said. "But we never even feel it. Trust me, if you were on the ground, you'd feel it! But this tower was built to absorb the shock and send it through the ground. It's safe." She went on to explain that the winds were so high that the tower was swaying with the wind; it was designed to do this to improve the building's safety.

"If you were on the ground right now, you'd be inside because these winds are dangerous." Sure enough, we got down to the ground, where the storm was worse. The officials wouldn't even let us go outside down there because it wasn't safe.

Inside the tower, we were safe. Outside, we were not.

The writer of Proverbs calls God a strong tower. The strength of his protection never gets weaker, even if there's a gigantic storm going on. Just like the CN Tower, safety isn't found on the ground. It's always safest up in God's tower.

Prophet-Doodles

Bible Blast: Read Mark 13:22-23

Jesus told him, "I am the way, the truth, and the life. No one can come to the Father except through me." JOHN 14:6

I sure am glad for one man in Hawaii who had a runny nose and scratchy eyes every time he was near a dog. You see, he's the reason I have my lovable dog, Stormie! In 1988, Wally Cochran of the Royal Guide Dogs organization in Victoria, Australia, got a request from a blind woman living in Hawaii. She needed a guide dog that wouldn't aggravate her husband's allergies. Wally asked the manager of the Royal Guide Dogs about crossing one of their Labrador retrievers with a standard poodle. He agreed, and so the first labradoodles were bred. And guess what? "Mr. Allergy" had no reaction!

The result of the crossbreed was adorable—not to mention clean because the dogs don't shed and are practically allergen free. "Labradoodle Fever" soon hit Australia and spread farther and farther until it hit the Gresh family five years ago, giving us Stormie.

But the Labradoodle craze created a situation in which all sorts of poodles were being bred to just any Labrador. The result has been a lot of hairy houses and a lot of itchy eyes.

God tells you and me to "be careful" when we hear people speaking about Christ. On the outside, they might look, act, and sound like "prophets" of God, but they may actually be false prophets—like those fake Labradoodles who look just as cute and cuddly, but don't have the right genetics *inside* of them to be legitimate.

When someone says he or she has a message from God for you, always check it with Scripture. If you hear a teaching or read a book, make sure what you're learning is truth, not some twisted version of the truth.

Remember that 1 Samuel 16:7 says God doesn't look at the outward appearance. He looks at the heart. Ask God to help you see the heart behind what people say. If there's truth, apply it to your life. If there's something untrue, just toss it aside. Don't be fooled by "crazy prophet-doodles!"

Girl Gab: Did you know a pug/beagle mix is called a "puggle"? Think of funny dog combinations, like Great Dane and chihuahua or dalmatian and pug, and make up names for them. Ask God to give you wisdom to know what's false and what's true.

Amazing Animals: Bottlenose Dolphins

Bible Blast: Read Psalm 125:1-5

You hem me in—behind and before; you have laid your hand upon me. PSALM 139:5 (NIV)

Most people *love* dolphins! I think every girl has dreamed of petting dolphins, riding dolphins, or training dolphins. A few years ago our family was vacationing when a pod of dolphins came up to our boat. We actually jumped in the water with them, and one of the dolphins stayed and played with us for about thirty minutes.

There are several stories of bottlenose dolphins actually saving people's lives. On October 30, 2004, four New Zealand lifeguards were swimming when a group of dolphins came to them and started "herding" them like a sheepdog herds sheep. When one of the swimmers tried to swim away from the dolphins, two of the larger ones herded him back into their circle. That's when the lifeguards saw a great white shark circling nearby. The pod of dolphins surrounded the swimmers and slapped their tails in the water for over half an hour to confuse the shark and keep him from attacking the four men.

And on August 28, 2007, Todd Endris was surfing with some friends off the coast of California when a great white shark attacked him. Todd was losing a lot of blood. Just then a group of bottlenose dolphins that had been playing in the waves went into action. They placed themselves between the shark and Todd so that Todd could catch a wave back to the shore. A friend of Todd who was with him that day was able to help him stay calm until they were able to get him to the hospital. Today, apart from an amazing scar on his torso and some muscle damage, Todd is fine and still surfing.

Aren't those stories just amazing? I love thinking of those men being surrounded on all sides by "dolphin bodyguards!"

In the psalms of David, he regularly praises his Creator for his love, care, and protection. Today's focus verse says that God hems him in on all sides. David knew that he was surrounded by God's goodness, strength, and love.

I wonder if any of those swimmers thought of Psalm 139:5 when they were surrounded by the bottlenose dolphins?

Louder! Louder!

Bible Blast: Read Psalm 143:1-12

Come, everyone! Clap your hands! Shout to God with joyful praise! PSALM 47:1

Grace's best friend, Raye, was going through a hard time. So many things seemed to be going wrong for her, and she was starting to feel lost. Raye's faith in God had always been strong, but with all the bad stuff swirling around her, she was beginning to doubt his love for her.

Grace's heart broke for her friend. She encouraged her as much as she could with truth from God's Word. At times she was afraid Raye would turn her back on God altogether if something didn't change soon.

After catching a movie at the local theater one night, they drove down the flat roads of Ohio toward Raye's home.

Suddenly Grace said, "Raye, put down your window, and I'll put down mine."

Raye said, "Okay," and did as Grace said.

Grace looked at her and said, "We're going to take turns shouting out these windows at the top of our lungs about who God is in our lives. I'll go first." She stuck her head out the window and yelled as loud as she could, "God, you are my healer!" Then she turned to Raye and said, "Your turn!"

Raye hesitated a moment and screamed out the window, "God, you saved me!"

Along that long country road they took turns, yelling the truth about who God is out into the world. Did it change Raye's circumstances? Nope. Did it change Raye's heart? Maybe. Did it change Raye's language? Absolutely.

She had spent a lot of time talking about her doubt of God's character. When she was "forced" to proclaim truth of who God is, she was reminded that God never changes. He's the same God who has rescued Raye time and time again over the course of her life. He would definitely rescue her again.

At certain points in life, you may need to praise God for who he is just because it's the right thing to do, not because you feel like it. Every word written about him in the Bible is true. Go ahead and shout them out!

Girl Gab: When it's appropriate during a car ride with your mom, roll down the windows as your mom drives and take turns yelling out truth about God. Each of you should try to yell at least five things. (A remote country road works best for this so you don't freak anybody out!)

Breathing Courage

Bible Blast: Read 1 Thessalonians 5:14-16

Encourage each other and build each other up, just as you are already doing. 1 THESSALONIANS 5:11

Girl Gab: Mom, talk to your daughter about practical ways to "breathe courage" into the kids in her class. Pray that others in her grade would be full of grace and love as they change and grow.

By now you may have figured out that around your age, guys and girls start to change, especially in the way they look. Suddenly, a boy who's always been shorter is towering over everyone. And a girl with fine, straight hair might start to have thicker, wavier hair. You especially notice these changes after summer is over and you're back for the first day of school. Boys can change so much in such a short amount of time that you may not even recognize them at first!

It's an exciting and weird time of life, don't you think? I mean, it's so wonderful to grow up and start looking and feeling older, but sometimes it can be hard, especially because everyone changes at different times. Some girls' bodies will start to mature when they're eleven, and some won't until they're fourteen or older.

If there's a girl whose body has started to develop (especially in the chest) before everyone else's, she can feel awkward. Sometimes boys and others will say silly things because she looks different from the way she used to, and that can be embarrassing for her at times.

If that girl were you (and maybe it is), how would you want to be treated? It seems like a great time to offer some encouragement, wouldn't you agree? When you encourage someone, it literally means you "breathe courage" into someone. A girl whose body is changing into a young woman's could probably use some courage from a good friend. If you see people saying rude things to her, stand up for her. As you can tell by today's focus verse, we're actually *commanded* to encourage each other. Encouragement is supposed to be a natural part of a Christian's life.

Eventually, everybody's body gets to a similar place of maturity, and the changes become no big deal. But until then, everyone needs a lot of encouragement and building up. Pray for your friends and classmates during this time. It can make a *huge* difference in your school.

A Different Kind of Yo-Yo

Bible Blast: Read Ephesians 1:19-23

Open your mouth wide, and I will fill it with good things.
PSALM 81:10

If you were naming a child, "Yo-Yo" would probably not be the first name that popped into your brain. Yo-Yo Ma was born to his Chinese parents in Paris, France.

Yo-Yo and his sister were taught music from the beginning of their lives. By age five, Yo-Yo played the cello and the piano at a concert at the University of Paris.

The cello is kind of like a really big violin. It's so big that it isn't held up under the chin. It is set down on the ground to be played. It makes a lower, deeper sound than a violin. A person who plays the cello is called a "cellist."

Yo-Yo was already well on his way to becoming a great cellist at the age of seven when his family moved to New York City. He did great in his studies and amazed his music teachers. When he became a teenager, he went through a time when he didn't feel like practicing, but he didn't give up on the cello because it was important to him.

Over the years, Yo-Yo Ma has become one of the top cellists in the world, performing with the best-known orchestras and performing solo concerts. He even had the privilege of playing for Barack Obama's presidential inauguration.

When Yo-Yo was younger, his dad played music by Johann Sebastian Bach for his son before bed. He would tell him, "This is not practicing. This is for you."

Yo-Yo spent a lot of time in his life giving the gift of music to others, but his dad was there to remind him, "You can't keep giving, giving, giving if you're not also receiving."

That's true in our lives with Christ, too. It's important to give, serve, teach, and help others, but we must also get filled up by God with times that are just for us. Otherwise, we're going to eventually run dry.

Spend time in God's Word. Take time to have conversations with the Lord. Have times of private worship with him. Meditate on his truth. These things will fill you up and allow you to give to others without drying up.

Girl Gab: Plan to take in a lot of water today. Try to drink eight full glasses of water before you hit the sack tonight. (That's the daily recommendation.) Every time you drink, thank God for something specific he's done for you.

Girl Gab: Have fun talking with your mom about what you would do if you found out today that you were going to live for 969 years. Do you think you would want to live that long?

Bible Blast: Read Deuteronomy 5:7-21

"Honor your father and mother." This is the first commandment with a promise. If you honor your father and mother, things will go well with you, and you will have a long life on the earth. EPHESIANS 6:2-3

Kama Chinen was old. When she died on April 10, 2010, she was 114 years old. She had a ways to go to break the record though. The oldest person who ever lived was a guy named Methuselah who lived way back before Noah built the ark. He isn't mentioned very much in the Bible, but he's still kind of famous. Read this verse from Genesis 5, and you'll see why: "Methuselah lived 969 years."

He didn't die until he was 969 *years old!* Can you imagine watching the ball drop in Times Square on New Year's Eve almost a thousand years in a row?

There are many reasons a person lives a longer life than others. Healthy living has something to do with it. Some people just seem to have it in their blood. But one solid reason the Bible gives is honoring our parents. Maybe honoring them helps us make safer and healthier choices, or maybe God just delights in blessing us for honoring our parents. We don't know. We just know that he desires us to honor our parents and promises us longer lives if we do it.

A lot of people think that "honoring your parents" is something they should do in order to pay their parents back for taking care of them, giving them food, clothes, etc. But God first gave that commandment to the Israelites when they were wandering in the desert for forty years. During that period, the Israelite parents didn't really provide food and clothes for their kids—God did. God provided manna from heaven for them to eat every day. The Bible even says that God made it so their clothes didn't wear out and their feet didn't blister for the whole forty years (see Deuteronomy 8:4).

Honoring your parents isn't about paying them back. It's about thanking them for giving you life. It's about knowing they are wiser than you are and respecting that wisdom. It's about loving others as you love yourself.

Your Strongest Tooth

Bible Blast: Read Mark 2:1-12

Seeing their faith, Jesus said to the paralyzed man, "My child, your sins are forgiven." MARK 2:5

Is it an alligator or a crocodile? Can you tell the difference?

In most cases an alligator has a wider, u-shaped mouth, while a crocodile has a longer, skinnier one. Also, when a crocodile's mouth is closed, you're still likely to see all of his teeth sticking out, whereas alligators usually keep most of their biters covered up.

Speaking of teeth, did you know baby crocs have a special tool for getting out of their eggs? It's called an "egg tooth." The egg tooth is an extra bit of hard skin located at the front of the croc's snout. When it's time to hatch, the baby croc uses that little tooth to break out of the captivity of the eggshell and enter the world. The egg tooth is reabsorbed back into the crocodile's body just a few months after it's born. Isn't it just amazing that God didn't just leave those little guys in their eggs without a way to get out?

Did you know that you have a sort of "egg tooth" too? It's your faith!

Before you gave your heart to Jesus, that was sort of like being in a dark place, like an egg. You knew there was something outside of that egg, but you weren't sure what. The moment you decided to give Jesus a try, you cracked a hole in that shell and began to see everything Jesus had to offer you, a whole wonderful world of his love.

Without that first bit of faith, you never would have given your heart to Jesus. That first "egg tooth" time of believing in Jesus was the first step to the amazing journey you're on right now of following Jesus and sharing him with others.

Now, on crocodiles the egg tooth gets smaller and smaller until it disappears, but that's very different from what happens to your faith. As you come out of your shell and grow in your relationship with Christ, your faith will get bigger and bigger and bigger! The farther you go from your "egg," the more you trust God and the stronger your faith becomes.

Girl Gab: Do you have some friends who are still stuck in the egg? I mean, do you have friends who haven't made that first step of faith in God? Pray for them right now with your mom. Ask God to show them that they have enough of an "egg tooth" to get out of that dark place of not knowing Jesus.

Let Go and Let God

Bible Blast: Read Exodus 14:10-14

The LORD himself will fight for you. Just stay calm. EXODUS 14:14

Girl Gab: Have you ever been in a situation that caused you to panic? Talk about how doing that helped or didn't help the situation. Ask God for the ability to stay calm and let him fight for you during panicky times.

I'm a fan of the Disney movie *Finding Nemo*.

After Marlin and Dory find Nemo, they're swimming around in a big school of gray fish when suddenly the fish start panicking. A fishing net has gathered around them and is getting ready to pull them up out of the water onto a fishing barge. All the gray fish totally freak out and just start yelling while they swim in all different directions. Nemo and Marlin are small enough to get through the net, but Dory's caught.

Nemo gets an idea and says, "Dad! I know what to do! We need to tell all the fish to swim *down*!" Then, he swims into the net with all the other fish. Marlin, Nemo, and Dory go around to the fish yelling, "Swim down! We all need to swim down together!"

The gray fish catch on and start working together, swimming in the opposite direction of the boat. The strength of their teamwork pulls against the barge; eventually, the line breaks, the net drops into the water, and the fish are all free!

Panic can be a natural reaction to situations that get beyond our control. But panic doesn't produce anything good. Panic is not self-control or trust. It's letting fear and worry control you, and that's not how God wants you to live.

The Israelites were in a state of total panic when they saw the Egyptians coming after them. All Moses could do was remind them that God was in control and that he would fight for them. They just needed to chill out in a major way and let God protect them.

Even if the Israelites could have arranged themselves to fight against the Egyptians, they never would have won. The Egyptians had chariots, weapons, and soldiers. The Israelites had just been released from years of slavery and only had their few belongings. God was their only defense.

Panic may feel like the natural thing to do sometimes, but it won't be effective. God may need you to do the opposite of what feels right, just like the gray fish and the Israelites.

Loving Arms

Bible Blast: Read Deuteronomy 32:7-14

Like an eagle that rouses her chicks and hovers over her young, so he spread his wings to take them up and carried them safely on his pinions. DEUTERONOMY 32:11

Father Carlos runs a little farm in Brazil with some goats, chickens, roosters, and other common barnyard animals. But he has one set of animals that are anything but ordinary: six kittens. You might think that kittens are quite ordinary, but these kittens had a barnyard chicken that took to mothering them.

Mama Cat went to her kittens a few times a day to make sure they got the milk they need to live, but that's all she did. The Mama Chicken took over. She cleaned the kitties and kept them from danger. They rubbed up against her, and she nuzzled them with her beak. She never took her eyes off those kittens.

The kittens were just as comfortable snuggling with Mama Chicken as they were with Mama Cat. They didn't realize that cats and chickens are natural enemies. They didn't care because the chicken was caring for them and loving them as if they were her own babies. The Mama Chicken would even put her wings over the kittens to keep them safe and warm. That's how lots of birds protect their young. They gather the babies under their wings to hide them from predators. And that's what God longs to do with us.

It's a beautiful picture to think of God gathering all his children together and covering them with incredible, strong wings. It's a perfect picture of his protection and love. He doesn't need big steel walls or metal bars to protect us from evil. His love and affection for us are stronger than any weapon.

Real love attracts people to it. God has loved us with a love that never dies or goes away. It's a forever love, and it draws us to him. It's like a magnet. We are attracted to a relationship with God because his love pulls us closer and closer to him.

As Father Carlos's kittens felt secure with Mama Chicken close by, we can count on the Lord to cover us in his great love forever.

Girl Gab: God gives us parents to shelter us and cover us with protective "wings." Today, why not enjoy a prolonged mother/daughter hug. Daughter, really snuggle under your mom's "wings"!

Meditation Moment: Colossians 3

Work willingly at whatever you do, as though you were working for the Lord rather than for people. COLOSSIANS 3:23

"Work hard."

"Finish putting the dishes away."

"Did you finish your homework?"

You receive a lot of messages about work, don't you? Every now and then work can be fun or entertaining, but there's a lot of work we have to do that we don't necessarily want to do, right?

Maybe Colossians 3:23 will give you some wisdom for how to deal with the work you don't feel like doing. It doesn't say, "Work willingly when you are doing something you like." Nor does it say, "Work willingly when you are working for God." It says, "Work willingly at whatever you do." Taking out the trash? Work willingly. Studying your spelling words? Work willingly.

Pray first, and then go over the verse several times.

Wait to hear from God. He would love to teach you through the truth of his Word today.

When you feel that God has spoken to you through an idea, picture, or thought, go ahead and write it down.

Smoke and Mirrors

Bible Blast: Read 1 Timothy 2:9-10

Sixty queens there may be . . . but my dove, my perfect one, is unique. SONG OF SONGS 6:8-9 (NIV)

Since 1959 Barbie dolls have been thrilling girls all over the world. Barbie has done some amazing things over the years. She's been a veterinarian, a cowgirl, a pediatrician, a businesswoman, and even an astronaut. There have been celebrity Barbies, Barbies from different countries, dancing Barbies, singing Barbies, and Barbies with wings.

As amazing as Barbie may seem, there's one really big problem with her: her body.

Did you know that if Barbie were a real human, her neck would be nine inches long!? That's one serious bobblehead! And her chest would be so incredibly gigantic that she wouldn't be able to walk upright! Just imagine Barbie moving around the mall on all fours! Not very glamorous, right?

Barbie is fun to play with, but she represents a completely unrealistic picture of beauty. She's made out of plastic. We can't possibly look like Barbie, and God never wanted us to.

Unfortunately, Barbie is not the only standard of impossible beauty that you and I see. Remember how I described how the models' pictures on the cover of fashion magazines have been changed by computer programs to make the models look "perfect"? I'm not just talking about getting rid of a zit or a wrinkle. They make their eyes bigger, their hair fuller, their legs skinnier, their lips poutier, and their teeth whiter. By the time that magazine hits the newsstands, the model may look entirely different than she does in real life!

The women you see on magazines and commercials and other places have been changed in order to trick you into believing they are perfect. The problem with that is it can make you believe that you need to look as perfect as they do, which is impossible because the way they look in those pictures is not even real.

Today's focus verse reminds us that our beauty springs out of our uniqueness. The things about you that make you unique are the very things that make you beautiful.

Girl Gab: Mom, pick something out about your daughter that is unique. Tell her why that quality is part of her beauty. Daughter, you can do the same thing for your mom! Pray together that God can help you embrace how he created you to be unique.

22 August

In the World, but Not of the World

Bible Blast: Read Matthew 9:9-13

When Jesus heard this, he said, "Healthy people don't need a doctor—sick people do." MATTHEW 9:12

Girl Gab: Mom, talk to your daughter about "being in the world, but not of it." Pray for her as she determines to minister to the "sick" in the world. Then, Daughter, you pray the same for your mom.

Herod the Great built an incredible fortress called Masada south of Jerusalem and overlooking the Dead Sea. What made Masada so cool was that it was a small city built up on top of a plateau. The only way to get to it was by a couple of long, twisty "snake" paths, making it pretty much impossible for enemies to get to the city and take it over. To Herod, being separated was the ultimate protection.

As far as battle goes, I guess Masada was a pretty great idea, but it's not a good model for how we should live as Christians.

What if, when Jesus came to this earth, he placed himself high up on top of a mountain, way out of reach of the people, and just preached? I guess we might still respect him, but that's not what he did at all.

Jesus walked among all kinds of people, including some pretty major sinners. He touched sick people whom no one else would touch with a "thirty-nine-and-a-half-foot pole!" (Remember that from *How the Grinch Stole Christmas?*) Jesus ate meals served by tax collectors, who were hated by everyone. He forgave women who led sinful lives. He held all sorts of children. Jesus got right into the thick of life on earth, and he loved anyone and everyone who would receive his love.

Today's focus verse is powerful and yet really simple at the same time. After I read it, I think, *Of course healthy people don't need a doctor.* But Jesus was telling the church leaders of that time to get off their clean, healthy thrones and get dirty with those who really needed help.

That can be hard. It's hard to talk to someone who doesn't smell very nice because she lives on the street. It's hard to send a card to a prisoner even though she's done something terrible. It's hard to eat lunch with a girl at school that nobody else likes. But God never intended for us to build a Masada way far apart from everyone else so that we'll stay clean and not get hurt.

There are a lot of "ill" people out there. If Jesus is controlling your life, you have just the medicine they need.

Language Lab: What Is "Condemnation"?

Bible Blast: Read Romans 5:17-19

Anyone who believes and is baptized will be saved. But anyone who refuses to believe will be condemned. MARK 16:16

Today's Language Lab might make you picture an old, evil-looking judge sitting up on his throne. He points his long, bony finger at the accused in front of him and says in a booming voice, "You are condemned to the dungeon *forever!*" When someone is condemned, it usually means that person was tried and found guilty and will spend the rest of his or her life in prison, or something like it.

The Bible talks about condemnation as what happens to those who don't believe in Jesus and follow him. In your Bible Blast today the passage explains how Adam's disobedience brought sin and death into the world. Before he and Eve ate that fruit in the Garden of Eden, nobody was condemned to death. But after their sin, every other living human being on earth would follow in sin. We are born sinful (Psalm 51:5), and because of that we are condemned—or sentenced—to die physically and spiritually.

But the story doesn't end there.

When Jesus came and died for our sins, he made a way for us to be made right with God even though we are guilty of sin. Because of that free gift of salvation, we will live for eternity with Jesus.

It's so discouraging to look around and see so many people making the choice to live in sin, especially since you know the truth of Romans 8:1, which says there is no condemnation for those who live in Christ Jesus. If you know Jesus, you are totally, 100 percent free from condemnation and death. Death is never the winner when someone follows Christ. Even after our bodies die here on earth, we'll keep on living in heaven forever and ever and ever and ever and, well, you get the picture.

Now that you know what condemnation is, I hope you'll realize what a responsibility you have to share Jesus and his free gift of salvation with others. Jesus is the only remedy for someone who is on a road of condemnation.

Girl Gab: Pray for your town or city, believing that everyone living there can be brought into a relationship with Jesus. If the weather is nice today, take a prayer walk through your neighborhood, and pray for everyone you can by name.

24 August

Famous Last Words

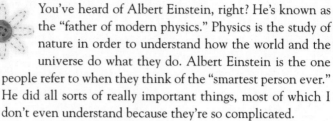

Bible Blast: Read John 19:28-30

When Jesus had tasted it, he said, "It is finished!" Then he bowed his head and released his spirit. JOHN 19:30

Girl Gab: You totally have to look for a pic of Albert Einstein. Do you think he used hairspray, or did his really smart brain make his hair stand up? Just for fun, some night this week try to give you or your mom Einstein hair! (Your mom may know how to tease hair and make it stick up.) Thank God for his perfect plan to give you eternal life.

You've heard of Albert Einstein, right? He's known as the "father of modern physics." Physics is the study of nature in order to understand how the world and the universe do what they do. Albert Einstein is the one people refer to when they think of the "smartest person ever." He did all sorts of really important things, most of which I don't even understand because they're so complicated.

One odd thing about Einstein's death is that nobody knows what his last words were. When he died in a hospital in 1955, he spoke something in German. Unfortunately, the nurse who was with him at the time didn't understand German. So we don't know the last words of one of the most intelligent men who ever lived.

The last words someone speaks are usually important, especially to those closest to the one who speaks them. Jesus' last words were no exception. He spoke a few things while he hung on the cross in the moments before his death but maybe one of the most well-known sentences is, "It is finished."

When you look at the Greek meaning of "It is finished," it means

"It is the end."
"I've reached my goal."
"It is accomplished."
"It is complete."
"It has been made perfect."

It was an announcement that what Jesus had come to do was done. He came to die on the cross so humans could have eternal life, and that's exactly what he did.

God's perfect plan of salvation through his Son, Jesus, had been completed.

One really cool thing about Jesus' last words, "It is finished," is that it didn't mean the end. In fact, it meant that for you and me and everyone else who believes in him, it was just the beginning.

Big Things Come in Small Packages

Bible Blast: Read John 6:1-14

Don't let anyone think less of you because you are young. Be an example to all believers in what you say, in the way you live, in your love, your faith, and your purity. 1 TIMOTHY 4:12

You may know *Thumbelina* as Hans Christian Andersen's fairy tale about a thumb-sized girl's adventures. But Thumbelina is also the world's smallest horse. She was born to two miniature-horse parents. Miniature horses usually grow to weigh about 250 pounds and stand thirty-four inches tall. But Thumbelina was only eight pounds when she was born. Today she only weighs about sixty pounds and is seventeen and a half inches tall! They say that Thumbelina is a dwarf miniature horse; her owners call her a "mini-mini."

In spite of her tiny size, Thumbelina acts like she's the biggest horse around. She bosses Clydesdale horses around. She doesn't seem to realize she's smaller and physically weaker than every other animal around her.

Thumbelina travels all around the country, visiting children who are disabled or experiencing difficult situations. Those children are inspired by her because she doesn't give in to the fact that she's little. She pushes on and does whatever she wants to do.

You don't have to wait until you're older to do great things. If God has placed a dream in your heart, why not start taking steps toward it right now? God doesn't expect you to wait to grow up into an adult so he can use you. He can use absolutely anybody at any age and any size! He delivered an entire nation (Israel) by a boy named David when Goliath the giant was after them!

Don't use your age as an excuse not to encourage, love, and help others. God will use you for his glory every single day if you make yourself available to him. There are ways you can minister to those around you that your parents could never do.

Like Thumbelina, don't be afraid because you're young. You have the power of God in you, and nobody can beat that!

Girl Gab: You definitely have to look up Thumbelina, the World's Smallest Horse, online. She's the cutest little thing ever! Turn today's focus verse into a prayer like this: "Don't let anyone think less of me because I am young. Make me an example to all believers in what I say, in the way I live, in my love, my faith, and my purity. Amen."

26 August

Paws for a Moment

Bible Blast: Read Matthew 6:1-4

When you give to someone in need, don't let your left hand know what your right hand is doing. MATTHEW 6:3

Girl Gab: If you have a cat (or dog), do a test like putting tuna in a container to see if your pet is right- or left-handed. Then try to do something kind for someone else in your family without anyone noticing. Your kindness will be a gift given in secret!

You might not believe this, but it looks like cats can actually be right-handed or left-handed. After playing with kitties for an extended period of time, scientists agreed that cats actually favor using one paw or the other. The scientists especially noticed this in a test they conducted in which they put a piece of tuna fish in a container that was too small for the cat's head to fit through. The cats had to use a paw to get the tuna out in order to eat it.

I guess if cats gave to the poor, today's focus verse would apply to them, too.

Obviously, your hands don't actually "know" anything because they don't have brains. The idea behind this Scripture is that when you give to someone who's in need, don't make a big deal out of it so that the whole world knows.

There are a lot of celebrities and TV shows that focus on giving extraordinary gifts to people. It's exciting to watch, but it makes me wonder: Would those celebrities and TV shows give in such big ways if they didn't get to show off while doing it?

God's way of giving is to give with humility and sometimes with total anonymity (without anyone knowing who did it). Once when my husband and I were very young parents, we were out of money. We had very little food at home, and we were out of diapers for baby Robby. When I got home that day, there was a cashier's check in my mailbox. I never did know who that money came from, but I bet God blessed the givers for that gift!

It can be hard to give quietly or in secret, because it feels good to have other people say, "Wow! I can't believe you gave that to them! What a sacrifice! You're an amazing person!" But God says he will reward us for giving. We may have to wait until heaven to get that reward, but it will be far greater than any pat on the back someone gives us on earth.

Amazing Animals: Loggerhead Turtles

Bible Blast: Read Matthew 11:28-30

Jesus said, "Come to me, all of you who are weary and carry heavy burdens, and I will give you rest." MATTHEW 11:28

Loggerheads are a type of sea turtle, so they have flippers instead of feet—perfect for living in the ocean. They live in the warmer ocean waters all over the world, including off the coasts of the United States. Just a few weeks ago, my husband and I were out in the ocean, and I saw several of these amazing creatures.

When Mama Loggerhead is ready to lay her eggs, she actually leaves the water and scoots up onto a beach. The mother loggerhead digs a hole and very carefully lays as many as one hundred eggs in it.

After Mama Loggerhead buries her eggs, she heads back out to the ocean. In about sixty days, something amazing happens when the sun goes down. Those babies—who won't be burned by the hot rays or nabbed by predators—peck their way out of their eggs. Then they dig their way up to the surface and head toward the ocean. Now remember, these little guys are tiny. They would fit in the palm of your hand. And they don't have feet made for walking on land. Traveling any distance with their little flippers is quite a chore. If you get a chance, go online and check out a video of little loggerheads making their way to the ocean. It's pretty cute.

My question has always been, how do the baby loggerheads know which way is the ocean? Loggerheads naturally head toward the brightest light on the horizon, and because of the water's reflection, it's almost always where they head.

Once the baby loggerheads get in the ocean, you can just imagine them breathing a huge sigh of relief like, "Whew! I made it! I didn't get eaten by a seagull or crab, and I went in the right direction! Now I'm just going to float and rest because my little flippers are pooped!"

If you think about it, we're kind of like those baby loggerheads, and Jesus is like the ocean. When he said, "Come to me, and I'll give you rest," he knew that we would have to keep focused on his "light" as we scurry toward his safe arms.

Girl Gab: If you can, check out an online clip of the baby loggerheads making their way to the ocean after they hatch. Today, if you're feeling tired or bummed out about something, take it to Jesus in prayer.

28 August

Charge!

Bible Blast: Read Matthew 21:12-13

Don't sin by letting anger control you. Think about it overnight and remain silent. PSALM 4:4

The matador enters the ring holding a red cape.

A beautiful, gigantic bull enters the ring and stares at him.

The matador grandly takes his cape and flips it out to the side, taunting the bull.

The bull snorts loudly and stomps at the ground.

Suddenly the bull runs full speed toward the red cape, and just before it gets there, the matador swings the cape out of the way.

The crowd yells, "Olé!"

Many people say the bull gets angry when he sees the color red, and that's why he charges at the cape. When you hear the saying that someone "sees red," it means he or she is getting really angry, just like the bull.

Here's the thing, though: Bulls are color-blind. They can't see red at all. The reason they charge at the cape isn't because of the color. It's because of the movement of the cape.

"Seeing red" isn't necessarily a sin. Getting angry and letting that anger control you is the problem. Jesus was filled with anger in the Temple because people were selling stuff in there, and God meant for it to be a place of prayer. Jesus wasn't controlled by anger when he knocked the tables over and told people to get out. He was controlled by love for God's purposes and God's house.

When you're angry, it's always a good idea to keep your mouth closed. Hold your tongue, and give it some time. Waiting overnight is fabulous for fighting anger. It's amazing how a good night's sleep can make your mind think more clearly about a situation.

If you can learn how to deal with anger in a godly, controlled way, you'll be a better friend, sister, daughter, and mother. When you see a red flag waving, don't charge at it. Turn around and walk away for a bit. You'll never regret it.

Girl Gab:
Memorize today's focus verse with your mom. Ask God to help you do the right thing when you're angry.

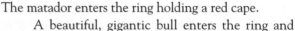

Ring the Dinner Bell, Y'all! I'm Hungry!

Bible Blast: Read Deuteronomy 8:2-3

My heart has heard you say, "Come and talk with me." And my heart responds, "LORD, I am coming." PSALM 27:8

Have you ever seen an old movie or TV show about pioneer families that shows Ma working over a hot stove, preparing dinner, while the kids play outside and Pa works in the fields? When the beef and potatoes are cooked and the hot rolls are on the table, Ma walks out to the front porch and rings a dinner bell that can be heard all across the land. It goes, *"Clang! Clang! Clang!"* and the family knows that it's time to come in and wash up for dinner.

There's a good chance your mom doesn't ring a dinner bell to get you to come and eat. However, when you smell your favorite meal simmering on the stove and Mom calls to you, "Dinner's ready!" you probably don't waste much time getting to the table. You know you're going to sit down and taste something wonderful and your body's going to get nourished from the food.

If you read today's Bible Blast, you know that we can't live just by eating food. Our most essential nourishment comes from spending time with God and listening to his Word.

Imagine that every morning, God has prepared something for you—an encouragement, a challenge, a warning, or even a good laugh. And he walks out onto the porch and rings that bell, loudly proclaiming, "Hey! I've prepared something for you! Come on in! Stop what you're doing, and let's talk! I really want to spend time with you, and you need to spend time with me, so let's do this! Let's enjoy each other!" You have a choice right then, don't you? Either you stop what you're doing and yell, "Lord, I am coming!" or you continue what you're doing and say, "Sorry, Lord, but what I'm doing is better for me than what you've prepared for me! I'll catch you next time!"

God loves to spend time with you. If you make a point to have time alone with him, you'll grow to really love it. My time with Jesus is some of the most precious time I have. I look forward to it, and I love it. I make time for him because I can't live just by "bread alone." I need every word that comes out of his mouth and I don't want to miss it!

Girl Gab: Today I want you and your mom to repeat Psalm 27:8 to the Lord as a prayer. Very simply, say, "My heart has heard you say, 'Come and talk with me.' And my heart responds, 'Lord, I am coming.'"

Kickin' Kraft:

Dazzling Doorway!

(Check out p. 374 for a great mother-daughter craft that helps reinforce today's devo!)

Kickin' Kraft: Keep on Knockin'

Bible Blast: Read Matthew 7:7-11

Keep on asking, and you will receive what you ask for. Keep on seeking, and you will find. Keep on knocking, and the door will be opened to you. MATTHEW 7:7

I have a friend named Andy Mylin. He actually works at my ministry with me. Well, ten years ago, God gave him a dream: to raft through the Grand Canyon in the river down in the bottom. To fulfill his dream, Andy needed to take a lot of time off work after saving up enough money to pay for such a trip, which requires a lot of special equipment and a private guide. So at the age of twenty-eight, Andy began praying that he'd be able to take this trip before he turned thirty-eight.

A few years ago, God prompted my husband and me to offer all of our full-time staff a one-month Adventure (or sabbatical) Plan to refresh themselves. Since we minister to roughly sixty-five high school students daily at our local ministry and take many long nights and trips for our tween and teen ministry nationwide, our staff needs special time to rest as God commands us to do. (We rarely work normal hours.) After several years of praying, Andy had the time to go on the trip available to him, thanks to our Adventure Plan. He just needed the money.

His sabbatical was coming up the year that my friends at Tyndale asked me to write this devo for you. Guess what? Not knowing that Andy had this dream and didn't have the money for the trip, I was led by God to ask his wife to help me write this book with me. The money I'm paying her to help me was enough to pay for Andy's adventure! Just about the time the first girls and moms read this, Andy will be hiking several hours to the base of the Grand Canyon, breaking out his camping gear, and checking out his raft! After almost ten years of asking, God finally opened the door for this unique dream!

If there is something you desire that seems impossible, keep asking.

The Ultimate Promise Keeper

Bible Blast: Read Genesis 17:15-19

The LORD kept his word and did for Sarah exactly what he had promised. GENESIS 21:1

Today in America many people have children or at least want to have children. However, there are a good many people who remain childless. Sometimes couples choose never to have a child, but often a husband and wife find themselves unable to have a baby. This is called being "barren."

When a woman is barren, something in her body isn't allowing her to have a baby. This can be devastating news to a hopeful couple. There's a really good chance that your family knows someone who desperately wants a baby but can't have one. It's good for you to pray for them. Take a moment to ask God to bless them with a healthy child.

When God told Abraham, as recorded in Genesis 15:5, "Look up into the sky and count the stars if you can. That's how many descendants you will have," Abraham was encouraged because, up until that point, he and his wife, Sarah, weren't able to have children though they desperately wanted them.

Genesis 17 records God's covenant promise that he would give Abraham and Sarah many descendants. But a lot of time had gone by since the first promise from God. Do you know what Abraham's response was? It's in verse 17: "Then Abraham bowed down to the ground, but he laughed to himself in disbelief. 'How could I become a father at the age of 100?' he thought. 'And how can Sarah have a baby when she is ninety years old?'"

Okay. Abraham was *a hundred years old* and his wife was *ninety years old*! No wonder Abraham laughed. Of course, about a year later Sarah gave birth to a son, Isaac, and ultimately Abraham's descendants did outnumber the stars in the sky, just like God said.

Not everyone who prays for her own baby receives one like Sarah did, and I don't know why that is. God has personal plans for each wife and husband. But you can pray for people who are longing for and waiting for children.

Girl Gab: Take some time now to kneel down with your mom and pray for someone you know who wants a child.

1 September

Fanny Crosby

Bible Blast: Read Ephesians 5:15-20

Sing and make music in your heart to the Lord, always giving thanks to God the Father for everything, in the name of our Lord Jesus Christ. EPHESIANS 5:19-20 (NIV)

Girl Gab: Do you feel like some of the things you see around you distract you from praising Jesus? Pray with your mom today that your eyes would always focus on Jesus more than anything else.

Fanny Crosby was born in 1820. When she was six weeks old, she developed a cold in her eyes. The doctor who treated her didn't know what he was doing. He treated Fanny by placing hot packs of some sort on her eyes. That made the inflammation in her eyes get worse and caused her to become completely blind.

In spite of her blindness, Fanny was an incredibly happy kid. She still jumped over fences and climbed trees, just like any other kid. It was as if her blindness never bothered her.

Fanny Crosby had a gift for poetry. When she was only eight years old she wrote this:

> Oh! what a happy soul I am!
> Although I cannot see,
> I am resolved that in this world
> Contented I will be.
> How many blessings I enjoy
> That other people don't!
> To weep and sigh because I'm blind
> I cannot nor I won't.

She eventually got teamed up with people who wrote music, and her poems became songs called "hymns." In case you don't attend a church that sings hymns, they are worship songs that usually have a few verses and a chorus. By the time Fanny died in 1915, she had written about eight thousand hymns and poems! A couple of her most famous hymns are "Blessed Assurance" and "To God Be the Glory."

I think if I were unable to see, I would jump at any chance to get my sight back, but Fanny didn't feel that way at all. She said, "If I had a choice, I would still choose to remain blind . . . for when I die, the first face I will ever see will be the face of my blessed Saviour."

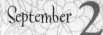

Meditation Moment: Acts 2

All the believers met together in one place and shared everything they had. They sold their property and possessions and shared the money with those in need. ACTS 2:44-45

The second chapter of Acts is so inspiring. It describes the way the first group of Jesus' followers came into fellowship with each other as a church. The Christians shared everything. They sold their stuff so they could give the money to people who needed it. My husband thinks it would be so cool if we didn't live on a cul-de-sac where everyone owns his own lawn mower, snow blower, camper, and gas grill. He often imagines what we could do with the money we would save if we all shared our possessions and didn't feel so much like we needed them. I bet we could change the world! The early believers did!

What if everything you had wasn't just yours?

What if you shared all your belongings with other Christians?

What if you sold stuff you didn't need and gave the money to the poor?

What if church were less like a meeting and more like a family?

As you meditate today, run some of these "what ifs" through your mind. Pray first and then read over the focus verses. Ask God to speak to you as you wait on him. When you feel that he's telling you something through an idea, word, picture, or thought, go ahead and write it down.

Girl Gab: What would you share, if your neighborhood got into the community spirit? Talk about it together. Pray that God would help you to be willing to sell anything he asks you to so that you can give to those who have need.

3 September

Bible Blast: Read Galatians 5:19-25

Those who are dominated by the sinful nature think about sinful things, but those who are controlled by the Holy Spirit think about things that please the Spirit. ROMANS 8:5

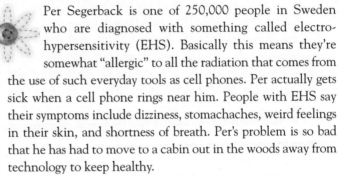

Girl Gab:

Imagine what life would be like if you had SHS (sin-hypersensitivity). No one would be able to hide sin anymore, would they? Ask God to help you be totally uncool with sin and evil.

Per Segerback is one of 250,000 people in Sweden who are diagnosed with something called electrohypersensitivity (EHS). Basically this means they're somewhat "allergic" to all the radiation that comes from the use of such everyday tools as cell phones. Per actually gets sick when a cell phone rings near him. People with EHS say their symptoms include dizziness, stomachaches, weird feelings in their skin, and shortness of breath. Per's problem is so bad that he has had to move to a cabin out in the woods away from technology to keep healthy.

Per's allergy got me thinking about sin. What if every time you got close to sin you felt physically sick? Can you imagine what it would be like if someone told a lie near you and you would have to grab your stomach and head for the bathroom? Or if you disrespected your parents, you got red blotches all over your skin? Or how about if someone stole something, you suddenly passed out? Bizarre!

Maybe we *should* have some sort of "sin-hypersensitivity" (SHS). I'm not saying I want to "toss my cookies" every time someone does something bad, but I think it would be good if sin made me really, really uncomfortable. The more I grow in my relationship with Jesus, the yuckier I do feel in sinful situations, and that's good. But there are times when I let sin slip on by without its bothering me at all.

Here's the catch. Even though we're supposed to hate evil and cling to what is good (see Romans 12:9), God doesn't want us to remove ourselves entirely from the world, like Per Segerback has had to do. We would have an awfully hard time seasoning the world with the message of the gospel if we lived an entirely separated life from those who need to hear the gospel.

Yes, we need to hate sin and evil. But, no, we can't just completely cut ourselves off from the lost. If we don't tell them about Jesus, who will?

Breaking Habits

Bible Blast: Read Matthew 6:9-13

We are confident that he hears us whenever we ask for anything that pleases him. 1 JOHN 5:14

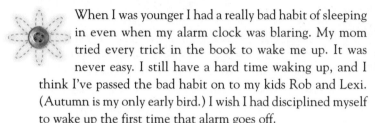

When I was younger I had a really bad habit of sleeping in even when my alarm clock was blaring. My mom tried every trick in the book to wake me up. It was never easy. I still have a hard time waking up, and I think I've passed the bad habit on to my kids Rob and Lexi. (Autumn is my only early bird.) I wish I had disciplined myself to wake up the first time that alarm goes off.

Lots of people have bad habits. Some of the most common bad habits are

nail biting

knuckle cracking

hair twirling

late-night snacking

gum popping

The list could go on and on. Habits can be really hard to break, especially since something about the habits feels good and is somehow satisfying.

One way to deal with a habit is to have someone else alert you when you're doing it without realizing it. This can be tough, but it's effective. Think how quickly you would stop cracking your knuckles if every time you did it your brother threw a Nerf football at you!

Another great way to stop a bad habit is prayer. I don't mean you need to sit down and give God a three-hour explanation of why you feel bad about twirling your hair. I recommend that you pray an honest prayer, talking to God as if he were sitting across from you listening—because he is.

People can slip into lazy, repetitive habits in their prayer lives. You know what I mean. Do you pretty much pray the same thing every time you get ready to eat? It becomes like more of a habit or a poem you recite instead of a real prayer.

Jesus encouraged people to pray from their hearts. Talk to God from your heart about your bad habit, and he will help you.

Girl Gab: Mom, did you have any bad habits when you were a kid? How about now? Daughter, talk to your mom about any bad habits you want to be rid of. Pray together from your hearts about your bad habits and help each other overcome them.

5 September

Girl Gab: Talk about this question with your mom: If you could have only one thing for breakfast for the rest of your life, what would you choose? How does God's Word "feed" you? Make a commitment to "dive right in" when God is waiting to spend time with you.

A Real Grand Slam Breakfast

Bible Blast: Read John 21:1-14

"Now come and have some breakfast!" Jesus said. JOHN 21:12

Not too long ago, Denny's restaurants were offering free Grand Slam breakfasts to anyone who came in really early in the morning. Free food is always a good idea, so my friend Kim and I grabbed our daughters and headed to Denny's at 5:45 a.m. We arrived to find about a gazillion other people waiting for their free Grand Slam breakfasts.

We girls were feeling kind of giddy about our fun breakfast adventure, so we thought we would do something to get everyone in the restaurant as excited as we were. We counted to three, stood up, and yelled, *"Grand Slam!"* thinking that all the other folks waiting around would respond with cheers or at least yell it back to us. But that's not exactly what happened.

After we yelled, the place was completely quiet. No one cheered, yelled, or even cracked a smile. They just stared until we sat back down in our seats. Awkward!

Do you know why we call the first meal of the day "breakfast"? Most of us eat dinner and maybe a little snack before bed, but then we spend all night sleeping, not eating. That's a "fast" because we go for a period of time without eating or drinking. When we wake up and eat that first meal, we are "breaking" the "fast" from the night before. So breakfast has nothing to do with getting up, eating your food super "fast," and making a "break" for the school bus!

Jesus once made breakfast for the disciples. (You can read about it in today's Bible Blast.) He prepared fish and bread for them, cookout style.

The wildest thing about this story is that Jesus conducted this breakfast meeting *after* he had been resurrected from the dead. The disciples must have been blown away with amazement. When Peter realized he was seeing Jesus, he just jumped into the water and swam for shore. He had to get to Jesus.

Every day it's like Jesus is saying to us, "Now come and have some breakfast!" Not so we can sit down and have bacon and eggs (or bread and fish!), but so he can feed us with the truth of his Word.

Amazing Animals: The Lionfish

Bible Blast: Read Romans 12:3-8

In his grace, God has given us different gifts for doing certain things well. ROMANS 12:6

Do you have a fish aquarium? I don't have one, but I think they're really beautiful. Once I had a tiny fishbowl. It held two goldfish, Jet and Fruit Juice, we had won at the Grange Fair. We loved the quiet comfort and entertainment that Jet and Fruit Juice provided to our family. Unfortunately, Fruit Juice died one day. My husband was worried that Jet was lonely, so he went out and bought a little glass crab that floated in the tank so Jet would have a friend. That glass crab terrified the goldfish! Poor Jet jumped right out of that bowl! He made it three feet across the table. Jet was scared out of his mind.

I love snorkeling, so I've seen some pretty cool "wild" fish, too. One of the most impressive saltwater fish I've ever seen is the lionfish. With zebra-striped spikes extending from their bodies, they can mesmerize a snorkler with their beauty. They're native to the oceans around Australia, but recently they've been spotted below Florida. How'd they get there? Perhaps when an aquarium in Florida was destroyed in a hurricane. While it's fun to look at them, it is *not* good to have them in those Atlantic waters.

Not only can lionfish be supergrumpy, but those beautiful spikes are highly venomous. A group of lionfish can kill off the native population of fish around a coral reef by 80 percent in just five weeks! While lionfish will not be aggressive toward humans (although you should be careful to avoid touching them if you come near them in the ocean), they will not hesitate to kill off fellow fish. These fish were born to fight.

I'm thankful for the beauty and strength of the lionfish, but I'm also thankful for simple pet goldfish you can win at the fair. They both have important roles in the world, but they're very different from each other, just like us. God made some people to be flashy fighters and others to be quiet encouragers.

What kind of "fish" are you?

Girl Gab: After the description I gave of the lionfish, you probably should look for a photo or video clip of one online or in the encyclopedia! Aren't they beautiful? Maybe you've never prayed for the animals in the ocean before, but take a sec to pray for the coral reefs in the Caribbean.

Bells Are Ringing

Bible Blast: Read Exodus 28:31-35

Aaron will wear this robe whenever he ministers before the LORD, and the bells will tinkle. EXODUS 28:35

Girl Gab: Do you have any objects that produce tintinnabulation in your house? Go ahead and ring them for a moment before you pray for your pastor, children's ministry director, or other church leaders.

On days you're having a hard time figuring out what to wear, your mom might tell you, "Honey, it's not a matter of life or death." Well, in the case of Aaron—Moses' brother who was the priest of Israel—it totally *was* a matter of life or death! If he didn't wear every piece of clothing that God had called him to wear to do his work at a certain time, he would die. What on earth was he wearing anyway?

The clothes Aaron was instructed to wear for worship and sacrifices were made "with fine linen cloth, gold thread, and blue, purple, and scarlet thread" (Exodus 28:5). The chest piece had actual gemstones, like emerald, turquoise, blue lapis, moonstone, amethyst, and onyx, all set in gold. These are the kinds of things modern women wear on their fingers in rings. Verse 36 describes a gold medallion that had "HOLY TO THE LORD" inscribed in it. The medallion was worn on Aaron's forehead over his turban.

Perhaps most interesting is the hem of Aaron's garment. Verses 31-35 say that the hem of Aaron's robe had two things attached to it—embroidered pomegranates and bells. The pomegranate tassels were made out of blue, purple, and red yarn, and a gold bell hung between each of the pomegranates. So if you were an Israelite relaxing in your tent, you would know when Aaron was going to do his priestly job because you would hear the tintinnabulation of the bells on his garment.

Tintann—what? That's a cool new word I learned. Tintinnabulation is the sound produced by the ringing of a bell—and Aaron's hem was full of them! Why? Some Bible scholars believe the bells were necessary so that the people of Israel could hear him walking through the camp and know that he was about to go into the presence of God. The bells called out to remind the people to pray for Aaron.

Today, our church leaders don't wear bells on the hems of their garments, but we are still called to pray for them in humility. Have you been praying for your church leaders?

The Beatitudes: He Satisfies

Bible Blast: Read Matthew 5:1-12

God blesses those who are poor and realize their need for him, for the Kingdom of Heaven is theirs. MATTHEW 5:3

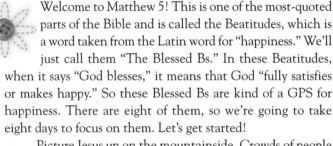

Welcome to Matthew 5! This is one of the most-quoted parts of the Bible and is called the Beatitudes, which is a word taken from the Latin word for "happiness." We'll just call them "The Blessed Bs." In these Beatitudes, when it says "God blesses," it means that God "fully satisfies or makes happy." So these Blessed Bs are kind of a GPS for happiness. There are eight of them, so we're going to take eight days to focus on them. Let's get started!

Picture Jesus up on the mountainside. Crowds of people have gathered to hear him talk. Jesus opens his mouth and says, "God blesses those who are poor."

Some of his followers may have whispered, "What? God blesses the poor? I'm poor and he's not giving *me* any money!"

Then they hear the second part: "And realize their need for him."

The lightbulb may have gone on in their heads. "Oh, I get it! I'm not supposed to be focused on my need for cash. I have to realize that I need the Lord more than anything, even money."

When Jesus was talking about the poor in this verse, he wasn't just talking about people who don't have money. He was talking about those who are "poor in spirit," desperate for love because they didn't have any in their own lives.

What does Jesus say the poor and poor in spirit get to look forward to? He promises a closer relationship with God. God was redirecting their focus.

Do you focus on what you don't have? Maybe you don't get to go on big vacations like some people, or maybe your mom is single and struggles to put good food on the table. Maybe you don't have a dad who spends time with you. Don't focus on those things, Jesus encourages. Focus on Christ's promise of heaven, and you'll feel happier.

That's an awesome Blessed B!

Girl Gab:

Daughters, tell your mom some experience or feeling that you tend to focus on that's negative. Mom, help your daughter think of a few ways that this hardship can be a blessing if she focuses on the good rather than the bad. Pray about that hardship, and look forward to God making it all right when you get to heaven one day.

The Beatitudes: No More Sadness

Bible Blast: Read Revelation 21:1-4

God blesses those who mourn, for they will be comforted.
MATTHEW 5:4

A few years ago, our beloved dog Tippy died. She was the sweetest little cocker spaniel ever seen. Those big, pouty, cocker spaniel eyes and that soft, droopy nose made a person just want to squeeze her.

It became apparent, as is often the case with beloved pets, that it was cruel to keep her alive on medication, and we knew we needed to take her to the vet to say good-bye. The sadness nearly broke us. My husband was the one who had to take her. He stopped at the McDonald's drive-through and bought her an entire bag of hamburgers to munch on that morning. When he came home, all he had with him was Tippy's collar and the purple bandana she had been wearing.

I kept that bandana handy for days, sniffing it so I could be "near" my sweet, furry friend. For three days, no one in the family wanted to do anything. We were so sad.

When you are in mourning, it feels as if the pain is never going to end. But God does provide comfort for those who are grieving on this earth. If we let him, he'll meet our pain in various superpersonal ways that will help us get through each day without the friend we miss so much. God will use other people to help you, hold you, and cry with you. Just ask him.

In the days following Tippy's death, friends came to tell us funny stories about her, and hearing the stories made us feel better. If you are mourning a pet—or a friend or family member—ask God to comfort you. And know that as time goes by the pain will be more bearable.

If you are not, look around and see if you need to be the source of comfort for someone else. It can be hard to know what to say, but God will give you the words to speak. Just take the time to try. I had a friend whose daughter died in a car crash, and no one knew what to say. God gave me the words. Do you know what they were? "I'm not really sure what to say. I just know this must be painful." They were the most comforting words she'd heard all week.

The Beatitudes: Is Meekness Weakness?

Bible Blast: Read Psalm 37:5-11

Blessed are the meek, for they will inherit the earth.
MATTHEW 5:5 (NIV)

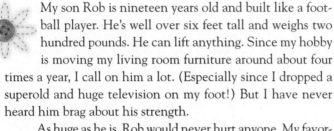

My son Rob is nineteen years old and built like a football player. He's well over six feet tall and weighs two hundred pounds. He can lift anything. Since my hobby is moving my living room furniture around about four times a year, I call on him a lot. (Especially since I dropped a superold and huge television on my foot!) But I have never heard him brag about his strength.

As huge as he is, Rob would never hurt anyone. My favorite photos of him are from our missions trips to Zambia, with little orphans hanging onto him while he walks. They just loved climbing up him and knowing his affection for them. He'd just tap them gently on their heads and smile. Rob is meek.

Meekness isn't the same thing as being weak. It's more like knowing you have power and strength inside of you, but knowing when to tuck it away and when to use it. Meekness is a lot like self-control. Meekness is a difficult choice because it means you back off of every fight you could win—whether it's a physical fight, a mental fight, or a power struggle. The world seems to send the message, "If you're meek, you're a wimp! You need to stand up and fight! Show the world what you can do! Fight your way to the top! Meek people won't ever be successful!" Well, according to this focus verse, the meek will ultimately be supersuccessful. They will get the entire earth! How can that be?

Toward the end of the book of Revelation, John describes what he sees in a vision God has given him. It's a vision of heaven. John says that he saw the old heaven and earth that had passed away. In its place came a brand, spankin' new heaven and earth for us to live on! And guess who will be living on that new earth with us? The meek who love Jesus, that's who (see Revelation 21).

In every situation it's important to ask God how we should act and respond. If we do that and obey what he says, meekness will naturally happen.

Girl Gab: Can you and your mom think of someone who's meek? It doesn't have to be a big guy like Rob. An eighty-year-old woman can be meek. Encourage that person today, saying that you notice and admire her meekness.

Kickin' Kraft:

**Treasure
Hunt Bottles!**

(Check out p. 375
for a great mother-
daughter craft that
helps reinforce
today's devo!)

Kickin' Kraft:
The Beatitudes—Thirsty?

Bible Blast: Read Psalm 107:1-9

Blessed are those who hunger and thirst for righteousness, for they will be filled. MATTHEW 5:6 (NIV)

Imagine that a dude named Mortimer is trudging through the desert. The sun is beating down on him, and sweat is pouring off his body. Suddenly Mortimer is filled with excitement and energy. He looks down into a valley and sees a lake of crystal-clear water. Mortimer runs toward it, anxious to drink until he can't drink anymore. He jumps up in the air and dives into the water, only to find himself surrounded by sand. The refreshing lake was only a mirage.

A mirage is kind of a trick that your eyes play on you when they see the sun's rays playing around with certain surfaces of the earth. You can "see" something that's not really there. It usually happens in the desert or on the water.

The things the world offers for "satisfaction" are like a mirage. Say your family moves into a bigger house and you think, *This will make me feel important,* but eventually it's just a house, and you don't really care anymore. Maybe when you are a teenager, you'll be feeling lonely and there's a boy who tells you he "loves" you. You become his girlfriend and find out he's not a nice boy at all. Those things are all mirages. They all may look as if they'll satisfy you, but when you get close to them, you find they don't measure up to your expectations, and your feelings of contentment don't last.

When God fills you up, you'll be satisfied *and* you'll want more. He never breaks his promises, and he loves you more than anyone ever has or ever will. If you see an opportunity to learn more about God and become more like him, dive right in!

The Beatitudes: Mercy Me!

Bible Blast: Read Matthew 9:35-37

God blesses those who are merciful, for they will be shown mercy.
MATTHEW 5:7

My second daughter, Autumn Qiu Yun Gresh, was thirteen when we met, and I didn't know then just how merciful she was. But it didn't take long to see it. The first time I saw it was when she met one of my husband's best friends. When she heard he was a single dad, she began asking me almost every night if we could take food to him and his children. That's just how Autumn Gresh rolls. She sees people's needs and wants to help them. That's mercy.

Mother Teresa is thought by many to be one of the most compassionate people in history. (Of course, we know Jesus is *numero uno* in compassion!) Below is part of one of her most beloved prayers.

> Dear Jesus,
> Help us to spread your fragrance everywhere we go.
> Flood our souls with your Spirit and life.
> Penetrate and possess our whole being so utterly
> that our lives may only be a radiance of yours.
> Shine through us and be so in us
> that every soul we come in contact with
> may feel your presence in our soul.
> Let them look up and see no longer us but only
>   Jesus. . . .
> The light, O Jesus, will be all from you.
> None of it will be ours.
> It will be you shining on others through us.
> Let us thus praise you in the way you love best
> by shining on those around us.
> Let us preach you without preaching
> not by words, but by our example
> By the catching force
> the sympathetic influence of what we do
> the evident fullness of the love our hearts bear to you.

Girl Gab: If there was a word or two you don't entirely understand from this prayer, ask your mom to explain it to you. Now pray the prayer together, not because the words are special or anything, but because the words are all about showing God's compassion to others through how we live.

The Beatitudes: Tiny Water

Bible Blast: Read Psalm 24:1-4

God blesses those whose hearts are pure, for they will see God.
MATTHEW 5:8

Did you know that about 1.1 billion people around the world do not have access to clean water? That's about 20 percent of the world's entire population! Many people in developing countries use the same pool of water for bathing, laundry, and drinking. Sometimes they allow their animals to get in that water, too, and we all know what they do in there!

Pure water is a fantastic blessing. The most pure natural groundwater in the world is found in Tiny Township, Ontario, Canada. The only water found to be more pure than Tiny Township's water is found in the center core of glaciers! In Tiny Township, the rocks that surround the water don't have tons of metal and junk minerals in them, so the water is pure because it comes out from a clean place.

Our hearts work the same way. If we do something pure, it's because our hearts are pure. Think of your heart as being like those rocks in Tiny Township. If your heart has junk in it, what comes out of it will be junky too. If it is clean, what comes out of it will be clean.

Having a pure heart means that your motives honor God. You don't do something nice for someone so that everyone can see how amazing you are. You share a prayer request out of genuine concern, not for gossip's sake. You're friends with the new girl because you like her and want to make her feel welcome, not because her parents are rich. You share something with your brother because you love him, not because you want to bribe him later. You clean your room out of respect for your mom, not because you want something. Do you see how motives show the purity of your heart?

The only way to get a pure heart is to put pure things into it. By now you know that one fab way to do that is reading God's Word. Also notice if what you're watching on TV will give you a pure heart or a cloudy heart.

If your heart is clean and pure, your life will be too.

The Beatitudes: Peacemakers

Bible Blast: Read Isaiah 26:3

God blesses those who work for peace, for they will be called the children of God. MATTHEW 5:9

It seems as though every family has one peacemaker. This is the person who steps into every argument and tries to get everyone calmed down and happy again. In my house, that person is my son Rob. Who's the peacemaker in your home?

According to the Bible, a person who "works for peace" isn't just someone who keeps two people from being mean to each other. It's not someone who is against war. A peaceful person isn't someone who's just quiet and smiles knowingly all the time. A peacemaker is a person who has received peace from God and passes it on to others. True peace can only come through someone who experiences true God-given peace.

One big key to having godly peace is found in Romans 8:38-39: "I am convinced that nothing can ever separate us from God's love. Neither death nor life, neither angels nor demons, neither our fears for today nor our worries about tomorrow—not even the powers of hell can separate us from God's love. No power in the sky above or in the earth below—indeed, nothing in all creation will ever be able to separate us from the love of God that is revealed in Christ Jesus our Lord."

Knowing that God's love is mine forever, no matter what happens around me, allows me not to be shaken by bad circumstances. David Wilkerson, author of *The Cross and the Switchblade*, says this: "Simply put, peace is the absence of fear. And a life without fear is a life full of peace."

Much of the world thinks that if people stop fighting each other, peace will rule, but that's not true. It would be awesome if war stopped, but that doesn't guarantee no more fear. People who don't put their faith in God will always find something to be afraid of, and fear is the enemy of peace.

The peace you have in God was meant to be shared. You can bring peace into situations at school and in your family. You can be a peacemaker.

Girl Gab: Look at that passage from Romans 8 again. How does it make you feel to know that not even death can separate you from God's love? Ask God for total peace in your life.

15 September

The Beatitudes: Language Lab— What Is "Persecution"?

Bible Blast: Read Matthew 5:10-12

God blesses those who are persecuted for doing right, for the Kingdom of Heaven is theirs. MATTHEW 5:10

Girl Gab: Take time now to pray for at least one of the countries I listed in the devo where Christians aren't free to worship. Pray that the believers will remain strong in their faith and that they will not be afraid.

A few years ago, a young girl was invited to make a piece of a quilt that was to hang in her public school. She made a picture of the cross on her square because she loves Jesus. The next day when the quilt was displayed, her square was missing. The teachers and some parents didn't want a symbol of Jesus up in the school. The little girl and her family decided they were going to stand up for her right to display her art. The attacks became very vicious, and some Christian lawyers had to come in to defend the little girl and her family. The little girl was being "persecuted."

Persecution is when someone stands up for what is right, and another person makes fun of her or even hurts her for that decision. A lot of Christians are persecuted for their faith. If you are ever teased for being a Christian, pray for the stamina and comfort of the persecuted believer but don't be all bummed out. We're actually told to be happy because God will reward us for it. When we're persecuted for our faith in him, that means we have chosen righteousness instead of being accepted or "cool."

Jesus warned the disciples in John 15 that persecution would come. He said, "Since they persecuted me, naturally they will persecute you." Maybe that didn't scare the disciples too much until they watched Jesus dying on the cross. They must have realized then that their lives could be at risk for standing up in their faith in God. And eventually many of them did pay for their faith with their lives. Believe it or not, Christians all over the world are being persecuted and killed even today in Morocco, Iraq, Laos, Iran, Nigeria, Myanmar, Algeria, Malaysia, Indonesia, Azerbaijan, China, Pakistan, Somalia, and many other nations.

Pray for believers in parts of the world where there is no freedom to worship God. And pray that we will keep the freedom to worship him freely in the United States.

No Worries

Bible Blast: Read Psalm 23

He makes me lie down in green pastures, he leads me beside quiet waters. PSALM 23:2 (NIV)

I really don't like snakes.

So I guess if God ever asked me to move to New Zealand, I'd be happy.

Why? Because there are no snakes in New Zealand! I'm totally not kidding.

In fact, it's against the law for snakes to be in New Zealand. They don't even have snakes in their zoos! There's a special group of New Zealanders who are trained to catch snakes in order to keep them out of the country. They search incoming boats and shipments for slithering stowaways.

If I were to lie down in a green pasture, a snake-less New Zealand would be a good place to do it. However, today's focus verse isn't necessarily talking about an actual pasture.

David wrote Psalm 23 as if he were a sheep and God was his shepherd. When he writes that God makes him lie down in green pastures, he's talking about a place of peace, a place with no worries. *Hakuna matata.* Remember that Swahili phrase from Disney's *The Lion King?*

When a sheep folds all four legs underneath its body and lies down, it's totally at rest. That sheep is enjoying the lush, green grass. It's not worried about wolves or any other predators. It feels safe. *Hakuna matata.*

Since we're God's "sheep," too, we don't need to worry either. It's not as if we ignore the fact that evil things go on in the world. Not worrying also doesn't mean we will never be hurt by another person or situation. It does mean that no matter what happens God has our back. He's totally fighting for us, and it's not up to us to take the battle into our own hands.

God has such beautiful plans for you. He really wants you to rest and enjoy the world he created. He wants you to lie down in the rich safety of his love for you. Today make a choice not to worry about whatever is on your mind. Let God be the one to take care of it as you trust him.

Girl Gab: If it's nice outside where you live, go ahead and lie down in the grass with your mom for two minutes. Lay side by side with your eyes closed and don't say anything. Just think about God taking all your worries while you enjoy his creation. (You can also pretend you're outside and do this inside on a cushy rug or bed!)

17 September

Amazing Animals: Barn Owls

Bible Blast: Read 1 Corinthians 6:19-20

You must honor God with your body. 1 CORINTHIANS 6:20

Girl Gab: Mom and Daughter, talk about your family's eating habits. Do you eat plenty of veggies and fruit? How much water do you drink every day? Do you always eat on the go, or do you sit down and slowly eat your meals? Ask God together to help your family set and maintain good eating habits.

I have to admit, I don't see many barn owls where I live. But I have heard one up on my parents' mountain property.

You can find barn owls all over the world except in supercold or desert regions. And guess what? They don't just live in barns, although some people actually make special holes in the tops of their barns, hoping the owls will nest there because they get rid of pests.

Barn owls are also called screech owls because they don't say, "who-who-whooo," like other owls. They give off an eerie screeching sound. These birds can also make a hissing sound to scare off predators. If it's captured or trapped, the barn owl throws itself on its back and lashes out with its sharp talons.

One of the most interesting, and maybe most disgusting, things about owls is how they digest their food. They eat mostly small rodents and critters, tearing them into chunks so they can swallow the bits. (That's not even the gross part.)

Owls can't digest the bones, feathers, fur, and teeth of their prey. So when an owl swallows the food, it passes through an organ that filters out all that indigestible stuff. That organ is called a "gizzard." The rest of the good stuff goes through the body and nourishes the owl.

Here comes the gross part: When the gizzard gets full of all that hard stuff, the owl has to get rid of it. So it regurgitates (coughs up and spits out) the contents of the gizzard, and what comes up is called an "owl pellet." It's full of bones, feathers, fur, and teeth.

Even though owl pellets are nasty, it's wonderful how God provided the gizzard as a filter so the owl wouldn't digest stuff that would be bad for its digestion. We humans don't have a gizzard. We have to be the ones to filter what food we eat. We need to be aware of what's in our food so we don't digest a bunch of junk that will make our bodies unhealthy.

Eat healthy, because "owl" be watching you! (Not really, but I couldn't resist the joke!)

He Holds the Keys

Bible Blast: Read Revelation 1:17-19

This is the message from the one who is holy and true, the one who has the key of David. What he opens, no one can close; and what he closes, no one can open. REVELATION 3:7

I bet I can guess something that's true about you. I bet that you and your mom have missed some devos this year. It's easy to do. I miss devos myself, but something I never miss is praying first thing in the morning and last thing at night. I might only say, "Good morning, Jesus" or "Good night, Lord," but I always start and end my day with prayer.

There was a well-known writer from England named Thomas Fuller. One of the things he's kind of famous for saying about prayer is this: "Prayer: the key of the day and the lock of the night." Even though that's not a Bible verse, it's so true. Let's look at how prayer is a key for the day and a lock for the night.

Prayer is the **"Key of the Day"**: Psalm 118:24 says, "This is the day the LORD has made. We will rejoice and be glad in it." If it's true that God made each day, then doesn't it make sense to go to him to find out *why?* He doesn't waste time, and he doesn't do things "just because" or for no reason at all. So it must be that each and every day has something for us. I don't believe the day can be fully opened up until we've spent time in prayer.

Prayer is the **"Lock of the Night"**: At the end of every day, the sun goes down, the moon comes up, and eventually our heads hit our pillows. What a great time to think about the day and talk to God about what happened. It's good to remember the day's events with the Lord and to ask him questions. Another good thing about locking up the night with prayer is knowing that he keeps you safe while you sleep. Check out Psalm 4:8: "In peace I will lie down and sleep, for you alone, O LORD, will keep me safe." Tell God that you know he takes care of you and that you have no reason to be afraid.

It really is like you have two prayer keys in your hand—one for opening your day and one for sealing it up at night. Of course, you can pray to God all the time, but don't forget that each day he gives you is a personal gift.

Girl Gab: Ask your mom for an old key she doesn't need or use anymore. Take a tiny piece of paper and write "PRAYER" on it. Tape or glue that word to the key. Keep the key in your wallet or change purse. Let it remind you of today's teaching.

Girl Power or God Power?

Bible Blast: Read 1 Timothy 1:12-17

That's why I take pleasure in my weaknesses, and in the insults, hardships, persecutions, and troubles that I suffer for Christ. For when I am weak, then I am strong. 2 CORINTHIANS 12:10

There are a lot of programs and things going on to get girls your age to have a good self-esteem. Today I want to show you what "self-esteem" means. When you "esteem" something, you're saying it's good and has value. So when you hear that someone has a low self-esteem, it means she doesn't think she has much good or value to offer.

It breaks my heart when I see a young girl crying because she doesn't feel special. I can remember a time in my life when I felt that way too. What if I told that girl who has "low self-esteem" she just needs to think about positive things and believe she can do anything because she's a girl? And what if I put a T-shirt on her that says in bold, pink puffy letters, "GIRL POWER!"? And what if I covered her in buttons and pins that say, "GIRLS RULE" and "SUPER GIRL" and all sorts of other wonderful things about girls? Will that solve her low self-esteem problem? Uh . . . I doubt it.

In today's Bible Blast, Paul gives the real medicine for a low self-esteem sickness. You see, when Paul says he was the worst of all sinners, he really meant that. His job before he gave his life to Jesus was to hurt Christians and sometimes even have them killed! He absolutely *hated* people who loved Jesus. Yet God used Paul's life to bring millions of people to Christ.

Paul knew that anything good that came out of his life was because of God. In verse 12 he thanks Jesus for giving him strength to do what he did. Paul didn't have any faith in himself, but he had all kinds of faith in God. He had a serious case of a healthy God-esteem.

It really is fun and special to be a girl, but that's not going to keep you encouraged when you're not feeling good about yourself. Knowing that you can do all things through Christ is where real value comes from (see Philippians 4:13). The answer to self-esteem problems doesn't come from believing in yourself. It comes from believing in God *through* you.

Kickin' Kraft: Bucket o' Thoughts

Bible Blast: Read Psalm 139:23-24

You know my thoughts even when I'm far away. PSALM 139:2

I love my mom. I'm so blessed to have her live in the same town I live in so I can see her whenever I want. She's so wise and full of faith. This morning my mom said the coolest thing to me.

I was telling her that I was feeling kind of yucky and overwhelmed by everyday pressures. My feelings were making me unsure of what to do, say, or even think. Mom arranged to have lunch with me the next day, and then she said, "Bring a bucket of thoughts. We'll empty it out."

Isn't that just what a mom does? My whole life long, Mom has been the best listener. There are many, many times that I have picked up my "bucket of thoughts" and gone to empty it out with my mom.

Did you know that God knows all your thoughts? He loves knowing them and helping you think through them too. If your mom isn't around, you can just talk to God. But I'm so glad he's given you your mom, too!

Do you take your bucket of thoughts to your mom? I think sometimes just hearing myself say my thoughts out loud can be a huge help. It helps me see things more truthfully. Whether my mom gives advice, listens silently, or just hugs me, I always feel better when my thought bucket is empty.

Kickin' Kraft:
Bucket o'
Thoughts!

(Check out p. 375 for a great mother-daughter craft that helps reinforce today's devo!)

21 September

Girl Gab: It's important to take care of your hair and scalp. When you wash your hair, use your fingertips to scrub your entire scalp with shampoo. That will lift up dirt and oils so your hair will be clean. If your hair is really thin, don't use a heavy conditioner. Just use a detangling spray. If your hair is thick, a conditioner might help keep it tamed down.

No Shampoo Can Do *That!*

Bible Blast: Read Judges 16:15-19

Delilah lulled Samson to sleep with his head in her lap, and then she called in a man to shave off the seven locks of his hair. In this way she began to bring him down, and his strength left him.
JUDGES 16:19

The story of Samson and Delilah is a wild one. In case you didn't read the section before today's Bible Blast, I'll fill you in. Samson was crazy strong. He was so strong that no one could ever capture him. Yet I guess I should say he was *physically* strong, because he didn't always show good judgment and he was easily overcome by one beautiful lady named Delilah.

Samson fell head over heels in love with Delilah, who was not an Israelite woman. When the Philistines (the bad guys) found that out, they told her to find out what gave Samson his strength so they could take it from him and make him their prisoner. The Philistines offered to pay her a huge amount of silver if she obeyed them. So every day Delilah asked Samson what was the secret to his strength. Samson told her a few lies to get her to stop asking him about it.

Finally he told her everything (see verse 17). He said, "No razor has ever been used on my head . . . because I have been a Nazirite set apart to God since birth. If my head were shaved, my strength would leave me, and I would become as weak as any other man" (NIV). And that's exactly what she did. Delilah had Samson's head shaved while he slept, which allowed the bad guys to capture him.

Delilah was a deceitful woman. She used lies to get Samson to compromise his strength, which had been a tool for God. If Samson had not chosen to hang out with her, he may never have been captured.

If you read to the end of the chapter, you'll see how God used Samson one more time, but it's still a pretty sad story. In the end, he dies trying to please God with his death.

If a strong guy like Samson can be foolish enough to choose bad friends, so can we. Are your friends bringing you closer to God or farther from him?

A Greater Great

Bible Blast: Read Numbers 20:6-12

The LORD said to Moses and Aaron, "Because you did not trust me enough to demonstrate my holiness to the people of Israel, you will not lead them into the land I am giving them!"
NUMBERS 20:12

Whenever I hear my friends from California talk about walking into the backyard to pick fresh avocados, mangoes, and other fruit right off the tree, I get so jealous!

In fact, one friend is kind enough to send me avocados and oranges whenever I ask. Where I live, I can find apple and pear trees but not any of those tasty, exotic fruits I love.

If I want an avocado, I go to the grocery store and buy one. Sometimes it will have a sticker on it that says, "RIPE." Yet when I take that "ripe" avocado home and cut into it, it's not very ripe at all. I can still eat it and it tastes okay, but it's not fantastic. Bummer. But if I have a little patience and wait just a couple of days, the avocado will ripen and get softer. Then it's absolutely perfect for making guacamole!

Sometimes it takes self-discipline to wait for something; other times it takes self-control to do something exactly the way it should be done. Moses learned this the hard way. God gave Moses some specific instructions, but because he didn't obey God's exact commands, Moses suffered a terrible consequence. God was using Moses to lead the people through the wilderness to a beautiful land full of food and good things. God told Moses to speak to the rock, but instead Moses struck it. Since Moses hit that rock with his staff instead of just speaking to it like God said, he lost the privilege of ever going into that Promised Land.

Does that sound like heavy discipline to you? We don't know if Moses hit the rock because he wanted to be more "showy" or if he just didn't believe that speaking to the rock would produce water. Either way, if he had known what the consequence would be for his disobedience, I bet Moses wouldn't even have thought about striking that rock!

God still gave the people water. But Moses didn't get to live in the Promised Land. If only he had been obedient.

Girl Gab: In your relationship with God, don't settle for "good." Obey him completely and receive his *best* for your life! If you like avocados, make guacamole this week with your mom. (It's okay if you don't!) Make sure you ask God for patience and self-control to obey him 100 percent.

23 September

Rock On

Bible Blast: Read Joshua 4:1-9

You can tell them, "They remind us that the Jordan River stopped flowing when the Ark of the LORD's Covenant went across."
These stones will stand as a memorial among the people of Israel forever. JOSHUA 4:7

Arizona State University is a really rockin' place! Literally.

Since 2004, the University's Rock Around the World (RATW) program has had people mailing rocks to them from all over the place. If you mail them a rock, they'll investigate and scan it and tell you what it's made of and maybe some other interesting factoids. The Rock Around the World program receives an average of fifty to a hundred rocks each month. (I hope their mailperson does some serious back exercises!)

In the story from our Bible Blast reading today, Joshua made his own pile of important rocks—actually, he made two piles. God had just done a big miracle: He held back the water of the Jordan River so Joshua could lead the Israelites across into the land God had promised them. God had done the same thing with the Red Sea back when Moses took everyone out of Egypt.

Afterward, God instructed Joshua to set up a memorial of twelve stones to remind the Israelites forever that God had worked a miracle for his people. Can't you just see a grandpa taking his grandson out to that memorial and saying, "Now, Grandson, this is here because back when we first came to this land, God held back the river to let us walk across!"

Joshua also set up another pile of twelve stones on the riverbed before God released the waters again. Verse 9 says, "And they are there to this day." Okay. If I were a superadventurous traveling scuba diver, I would *totally* be going to the Jordan River, trying to find that pile of stones, wouldn't you?

It's good to remember what God has done. Even if we think we'll never forget, sometimes we do unless we write it down or make a pile of twelve huge rocks in memory of it.

What has God done for you?

Girl Gab: Here's today's challenge for you and your mom: List five amazing things God has done for you. If neither of you have ever written those things down, take time to do it now. Praise God for his miracles!

Language Lab: What Is "Submission"?

Bible Blast: Read Hebrews 12:9-11

Submit yourselves, then, to God. Resist the devil, and he will flee from you. JAMES 4:7 (NIV)

Before we can talk about submission, I need to make sure you understand the meaning of another word: *authority*. This is a person who is like your leader or boss and has more power than you. That may sound like a bad thing at first, but God established authority, and everybody has all kinds of authorities over him or her. Go ahead and answer these questions:

Who is your authority at home?

Who is your authority at school?

Who is your authority at church?

Who is your authority when you're at a friend's house?

See? Authority figures are everywhere, and that's not always such a terrible idea, is it? I mean, imagine if you went to your school (even if you're homeschooled) and you sat down at your desk and no one was there to tell you what work to do or how to do it. At first that might be fun, but eventually that would be terrible, especially if you want to graduate! Authorities are so necessary.

Submission is what we do when we listen to and obey those authorities. It means that we realize someone holds authority over us and that we're going to respect that. Think about the questions you just answered: How do you submit to those authorities?

Submission isn't always easy, especially if you don't always agree with or even like someone who's in authority over you. One year you might have a great teacher, and the next year you might have "that" teacher whom nobody likes. Do you have to submit to that not-so-nice teacher, too? Yep.

The most wonderful authority we need to make sure we submit to is God. When we know he wants us to do something, we need to submit to that and do it. This will end up being a great blessing in our lives.

Submission is a fantastic way to show God's love to authorities.

Girl Gab: Is there someone you have a hard time submitting to? Take time to pray for that person. Ask God to show you how to submit to him or her out of love and respect.

Talk to your mom about slavery. How does it make you feel to know it used to be "normal" in the United States to have slaves? Pray that God would stop slavery all over the world.

Real Help

Bible Blast: Read Luke 10:25-37

Going over to him, the Samaritan soothed his wounds with olive oil and wine and bandaged them. Then he put the man on his own donkey and took him to an inn, where he took care of him.
LUKE 10:34

There was a time in United States history when it was actually legal to own people as slaves. Harriet Tubman was born as a slave in Maryland in 1820. She managed to escape from her owners and fled to the North where she could live freely. But instead of staying safely there, she sneaked back into the southern part of the country many times to help other slaves escape too.

She worked with something called the Underground Railroad, which wasn't actually a railroad at all. It was a secret system created to get slaves away from their owners and to safe free places in the North. Harriet Tubman helped move slaves from safe place to safe place until they finally found freedom from the terrible life of slavery.

Harriet ended up helping more than three hundred slaves find freedom in the North.

Jesus once told a teaching story with a character who was a lot like Harriet Tubman. We just call this character "The Good Samaritan" because Jesus didn't give him a regular name.

The Good Samaritan helped a man who was in bad shape. He had been badly beaten, robbed, stripped, and left on the side of the road to die. The Samaritan used his own wine, oil, and bandages to soothe the the man's wounds; then he carried him on his donkey to an inn. He paid the innkeepers to take care of the man and promised to pay any extra costs that came up. As the parable goes, this Samaritan went out of his way to help a stranger—a stranger from Israel, which was a community Samaritans typically despised.

God wants us—like Harriet Tubman and the Good Samaritan—to help people because we love them, not just because we know them.

Can You "Bee" Too Sweet?

Bible Blast: Read Proverbs 25:14-17

Do you like honey? Don't eat too much, or it will make you sick!
PROVERBS 25:16

Honey is such a tasty, gooey mess of goodness! I sometimes can't believe how it's made. Basically the honeybee sucks sweet liquid called "nectar" out of flowers and stores it in his "honey stomach." Stuff mixes with the nectar turning it into honey. The bee goes to the hive, finds a hole in the honeycomb that isn't full, and spits the honey into that hole. Yes. Honey is, well, kind of like bee vomit.

The bees fill the "cells" of the honeycomb and cap them off with a seal of beeswax. They use the honey for food. No wonder they get so mad when you try to take their honey: They want to eat it too!

I love it when I come across a verse like Proverbs 25:16 that's so practical. It makes sense, right? If you eat too much honey, you'll get sick. If you eat too much of *anything*, you risk getting sick. Have you ever learned that by experience? I have! Well, not with honey. But once at a turkey dinner, I ate so many noodles that I could not stand up after I finished eating. I was so sick!

When you're really superhungry and the first thing you see is a package of cookies or a bag of chips, don't you just want to sit down and eat the whole thing? There's a good chance you won't feel very well if you do. And not only that, but you will also have filled up with junk food and won't have room for food that will actually be good for your body. That's the point of today's Bible verse; it's a reminder to eat well.

One good word to remember when you're filling your plate at mealtime is this: color. If your plate is filled with pale, white, or brownish foods, you probably have too much of one kind of food. The more colorful a food is, the healthier it is. So foods like broccoli, carrots, and apples are full of more vitamins than things like rice, white pasta, and potatoes.

The next time you eat, add some color to your plate! Make it an artistic masterpiece of red, green, and yellow, with a dash of white!

Girl Gab: If you have a hard time eating colorful food, tell your mom which veggies and fruits you like the most. Also, talk about tastier options, like dipping vegetables in ranch dressing or drizzling honey over fruit. God will help you find creative ways to enjoy healthy foods. Go ahead and ask him!

27 September

Girl Gab: Is there something you've lost that you just can't seem to find? Ask God to show you where it is or to help you find it. He knows exactly where it is.

God's Eyes

Bible Blast: Read Proverbs 15:1-3

The eyes of the LORD search the whole earth in order to strengthen those whose hearts are fully committed to him.
2 CHRONICLES 16:9

Brenda stared up at the rock wall towering in front of her. Could she really climb *that*? Her friends had invited her to go rock climbing, and she was kind of nervous about it. In spite of her fear, she put on all the proper equipment, grabbed onto the rope, and started climbing.

When Brenda stopped on a ledge to take a breath during the climb, the rope somehow snapped against her face, knocking the contact lens out of her eye. There she was, hanging by a rope and harness on the face of a giant rock with one good eye and one blurry eye. It was not an ideal situation.

Brenda looked all over the rock in front of her for that little clear disk, but she couldn't find it. When she reached the top of the climb, her friend inspected her clothes, looking for the contact lens, with no success.

As Brenda waited for everyone else to reach the top, she looked out over the tops of the mountains and thought about today's focus verse: "The eyes of the LORD search the whole earth in order to strengthen those whose hearts are fully committed to him," and she prayed, "Lord, you know exactly where my contact lens is. Please help me."

Eventually, everyone made it to the top. Then they all hiked down the trail to the bottom of the rock. When they got there, they met another group of climbers. You can imagine Brenda's surprise when one of them shouted, "Hey, you guys! Anybody lose a contact lens?" Can you guess how he found Brenda's contact lens? He saw an ant scurrying across the rock carrying the lens on its back!

Brenda was right to trust that God sees everything. Instead of freaking out, she chose to trust God and ask him for help. God's eyes really do see absolutely everything in every part of the world. He even sees all the things no humans see.

God loves you very much, and he cares about the things you might think are "little."

Meditation Moment: Psalm 73

Whom have I in heaven but you? I desire you more than anything on earth. My health may fail, and my spirit may grow weak, but God remains the strength of my heart; he is mine forever.
PSALM 73:25-26

Forever. Have you ever tried to really think about *forever*? Take a minute and try. It can be kind of frustrating because your mind doesn't have a place to stop and rest as it thinks about eternity.

Some people believe that when we die, that's it. Everything is over—the end. But those who trust in the Lord know something different. We get to be with God in heaven forever and ever and ever! Our relationship with God never ends because he never ends. You aren't going to wake up one morning and say, "Something's different. Oh, it must be time for God to end his relationship with me."

God is there. He'll never go away or leave. He is always available to be your strength.

Before you meditate today, don't forget to pray and ask God to open your heart and mind to his truth that's found in Psalm 73:25-26. Then after you read it through, wait on God and see what he says to you. Whether it's a phrase, a picture, or an idea, write it down.

Girl Gab: Talk to your mom about these verses, and ask her what truth stands out to her when she reads them or meditates on them. Praise God for eternal life!

29 September

Good Friendship

Bible Blast: Read Ruth 1:1-18

There are "friends" who destroy each other, but a real friend sticks closer than a brother. PROVERBS 18:24

Girl Gab: Think about some of the little things that make your friendship as mother and daughter one that sticks closer than a brother (or sister). Thank each other for those little things.

Lisa is a dear friend of mine. She's kind, soft-spoken, and a fantabulous cook. She recently opened up her home as a bed-and-breakfast. A bed-and-breakfast is a place a lot like a hotel where people can stay overnight, but it's in an actual home. It feels much cozier and warmer than most hotel rooms, and the breakfast is always super fantastic!

One of the bedrooms in Lisa's bed-and-breakfast is a girly-whirly dream. It's decorated mostly in beautiful pink roses. The bed has lots of cushy pillows with roses stitched on them. The lacy curtains have tiny pink flowers embroidered on them. Lisa placed itty-bitty bouquets of roses in the shower by the shampoo and body wash. That room is so adorable! And you won't believe this, but she somehow shapes the beginning of the roll of toilet paper to look like a white rose!

In that very beautiful bedroom, I saw a painted wooden sign that says, "Share Faith. Offer Prayer. Gather Hope." I looked at that sign and thought, *Yep. That's real friendship.*

Then I went downstairs to the gorgeously decorated TV room in Lisa's bed-and-breakfast and saw another sign. This one is actually embroidered onto fabric and framed. It says, "Friendship isn't a big thing. It's a million little things."

Both of those signs are so right. The one in the rosy bedroom reminds me of all the times I've called on a trusted friend when I needed some encouragement. Almost every time, my friend will share her faith in believing God can do anything. Then she'll offer to pray for me, and finally she'll start pointing out the reasons I can have hope.

Friendship is so much about everyday little things. Sure, big, traumatic events or circumstances do come along, and we need others to help us get through those times, but those smaller bumps in the road are where we need a good, consistent friend to keep us focused on God. When we learn to focus on him during the "smaller" things, it will be more natural for us to do the same thing when we face a "bigger" thing.

When? When? When?

Bible Blast: Read Matthew 24:30-36

No one knows the day or hour when these things will happen, not even the angels in heaven or the Son himself. Only the Father knows. MATTHEW 24:36

I remember the day my son Rob was born as if it were yesterday—even though he's a young adult now! Certain things had started happening in my body to let me know the time was coming, so I got my bag ready to go to the hospital. When my husband, Bob, got home, I said, "It's time!" It took him a minute to understand what I was talking about, but once he did, he went completely nuts, yelling and jumping up and down. He even ran into the nursery, grabbed all the little cute stuffed animals people had given us for our new baby and spiked them onto the floor like footballs. I'm surprised that he actually remembered to drive me to the hospital!

Waiting for a baby to come is such an exciting time. Most of the time, a couple only knows generally when the baby should arrive, but only God knows exactly when it's coming. It's funny to watch a husband as he watches his wife get closer and closer to the Big Day. If she makes a strange noise or just sneezes, he jumps for the car keys, ready to drive her to the hospital!

The way Matthew 24 talks about Jesus' return to earth reminds me of that anxious, happy anticipation. Matthew 24 says we'll be able to see certain signs that Christ's return is in the near future, but we won't be able to say, "I've done all the calculations, and Jesus is coming back on the third Thursday of next month!" So if you hear someone saying he or she knows the exact date of Jesus' return, don't believe that person. Scripture tells us that God the Father is the *only* one who knows when that day will be.

So what do we do while we wait for Jesus to come and get us? Tell everyone we know about him! We'll let them know he's coming back, and it really could be tomorrow.

We'll also commit to knowing Jesus as much as we can while we're here on the earth. Then when we see him in the sky, we can say, "I know you!"

Girl Gab: Do you know someone who's pregnant right now? Bless her with an encouraging note today.

1 October

Girl Gab: You can reenact Bessie's Great Well Escape with a miniature animal toy, a spoon, some dirt, and a glass, if you want. Tell God that you want the kind of life he has planned for you.

Cow Sense

Bible Blast: Read 1 Peter 2:21-25

The thief's purpose is to steal and kill and destroy. My purpose is to give them a rich and satisfying life. JOHN 10:10

There once was a cow whose name was Bessie who was caught up in the beauty of the day. She was smelling flowers, chewing grass, and gazing up at the cotton-ball clouds—and then she fell in a well.

Luckily the well was dry, so she didn't fall into water, but she was still freaked out since there was no way out. Bessie did what any sensible cow would do and started to moo loudly for Farmer Skip.

"Mmmoooooooooo! MmmoooooooOOOOO!"

Farmer Skip came running from the barn and saw Bessie's predicament. Suddenly he got an idea, and he called his neighbors to grab their shovels and come over. When everybody got there, Farmer Skip said, "Bessie has fallen into this old dry well. I've been meaning to fill it in with this here pile of dirt, so why don't you help me do it now?"

The neighbors looked confused. Why would Farmer Skip want to fill up the well *before* he got Bessie out? Because the neighbors didn't talk much, they just did what he told them.

Bessie didn't respond well when she started to feel piles of dirt hitting her back. "I thought Farmer Skip was my pal! He raised me from a calf!" She began to cry. Then she sneezed a really big cow sneeze. "Ah-ah-aaa-CHAMOOOOOO!" The sneeze caused her whole body to jerk, which shook the dirt off her back and onto the ground. Then Bessie stepped up onto that pile of dirt. *Aha!* she thought.

Every time a pile of dirt collected on the floor, Bessie stepped up onto it. Eventually, the dirt that everyone was shoveling into the well started to fill it up as Bessie slowly climbed the dirt to the top of the well.

Sometimes God does things we don't understand, but we have to trust that he's always doing what is best. He has a reason for everything he does, just like Farmer Skip did. Trust God with your whole life, and you'll experience a very satisfying life.

Language Lab: What Is "Discernment"?

Bible Blast: Read Proverbs 3:21-24

My child, don't lose sight of common sense and discernment. Hang on to them, for they will refresh your soul. They are like jewels on a necklace. PROVERBS 3:21-22

A friend recently gave eight-year-old Lucy some trading cards with different characters on them. Lucy had never seen those kinds of cards before and had never talked about them with her parents or anybody. As Lucy looked down at the colorful pictures on the cards, she thought for a moment and said, "Mom, do these cards not make God happy?"

Her mom said, "I'm not sure, honey. Why?"

"I don't know. I just think maybe they don't," Lucy answered.

"Well, if God is talking to you about those cards, you should probably listen to him," her mom said.

Lucy said, "I think he is."

Her mom asked, "Do you see anything on the cards that makes you think they're not good?"

"No," Lucy said. "I just think they're not."

Her mom came over to look at them, and they had some symbols on them that she, as a grown-up, knew were not good. Lucy could not have known, but God was telling her. That's discernment.

Discernment is having the ability to tell right from wrong. God gives us the ability to discern what's good and what's evil even when it doesn't seem very obvious. At times God has told me that a certain song was bad, or that a conversation with someone wasn't safe and that I should leave. Sometimes he gives me a sense that I need to pray for someone. It's not as if God says it out loud to me. But I get a feeling in my heart that God is speaking to me. Some people call it "women's intuition," but I think God gives girls discernment.

Philippians 1:9-11 talks about discernment, saying that it helps keep us "pure and blameless" for the day of Jesus' return.

Do you remember a time when, like Lucy, you felt God telling you something was bad?

Girl Gab: Discernment grows as you grow in your faith, so always dig in for more wisdom and knowledge from God's Word. Also ask him for discernment like this: "Dear God, I want you to tell me what's right and what's wrong so I can make the best decisions to love you. Give me discernment, and help me to trust your voice. In Jesus' name, amen."

It's a Great Big World

Bible Blast: Read Psalm 104:1-4

God sits above the circle of the earth. The people below seem like grasshoppers to him! He spreads out the heavens like a curtain and makes his tent from them. ISAIAH 40:22

Girl Gab: What part of the world would you love to see? What's the coolest place you've ever visited? If you have big dreams to see different parts of the world, tell your mom about it, and ask God to make that dream a reality.

Amelia was born in Atchison, Kansas, in 1897. When she became an adult, she started out as a nurse for the soldiers who got wounded in World War I. It didn't take her long to realize she didn't really want to be a nurse. Amelia really wanted to become a pilot.

By now you might know I'm talking about Amelia Earhart.

Now you might be thinking, *What's the big deal? Why didn't she just go to pilot school and become a pilot?* Well, things were much different for women in Amelia Earhart's time. Airplanes had just been invented when Amelia was born, and only brave, strong men flew them, not women. But Amelia wasn't the type of girl who gave up easily.

While living in California, Amelia got a job and saved money so she could take flying lessons. In 1928, she became the first woman to fly across the Atlantic Ocean as a passenger, and she loved the experience.

In 1932 Amelia became the first woman to fly across the Atlantic Ocean as the pilot. It took about fifteen hours, but today that would only take about five hours. She became the first woman to attempt many flights, but her biggest goal was to fly around the world.

She and a copilot began the trip around the world in 1937, but they didn't make it. It's actually quite a mystery because Amelia Earhart was never seen again after she left for that trip. Friends on the ground kept contact with her until she was somewhere over the Pacific Ocean, but no one knows what happened after that.

Can you understand Amelia's desire to see the whole world? I think it would be amazing to have God's view of the earth. He sees every animal, person, tree, flower, body of water, and snowcapped mountain.

The world is truly an amazing place. Let's enjoy it.

Kickin' Kraft: Dance like David

Bible Blast: Read Psalm 150:1-6

Praise him with the tambourine and dancing; praise him with strings and flutes! PSALM 150:4

**Kickin' Kraft:
David's Disco Ball!**

(Check out p. 376 for a great mother-daughter craft that helps reinforce today's devo!)

Chizuruoke (pronounced "cheez-uh-roe-kay") has a gift for dance. Born to Nigerian Christian parents, she began to use dance as a normal way of expressing worship. Every now and then she'll prepare a special dance for our church. I don't know how to explain how I feel when I see her move in such worshipful ways to the rhythm of music that glorifies God. I cry almost every time.

I'm not such a gifted dancer as Chizuruoke, but I have had times in my life when I've danced before God to praise him. It's kind of like when you're getting ready finally to see your favorite singer in the world in concert, and you're so excited you just start jumping up and down and spinning around, squealing happy squeals. That's how I get about Jesus sometimes. I just love him so much that I can't possibly hold it in anymore.

In the Bible, David was a serious dancer. It says in 2 Samuel 6:14 that he "danced before the Lord with all his might." For a moment, picture what it would look like if a man danced with all his might. We're not talking about a slow, controlled waltz, are we? David was totally giving his entire body to worship God. He just couldn't contain his worship, and he didn't care who knew it.

Psalm 150 sounds like a party to me. Just look at all the instruments listed in there: horns, harps, tambourines, flutes, cymbals. The idea behind that psalm is that we absolutely, positively, 100 percent need to give everything we have when we praise and worship God. Don't let anything hold you back from giving it all in worship. Dance like David if you want to!

I'm Sorry

Bible Blast: Read James 5:13-16

Confess your sins to each other and pray for each other so that you may be healed. The earnest prayer of a righteous person has great power and produces wonderful results. JAMES 5:16

Girl Gab: Ask your mom about the right way to apologize when you've hurt someone. Here's a hint or two: Don't list a bunch of excuses for why you hurt the person, and make sure it's really clear that you're apologizing. Do you need to apologize to someone today?

When Yasmine received the notice from the school librarian that her book was overdue, she got frustrated because she couldn't find it. She looked everywhere, but she couldn't find it anywhere.

She stomped in the door after school, threw her backpack down on the floor, and announced, "I can't find my library book anywhere! If I don't return it, they're probably going to send me to library jail or something!"

Yasmine's mom assured her that she wouldn't go to any type of jail and said, "We'll all help you look for it, honey."

That entire weekend Yasmine's family helped her search for the missing book. They looked through backpacks, cleaned out the stuff under the beds, and went through the car. Every time they didn't find it, Yasmine accused her little sister, Alexis, of hiding it even though Alexis said she hadn't.

Monday morning in school, Yasmine opened her desk to get her math workbook. When she pulled it out of her desk, she squealed because lying underneath it was her long-lost library book!

At home she shared her excitement with everyone about finally finding the book. Alexis just went into her room and shut the door.

"Yasmine, I'm glad you found your book," her mom said. "But don't you think you need to talk to Alexis about accusing her of something she didn't do?"

Yasmine looked down at her feet and swallowed hard. "Yeah. I guess I'll go apologize."

She went into her sister's room and sat down on the bed. "Lexi, um, I'm really sorry that I kept saying you took my book. And I'm sorry I didn't believe you. Will you forgive me?"

Alexis had tears in her eyes when she answered, "That was pretty lame, but I do forgive you."

They hugged and were glad to be okay again.

Meditation Moment: Hebrews 13

Don't love money; be satisfied with what you have. For God has said, "I will never fail you. I will never abandon you." So we can say with confidence, "The LORD is my helper, so I will have no fear. What can mere people do to me?" HEBREWS 13:5-6

"If I just had more money, I would be satisfied, and I would never have to be afraid of anything ever again!" That's what a lot of people think, but it certainly isn't true.

Today as you meditate on these verses, the challenge will be to figure out how money and God's commitment to you are connected.

How would knowing God will never abandon you help you not love money?

If the Lord is your helper, how does that help you not be afraid?

Why do people think money will give them total freedom from fear?

I have an idea that God has a lot he wants to teach you today through these verses, so go ahead and dig right in!

Take time to talk to God about your desire and to hear his voice about Hebrews 13:5-6 today. Then, after you read through the verses a couple of times, be still for a moment and wait for God to give you a juicy tidbit of truth for today. Once you feel that God has shared something with you, write it down. Don't forget to thank him for teaching you today.

Girl Gab: Now share what you've learned with your mom. Have a chat with her about money and being satisfied with what you have. Tell God "thank you" that since he's with you, you don't have to be afraid.

Preteen Truth

Bible Blast: Read 1 Peter 2:1-3

I had to feed you with milk, not with solid food, because you weren't ready for anything stronger. 1 CORINTHIANS 3:2

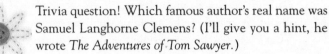

Trivia question! Which famous author's real name was Samuel Langhorne Clemens? (I'll give you a hint, he wrote *The Adventures of Tom Sawyer*.)

It's Mark Twain. Maybe you haven't read anything by him yet, but there's a good chance you will. Mark Twain is famous for writing stories like *The Adventures of Tom Sawyer* and *The Adventures of Huckleberry Finn*.

You may wonder why he would pick a different name, but that's actually pretty common for fiction authors. It's called a "pseudonym" (pronounced "soo-doe-nim").

Aside from having written a lot of books and stories, Mark Twain is one of the most quoted people around (although he died in 1910). He said some really funny and smart stuff.

It doesn't appear as though Mark Twain was a follower of Jesus Christ, but he did say one really interesting thing about the Bible. He said, "Most people are bothered by those passages of Scripture they do not understand, but the passages that bother me are those I do understand."

Even though he didn't believe the Bible was 100 percent truth, he made a perceptive comment. The passages he did understand were already convicting him with their truth. Besides, it simply makes sense to begin with the parts of Scripture that you can understand. It can be totally overwhelming to open the Bible and see a bunch of weird names and phrases that you don't understand. Don't worry too much about the things that you won't understand until you get older. For now, focus on the bunches of things you totally understand, like, "Do to others whatever you would like them to do to you" (Matthew 7:12)

When you come across something that you don't quite get in the Bible, ask God for understanding, or ask your parents or an adult at church to help you. If you still don't understand, just set that passage aside. God will reveal it to you when you're ready.

Girl Gab: If you were an author and you could pick a pseudonym (fake name) to write under, what would you choose? How about "Pen N. Paypurr"? Talk to God about the Bible today. Tell him how it makes you feel. Ask him to help you understand what you read.

Money Matters

Bible Blast: Read Luke 18:18-25

It is easier for a camel to go through the eye of a needle than for a rich person to enter the Kingdom of God! LUKE 18:25

Karl Rabeder is a guy from Austria who has a ton of money—4.7 million dollars, to be exact.

It might be easy to think that, if someone has millions of dollars, he must be really happy. However, at least in Karl Rabeder's case, that's not true at all. That's why he chose to start giving it all away in 2010. He realized his wealth wasn't making him happy at all. So Karl began selling his homes, fancy car, glider planes, and other stuff. He's doing some great charity work with his money, and he plans to live in a small cabin somewhere instead of in a great big villa. He said his goal is to have nothing left. He really feels that having so much money can get in the way of real happiness.

I can't help but think of the dude in the Bible we call the "Rich Young Ruler." You read about him in the Bible Blast. When Jesus told him to sell everything he had and give it to the poor, the young man had a really hard time with that command, "for he was very rich." I doubt it was because the young man was an especially greedy guy. I think Jesus knew it would be *very* difficult to give away all of his riches to help the poor.

Jesus leaves us with a funny word picture at the end of that section of Scripture: "It is easier for a camel to go through the eye of a needle than for a rich person to enter the Kingdom of God!" The bottom line there is, if someone has lots of riches, his or her wealth can really become a big fat distraction from God because people often end up worshiping the money and the happiness they think it brings instead of worshiping their Creator.

Now, I hope you're not running around the house right now yelling, *"We have to sell everything and give everything to the poor!"* Don't rush out and put a For Sale sign on the family car. The whole idea here is that no matter how much money you have or don't have, you must not worship it. Put your faith in God. Then you will have true happiness.

Girl Gab: Pray this today: "Dear God, help me to realize that any money I make is really your money. Let me always obey you in how I spend it. In Jesus' name, amen."

That's Blibber-Blubber!

Bible Blast: Read 1 Peter 3:13-17

Let your conversation be gracious and attractive so that you will have the right response for everyone. COLOSSIANS 4:6

Girl Gab: Have a Blibber-Blubber bubble-blowing contest with your mom! Do the biggest bubble, smallest bubble, most bubbles in twenty seconds, and most creative bubble. Ask her any questions you have about today's devo.

Gum is so great. I love popping a piece of fresh mint gum in my mouth after eating a meal that was full of garlic and onions. In just a moment of time, the cool minty-ness just washes away the bad breath so people don't drop over dead when I open my mouth to talk to them.

And don't even get me started on bubble gum! Can you blow bubbles? Have you ever blown a bubble so big that when it popped you actually got some on your eyebrows? Awesome!

People have been chewing some sort of gum for, like, a really long time, but old-fashioned gum didn't look like what we chew now. People used to take different types of tree sap, resin, or even wax, and chew it. Eventually, someone discovered the stuff could be made into chewing gum.

Frank Henry Fleer invented the first real bubble gum in 1906, but it didn't really take off. He called it Blibber-Blubber. I think that's such a great name! Can you imagine saying to your friend, "Hey, do you want a piece of Blibber-Blubber?" I grew up believing that if you swallowed gum, it would just sit in your stomach for about seven years. Have you ever heard that? That was always a kind of scary thing to think about. If you swallowed a lot of gum, how would there be room for anything else in your stomach?

Well, I've done a little research and found out that's not true! In some really weird cases, gum can get caught on something else like nutshells and get stuck somewhere, but generally it passes through the body just like anything else you eat. It doesn't get broken down and absorbed like food does, but it doesn't set up a beach house in your tummy.

It's important to know why we believe things. Like, if someone asked you why you believe Jesus is the only way to heaven, what would you tell that person? As you go through this devotional book, I hope you start to figure out why you believe what you believe.

Amazing Animals: Chinchillas

Bible Blast: Read Psalm 51:7-10

Purify me from my sins, and I will be clean; wash me, and I will be whiter than snow. PSALM 51:7

Have you ever seen a chinchilla? Oh, my goodness. They are one of the cutest little animals God ever made! Their heads kind of look like a mouse's, their bodies resemble a rabbit's, and their long puffy tails look like a squirrel's. Chinchillas are naturally found in the Andes Mountains in South America, so they prefer dry and cool weather.

One of the most unbelievable things about chinchillas is their fur. If you've ever touched one, you know exactly what I'm talking about. They have fifty or more hairs coming out of one hair follicle in their skin. (To give you an idea of what that's like, we humans only have one hair per follicle.) Their fur is so soft and so fluffy!

Chinchillas aren't superaggressive, but they do have one funky way of defending themselves. If an enemy grabs onto its fur, the chinchilla will actually release that fur from its body in order to get away.

Anyone who has a pet chinchilla will tell you that the most entertaining thing about owning one is the dust bath. In order to keep a chinchilla's fur clean, you don't wash it down with shampoo and a hose like you would a dog. A chinchilla cleans itself with dust. The dust is superfine powdery stuff made especially for chinchillas. Every now and then, you take a bowlful of chinchilla-cleaning dust and set it down near the rodent. He'll very happily climb into that container and start flipping and rolling all around in it like it's the best thing that's ever happened to him. The dust gets into his fur and cleans all the oils and yucky stuff that gets in there. It's funny that dust—really fine dirt!—gets the chinchilla clean!

When you want to be clean from something bad you've done, the only way to do that is by telling Jesus about your sin and accepting his forgiveness, just like David did in today's Bible Blast. God has forgiveness available for anyone who wants it. We just have to jump in and give it a whirl.

Girl Gab: If you've never seen a chinchilla take a dust bath, go online or to a pet store and check it out. It's really cute. If there's something you need to confess to God, go ahead and do that now. Thank God for his forgiveness.

11 October

Crocodile Tears

Bible Blast: Read Psalm 56:8-11

You keep track of all my sorrows. You have collected all my tears in your bottle. You have recorded each one in your book.
PSALM 56:8

Have you ever heard someone's tears described as "crocodile tears"? It's a weird phrase, right? People began saying that as a way of describing the tears of someone who didn't feel bad, but was pretending that she did. It turns out that crocodiles actually cry when they eat their prey, as if they feel bad about what they're doing. Like the crocodile is chowing down on an antelope and saying through tear-stained eyes, "I'm so sorry, antelope. I don't really want to eat you. I just have to. It's the way I am! I'll never be able to change!"

No one is really sure why crocodiles "cry" when they eat; biologists think it has something to do with all the hissing and puffing crocodiles do while they're eating, which may push tears through their sinuses somehow. One thing crocodile experts will agree on is that the gigantic animals don't feel bad about eating their prey.

There are three types of tears our human eyeballs create. One type keeps our eyes moist and protects our eyes from getting dried out. The second type of tears kick in when you get something in your eyes or when they burn from cutting raw onions. Those tears are meant to wash your eyes out and get rid of whatever's causing the problem. Finally, we cry emotional tears. Those are the ones that stream down our faces uncontrollably when we're sad or really happy. When we cry those emotional tears, chemical things happen in our bodies that make us feel better after we've cried. Isn't that so cool?

Today's focus verse is so beautiful. Imagine God taking some beautiful bottle and holding it under our eyes to capture our tears. He knows the reason for every single teardrop, and he cares about them.

You are so valuable to God. In fact, you're invaluable. That means you're worth so much that you're priceless! Your happy tears and your sad tears matter to God. So go ahead and pass the tissues!

Girl Gab: Between you and your mom, which one of you cries more easily? How does it make you feel to know that God knows about each one of your tears? Pretend the word *invaluable* is written across your shirt today. But watch out—it just might make you smile!

Gold Nose Rings

Bible Blast: Read Proverbs 31:28-31

A beautiful woman who lacks discretion is like a gold ring in a pig's snout. PROVERBS 11:22

Picture a beautiful queen who's getting ready for the royal ball. Her servants help the majestic lady put on her hand-stitched, 100 percent silk gown. It has crystals delicately placed all over the fabric, making the gown appear to twinkle under the candlelight. Her slender feet slide into shoes that look more like jewelry than something you should walk around in. Her personal hairstylist pins her hair up into an elegant sculpture of curls and twists. The queen's neck is covered with a necklace holding hundreds of different colored gemstones. After the makeup artist has made her skin look like a perfectly painted art canvas, the queen is ready to enter the ball.

She stands at the top of the grand staircase with her handsome king at her side. The people gasp at her beauty and bow as the royal couple slowly walks down to the ballroom floor. As they begin the first waltz with everyone watching, the queen reaches up with her bejeweled hand and . . . picks her nose. Then she gets an itch on top of her knee. So she hoists up her gorgeous gown and crazily scratches like a dog with fleas. And finally, shocking everyone in the room, she grabs a can of soda, drinks it as fast as she can, and lets out a *huge* burp that echoes through the palace walls.

That was a detailed description of today's focus verse. The queen was a beautiful woman who didn't have any discretion or good judgment. Can you see how that's like a gold ring in a pig's nose? You can wash a pig, put piggy perfume on it, put a big bow around its neck and a shiny pure gold ring through its nose, and one thing won't change. It's still a pig. If it were near a mud puddle, it would roll in it with great joy in spite of its pretty jewelry.

It doesn't matter how good you look on the outside; if you don't make good choices to live as one of God's girls, how you look on the outside is like a gold ring in a pig's snout. True beauty comes from becoming more like Jesus. Keep spending time with him. Let his love be your jewelry.

Girl Gab: Mom, what do you think it means to "be a lady"? Daughter, do you agree with your mom about this? Pray that God would give you both good judgment.

Girl Gab: Look over these five ideas with your mom. Are there any that really stand out to you? If so, that may be God giving you a little nudge, saying, "Why don't you give this a shot?" If you don't already have some sort of Bible reading plan you're following, come up with one with your mom's help. Maybe she'll want to have a plan too!

Do What You Can

Bible Blast: Read 2 Thessalonians 2:4-6, 13

Do your best to present yourself to God as one approved, a workman who does not need to be ashamed and who correctly handles the word of truth. 2 TIMOTHY 2:15 (NIV)

The pastor of a church was encouraging the people in his congregation to get into the Word of God. One Sunday he stood in front of them and preached a message called, "Five Ways to Get the Most out of Your Bible." Do you want to know what those five ways are? Here you go!

1. *Get started right away.* As the saying goes, "There's no time like the present." Start reading it today. Don't wait until the full moon or until your sixteenth birthday.

2. *Read every day.* Even if it's just one verse, it's a great thing to make reading your Bible a number one priority for every day. It gets truth into your mind and heart, and that's really going to help you live a godly, truthful life.

3. *Begin with prayer.* Before you sit down to read God's Word, pray. Ask God to help you focus on what you're reading and ask him directly to teach you something. I believe he will teach you every single time you ask him.

4. *Have a plan.* Instead of just flipping the Bible open, closing your eyes, and blindly pointing to a verse to read, start somewhere. Maybe you'll want to read a verse from Proverbs every day. Or maybe you'll want to read a little more so you'll read a psalm. A lot of people like to read an action-packed Gospel, like Mark. Others like just to start in the beginning with Genesis 1:1. Having a plan will help you do it more regularly.

5. *Ask yourself three questions:*

1) What does this Scripture say? Like, what are the facts?
2) What does this Scripture mean?
3) What does this Scripture mean *to me*?

There really are no rules to reading the Bible, but these are definitely guidelines to help you fall in love with God's Word.

Language Lab: What Is "Evil"?

Bible Blast: Read Genesis 2:15-17

Don't let evil conquer you, but conquer evil by doing good.
ROMANS 12:21

Now before we even begin today's Language Lab, I want you to pray: "God, be my teacher today. Show me that you have power over all evil. That makes me feel good because you live inside of me. Thank you for that! In Jesus' name I pray, amen."

The reason we're talking about evil today isn't so that we can learn all the evil stuff we can and get creepy feelings. We're learning what evil is so that we can learn *more* about who God is. Knowing about God and knowing God are the most important things!

Evil is the opposite of good. It's bad stuff. It's sin. God has nothing to do with evil.

Now the one who started the whole evil thing is the devil, or Satan. He's the ultimate bad guy, and he totally hates God. Most people believe (based on Isaiah 14 and Ezekiel 28) that the devil was originally a worship-leading angel in heaven. Then he got too stuck on himself, so he tried to make himself more important than God, which, of course, doesn't work! So God kicked the devil and a bunch of the angels who were with him out of heaven.

If the devil is able to love anything, he loves evil. He wants everyone to do bad things that don't honor God, and he does his best to get people as far from God as he can. He's kind of like the kid who didn't get invited to a party, so he tries to get as many people as possible to not go to the party too.

Here's the good news: "The Son of God came to destroy the works of the devil" (1 John 3:8). And that is exactly why we don't have to get totally freaked out or afraid of the devil. Jesus has all the power to get rid of the devil's plans to keep us far from God. All we have to do is ask!

Revelation 20 tells us about a day when God will get rid of the devil forever. So no matter what, the end result of that evil guy is *extinction*. Awesome!

Girl Gab: Talk to your mom about today's lesson. Ask God to help you "overcome evil with good" like it says in Romans 12:21. Thank God for his goodness today.

15 October

Fancy Feet

Bible Blast: Read Romans 10:13-15

How beautiful on the mountains are the feet of the messenger who brings good news, the good news of peace and salvation, the news that the God of Israel reigns! ISAIAH 52:7

There is a hilarious bird that lives way down at the bottom of South America. It has a really comical name, so prepare yourself. It's a Blue-footed Booby. Now go ahead and say that five times in a row as fast as you can and get all your giggles out.

A Blue-footed Booby is a funky bird that might remind you of a seagull. Blue-footed Boobies nest on land, but they dive into water for their food. As you might be able to tell by the name, Blue-footed Boobies have very unique feet. Their bodies are mostly black, white, or grey, but their feet and legs are a vibrant light blue. And as if their feet weren't crazy enough, what they do with their feet is even funnier. When a boy Blue-footed Booby is trying to get a girl Blue-footed Booby's attention, he does a funny little dance. He walks kind of slowly and lifts his blue feet up high, one at a time in a sort of clumsy waddle. He looks so serious and proud about his dance, but the dance itself is so awkward.

Your feet may not be blue, but they are beautiful if they take you out to share the gospel. Today's Bible Blast is so great because it makes sense. Let me rewrite it for you differently:

Everyone who calls on the name of the Lord will be saved. But how can they call on him to save them unless they believe in him? And how can they believe in him if they have never heard about him? And how can they hear about him unless someone tells them? And how will anyone tell them without being sent?

And now, ladies, that's where your pretty feet come in!

When someone chooses to go and tell others about Jesus, her feet are blessed. That means that God sees what you're doing, and he likes it. He will make a way for your feet as they walk toward the lost.

Those who take the Good News of salvation in Jesus Christ to others have truly gorgeous piggies!

Girl Gab: I know summer is over and fall has officially begun, but wouldn't it be great to paint your toenails a bright, hot pink today? Don't forget to do your mom's, too! You could even get creative and paint or draw little designs on them. Thank God for blessing your beautiful feet!

A Big, Big House

Bible Blast: Read 1 Chronicles 4:9-10

Oh, that you would bless me and expand my territory! Please be with me in all that I do, and keep me from all trouble and pain!
1 CHRONICLES 4:10

Some girls dream of living in a huge palace with tons of rooms, indoor swimming pools, air-conditioned stables with hundreds of horses, and a team of maids and butlers to help them take care of it all. Other girls dream of living in a house that's only as big as some walk-in closets. Dee Williams got tired of maintaining a big house with a big payment, so she built something a little smaller. Actually, it's *a lot* smaller.

Dee's home is what they call a "tiny house." It's a cute, cozy, wooden cottage with a little front porch, kitchen area, living room, bedroom, and restroom. The little home is built on a trailer so Dee can pull it anywhere with her truck. Oh, and did I mention it's only eighty-four square feet? That's about the size of one average parking space, ladies. Dee said she built her tiny house because it's really all she needs, and now she doesn't have a big house payment every month. It only cost her about $10,000 to build, and a lot of the materials she used were things other people were getting rid of.

In 1 Chronicles 4, you read about Jabez, who wasn't asking for a smaller house. In fact, he prayed, "God! Make my territory bigger!" Jabez may have been asking for more land, but we can look at that in a different way too.

What if we began asking God to increase the number of people we bless? Or the number of people we tell about Jesus? Or the number of people we pray for?

That's a different kind of "territory," but God can enlarge it. He can make our influence in the world and with our friends even bigger so that more people come to know and follow him.

Whether you live in a huge palace or a tiny house, you can ask God to expand or enlarge your "territory." Then watch how he answers that prayer. He knows your heart, and he knows what is best for you.

Girl Gab: You will be amazed if you go online with your mom and do a search for tiny houses. There are tall houses, skinny houses, short houses, fat houses, square ones, and even round ones. Have fun imagining what it would be like to live in a tiny house. Pray Jabez's prayer today, and see what God does.

17 October

Kickin' Kraft: Magnetic Words

Bible Blast: Read Proverbs 12:17-22

Wise words satisfy like a good meal; the right words bring satisfaction. PROVERBS 18:20

Kickin' Kraft:
Sticky Word Game!

(Check out p. 376 for a great mother-daughter craft that helps reinforce today's devo!)

What's the nicest thing you think anyone has ever said to you? Okay. Now what's the meanest thing anyone has ever said to you? I wonder if you remember the hurtful comments more quickly than you remember the affirming words.

I can still remember good things and bad things people said to me when I was a little girl as if those conversations happened yesterday. Words have power.

Every day we have a choice: Are we going to use the words we speak to bring life to someone, or are we going to use them to drag a person down? I wish I could say that every word I've ever spoken has been good and uplifting and wonderful, but unfortunately, that isn't true. I have sometimes used my voice to hurt others. I wish I could take all those hurtful words back, but I can't. That's the thing with words. We have the ability to remember words for a long, long time because words stick.

The big challenge with our speech is thinking about what we say before it comes flying off our tongues. Ask the Holy Spirit to give you a big red flag when you're about to release uncool words from your mouth.

Your sticky words have great power, so use that power for good!

He Is the Shepherd; We Are the Sheep

Bible Blast: Read John 10:11-15

I am the good shepherd; I know my own sheep, and they know me, just as my Father knows me and I know the Father. So I sacrifice my life for the sheep. JOHN 10:14-15

The animals wait at the starting line, impatiently stomping their hooves on the track beneath them. They know their time is coming. They know in a matter of seconds the gate will be lifted, and they will be set free to run like the wind toward the finish line. Finally, they hear, "The race begins in five, four, three, two, one! And they're off!" The crowd goes wild as the racers take off toward their goal.

That's the scene in Emmaville, New South Wales, Australia, when the town's Mining Museum hosts its most popular fund-raising event: sheep-racing. You heard me correctly. *Sheep*-racing. One of the town's roads is blocked off for the event, and people pay a few dollars to watch the race. You may wonder what would motivate a sheep to run. The group of woolly racers are being moved along by sheep dogs, but that doesn't always go as planned. In many such races, the sheep just kind of stop before they reach the finish line, or they turn around and start heading back toward the starting gate. If a sheep does actually become the winner, its owner wins about $100.

We may not be racers, but the Bible tells us that those who follow Christ are sheep. In Matthew 25 you can read about a time when Jesus separates people into two categories: sheep and goats. He refers to those who don't follow him as goats and those who do as sheep.

You could do a whole separate study on why the Bible says we're like sheep, but probably the most important reason is that sheep are great followers. Sheep know the voice of their shepherd, so when he calls they follow.

Jesus is our Good Shepherd. He does know us, and we know him. When he calls us, we need to stop what we're doing and follow him, knowing we can totally trust him.

Girl Gab: If you know someone who has sheep, set up a time to go and ask questions about sheep and what they do. In the meantime, why don't you and your mom come up with other reasons why Christians might be like sheep? Ask God to help you know his voice when he's speaking to you.

He Is the Vine; We Are the Branches

Bible Blast: Read John 15:5-8

Yes, I am the vine; you are the branches. Those who remain in me, and I in them, will produce much fruit. For apart from me you can do nothing. JOHN 15:5

Girl Gab: Play a game of Bobbing for Grapes with your mom. Put a handful of grapes in a large, shallow bowl. Fill the bowl about three-quarters full with water. Take turns, and see who can stick her face in the water and pull out the most grapes using just her mouth in one minute! The winner gets a back rub!

When a grape is dried, why is it suddenly a "raisin"? Why wouldn't it just be a "dried grape"? I may never know the answer to those questions, but I do know about the oldest grapevine in the world. It's found in England at the Hampton Court Palace garden. The palace isn't home to royal families anymore, but it's a great place for tourists to visit. One of the things those visitors can see is a huge grapevine that the groundskeepers believe was first planted in the year 1768! So not only is it more than 230 years old, it's about 120 feet long! For good reason, people call it the Great Vine. The vine's keeper harvests roughly 507 to 705 pounds of grapes off of the Great Vine every year. Once, back in 1807, the keepers harvested three times that many!

Our focus verse today tells us that Jesus is the true Great Vine, and we are the branches. Now, I could sit and tell you all the reasons why I think Jesus is like a vine and we are like the branches, but I want to give you a moment to think of some reasons for yourself. So go ahead and take a minute to do that.

Okay. Did you come up with some possible answers?

One possibility that really stands out to me about Jesus being the vine is that he is our source of power, strength, and life. A branch can't grow unless it's connected to something. Jesus is our constant power supply.

It's not like an MP3 player or video game that you plug in until it's charged up, and then you unplug it until the battery dies again. It's more like your family's television set. If it isn't plugged in to the electrical socket, it's not going to show your favorite TV shows or movies.

When you live your life for Jesus, you are his. Take the time to stay connected and plugged in to his love and power. If you do, your life will grow a lot of fruit.

He Is Bread and Water;
We Are Hungry and Thirsty

Bible Blast: Read John 6:28-35

I am the bread of life. Whoever comes to me will never be hungry again. Whoever believes in me will never be thirsty. JOHN 6:35

There aren't many things better than a loaf of warm, freshly baked bread. My tummy's growling just thinking about it! So obviously when you read the title of today's devo, you can know I'm not saying that Jesus is a loaf of bread and a glass of water. The devo title points to Christ being the ultimate source to meet our most essential needs.

The people described in John 6 were demanding miracles. They figured that since the Israelites way back in the Old Testament got manna (bread) sent to them from heaven every day, then they should get something like that, too. They didn't realize that the real "Bread" from heaven was standing right in front of them, looking them right in the eyes.

When Jesus called himself the bread of life, he was saying that he came to completely fill and satisfy everyone who is hungry. What are people hungry for? Lots of things: forgiveness, hope, joy, happiness, love, peace, and feeling as if they're important. Jesus fills all those needs.

Verse 35 says that Jesus claimed that whoever believes in him won't ever be thirsty again. In John 4 there's a story about Jesus and a woman he meets at a well. Jesus pointed at the water in the well and told her, "Anyone who drinks this water will soon become thirsty again. But those who drink the water I give will never be thirsty again. It becomes a fresh, bubbling spring within them, giving them eternal life."

The ultimate way Jesus satisfies those who are hungry and thirsty is by giving them eternal life. In heaven all of our needs will be met. We'll never be starving or dying of thirst again. But until we get to heaven, Jesus fills us up every day with the bread of his Word and the water of the promise of eternal life.

Girl Gab: Are you feeling empty in any way today? Ask your mom to pray that God will fill you up and satisfy you. Do the same thing for her.

21 October

Loving the Critters

Bible Blast: Read Matthew 10:29-31

God said, "Let us make human beings in our image, to be like us. They will reign over the fish in the sea, the birds in the sky, the livestock, all the wild animals on the earth, and the small animals that scurry along the ground." GENESIS 1:26

Girl Gab: Do you have a special place in your heart for animals? If you could plaster your bedroom walls with posters of an animal, what animal would you choose? What animal would your mom choose? Take some time to pray that people would not be cruel to animals. Then take some time and pray for the people you know who aren't saved.

When I look into the eyes of any animal, it's hard for me to understand how anyone could be cruel to it. Unfortunately, it happens all the time. People have done some really horrible things to all kinds of animals.

In Virginia a man had thirty horses taken from him because he simply was not feeding them. And as if that wasn't terrible enough, some of those beautiful animals were pregnant! The veterinarians who are helping nurse the horses back to health said many of the patients weighed two hundred pounds less than a healthy weight for a horse. You could almost count the animals' rib bones because they were so thin and malnourished.

This story of the starved horses may have made you feel really sad, but sometimes it's good to feel sad. I know that God is sad when animals are treated with such meanness. Our focus verse today reminds me that God made me and he made the animals, and it's part of my job to help take care of them.

As Christians, we can find it hard to know what our view of animals should be. Jesus gives us a little teaching on that in Matthew 10:29-31. He talks about sparrows, which are little birds that are very common. He said that "not a single sparrow can fall to the ground without your Father knowing it." God cares about those little unfancy birds. Then it says, "Don't be afraid; you are more valuable to God than a whole flock of sparrows!" It's good and godly to take care of animals, but we need to also keep in mind that humans are more valuable to God than animals.

To sum it all up, when you love animals, you're loving God's creation. But, if you value animals more than you value humans, that's not God's plan. So go ahead and save the whales, the rainforests, and the polar bears, but don't make protecting animals more important than saving humans.

Share and Share Alike

Bible Blast: Read 1 Samuel 30:8-25

David said, "No, my brothers! Don't be selfish with what the LORD has given us." 1 SAMUEL 30:23

Katherine Reutter is big into necklaces, or should I say she's into big necklaces? Katherine competed in the 2010 Winter Olympics in the short-track speed-skating competition, and she ended up winning two very large necklaces—a silver one and a bronze one. Those necklaces happened to be Olympic medals!

You may not know this, but some countries, including the United States, pay Olympic athletes a bonus for each medal they win. Katherine won $25,000 with her silver and bronze medals. And do you know what she did with that money?

She gave it to her parents to get some work done on their house.

Why?

Because Katherine's parents had sacrificed a lot of time and money over the years to help Katherine become a professional speed skater, and one thing they weren't able to take care of was their house. Mr. and Mrs. Reutter's home was in desperate need of serious repairs and remodeling, but they just didn't have the cash to take care of it.

Katherine could have been really selfish with her fame and money, but she wasn't just thinking about herself. She wanted to give back to her parents to honor them for all they had sacrificed for her.

Love isn't self-seeking (1 Corinthians 13:5). That means a girl who truly loves doesn't just think about herself and how to make her life easier. She thinks about others. She loves and gives freely, even if she doesn't get anything in return.

Most parents don't give to their kids because they want something back from them. They give because they love their kids. You don't need to feel that you have to pay your parents back for everything they've done, but it's important to realize how they've sacrificed for you. When you understand that, it will be a good motivator for you to give back to them freely when they need it most.

Girl Gab: If someone gave you $25,000 right now, what would you do with it? What about your mom? Pray that God would open your eyes to give generously to those in need.

Bird vs. Window

Bible Blast: Read Ecclesiastes 1:3-8

I observed everything going on under the sun, and really, it is all meaningless—like chasing the wind. ECCLESIASTES 1:14

Girl Gab: What would you do if a big wild turkey kept flying into your window? I would grab the video camera! Ask God to help you think about heavenly things, not earthly things today.

It's Saturday morning. You're sitting on the couch watching Saturday morning cartoons in your cozy jammies and slippers. Just as you put a spoonful of your very fave cereal into your mouth, you hear a *thud.* Then you hear it again. *Thud!* Something is hitting the window. *Thud!* Could it be? Is it really? A bird! A bright red cardinal! It's repeatedly flying into your living room window. *Thud!*

Have you ever seen such a weird thing? It happens quite a lot—and not just with cardinals. Robins do it, and apparently larger birds like wild turkeys fly into windows too.

Some birds are really territorial. That means when a bird builds a nest, it becomes the king of all the area, or territory, surrounding that nest. So if it sees another bird or animal coming too close, it will try to scare it off, which brings us to the window war. Birds don't have the kind of brain that can understand the difference between what's a reflection and what's real. So if a territorial bird like a cardinal sees its own reflection in something like a window, it will attack it over and over. It doesn't understand that the "other bird" isn't real.

There's really not much you can do if this happens except to cover the outside of the window. But that's not really a great solution because birds will try to find their "opponent" in some other window and attack that reflection. It will find the "other bird" in every window it sees. It's such a meaningless battle for the poor bird to fight. Solomon calls that kind of fruitless endeavor a "chasing after the wind."

Ecclesiastes 1 is full of Solomon's thoughts about everything the world chases after, and he concludes that the behavior is pointless. It won't result in anything good or useful, just like that bird attacking its own reflection.

In Colossians 3:2, Paul says that we need to "think about the things of heaven, not the things of earth." Focusing on what's important to God will keep us from doing silly things that would be like chasing the wind.

Don't Travel in a Barrel

Bible Blast: Read James 1:5-8

When you ask him, be sure that your faith is in God alone. Do not waver, for a person with divided loyalty is as unsettled as a wave of the sea that is blown and tossed by the wind. JAMES 1:6

On this very date in 1901 Annie Edson Taylor did something incredible—and very dangerous. Annie was looking for a way to make some money, so she decided that at the age of sixty-three, she would be the first person to ever go over Niagara Falls in a barrel.

Annie had a barrel, crafted of oak and iron, made just for her trip. She padded it with a mattress. On her sixty-third birthday, October 24, 1901, Annie climbed into the barrel, clutching her favorite heart-shaped pillow. Her friends screwed down the lid, pumped some air into the barrel, and set Annie and her barrel in the water above the falls. The current carried her down, down, down into the rushing, roaring water. Of course, everyone was thrilled to see Annie still alive and well when they opened the barrel after her twenty-minute adventure ride. So she became the very first person ever to survive a trip over Niagara Falls in a barrel.

When Annie was interviewed about her trip, she said she would caution anyone against doing what she did and that she would never, ever want to make another trip over the falls.

Floating around a river in a barrel would be dangerous because you would have no control about where you went. The book of James says that's like people who ask for God's wisdom and then don't do what God tells them. It's like they say they believe God, but they act as if they believe more in themselves. That's why they're so unstable. They're being tossed around by their own ideas, even though God has already given them clear answers and guidelines.

If you have to go on a river trip, take a boat that you can steer. In fact, let God steer you with his wisdom. Barrel travel is not the way to go.

Girl Gab: If you need wisdom about something today, ask God for it, and then act on that wisdom. Don't doubt it.

25 October

Meditation Moment: Proverbs 15

If you reject discipline, you only harm yourself; but if you listen to correction, you grow in understanding. PROVERBS 15:32

Girl Gab: Talk to your mom about discipline. Ask her how her parents handled discipline when she was growing up. Ask God to help you learn how to love discipline and to make you wise.

Okay, let's just imagine that you keep forgetting to feed your hamster. (It doesn't matter if you have a hamster. We're imagining.) Let's say your mom notices that "Mighty Mouse" has almost died twice from starvation. So you get in trouble. Mom no longer feeds you dinner unless you have fed Mighty Mouse. After two days of being very hungry at bedtime, you start remembering. Now your dear furry friend is much better off. What your mom did to help you make a change in your habits is called discipline. Discipline is good for you and for everyone else who comes into contact with you!

When you are disciplined, it's a chance to grow up a little. People who are never disciplined have a hard time maturing into adults because they never really learn how their actions affect other people. In short, they stay somewhat selfish.

Today you get to meditate about the idea of discipline. That may not sound like fun, but God has stuff to teach you today, so open your ears and your heart.

Take a moment to pray. Now read Proverbs 15:32 a couple of times. Ask God to speak to you through an idea, thought, picture, or whatever. Then wait and see what he says to you. Go ahead and write it down.

He's God, and We're Not

Bible Blast: Read Isaiah 40:12-15

Has the LORD ever needed anyone's advice? Does he need instruction about what is good? ISAIAH 40:14

I love to read letters that kids write to God. Here are some of my favorites:

"Dear God, If you will watch in church on Sunday, I will show you my new shoes."

"Dear God, Instead of letting people die and having to make new ones, why don't you just keep the ones you got now?"

"Dear God, Thank you for the baby brother, but what I prayed for was a puppy."

Aren't those great?

A lot of people wish they could write letters to God so they could tell him how to do his job. There are a lot of problems with wishing you were God or thinking that you're smarter than God. First of all, that kind of behavior is exactly what got Satan kicked out of heaven. If you want to be God, you're going to have a very hard time being close to him.

Remember that you are human and even though your brain is amazing, you're not smarter than God. God created you. You didn't create him. There's no way in the world you could ever know as much as he does. You can't see everything that goes on everywhere all the time the way he can. You can't always see how a bad thing that happens today can end up being a really great thing for your future life, but God can. Ecclesiastes 5:2 says, "God is in heaven, and you are here on earth. So let your words be few."

Finally, keep in mind what you learned in today's Bible Blast: God's power and size is *much* greater than yours. It's amazing to think that God is so big the oceans fit in his hands and the earth is like a grain of sand compared to him. That doesn't mean the earth isn't important to him, but it does mean he's far more important and more powerful than anything or anyone on the earth.

Be happy today that your God is *gigantic* and he loves you sooo much!

Girl Gab: If you wrote a letter to God, what would it say? What questions would you ask? Today tell God how you feel about his power and bigness.

Prayer = Love

Bible Blast: Read Psalm 18:1-6

In my distress I cried out to the LORD; yes, I prayed to my God for help. He heard me from his sanctuary; my cry to him reached his ears. PSALM 18:6

Emma is a beautiful preteen girl. She has thick, gorgeous hair. Her smile is warm like a sunshiny day, and her eyes—oh my! They're the biggest, bluest eyes *ever*, and they sparkle behind her superadorable glasses. But even more than her outside, Emma has a stunningly beautiful heart.

Emma found out about a girl who was having some health problems. The girl's family didn't have a lot of money, so it was hard for her to get the medical help she needed. Emma went home and told her mom about it. Emma knew her church had money set aside to help people like her new friend. She had her parents call and offer that money to the girl's family. Emma even spoke to her teacher about it, hoping she could help.

All those things are fantastic! But Emma did one thing that was the most important thing she could do for that girl and her family. She started to pray. God actually worked out a way for Emma to get to know the girl and her family even better!

Don't catch yourself saying things like, "Well, all I can do is pray." Prayer is the absolute most amazingly powerful thing you can do! When you pray to God, you're going to the one with more power and love than anyone else and asking him to help. And since he's so full of love for you, he answers those prayers!

Your prayers for others don't need to be superlong and packed full of fancy words. Just talk to God. If you want God to heal someone, just ask God to heal that person. He can see your heart, and that's what matters the most.

Amazing Animals: Space Monkeys

Bible Blast: Read Judges 6:11-16

"I know the plans I have for you," says the LORD. "They are plans for good and not for disaster, to give you a future and a hope." JEREMIAH 29:11

Monkeys don't have dreams—not "I was in front of the class in my underwear" types of dreams, and not the kind of dreams that are like goals. Even if they have a nice tree-swinging image in their sleep, monkeys probably just wake up in their trees every morning and think about eating bananas.

Miss Baker and Able are two monkeys that may have simply dreamed about bananas, but they got a whole lot more. On May 28, 1959, they became the first monkeys to travel into space and back again successfully. Miss Baker was a little squirrel monkey, and Able was a rhesus monkey.

The whole space expedition only lasted about fifteen minutes, but during that time the little astronauts experienced nine minutes of weightlessness. Since they were strapped in, they didn't get to float around or anything, but I bet they thought it felt really weird!

When the space capsule was recovered and Miss Baker and Able appeared to be okay, everyone was excited. After relaxing in an air-conditioned room for a bit, the monkeys were sent off to a press conference! The whole world was interested in their space flight, because if Miss Baker and Able were able to fly into space and back again successfully, then it probably was possible for a human to go into space too.

That is exactly what happened. On April 12, 1961, a Russian guy named Yuri Gagarin became the first human to visit outer space and the first human to orbit the earth. Since then, hundreds of humans have gone into space.

Miss Baker and Able will always be two of the most famous monkeys in the world because of what they did. Two normal little monkeys. One day they're sitting in a tree. The next day they're changing the course of history.

No matter who you are or what you do, God can use you to do great things.

Girl Gab: What great thing do you dream of doing? What did your mom dream about doing when she was your age? Tell God that you want to do big things for him with your life.

29 October

Girl Gab: Does your family have any made-up words for things around the house? Ask God to give you patience and love for others who speak different languages.

Howdy, Pardner!

Bible Blast: Read Genesis 11:1-9

That is why the city was called Babel, because that is where the LORD confused the people with different languages. In this way he scattered them all over the world. GENESIS 11:9

Did you read the first verse of today's Bible Blast? It says, "At one time all the people of the world spoke the same language and used the same words."

That is so wild to think about, isn't it? *Everybody* in the entire world spoke the same language. That definitely made things easier for them as they built the huge tower to make themselves famous. But since God doesn't want people to focus on making themselves greater than everybody else, he intervened and made them speak different languages. This scattered those people all over the earth.

Languages are so interesting. Most people learn to speak the languages spoken by their parents and neighbors. Sometimes people make up language as they go along—like the cowboys did. Did you know they had different cowboy words for common everyday things? Here's a little cowboy language quiz for you. Try to figure out what cowboys were saying when they said these words:

1. "hot rock"
2. "splatter dabs"
3. "dough-wrangler"

The answers are on the left, but here's a hint for some of the words: Maybe for breakfast tomorrow morning you can ask the dough-wrangler to fix up some splatter dabs and hot rocks!

If you meet someone who speaks a different language or has trouble speaking your first language, don't just ignore her or make fun of her. Put yourself in her shoes. (That means, try to think about how it would feel to be that person.)

It does take a little more work to be friends with someone who speaks a different language, but reach out to and love that stranger, just like Jesus would.

Answers: 1. biscuit 2. pancakes 3. a cook

It's a Snake! No, It's a Moth?

Bible Blast: Read Acts 2:42-47

Your love for one another will prove to the world that you are my disciples. JOHN 13:35

Do you know how to tell the difference between a butterfly and a moth? I used to think that butterflies were pretty and colorful and moths were ugly and plain, but that's not necessarily true.

Butterflies rest with their wings held high, while the wings of a moth lie flat when the moth is sitting still. Moths have fatter bodies than butterflies, and moths' antennae can be all sorts of different sizes and shapes. Since moths are mostly active at night, those feathery feelers help them find food and other moths to hang out with. Butterflies have antennae, too, but they're simpler because, since they flutter around during the day, they can also use their eyesight to get around.

While it is a fact that moths are usually less exciting to look at than butterflies, that's not *always* true. Take the Atlas moth, for example. It's found in Southeast Asia and is known to be the world's largest moth, with a wingspan of up to twelve inches! The Atlas moth got its name because the pattern on its wings resembles a map. This moth is also called the Snake's Head moth since the tip of its wings looks a lot like the head of a snake, complete with an eye. The fake snake heads help scare off predators.

Christians have a "pattern" that helps people tell the difference between them and people who don't follow Christ. That pattern is called *love*. Before Jesus was crucified, he told his disciples that their love for each other would let others know they were his disciples. What do you think about that? That sounds as if Christians should be going nuts expressing their love for each other, don't you think?

All through the Bible, you'll find the command to love each other. When we love each other, we are loving God. In a world where people aren't loving one other very well, others are going to notice when we love the way Jesus wants us to.

Do you have the mark of love on *your* wings?

Girl Gab: What would be another good pattern for a moth to have on its wings to get rid of predators? Ask God to give you his love for others as you go about your day.

31 October

No More Darkness

Bible Blast: Read 2 Corinthians 6:14-18

What harmony can there be between Christ and the devil? How can a believer be a partner with an unbeliever?
2 CORINTHIANS 6:15

Girl Gab: With your mom, pray for your neighbors and friends today. Ask that the light of Jesus would shine into their homes and give them hope. Talk to your mom about your family's view of Halloween. Ask questions and decide together if anything should change in how you approach this day.

Unless you haven't gone anywhere for the past month, you've seen the same things I have all over the place. Witches, ghosts, goblins, mummies, spiders, monsters, and all sorts of spooky decorations fill the stores and people's yards. Halloween is here. Whether you participate in trick-or-treating or not, those images can be really freaky.

I jump a little when I turn the corner in a store to find a cackling witch doll staring at me. I have to be careful not to get stuck watching one of the über-scary movies they're playing on TV so I don't have bad dreams. I make a choice not to take part in the scary stories on the news or in the paper. There's a reason why all of that makes us feel uncomfortable. You weren't created for that kind of darkness.

In today's Bible Blast you read about how light can't have anything to do with darkness. So who is "light"? You are. In Matthew 5:14-16 Jesus says, "You are the light of the world." If you are light, then the things of darkness should make you uncomfortable. The Spirit inside of you can't hang out with dark stuff.

Also, you represent life. In John 14:6, Jesus says that he is the way, the truth, and the life. He is life, and you are his follower. Tombstones and mummies have nothing to do with light and life. Halloween decor is all about darkness and death.

So what do you do when there are spooky things all over the place? The best thing you can do is pray. I always pray that God would protect my mind, because I don't like to be scared. You can also pray that people in your neighborhood just wouldn't put the scary decorations out this year. But most importantly, you can pray that Jesus' light in you would shine more brightly than anything else so that your friends wouldn't be attracted to darkness and death stuff. Instead, they would run toward the light and life they see in you.

That's Quite a Name

Bible Blast: Read Isaiah 9:6-7

He will be called: Wonderful Counselor, Mighty God,
Everlasting Father, Prince of Peace. ISAIAH 9:6

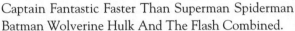

Captain Fantastic Faster Than Superman Spiderman Batman Wolverine Hulk And The Flash Combined.

That's the new name of George Garratt from England, who changed his name when he was nineteen. He had it legally changed to that thirteen-word wonder because he wanted to be unique, but people just call him Captain or Captain Fantastic.

In Isaiah 9 we see that Jesus' name is actually a lot longer than that. The book of Isaiah was written hundreds of years before Jesus would be born. The verses about his birth and his name were a prophecy. A prophecy is when God gives a message about something that is going to happen even before anyone knows anything about it. God was saying, "I'm going to send my Son, and this is what his name will be:

> Wonderful Counselor,
> Mighty God,
> Everlasting Father,
> Prince of Peace."

Those are some awesome names. We know that he really lives up to every single one of those names.

He counsels us.
His might and strength fight for us.
His "daddy's heart" for us never goes away.
His peace is available to us 24/7.

Knowing God's names really comes in handy during times of prayer and worship. When you see one of God's names in the Bible, stop for a moment and ask God what that name means. His names aren't empty and boastful. They have real meaning.

Girl Gab: Of the names of Jesus we talked about in the devo, which one means the most to you right now? Use that name in a prayer to him today.

Addy's Eyes

Bible Blast: Read 1 John 4:7-12

God is love. 1 JOHN 4:8

Addy's family planned to go on a cruise for a special vacation one year. Addy made some new friends in the Kids Club on the big ship and had a ton of fun. One friend Addy made was Melinda. Melinda had Down syndrome, a disorder that can make people look a little different and keep them from maturing as quickly as other kids. For one of the activities, Melinda was the designated writer for the project the kids were working on. She had a difficult time writing well, and the other kids started making fun of her. Melinda went to sit on the beanbags, and Addy went with her. They played together the rest of the afternoon.

Later Addy told her mom, "It doesn't matter what you can or can't do. It matters who you are." Addy knew God loved Melinda, and that meant she would love Melinda too.

In 2 Samuel 9, we see King David's having the same kind of eyesight that Addy had. When David became king, he found out that one of the former king's grandsons was still alive. He immediately sent for him. His name was (are you ready for this?) Mephibosheth. When Mephibosheth arrived, he was pretty nervous because it was common in those days for the whole family of the ex-king to be killed. David told him not to be afraid. He gave Mephibosheth his own land and told him that he would be brought to the palace to eat with the king regularly.

Here's something that makes this story a lot like Addy's. Mephibosheth was crippled in both legs. By today's terms, he was disabled. Back in those times, a handicapped person would have a difficult, if not impossible, time making a living. But David blessed Mephibosheth with land and good, solid meals for the rest of his life—even though Mephibosheth was the grandson of his former enemy.

When someone has a disease, disorder, or disability, life can be really difficult for that person. A little bit of kindness and love can go a long way to help someone feel important and special.

Sweet Water

Bible Blast: Read Exodus 15:22-27

He himself bore our sins in his body on the tree, so that we might die to sins and live for righteousness; by his wounds you have been healed. 1 PETER 2:24 (NIV)

It's November, and no matter where you live, the air is probably getting colder at night. Maybe you even have snow on the ground already. Do you remember just a couple of months ago, when you were complaining about how hot it was? On those really, really steamy days, all you wanted was to sit somewhere cool and sip an ice-cold drink, like a tall glass of freshly made iced tea.

Now, for you southern girls, iced tea has a very specific meaning. It's *sweet* tea. If you've never had sweet tea, I promise you that stirring a packet of sugar into a cold glass of tea is nothing like real southern sweet tea. To make sweet tea, the sugar is added to the tea after it's been brewed on the stove while it's still hot. That way the sugar completely dissolves into the tea and stays dissolved even after the tea has cooled off. It's great because you don't have to stir the tea up every time you drink it. Some people can't handle sweet tea because it really is very, very sweet, almost like syrup! And so yummy!

God gave Moses a recipe for turning the bitter water at Marah into sweet water. The recipe was simple; all Moses had to do was throw a tree in the water. It worked. The water turned sweet and good to drink. The Bible doesn't explain what kind of tree it was, but God somehow empowered that tree to heal the water so the people could drink.

I can think of another tree that heals bitter, yucky things. In the focus verse you'll see that sometimes the cross is called a "tree." Crosses were made of wood from a tree. When Jesus died on that tree and rose again, people could be set free from sin and healed through their faith in Jesus. That tree has the power to turn anybody's bitter water into something sweet and good, which is another way of saying that God can take any bad situation and make something wonderful come out of it.

Whether you drink sweet tea or unsweetened tea, Jesus hung on the tree to bring you freedom through faith in him.

Girl Gab: If you and your mom usually make sweet tea, make a big pitcher of it and take it to a friend with a bright summery note attached to it. If you've never made it, check out our recipe for sweet tea in the Wacky Appendix, and make some for dinner tonight. Talk about your favorite memories from the summertime with your family.

Girl Gab: If you have been to a parade, what's your favorite part? The horses? The clowns? The bands? The baton twirlers? Or *the candy*? Make a commitment to follow God today, just like the Israelites followed his fire.

I Love a Parade!

Bible Blast: Read Exodus 40:34-38

Whenever the cloud lifted from the Tabernacle, the people of Israel would set out on their journey, following it. EXODUS 40:36

Thanksgiving, that great time of eating and being thankful is just a few weeks away. When your family is preparing the day's feast, do you turn the TV on? Our family loves to watch the Macy's Thanksgiving Day Parade!

The Macy's Thanksgiving parade is one of the biggest parades in the United States, but it began as just a small celebration. In the 1920s, many of the people who worked at the Macy's department store in New York City were immigrants from Europe. They were really proud to be Americans and wanted to celebrate the American holiday in a European way. They dressed up as clowns, knights, cowboys, and other things. They made floats, and they even brought some animals from the zoo! So many people showed up to watch the parade that Macy's decided to sponsor the parade every year.

Have you seen those huge balloons that float through the streets during the parade? They used to let those balloons go at the end of the parade. Whoever found the balloon could mail it back and receive a gift from the Macy's store. They don't do that anymore, but I think it would be so cool to find a giant Mickey Mouse in the backyard!

Now imagine you're in the desert somewhere outside of Egypt sitting in a camp chair in the evening. Suddenly you see something coming up over the hill. It's a huge pillar of fire! And following the great fire are thousands of people with their tents, animals, and children! You ask your dad, "What is that fire?" He replies, "God is in that fire, and he is leading all of those people to freedom!"

That would be the most magnificent parade *ever*! God led the Israelite people with a huge cloud during the day and a huge pillar of fire at night so that everyone could see it and would know which direction to go.

God is leading you, too. Every day as you obey him, he's leading you to the places he needs you to be.

Mighty Men

Bible Blast: Read 2 Samuel 23:8-12

Walk with the wise and become wise; associate with fools and get in trouble. PROVERBS 13:20

I bet any guy would love to be called a "Mighty Man." That's what David called members of a special group of guys that surrounded him to protect him and help him defeat his enemies. They were strong warriors and champions. The Bible lists the amazing things those men had done in battle to earn the right to be one of David's Mighty Men. If you don't like battle-scene stuff, you may not like reading this very much, but the stories are incredible!

The Mighty Men were guys David could rely on and trust to fight for him and for the Lord. They were committed to David and his safety. More than likely, the Mighty Men were some really big dudes.

Who do you rely on? Do you have a team of Mighty Girls who do great things for God and love you very much? Do your closest friends encourage you to

- shop for modest clothes?
- not be boy-crazy?
- get into God's Word?
- be respectful to your teachers and parents?
- listen to music that honors God?
- exercise and eat healthy foods?
- always tell the truth?
- pray about everything?

If you want to live a life that pleases God, you definitely need at least one awesome Mighty Girl in your life. Just like Proverbs 13:20 says, if you hang out with wise girls, you'll become wise too. But if the girls you hang with do foolish things, you will too. That could get you into a lot of trouble.

David knew he needed some awesome people in his life, and you do too. Every girl who wants to follow Jesus needs some Mighty Girls to walk with her and fight for her. Are you a Mighty Girl?

Girl Gab: Have an arm wrestling match with your mom, Mighty Girl! If your mom beats you right away, you get to use both arms for the next match! Remember to keep your elbows on the table! Pray with your mom that God would give you both Mighty Girl friends.

Snow-woman

Bible Blast: Read Psalm 147:16-18

He sends the snow like white wool; he scatters frost upon the ground like ashes. PSALM 147:16

Girl Gab: How often do you go outside? I know it might be cold right now, but decide to bundle up and go outside today if you can. Maybe you can take the dog for a walk or go on a short prayer walk where you just talk to God. Thank God for his pretty creations.

When I read today's verse, I couldn't help but try to picture God in heaven getting ready to send snow. Of course, my imagination isn't the least bit scientific. I just think it's fun to imagine God gathering up a bunch of white, fluffy snow in his great big arms. Then maybe he takes in a deep, God-sized breath and gently blows the snow so that it falls onto the earth.

God sends so much snow to the town of Bethel, Maine, that they decided to do something extraordinary with it. So in 2008 they built the world's tallest snow-*woman*. She's 122 feet tall! To give you an idea of how tall that is, the Statue of Liberty is 151 feet from the base to the torch.

This gigantic snow-woman's name is Olympia. She was named after Maine's United States Senator, Olympia *Snowe*. (That's her real last name!) It took thirteen million pounds of snow to create Olympia. She had five-foot wreaths for eyes, and they used sixteen snow skis for eyelashes! Her scarf was 130 feet long, and instead of using sticks for arms, they used trees! To make sure the snow-lady had some bling, the people of Bethel gave Olympia a six-foot snowflake pendant to wear around her neck.

The sad thing about snowmen and snow-women is that since they're made of snow, they do eventually melt. Olympia the Snow-woman melted completely by July of 2008. I wonder what happened when thirteen million pounds of snow melted. Was there a flood?

God loves giving us things to enjoy—like snow. Or if you don't live in a place where you get snow, I bet you can think of things God has created around you that you enjoy like water, sand, trees, or flowers. Get out there and do something fun with it. Go swimming or fishing! Make sand angels! Build a tree fort! Pick a bouquet of flowers, or make a flower tiara for your hair!

Dive into the beautiful things God has placed all around you!

Little and Big Choices

Bible Blast: Read Genesis 3:1-6

When Adam sinned, sin entered the world. Adam's sin brought death, so death spread to everyone, for everyone sinned.
ROMANS 5:12

We don't always understand how one little decision we make can turn into something much, much bigger.

When Adam and Eve decided to eat from that tree they might have thought, *It's just a piece of fruit. What harm could it bring if we ate it?* The moment Eve took that bite, though, was the first time a human disobeyed God. With that first disobedient step, sin came into our world.

When we think about the message of God sending his Son, Jesus, to the earth to die for our sins, we don't always include Adam and Eve as part of that story, but they're a big part of the gospel. If sin had never entered the world through the first couple, Jesus never would have needed to come and give his life to provide a way for people to be forgiven for their sins. If no one had ever sinned, we would still be living in a perfect world with no death or sin. But God will restore us to a perfect world, like Eden but better, when we get to heaven. In heaven we'll be totally connected to God, just like Adam and Eve were in the very beginning. That's something to look forward to!

Sometimes "little" choices can lead to bad things, and sometimes they can lead to really good things. Do you know who Neil Armstrong is? He's the first man ever to walk on the moon. The whole world waited while Neil made his way down the ladder to place his foot on the surface of the moon. When his feet touched the moon, he said, "That's one small step for a man, and one giant leap for mankind."

Neil Armstrong was right in what he said. His tiny little step onto the moon changed history.

The choices you make every day really do matter. The steps you take can lead to big things. Choose to obey God today and every day.

Girl Gab: Your mom can help you find video clips of Neil Armstrong and Buzz Aldrin on the moon. Ask God to help you resist temptation today.

Language Lab: What Are "Angels"?

Bible Blast: Read Luke 1:26-33

Don't forget to show hospitality to strangers, for some who have done this have entertained angels without realizing it!
HEBREWS 13:2

Angels are everywhere these days. Images of "angels" appear on plates, blankets, cups, shirts, bags, ornaments, and jewelry. Most of the time, the pictures people draw of angels show one of two things. Either the angel looks like a tall, long-haired person in a white robe with large wings, or the angel is represented by a tiny baby with little fluttery wings wearing a cloth diaper of some sort.

Let's look at what the Bible says about angels.

In the Bible the word for *angel* means "messengers." They are sent to give messages to people. In the Bible Blast today you read about one of the greatest messages an angel ever gave when he announced the birth of Jesus to Mary. All through the Bible you'll find stories of angels delivering messages to people from God.

The big question is, do angels really have wings?

The answer is that some definitely do. The two types of spiritual beings that are described as having wings are cherubim and seraphim. When God told Moses how he wanted the Ark of the Covenant built, he said to have two cherubim on it with their wings spread over it for protection (Exodus 25:20). In Isaiah 6, seraphim are described as having six wings each. Now, do God's other angels have wings? There's nothing saying that they specifically do, but they could.

There are so many wonderful stories about angels in the Bible. We could spend weeks just going through those verses and learning all sorts of cool things about angels. But the main thing I want you to learn today is this: Angels are definitely real, but you are not supposed to worship them. In Revelation 22, John bowed down to worship at an angel's feet, and do you know what the angel said to him? "No, don't worship me. I am a servant of God, just like you. . . . Worship only God!"

Pictures of angels are pretty, but don't be tempted to worship them. Like the angel said to John, worship only God.

Twelve Important Guys, Part 1

Bible Blast: Read Matthew 10:2-4

He said to his disciples, "The harvest is great, but the workers are few." MATTHEW 9:37

Jesus had twelve guys who followed him all over the place, learning from his teaching and helping him with his ministry of teaching and healing. These guys were called the "disciples." Jesus trained them to take over sharing the gospel after he was gone from the earth. The Bible Blast today lists the names of the disciples. Today and tomorrow you'll learn who they were and what they did.

Simon Peter was a fisherman. He's usually just called Peter in the Bible. Peter's name means "rock," which was perfect for him. He was strong and really pumped about following Jesus, but sometimes that caused him to do dumb things, like cutting off a soldier's ear when they were arresting Jesus. Peter was very bold about preaching the truth of Jesus.

Andrew was Peter's brother; he was a fisherman too. When Jesus called Peter and Andrew, they were fishing. Jesus called to them, "Follow me, and I will show you how to fish for people!" (Matthew 4:19). They dropped their nets and followed him.

James and his brother **John** were sons of a man named Zebedee. (There was another disciple named James, but we'll talk about him later.) Jesus called James and John the "Sons of Thunder." They were fishermen, too, and were sitting in a boat repairing their nets with their dad when Jesus called them to follow him. Peter, James, and John were three of the disciples who were close friends of Jesus.

Philip was a fisherman too! Now when I say fisherman, I mean fishing was their job. It's what they did to make money. Philip asked a lot of questions.

Bartholomew may have also been called Nathanael. If that's true, then he was someone Philip brought to Jesus. He didn't like Jesus at first because Jesus came from the town of Nazareth, and Nathanael had some prejudice against people from that town. It didn't take long for him to realize that Jesus really was the Son of God.

Girl Gab: Which of today's disciples have you heard of? Tell your mom if there's anything else you know about these disciples. Would you leave everything to follow Jesus as these men did?

Twelve Important Guys, Part 2

Bible Blast: Read Matthew 10:2-4

In the same way, any of you who does not give up everything he has cannot be my disciple. LUKE 14:33 (NIV)

Girl Gab: What do you think about the men Jesus chose to be his disciples? Are you surprised by any of them? It's a good idea to go over this info so you can remember who the twelve disciples were. You could do a little "Disciple Trivia" with the family over dinner. Bonus points to anyone who can remember who replaced Judas Iscariot!

Yesterday we ended our introduction to the disciples with Bartholomew. Let's keep working down that list!

Thomas doubted a lot. He wasn't quick to believe something was true. That's why you might hear someone say, "He's a doubting Thomas." When Jesus came back from the dead and his disciples saw him, Thomas didn't believe it was really Jesus until he touched his actual wounds.

Matthew was an interesting choice for a disciple because he was a tax collector. Tax collectors were hated because they were known to be wealthy, selfish men who stole money. When Matthew left his job to follow Jesus, he left behind his passion for riches and wealth. He wrote the Gospel of Matthew.

James the son of Alphaeus was one of Jesus' disciples, but we don't really know anything about him, except that he was one of the twelve.

Thaddaeus is another one we don't know much about. He was also called Judas, but he wasn't the same Judas who betrayed Jesus. We'll talk about that Judas in a minute.

Simon the Zealot got his name because he was a fighter. He wanted the Roman government to be gone, and he was passionate about it. That's what *zeal* means: "passion."

Judas Iscariot is definitely one of the most interesting disciples. Jesus allowed Judas to follow him as his disciple, knowing that one day he would be the one to hand Jesus over to be killed. Judas was greedy. The chief religious leaders paid him thirty pieces of silver to betray Jesus, which is exactly what he did. Later, in despair over what he'd done, he killed himself.

Now we've talked about twelve disciples, but we're not quite done. The disciples chose another follower of Jesus to make up the twelve, replacing Judas Iscariot. **Matthias** was the one chosen. You can read about him in Acts 1:21-26.

What an interesting group, huh? They were ordinary men who became extraordinary through Jesus.

What People Really Notice

Bible Blast: Read Acts 4:8-13

The members of the council were amazed when they saw the boldness of Peter and John, for they could see that they were ordinary men with no special training in the Scriptures. They also recognized them as men who had been with Jesus.
ACTS 4:13

Girl Gab: Do you believe your relationship with Jesus is the most important thing? Spend time with Jesus today.

You have to go to school. You may be able to get out of it a few days a year, but for the most part, it's something you have to do. I hope you have a lot of school days that you enjoy. Learning new things can be awesome.

Even though school is very important, there are some famous people who never went to college. Some of them never finished high school! Andrew Jackson didn't go to college, but he was the sixth president of the United States! Steven Spielberg directed or produced major movies like *Transformers* and *E.T.*, and he was actually rejected from film school!

When Peter and John stood in front of the council (leaders) who were upset with them for preaching about Jesus, the council leaders were amazed. Those two disciples were just normal guys who had never been through any official training or study of the Scriptures. But the council could tell that Peter and John had been with Jesus.

Isn't that the most important thing? Isn't that what people should notice about Christians more than anything else? Shouldn't others know that we've been with Jesus?

If you become a rich movie star who's known all around the world, none of that will matter at all if people don't know that you love Jesus more than anything.

If someday you have the honor of being a stay-at-home mom and you raise your children to be amazing inventors and your house is the cleanest house on the block and you lead Bible studies and prayer groups, none of that means anything if people don't see you as someone who's been with Jesus.

Being with Jesus and loving him is number one. Spend time getting to know him. Let him teach you about Scripture. Follow him wherever he leads. You can have the highest honor of being recognized as "someone who's been with Jesus."

Kickin' Kraft:
Happy Hair Clips!

(Check out p. 377 for a great mother-daughter craft that helps reinforce today's devo!)

Kickin' Kraft: Big Hair

Bible Blast: Read Isaiah 30:18-21

I want to do what is good, but I don't. I don't want to do what is wrong, but I do it anyway. ROMANS 7:19

I bet if I asked who your favorite singer was you wouldn't jump up and down and say, "Crystal Gayle! I love Crystal Gayle!" Crystal Gayle is one of the most famous country music stars of all time. She has a really clear, pretty voice, but if you saw her, what you'd probably notice first—and find amazing!—is her hair. Crystal's shiny brown hair is so long that if she were barefoot, her hair would touch the floor! It's more than five feet long! She often wears it down and brushed, not up in braids or in some kind of bun.

Crystal has had a lot of hit songs since 1970, and one of them was called "Wrong Road Again." It was a song about how she was going to go down the wrong road, even though she knew it was bad. It sounds like a boy problem to me. Maybe she had a boyfriend who wasn't good for her. Maybe he wasn't kind to her, or maybe he ignored her when she was around her friends. Even though he treated her selfishly, she still wanted to be with him so she just kept being his girlfriend.

I see girls of all ages do that all the time. Something like thirty percent of eleven-year-old girls have boyfriends! For crying out loud! They just want a boyfriend so badly they don't really care if he's even *nice* to them. Even though the girl knows that boy is dragging her down and making her feel bad, she keeps going down that "wrong road again."

If a boy doesn't really care for you, why would you want to be called his girlfriend? You're probably not allowed to go on dates now, but start praying now that God would keep you from falling for boys who don't love Jesus and don't treat you with care or kindness.

No Caffeine Needed

Bible Blast: Read Psalm 121:3-8

He who watches over Israel never slumbers or sleeps.
PSALM 121:4

When a woodchuck hibernates from October to February, his heart rate drops from about eighty beats per minute down to about four beats per minute! His body temperature drops from 98 degrees to 38 degrees. Did you know that a woodchuck's front teeth never stop growing? That's why they always gnaw on wood—to keep them down. Yet when a woodchuck is hibernating, God stops those teeth from growing! Our Creator thought of everything.

Some animals need an extra dose of sleep, especially during the winter. God created these animals to go into a time of deep sleep, or hibernation, during the cold months as a way of dealing with the lack of food. Before hibernation begins, the animal eats like crazy to store up fat in its body to keep it alive while it sleeps. Then it finds a cozy spot to get some major beauty rest.

Knowing that God never sleeps is so comforting. It would be horrible if I needed to talk to him about something really important and he had a "Do Not Disturb" sign hanging on his door!

God doesn't need to rest in order to stay strong and healthy. Right now you might be thinking, *But after God created the world, it says he rested on that seventh day.* Yes, that's true. But that word rest isn't saying that he was exhausted and just couldn't hold his head up anymore so he napped on the couch for a day. It means that his work was done, so he stopped to enjoy his creation. He was setting an example that we need to take a day when we don't work.

Humans and animals need rest and sleep. If we don't get enough sleep we can have problems thinking clearly, we get upset easily, and we're more likely to get sick. Did you know getting enough sleep helps you grow?

The next time you notice your cat sleeping in a patch of sun, or you see your little sister yawn, be reminded that God is always awake and paying attention to your life.

Girl Gab: Do you think you would like to hibernate? What would some of the positives and negatives be if humans slept through the winter? Praise God that he never snoozes!

Bible Blast: Read Psalm 32:8-10

Do not be like a senseless horse or mule that needs a bit and bridle to keep it under control. PSALM 32:9

Girl Gab: Do you think you're "stubborn as a mule"? If so, ask your mom what you can do to become more "teachable." Talk to God about wanting to do the right thing in every situation.

A couple from Montana went for a ride on their mules out on the open range. Their dogs followed close behind. It was common for them to run into a mountain lion on their rides, so the man took a rifle. Sometimes just shooting a gun straight up into the air was enough to scare the mountain lions away.

On this particular day, a mountain lion decided it wanted one of the dogs for a snack. When the man realized the mountain lion was following them, he hopped off his mule and raised his gun in the air to scare the predator away. Before the man could shoot, the mountain lion raced after the dogs. And then the mule raced after the mountain lion!

That stubborn mule attacked the mountain lion before it ever even got to the dogs! The dogs just stood and watched while the mule fought the mountain lion, making sure it wouldn't attack anybody. The woman had brought her camera and actually got a few pictures of their mule hero in action. After the fight was over, the mule calmly walked over and stood by its owner, like fighting a mountain lion was no big deal. He was ready for his ride now.

That story circulated on the Internet. There are even photographs of the mule and the mountain lion. Some have said the story isn't possible, even if there are pictures to support it. Whether or not it is true, the story sure does tell us a little bit about just how stubbornness can come in handy when used for something good!

The mule did the right thing without anyone telling it to. That's what today's focus verse is all about. God wants you to get to a point where you naturally do what God wants you to without someone else dragging you into it. As you become more mature and learn more about his Word, obeying God will become a normal part of your thoughts and actions. You may not have to fight off any mountain lions, but God will definitely use you to do big, courageous things!

Are You Awake?

Bible Blast: Read Romans 13:8-12

This is all the more urgent, for you know how late it is; time is running out. Wake up, for our salvation is nearer now than when we first believed. ROMANS 13:11

Are you a morning person? Do you hop out of bed right away because you can't wait to start the day? Do you set your alarm to get up a little earlier because you want to read or do a craft? It's great if you're a person who loves the mornings, but not everyone is like that. Some people sleep right through regular alarm clock buzzing, so they have to get a clock with a little more kick. As it turns out, there are a lot of funky alarms to choose from.

What's better than waking to the smell of bacon cooking on the stove? You can get an alarm clock that actually cooks bacon for you. You put a piece of frozen bacon in it before bed at night, and it will start cooking ten minutes before you want to get up.

"Clocky" is an alarm clock that rolls off your nightstand and looks for a place to hide in the room if you don't get up right away to turn off his alarm. You have to get up and find him to make him stop buzzing.

If neither of those alarm clocks gets you out of bed on time, maybe you need something more "shocking." That's right; you can get a clock that shocks your hand every time you hit the snooze button. Apparently it's harmless, but what a horrible way to wake up!

Waking up can be hard, but we have to do it. We even need to wake up in our relationship with God because Jesus is coming back and time is running short. Just think! If we thought Jesus was coming back tomorrow, how would we live today? That's how we should live every day. It's kind of like getting your chores done *now* because your mom's going to be home soon. You're going to make sure they're done, right?

Obey God's Word today and every day. Then when Jesus comes back, you'll be ready.

Girl Gab: If it's hard for you to get out of bed in the morning, talk to your mom about what you can do to change that. Maybe you need to put your alarm clock on the other side of the room so you have to get out from under the comfy covers to stop its ringing. Ask Jesus to help you live as if he's coming back today.

Girl Gab: If you are a twin, how does this encourage you today? Talk to your mom about that. Love on your twin today! If you know twins, pray that they will enjoy being themselves.

Totally Unique

Bible Blast: Read Genesis 25:21-26

As the boys grew up, Esau became a skillful hunter. He was an outdoorsman, but Jacob had a quiet temperament, preferring to stay at home. GENESIS 25:27

Are you a twin? Do you know twins? It always blows my mind when I meet twins. If they're physically identical, I can't believe my eyes. It's amazing that two people could look so much alike. If they're not identical twins, I'm stunned at how two people born at the same time could look so different from each other. Twins truly are incredible.

Being a twin can be so much fun, but it can also be really challenging. Twins are often dressed alike, have similar names, and share everything. So when they get older and want to express themselves as individuals, it can be difficult to figure out just what they really like or don't like. They love having a twin, but they also want to be themselves.

Have you heard of Mary-Kate and Ashley Olsen? They took turns playing the character Michelle Tanner on the TV show *Full House*. For years they've been known as "The Olsen Twins," but now that they're adults, they don't want to be called that. They have different interests and gifts and want to be known for who they are as individual women.

Jacob and Esau are the first twins mentioned in the Bible. I love that, before they were even born, God told Rebekah (their mom) that the two boys each had a special purpose in becoming two nations that wouldn't get along. He didn't say that together they would lead a nation and they would never be separated and they would do everything the exact same way at the same time for the rest of their same lives. No, in fact, if you read on to verse 27, it tells just how different those two boys were. "As the boys grew up, Esau became a skillful hunter. He was an outdoorsman, but Jacob had a quiet temperament, preferring to stay at home."

Being a twin is wonderful. It's something to be enjoyed, but it's also important to know that just because you're a twin, it doesn't mean that you're not a very special, totally unique person.

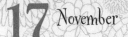

Meditation Moment: Psalm 119:105-112

Your word is a lamp to guide my feet and a light for my path.
PSALM 119:105

Conrad Hubert was the first person to bring flashlights into the world in 1903. To test them out, he gave a bunch of flashlights to some police officers to use while they patrolled the streets of New York City at night. The officers found the portable lights to be really helpful for their work. Now most people have a flashlight of some sort in their home, car, purse, or even on their keychain. I have a flashlight application on my iPhone! It's good always to have a light handy that you don't have to plug into an electrical outlet.

Psalm 119:105 says that God's Word is like a powerful source of light. It's always ready to show us which direction we should go. As you meditate on God's Word today, remember to ask God to speak to you before you dive in. As you read this psalm, you will notice how passionately the psalm writer loves God's Word. When the psalm mentions God's "laws" or "decrees," those are all references to the Scriptures. Take a moment to just focus on this section of Psalm 119, and then wait to see what God speaks to you about it through an idea, thought, picture, or anything else. Remember to write down what God teaches you, if you would like.

Girl Gab: If you have a flashlight handy, grab your mom, and talk to her about today's Scripture. Do it with all the lights off except for the flashlight.

18 November

Confusion-B-Gone!

Bible Blast: Read Proverbs 3:5-6

God is not a God of disorder but of peace, as in all the meetings of God's holy people. 1 CORINTHIANS 14:33

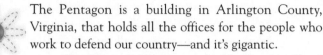

Girl Gab: What's the biggest building you and your mom have ever been to? Was it easy to find your way around or difficult? Tell God that you are choosing to trust him during confusing times.

The Pentagon is a building in Arlington County, Virginia, that holds all the offices for the people who work to defend our country—and it's gigantic.

The Pentagon sits on two hundred acres of land and has sixteen parking lots, which hold about 8,770 cars. It has more than 4,000 clocks, 691 water fountains, and 284 bathrooms. One of the really interesting factoids about the Pentagon is that it has seventeen-and-a-half *miles* of hallways! In spite of that, it only takes seven minutes for a person to walk from one point to any other point in the building!

I could see myself getting lost in a building like that, especially if I had to figure out where the seventeen miles of hallways led! Maybe I could leave a trail of breadcrumbs behind me so I could find my way out again. Big buildings like the Pentagon can be really confusing places to hang out, unless they have great signs and guides to help you find your way.

Like 1 Corinthians 14:33 says, God isn't the one who creates confusion. If a situation becomes crazy, you can know something isn't right. God clears up confusion if we let him.

Sometimes our lives feel twisted, whirly, and loopy when things happen that we don't understand, especially things like divorce, death, sickness, and fighting. Those things feel so confusing, don't they? But God wants you to trust in him with all of your heart so he can make those paths straight.

He may not tell you right away exactly why it's happening, but he can give you peace that he still has you in his hands and that he's not going to let go. He can give you trustworthy people to talk to and pray with when you're confused.

The Bible is a great tool for chasing away confusing thoughts, too. Even if you read something that doesn't seem to have anything to do with what you're going through, its truth can bring peace. If you find yourself overwhelmed by miles and miles of hallways, God is the perfect Guide to help you find your way.

Amazing Animals: The Four-Eyed Frog

Bible Blast: Read 2 Corinthians 4:16-18

We don't look at the troubles we can see now; rather, we fix our gaze on things that cannot be seen. For the things we see now will soon be gone, but the things we cannot see will last forever.
2 CORINTHIANS 4:18

Does it ever seem that your mom must have eyes on the back of her head? While it may feel as if she sees everything, she probably doesn't actually have four eyeballs. (If you're not sure, go ahead and check the back of her head right now!)

So if your mom doesn't have four eyes, is it possible for a *frog* to have four eyes? The gray four-eyed frog lives way down in Chile and other parts of South America. It's a cute little animal with two glands that look just like big eyes on its back end. When the frog is threatened by a predator, it tucks its head down, spins around, and sticks its rear up in the face of the bad guy. Sometimes this intimidates the attacker into leaving the frog alone. But if that doesn't work, the four-eyed frog has another secret trick. Those "eyes" release a bit of yucky-tasting poison if something bites them. That sends the predator running away looking for something tastier to eat!

The gray four-eyed frog isn't the only animal that has a set of fake eyes. Many fish, snakes, butterflies, moths, beetles, and caterpillars have some kind of pattern on them to look like an extra set of eyes. It's a fantastic weapon for animals that may not have other ways to defend themselves.

All this talk about eyeballs has got me thinking. What should we be looking at? Whether you have one eye or thousands of eyes like some butterflies do, all our eyes should be focused on just one type of thing: things that last forever.

If your mind spends all its time worrying about bad things going on around you, it will be very easy to get totally sad. God wants us to spend more time focusing on him and his promise of heaven. When we do that, we'll be full of hope, and that hope will attract other people to Jesus.

So keep your eyes open—just make sure they're eyeballin' the right things!

Girl Gab: If you had an extra pair of eyes that really worked, where would you want them to be? On your elbows? How about your knees? What if you had one big eye on the top of each of your big toes? Weird! Focus on "forever things" today.

20 November

Strong like a Tree

Bible Blast: Read John 17:20-22

I pray that they will all be one, just as you and I are one—as you are in me, Father, and I am in you. And may they be in us so that the world will believe you sent me. JOHN 17:21

It can be difficult to get along with others, even if they're Christians. Maybe in order to be more loving toward others, we need to be more tree-like. Let me show you what I mean.

There is a 107-acre patch of land in Utah that is covered in tree. That's right. I mean "tree," not "trees." It *looks* like the area is full of thousands of white-trunked trees called quaking aspens. (That name comes from the fact that their leaves shake really easily in the breeze.) The interesting thing about this patch of trees is they are actually all connected to each other. Scientists have discovered that they all share the same root system, and all the trees are exact clones of each other. So instead of it being thousands of trees, it's actually a colony of forty-seven thousand stems off the same root. They figure if you could weigh the whole thing, it would weigh more than six thousand tons. Some people call this colony of stems "*Pando*," which means "I spread" in Latin.

How can Pando help us learn to love others?

John 15:5 describes Jesus as the vine, while we are the branches. Sounds a lot like a "root system," doesn't it? If he is the vine that all the branches are connected to, then we all have the same power source, and we're all growing from the same place, right? When you meet someone who's a Christian, it's very important to remember that she is connected to the same Jesus you're connected to. That doesn't mean she's perfect and you'll be best friends forever, but it does mean that she is your sister in Christ. If you discover a new "holy sister," then you have a responsibility to love her by treating her like you would want to be treated.

For Christians, being connected by the same "root" means you both serve the same God and he loves you both the same. If Jesus loves somebody and Jesus lives inside of you, then you have the ability to love that person too.

Girl Gab: Is there a Christian person you know who's very difficult for you to get along with? How can you show love to that person? Ask your mom what she does when she wants to love someone she doesn't like very much.

Kickin' Kraft: The Glad Game

Bible Blast: Read 1 Chronicles 16:8-12

Give thanks for everything to God the Father in the name of our Lord Jesus Christ. EPHESIANS 5:20

Pollyanna is a classic novel written in 1913. It's all about a little girl who has to live with her wealthy but cold-hearted Aunt Polly in the town of Beldingsville, Vermont. Living with Aunt Polly would be really hard for most young girls, but not for Pollyanna because she plays the Glad Game. Pollyanna and her dad were poor, and their Christmas presents would come as donations from others. One year when Pollyanna was really hoping for a doll for Christmas, the only donation they received was a pair of crutches. Her dad immediately made up the Glad Game, a game that challenges the player to think of something to be thankful for even if it's hard. Pollyanna's dad looked at the crutches and said that she could be glad about those crutches because she doesn't need them. This began a habit of looking at the good side of things everywhere Pollyanna went.

So when Aunt Polly made Pollyanna sleep in the attic with no pictures on the walls or rugs on the floors, Pollyanna was glad for the beautiful view from her window. Her positive view of life soon spread throughout the whole town of Beldingsville, and her spirit of thankfulness really changed people's lives. Eventually even mean Aunt Polly gave in to the Glad Game, and her heart softened as she learned to love again.

Pollyanna learned a big lesson about being thankful when she had an accident, but I'm not going to tell you what happens. You'll have to read it for yourself!

Thanksgiving is right around the corner, and it's a great time to play the Glad Game! Today's Kickin' Kraft will help you get started!

Kickin' Kraft:
Pollyanna's Thanksgiving Turkey!

(Check out p. 377 for a great mother-daughter craft that helps reinforce today's devo!)

Bible Blast: Read Isaiah 26:2-4

I am leaving you with a gift—peace of mind and heart. And the peace I give is a gift the world cannot give. So don't be troubled or afraid. JOHN 14:27

When peace, like a river attendeth my way,
When sorrows like sea billows roll;
Whatever my lot, thou hast taught me to say,
It is well, it is well with my soul.

These words are the first verse of the well-known hymn "It Is Well," written by Horatio Spafford back in the 1800s. The words by themselves are beautiful and challenging; they remind us that no matter what happens, we have peace in Christ. But when you know the story behind these words, they mean so much more.

Horatio Spafford lived in Chicago with his wife, Anna, and their four daughters and one son. One year, the Spaffords decided to vacation in Europe, but right before they were to set sail, Horatio had to take care of some business. He told Anna to take their four daughters and go ahead of him. He would leave a few days later to meet them in Europe. So Anna and the girls boarded the SS *Ville du Havre* and began the journey across the ocean.

Along the way, the SS *Ville du Havre* was struck by another ship, and it sank very quickly, killing many people. Anna Spafford survived, but all four daughters drowned. Anna sent a telegram to her husband that read, "Saved alone."

Horatio made arrangements to get on a ship and bring his wife back to Chicago. As he sailed, the captain came to him at one point to tell him that they were going over the location where the SS *Ville du Havre* had sunk. As Horatio looked across the water, he was inspired to write the words to "It Is Well."

When our hearts belong to Jesus, peace is always there for us. We know that no matter what happens, good or bad, nothing can take Jesus or heaven from us. Horatio Spafford knew his girls were in heaven, and that gave him great peace.

Girl Gab: If you have a hymnal, look up the rest of the verses to "It Is Well." If you don't have one, go ahead and look them up online. Talk about what those words must have meant to Horatio and Anna Spafford.

Don't Waste Time

Bible Blast: Read Ecclesiastes 12:1-4

Don't let the excitement of youth cause you to forget your Creator. Honor him in your youth before you grow old and say, "Life is not pleasant anymore." ECCLESIASTES 12:1

Do you know what a "centenarian" is? It's a person who has lived to be at least a hundred years old. More and more people are living to be a century old. Right now the United States has more centenarians than any other country with about seventy-two thousand of them.[3] Everyone wants to know what it takes to live that long. Although there's no definite formula for living to one hundred, there are some things that come up when centenarians are interviewed about their lives.

Most of those century-old people keep their brains fresh by doing crossword puzzles, games, and jigsaw puzzles. A lot of them play instruments or dance, and most of them don't smoke. In general, most people who live to be one hundred don't stop enjoying life.

It's fun to think about getting older, but it's actually more important to God for you to think about your life right now. The Bible Blast today is a great chunk of wisdom for young people. Instead of waiting to live for God when you're older, this verse urges you to live for God right now! It's possible to get so caught up in all the fun things you want to do now that you forget about God. Do you see the danger in that?

If you get into a lifestyle of remembering God now while you're young, then when you're older, you won't regret the days of your youth. You won't be sitting on your deck at the age of 102 saying, "I really wish I had given Jesus my whole life back when I was eleven. I could have done anything for him with all that strength and energy!"

How do you "remember your Creator"? Spend time with him. Communicate with him and learn from him. Obey what he tells you to do. Get outside, and enjoy the things he's created, and, above all else, love!

Whether you live to be one hundred or not, you do have this day. Remember your Creator today!

---

3 See http://www.thecentenarian.co.uk/how-many-people-live-to-hundred-across-the-globe.html.

Girl Gab: Do you know any centenarians? Has anyone in your extended family lived to be one hundred? Do you think you would want to be around for a whole century? Tell God that you want to serve him completely today.

24 November

Take Time to Give Thanks

Bible Blast: Read Luke 17:11-19

One of them, when he saw that he was healed, came back to Jesus, shouting, "Praise God!" LUKE 17:15

Girl Gab: Talk to your mom about prayers you've seen God answer. Get excited together, and thank God for those answers!

Leprosy is a disease that covers a person's skin in painful sores. Before medicine was made to treat it, this disease was really contagious, so "healthy" people didn't go near lepers and certainly never touched them. During Bible times, lepers were treated as if they weren't even human.

There are several stories of God healing people from leprosy in the Bible, like in today's Bible Blast. There's one in Matthew 8 that tells how a leper knelt before Jesus and asked to be healed. It says that "Jesus reached out and touched him" and the man was healed. You have to understand: Nobody touched a leper. Nobody.

But Jesus did.

The story you read in Luke 17 today is so interesting. Can you picture ten outcast people with a terrible skin disease calling out to Jesus? They didn't even come close to him. They called to him from "a distance." He told them to go see their priests, and they were healed as they went on their way.

One guy was so amazed at his healed, clean, pure skin, he ran to Jesus, giving praise to God. He fell down in front of Jesus and thanked him for answering his prayer for healing.

Here's an interesting tidbit for you: If a person was healed of leprosy, the law said he had to go to his priest, who would pronounce the person "clean" so he could hang out with everyone else again. That's why Jesus told the ten lepers to head to their priests. Okay, here's the cool thing: The fifth chapter of Hebrews tells us that Jesus is our High Priest, meaning he's the one who pronounces us clean before God. So while the other nine lepers went to their priests, the tenth guy went directly to the High Priest, who was Jesus Christ! And Jesus gave him a new label of "clean."

When God answers prayers, it gives our faith a boost, and we feel like we're on top of the world. But make sure you take the time to go to Jesus and say, "Thank you."

Job's Job

Bible Blast: Read Job 1:20-22

In all of this, Job did not sin by blaming God. JOB 1:22

The book of Job starts off with a conversation between the Lord and the devil. When God remarked about how faithful and sinless Job was, the devil said, "Well, sure he's faithful now! He's rich and has everything he wants! Let me take all that from him, and then I bet he'll turn his back on you!" God said, "Okay. You can do whatever you like to him, but you can't take his life."

It's a weird beginning, right? But the awesome thing to remember here is that God knew Job would remain faithful to him, no matter what happened. I would love to have God brag about me like that!

The devil didn't waste any time. These are the things that happened to Job after that:

He lost all of his oxen and donkeys (1,500 animals) and all of the people who took care of them.

He lost all seven thousand of his sheep and the shepherds who watched them.

He lost all of his three thousand camels and the people who handled them.

His sons and daughters died.

He was covered in terrible sores from head to foot.

Basically, Job was stripped of everything he had, except for his wife—and she wasn't a great source of encouragement for him. After he was covered in sores, she told him he should just "curse God and die" (Job 2:9).

The big thing we can learn from Job is this: We aren't just supposed to praise God when things are going the way we want them to go. After Job's wife told him to curse God, he said, "Should we accept only good things from the hand of God and never anything bad?" (Job 2:10). Even though he had lost everything, he did not let go of his love for the Lord.

Whether God is giving to us or allowing things to be taken away from us, we still need to bless his name and love him with our whole hearts.

Girl Gab: To learn the rest of the story, read Job 42:12-17 right now. God rewarded Job's faithfulness *big time!* Pray today, and thank God for good things that are going on right now. Then praise him in spite of not-so-good things that might be happening right now.

26 November

Language Lab: What Is "Worship"?

Bible Blast: Read Deuteronomy 10:20-21

He alone is your God, the only one who is worthy of your praise, the one who has done these mighty miracles that you have seen with your own eyes. DEUTERONOMY 10:21

Girl Gab: Talk to your mom. Are you ever tempted to "worship" something or someone other than the Lord? Ask God to help you not to give in to that temptation. If there's something you're "bowing down" to instead of God, confess that to him.

In the United States, it's common to shake hands when you greet someone. In Korea, everyone bows. It's not a grand bow where you bend completely over and touch your head to the ground. It's just a little movement that communicates "thank you" to be courteous. You bow when you greet an elderly person. If you meet someone for the first time, you might bow a little more deeply. To Koreans, bowing to another person is a way of showing respect.

The word *worship* in the Bible means that you show respect to someone who is your authority or leader. It specifically talks about making yourself physically lower than the one being worshiped by bowing, kneeling, or lying down at his feet. When you kneel in front of someone, you're saying, "You are greater than I am, and so I'm going to bow down lower than you as a symbol that I submit to your power."

When you hear the word *worship*, you can picture somebody bowing in front of something else. We know that we're supposed to worship only God, but people worship all sorts of things. For example, when someone decides to believe what a fortune cookie says instead of listening for God's voice, it's as if that person is bowing down to that fortune, acknowledging its supposed power.

Sometimes people worship other people, too. In ancient times of Egypt, the people believed the man who ruled as pharaoh was a god, so they worshiped him, along with the other Egyptian gods they believed in.

When you worship God, you're honoring him; it's as if you're saying, "God, you are worth everything to me. You're greater than I am. You are my king." When you have a time of worship at church, it should be an experience of telling God how great he is.

God wants you to worship only him—not statues, TV shows, celebrities, boys, or hobbies. Bow down only to God.

Got Talent?

Bible Blast: Read Matthew 25:14-30

A man's gift makes room for him and brings him before great men.
PROVERBS 18:16 (NASB)

A man was getting ready to go on a long trip. He called his three servants together before he left. He gave one servant five talents, another two talents, and the third guy one talent. He gave them the money hoping they would make wise choices with it while he was gone.

The "five talent" guy used his money to make five more talents. He did this by investing and risking a little. Smart! The "two talent" guy worked hard and earned two more talents. He also invested by risking a bit. Another great idea! But the guy with one talent buried it in a hole in the ground. He didn't want to risk losing what had been entrusted to him.

When the boss came back, he asked the three men what they had done with their talents. The first two guys told their boss how they actually doubled the amount of money he gave them, and the boss was really proud of them. He said to each of them, "Well done, my good and faithful servant. You have been faithful in handling this small amount, so now I will give you many more responsibilities. Let's celebrate together!"

The third guy told his boss he had buried his talent because he was afraid. The boss was the opposite of happy about that. He made that guy give his talent to the first guy, who already had ten. Then he sent him away.

This parable, or story, teaches us that God has given each of us talents and gifts that are especially ours, and we shouldn't be afraid to use them. When we have courage in doing what we're good at, God will cause those gifts to grow in us for the blessing of others. It might mean taking some risks. For example, maybe you have a beautiful singing voice. It can be scary to try singing in front of an audience, but you'll never be able to use that gift for God unless you risk a little!

Chidi Ukazim, a beautiful Nigerian woman I know, said this: "The world is poorer when you don't share the unique gifts that God has given you." So let's make the world richer by using our gifts for God's glory!

Girl Gab: What gifts do you have? Talk about that with your mom. I bet she knows some gifts you have that you've never even thought of! What gifts does your mom have? Talk about using them in creative ways even today.

28 November

Boy Trouble

Bible Blast: Read 1 Corinthians 9:24-27

I do not run like a man running aimlessly; I do not fight like a man beating the air. 1 CORINTHIANS 9:26 (NIV)

Macy and Genevieve were great friends. They did everything together and almost never fought until one day when Macy ran up to Genevieve and said, "I totally have a crush on that new boy, Adam! He's so cute!"

Genevieve said, "You can't have a crush on Adam because I totally like him, and I'm pretty sure he likes me back! You'll have to find someone else to have a crush on."

Macy's face fell. "He doesn't like you, Genny! Kiersten told me she thinks that Adam said I'm cute. Why don't you start liking Chris instead? He's cool."

"Because I like Adam, Macy! How could this be happening? What are we going to do?" Genevieve pouted.

"I know," Macy said. "Let's have a contest and see who can get Adam to like her by the end of the week. Deal?"

"Deal!" Genevieve said with a huff.

The two friends did everything they could to get Adam's attention all week. They wore cute things in their hair. They laughed at everything Adam said. They even tried playing football with him when the class went outside.

By Friday, they weren't sure what Adam felt until they saw him pass a note with a big heart on it to Kiersten during class. The girls slumped down in their chairs and looked over at each other.

On the bus after school, Macy said, "I guess that contest thing was pretty dumb, huh?"

"It sure was," Genevieve agreed. "We almost let a boy get in the way of our friendship. Let's never do that again!"

Macy had an idea. "Let's promise not to let each other get boy crazy. I don't want to worry about boys all the time."

Genevieve liked that. "Yeah! If you start to think a boy is more important than anything else, I'll let you know."

"And I'll do the same for you, Genny!"

The girls made a "pinky promise" and talked about how Adam wasn't that cute anyway.

Meditation Moment: John 3

All who do evil hate the light and refuse to go near it for fear their sins will be exposed. But those who do what is right come to the light so others can see that they are doing what God wants.
JOHN 3:20-21

Have you ever driven past a big city at night? From a distance, it looks like a glowing world of all different colors and types of lights. The streetlights, headlights, neon lights from signs, and lights on skyscrapers appear so sparkly. In the dark you don't see all the garbage on the streets. From the car you don't smell the pollution from the factories or cars. You don't hear rude people yelling at other people because they're not moving fast enough. The darkness of night hides all the ugly stuff that can go on in a city. But if you were to drive into that city during the day, nothing would be hidden because nothing can hide in the light. The problems would all be exposed.

As you meditate on John 3:20-21, think about the difference between the light and the darkness. Pray and ask God to speak to you today through these verses. Read over the verses a few times, and then wait to see what God teaches you. You can write down what you've learned by drawing a picture or writing a prayer.

Girl Gab: Talk to your mom about today's Meditation Moment. Ask God to help you love living in his light.

Amazing Animals: The Mountain Goat

Bible Blast: Read 2 Samuel 22:31-37

He makes me as surefooted as a deer, enabling me to stand on mountain heights. 2 SAMUEL 22:34

Mountain goats actually aren't goats. They're really a part of the antelope family. Maybe we should call them "mountain antelopes"! If you've ever seen one, you know that they look more like white mini-buffaloes than goats. Their white, fluffy coats make them beautiful.

If you've ever seen a "regular" farm goat up close, it's hard to imagine they would be well suited for living in rocky places. The goats you might see at a county fair have hard, slippery hooves that work much better in grass or dirt. Mountain goats have a split hoof made for climbing rocks. The hoof spreads out a little when they step, which gives the goat a sturdier surface for climbing. And the bottom of the mountain goat's hoof has a leathery type of pad so it's not too slippery. God gave mountain goats special climbing shoes!

When I watch mountain goats in action on nature shows, I just shake my head in disbelief. They climb and climb on the very edges of rocky cliffs without falling. Since they live so high up in the air, they don't have many predators, either. The biggest dangers they face are landslides and avalanches.

When David wrote the song of praise you read in today's Bible Blast, he was amazed at how God helped him to do the impossible. God gave David great strength to protect himself. Maybe when David was hiding in the side of a mountain, he saw a herd of mountain goats climbing through the rocks. And maybe then he realized that the same God who created those goats created him and kept him from falling into danger.

God helps us walk through hard, rocky times. His faithfulness to us is like special pads on the bottoms of our feet that keep us from slipping. You don't need to be afraid of the climb because he's right there with you.

The next time you feel as if you're climbing to new heights in some special challenge or assignment, rest assured that you—just like mountain goats and King David—were made for this!

Bus to Freedom

Bible Blast: Read 1 Corinthians 10:12-13

Let's not get tired of doing what is good. At just the right time we will reap a harvest of blessing if we don't give up. GALATIANS 6:9

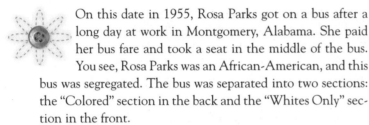

On this date in 1955, Rosa Parks got on a bus after a long day at work in Montgomery, Alabama. She paid her bus fare and took a seat in the middle of the bus.

You see, Rosa Parks was an African-American, and this bus was segregated. The bus was separated into two sections: the "Colored" section in the back and the "Whites Only" section in the front.

On this particular day, Rosa sat in the very front seat of the "Colored" section. The bus filled up. When four white passengers got on and didn't have a place to sit, the bus driver moved the "Colored" sign back a couple of seats behind Rosa and three other African-American passengers. He then told them to get up and move. After a little hesitation, the other three passengers around Rosa got up and moved to the back. But Rosa just scooted over toward the window.

The bus driver threatened to call the police and have Rosa arrested if she didn't move. And that's exactly what happened. The police took her off the bus and arrested her. Rosa didn't stay in jail very long because someone paid her bail. But that's not the end of the story.

The African-American community in Montgomery realized they needed to use this opportunity to do something really big. Led by a young pastor, Martin Luther King Jr., they organized a boycott against Montgomery's public buses. No African-American man, woman, or child would use the bus to get to work, school, or any other place until the buses were no longer segregated. The Montgomery Bus Boycott lasted for more than a year! Since so many of the bus riders were African-American, the bus company lost a lot of money during that time.

On December 21, 1956, Rosa Parks boarded a Montgomery public bus and was able to sit wherever she wanted. All the hard work and perseverance of the boycott had worked!

Girl Gab: Do you ever get tired of giving in to bad stuff going on around you? Is it time to take a stand? (Or to take a seat, like Rosa Parks did!) Talk to your mom about some things you need to boycott in your life. And maybe you can check out a book about Rosa Parks at your library sometime this week to learn more of her story!

Kickin' Kraft:
**Perfectly
Plump Pillows!**

(Check out p. 378
for a great mother-
daughter craft that
helps reinforce
today's devo!)

Kickin' Kraft: Head Rest

Bible Blast: Read Luke 9:57-62

*Jesus replied, "Foxes have dens to live in, and birds have nests,
but the Son of Man has no place even to lay his head." LUKE 9:58*

One thing Jesus told people over and over is that it's not always easy to follow him. The religious leaders and government guys hated Jesus and his disciples. Jesus never said, "Follow me! If you do, your life on earth will be full of daisies and sunshine! You'll be really rich, and everyone will love you everywhere you go!"

In today's Bible Blast passage, Luke records Jesus' words. Jesus made sure his followers knew that if they chose to walk with him, they might not even have a place to sleep at night. From what we read in the Bible, Jesus was constantly on the move, going from place to place sharing the message of God's Word everywhere he went.

God may ask you to live in a big house up on a mountain. He could say he needs you to set up your home in a grass hut in Africa. He might tell you to live on a boat that sails from port to port giving people medical care. Or he may need you to travel all around the world telling people about salvation in Jesus. The important thing is that you obey him, no matter what he needs you to do or where he asks you to sleep.

The Greedy Machine

Bible Blast: Read Luke 12:15-21

He said, "Beware! Guard against every kind of greed. Life is not measured by how much you own." LUKE 12:15

Once upon a time, there was an extremely bad famine in Germany, and the people were very hungry. One kindhearted, wealthy man took a basket of twenty loaves of bread to the courtyard where twenty children were playing. He said, "Children! I have a gift for you! In this basket you will find one loaf of bread for each of you. Take one and come back here tomorrow. I'll give you a loaf of bread every day until this famine is over."

The starving children fought over who got the largest loaf. Then they ran away without even saying thank you— all except for one little girl, Gretchen. She waited patiently until the other children grabbed their bread. Then she quietly reached into the basket and picked up the last tiny loaf. She thanked the man over and over for the food.

The next day Gretchen and the other kids were waiting for the bread. And once again, the other children acted like animals as they grabbed the biggest loaves from the basket. After the other kids were gone, Gretchen reached in and took the last loaf again. It was really small, not even half the size of the other loaves that had already been taken. She thanked the man again and took the bread home to her mom.

When her mother cut the tiny loaf of bread, six shiny silver coins dropped out of the center. Her mom said, "Gretchen! You need to go immediately and return this money to that gentleman! There has been a mistake!"

Gretchen did as she was told, but when the man saw her with the coins in her hand, he said, "No, dear girl. That wasn't a mistake. I had the silver baked into the smallest loaf of bread as a reward for you. You were content to have one small loaf of bread instead of fighting for the bigger loaves. This is your reward for not being so greedy."

Greediness is a nasty thing. It makes people fight over things. It causes jealousy. It keeps people from giving freely. A greedy way of life is not a life that will be blessed by God.

Girl Gab: Pray this prayer today: "Lord, help me to guard against every kind of greed. Remind me that life is not measured by how much I own. Amen."

Meditation Moment: Luke 2

Suddenly, the angel was joined by a vast host of others—the armies of heaven—praising God and saying, "Glory to God in highest heaven, and peace on earth to those with whom God is pleased." LUKE 2:13-14

Some shepherds were hanging out, making sure their sheep stayed safe through the night when they received a visitor. It wasn't just any visitor; it was an angel of God. The Bible reports that the shepherds were terrified. But the angel told them not to be afraid because he had brought great news: a baby had been born in Bethlehem. This baby was the Savior that people had been talking about for years and years. The angel told the shepherds they needed to go to Bethlehem and find the baby Jesus, who would be wrapped up in cloth and lying in an animal's feed bin.

What a night for those shepherds! They had been trained to know what to do if a wolf came to attack their sheep or if someone tried to steal one of their woolly creatures, but they didn't have any experience in how to respond when thousands of angels appeared to them and praised God!

Before you meditate on this wonderful part of the Christmas story in Scripture, pray and ask God to speak to you. Read over the verses, and then see how God speaks to you about it. He might show you a picture in your head, or share a thought or idea with you. No matter how he speaks, write it down to remember.

Amazing Animals: Woodpeckers

Bible Blast: Read Matthew 13:44-45

The laws of the LORD are true; each one is fair. They are more desirable than gold, even the finest gold. They are sweeter than honey, even honey dripping from the comb. PSALM 19:9-10

Woodpeckers come in several different colors and sizes. Some have bright red feathers on their heads, and some are just different shades of brown. The smallest woodpeckers are fewer than four inches long, while the bigger ones can be as big as two feet!

The tapping sound of the woodpecker is just their way of getting food. They have incredibly strong, pointy beaks that they use like little jackhammers to dig holes in trees or logs—or even the wood frame of your house! After the woodpeckers peck out a spot in the tree, they stick their really long tongue into the hole. God put a special, sticky goo on the ends of woodpeckers' tongues so that when they pull their tongues back into their mouths, they have a beakful of critters. Woodpeckers also use their beaks to pry up pieces of bark to reveal the scrumptious grubs and bugs underneath. Yum! (Not!)

Here's a little science experiment for you. Count one second. If you don't have a watch handy, just say "One Mississippi," and that's about one second. Did you do it? That's how long it takes for woodpeckers to peck *twenty times*! That's some crazy-fast pecking! It seems as if all that pecking should really hurt their little birds' heads, but the Creator took care of that. He put a spongy, soft spot behind their beaks to protect their heads and brains.

The tree-tappers have special talons on their feet—two facing forward and two facing backward so they can stay attached to the tree while they peck. The feathers on their tails are also really stiff so they can use them like a third leg for balance.

The woodpeckers work hard to get their food, but the reward is great. When we read God's Word, we need to keep digging and digging to learn as much truth as we can. His Word has something for you every single day for every single situation you face in life.

Girl Gab: Do you have a woodpecker that visits your yard? If you want to attract them, you can get something called "suet" to smear on a tree or put in a special feeder, and you might hear the tapping soon! Dig in to God's Word today!

6 December

God's Mind vs. Our Minds

Bible Blast: Read Isaiah 55:8-9

Just as the heavens are higher than the earth, so my ways are higher than your ways and my thoughts higher than your thoughts. ISAIAH 55:9

Girl Gab: Mom, tell your daughter about a time when God did something you didn't understand. How did that make your faith grow? Daughter, tell God that you trust him with your day today.

Look outside right now. What do you see? Is the grass still green where you live? Is it raining? Or do you see everything covered in a blanket of snow? Are there hundreds of icicles hanging from the power lines?

Maybe you're one of those fortunate few who look outside and see water and sand. But even if that's not you, you can still learn a lesson about the ways of God from the beach.

Picture yourself taking a bucket and a shovel and heading onto the shore of the ocean. The waves are crashing in. You can hear the seagulls chattering to each other. You can smell and taste the saltwater in the air. You dig a pretty big hole on the shore with your shovel. Now you get a bucket of water from the ocean and pour the water into the hole. And you do that over and over and over again. Finally, somebody who's been watching you comes up and says, "What are you trying to do?" You look up at him and reply, "I'm going to take all the water from the ocean and put it in that hole."

I hope you're sitting there, thinking, *That's a ridiculous story. I would never try to do that because it's impossible!*

You're right. Our human brains can only understand so much of who God is and what he does. His thoughts really aren't like ours at all. He's the perfect, all-powerful Creator, and we're not. Trying to "figure out God" is a lot like trying to empty the ocean one bucket at a time into a small hole on the beach. It's not possible, and we shouldn't attempt it.

We have a pretty good idea why God does some of the things he does. But there will be plenty of times when he will do something that simply seems mysterious to us. We won't understand why or even how he did it, and we just have to let that go. It's part of having faith. We need to believe that even though we don't understand everything God does, we can still trust him and know his way is much better than our own.

Now you can go back to daydreaming about the beach!

The M.A.P.

Bible Blast: Read Proverbs 16:1-3

I pray that God, the source of hope, will fill you completely with joy and peace because you trust in him. Then you will overflow with confident hope through the power of the Holy Spirit.
ROMANS 15:13

The next time you walk into a gas station with your parents, look for an atlas—a collection of maps. When you look on the cover of that atlas, there's a good chance you're going to see the words "Rand McNally." William *Rand* and Andrew *McNally* ran a printing company together in Chicago in the 1850s. Rand McNally was the first big map publisher to start using numbers to name roads. They actually put up a lot of road signs themselves. The government liked the idea and kept it up.

If you can read a map, you really can go just about anywhere. If you live in Tallahassee and want to get to Phoenix, all you have to do is find both places in the atlas and follow the roads that connect them.

There's another kind of M.A.P. It gives us the road to an amazing life with Christ.

The M stands for "**M**inistry of the Holy Spirit." John 14 tells how Jesus comforts his disciples by telling them that after he's gone from earth, God will send the Holy Spirit to be with them. The Holy Spirit ministers to us by helping us know what's wrong and right. He also fills us up and helps us minister to other people. We need to depend on him every day.

The A stands for "**A**uthority of Scriptures." Hebrews 4 tells us that God's Word is totally alive! It's not like any other book in the world. The Bible is the *numero uno* place where we go to find truth. Every Scripture you read is 100 percent true, and that makes the Bible the "boss" of everything else.

The P stands for "**P**ower of Prayer." Prayer is a *huge* part of loving God. If we don't talk to him and listen to him, how do we expect to become more like him?

Follow Rand McNally's map if you want to get to Phoenix, but follow God's M.A.P. if you want to experience an awesome life with him.

Girl Gab: Do you know how to read a map? Does your mom? Grab an atlas, and figure out the way to get to a dream destination of yours. Pray that you would love God more every day and become more like him.

Language Lab: What Is the "Lord's Supper"?

Bible Blast: Read Mark 14:22-26

He took some bread and gave thanks to God for it. Then he broke it in pieces and gave it to the disciples, saying, "This is my body, which is given for you. Do this to remember me." LUKE 22:19

The Lord's Supper is when we set aside a special time to remember Jesus' death on the cross by eating bread and drinking grape juice or wine. Different churches do this in different ways, but the meaning is the same.

Jesus had the first Lord's Supper, or Communion, with his twelve disciples the night before Judas handed Jesus over to the people who wanted to kill him. That first Communion was part of a Passover meal. So let's go back to the book of Exodus in the Old Testament and learn what the Passover is.

When the Israelites were being held as slaves in Egypt, God used Moses to set them free. In order to get Pharaoh to let the people go, God sent different plagues on the Egyptian people. It showed that God's power was greater than Pharaoh's and that God meant business. The final plague was that every firstborn son in Egypt would die on one particular night. If the Israelites spread the blood of a lamb or goat on their doorposts, their firstborn sons wouldn't be hurt. God's angel went through the land of Egypt that night, and when it saw blood on the doorpost, the angel "passed over" that house and didn't kill the oldest son. So this is where we get the name "Passover."

Every year after that the Jewish people celebrated the Passover with a feast, which is what Jesus and the disciples were celebrating the night Jesus gave them bread and wine and told them to eat those things "in remembrance of him."

When Jesus was crucified, he lost a lot of blood. The Bible says that sins can't be forgiven without the shedding of blood. Jesus wants us to remember his blood when we drink the juice at Communion. When Jesus died on the cross for our sins, his body was pierced with the crown of thorns, the nails in his hands and feet, and the spear of a soldier. Eating the bread during Communion is meant to be a reminder that Jesus' body was broken for us.

Deflated

Bible Blast: Read Proverbs 18:1-4

Fools have no interest in understanding; they only want to air their own opinions. PROVERBS 18:2

Girl Gab: Pray that you would receive wisdom from others today.

If you have a balloon that hasn't been blown up, go ahead and get it. If you don't have one, just imagine along with me. Give the balloon a good stretch or two and blow it up, but don't tie it shut. Just hold it closed with your fingers. As I tell this story, I'm going to have you let air out of the balloon bit by bit.

Danika had to do a creative book report on the book she had just read about Pocahontas. She sat on the couch beside her mom, who was looking through a magazine.

"Mom, I have to do a book report on Pocahontas, but it has to be creative. Do you have any ideas?"

Her mom thought a bit. "Well, honey, you could—"

"I know! I could make a real Indian headdress like she would have worn!" Danika interrupted. "What do you think?" *(Let some of the air out of that balloon.)*

"That's a fine idea, or why don't—"

"Oh wait! I could show a clip from the Pocahontas movie and talk about how it was different from the book. Is that a good idea, Mom?" *(Let some more air out of the balloon.)*

Danika's mom was quiet.

"Well, Mom. What do you think?" Danika asked.

Her mom just let out a big sigh and said, "Those are great ideas, honey."

"Thanks, Mom! You were a big help!" *(Let the rest of the air out of the balloon.)*

Danika didn't really want her mom's help. She just wanted to be able to voice all the great ideas she had. If she had listened to her mom's opinions, she may have discovered an even more incredible book report project idea, but she didn't give her mom a chance to speak.

People who only want to tell everything they know and think are like that balloon. They're so busy blowing out all of their "air" that they never receive anything back, and they just deflate.

Bible Blast: Read Romans 8:28-30

God knew his people in advance, and he chose them to become like his Son, so that his Son would be the firstborn among many brothers and sisters. ROMANS 8:29

Girl Gab: Have you ever wished you had more or fewer siblings? Did your mom ever wish that when she was your age? Have fun imagining what life would be like if you suddenly had zero siblings or twenty siblings. Make a list of your BFFs. Are they also your sisters in Christ?

Jeannie never had any brothers or sisters, but, boy, did she want them! She prayed for siblings and begged her parents to have more kids, but she remained an only child. Jeannie envied her cousins because there were four kids in their family. She totally wanted to be part of a bigger family.

When she got older she realized what a blessing it was to be an only child because of the attention and time her parents were able to give her. As an adult, Jeannie has superclose BFFs that love Jesus. They became the sisters she never had!

Shelly had the opposite "problem" that Jeannie had. She was the youngest of five kids. That's a big family! Sometimes she would sit at the dinner table and listen to everyone talking over each other and wish that she were an only child. It wasn't that she didn't love her siblings. She just thought it would be cool to have her parents to herself sometimes.

As Shelly grew older, she realized how much she loved the noisy, crazy holidays with people all over the house, and she saw the blessing that a big family can be. And, just like Jeannie, Shelly has some fabulous friends who love Jesus and help her stay close to him.

No matter what type of family you come from, one thing's for sure—God wants you to have people in your life who will be like sisters to you, even if you don't have the same mom and dad. In today's Bible Blast, you read that we are all brothers and sisters in Christ and that God is our heavenly Father. That means if you meet a *chica* who's in love with Jesus, she's your sister! And if you come across a boy who's totally into the Lord, he's your brother! How cool is that?

Whether you come from a big family or a little family, God wants you to be connected to other sisters in Christ. He doesn't want you to live your life all by yourself, so get out there and start lovin' your sisters!

Fruit in My Eyeballs?

Bible Blast: Read Psalm 17:6-8

Keep me as the apple of your eye; hide me in the shadow of your wings. PSALM 17:8 (NIV)

If a guy's feeling mushy gushy lovey dovey, he might tell his girlfriend that she's the "apple of his eye." That doesn't mean that he really loves apples and she reminds him of one and that's why he loves her so much. It's a saying that means his girlfriend is the most important thing in the world to him, that she's all he ever wants to see.

When you see that phrase in our focus verse today, it means pretty much the same thing. This reference to the "apple" of the eye is talking about the eye's pupil.

Quick Quiz: Which part of the eye is your pupil? What color is it?

The pupil is the very center of the eye. It looks like a black circle. The pupil is surrounded by the iris, which is the colored part of your eye. The pupil's job is to let in the right amount of light so your eye can see clearly. The iris causes the pupil to get bigger or smaller depending on how dark or light it is. If you hang out in a dark room for a bit, your pupils will get really big to let in as much light as possible. When it's really bright out, the pupil gets tiny to block some light.

So what could it mean when we ask God to keep us as the apple of his eye?

To figure that out, I want you to get your mom, if she's not already with you right now. Got her? Make sure you have a bright light on. I want you to look right into each other's eyes. You'll have to get pretty close, so if you haven't brushed your teeth yet or your mom has coffee breath, you may want to take care of that first! Now, when your eyes are wide open looking into your mom's eyes, do you see anything in her pupil? If the lighting is right and you're not *too* close to her, you should see your own reflection! Do you see it? Does she see her reflection in your pretty eyes?

Being the apple of God's eye means we're really close to him, and we already know he never lets us out of his sight. Get so close to God that he sees his reflection in your eyes.

Girl Gab: Really look into each other's eyes. Tell your mom every color you see in her eyes, and have her do the same for you. Make Psalm 17:8 your prayer.

Girl Gab: Harley
learned that being
the biggest isn't
always the best
idea. Do you
ever get distracted
from what's best
because you're more
concerned about
what others think
of you? Tell God
that you want to do
what's best, even if
it means you won't
get tons of attention
for it.

Harley the Skinny Chicken

Bible Blast: Read Romans 12:1-3

Do you want to stand out? Then step down. Be a servant. If you puff yourself up, you'll get the wind knocked out of you. But if you're content to simply be yourself, your life will count for plenty. MATTHEW 23:11-12 (THE MESSAGE)

Harley was the biggest, fattest chicken on Farmer Tuttle's farm. He worked very hard at being a big chicken by eating his food, plus any food that was left over at feeding times. Sometimes he even stole food from other chickens! Every day Harley went around, strutting his stuff and showing off his very plump self. The girl chickens thought he was the most handsome thing they had ever laid eyes on. Harley loved the attention he got. The only hen that didn't act that way around Harley was Martha, and she was his very best friend.

One day Martha ran as fast as she could to find Harley, who was eating, of course. She said, "Harley! *Harley!* Farmer Tuttle and his wife were just standing by the fence, looking at all the chickens. Mrs. Tuttle said Christmas is coming up soon and she wants the biggest, fattest chicken in the barnyard for their Christmas dinner, and she pointed right at you!"

Harley spit out his food. "Wh—what? They're going to eat *me* for Christmas dinner?! Oh no!"

Martha put her wing around him to help him feel better. "Harley, I think I've got a plan. They want a fat chicken, not a skinny one. Why don't you stop eating until you burst and instead just eat until your stomach's full?"

Harley squawked, "That's a great plan!"

Right away Harley began eating just until his tummy was full at mealtimes, and he started getting smaller and smaller. When the day came for Farmer Tuttle to get a chicken for his wife to cook, he stood in the barnyard and looked right at Harley and said, "Well, how did that happen? You used to be plump, and now you're skinny as a broom! Guess I'll have to get another chicken for the wife." And that's what he did.

Harley and Martha let out a big sigh of relief that day and had the best Christmas two chickens could have.

What about That Box?

Bible Blast: Read Romans 5:3-5

This hope will not lead to disappointment. For we know how dearly God loves us, because he has given us the Holy Spirit to fill our hearts with his love. ROMANS 5:5

We can learn some valuable lessons from stories, even when we know the story isn't true—like the story of Pandora's box.

Pandora was given a box (or jar) and was told *never* to open the box. (How lame is that?) She went to earth, and there her curiosity got the best of her. When she lifted the lid, all kinds of evil, disease, and hardships were released onto the earth. Once Pandora realized what she had done, she slammed the lid back on as fast as she could, but all the bad stuff had already gotten out. There was only one item left in her box: hope. Some versions of the myth say Pandora eventually released hope into the world, and others say she didn't.

People are going through hard times without hope all the time. We know that true hope comes from Jesus. He came to the earth and died for our sins so we could spend eternity in heaven with him. That is our hope. People who don't know Jesus and haven't given their hearts to him don't have that hope to help them through rough times, and that's very sad.

As we grow closer to Christ, hope will become like an instinct for us. Our brains will go straight to our hope in him instead of letting our problems be like a gray cloud over us all the time. We have to choose to let hope be free in our lives so we don't get really down, sad, depressed, and discouraged when things aren't going very well.

Today's Bible Blast shows us a pattern for how trials (or hard times) produce hope in us.

Problems produce endurance. (Endurance is the ability to hang in there.)

Endurance produces character. (Character is having a good reputation.)

Character produces hope.

And hope won't ever disappoint us because God won't ever disappoint us.

Girl Gab: What do you need to have hope for today? Talk to your mom about any hard thing you might be going through right now. Mom, pray for endurance, character, and hope for your daughter.

Yummy Yum-ness

Bible Blast: Read Proverbs 26:21-23

Rumors are dainty morsels that sink deep into one's heart.
PROVERBS 26:22

What is your favorite snack in the world? Do you love chips and salsa? How about ice cream? Or maybe you love chowing down on raw veggies?

A snack that most people can't resist is *chocolate chip cookies!* Sometimes it seems like we bake about three batches a week in my house! The funny thing is, this favorite snack was created totally by accident.

In the 1930s, Ruth and Kenneth Wakefield owned a little hotel in Massachusetts called the "Toll House Inn." Ruth enjoyed cooking homemade food for the guests who stayed there. One night she was baking butter cookies and thought it would be good to make them all chocolate instead. All she had was a bar of Nestlé chocolate, so she cut it up into tiny bits and stirred them into the cookie dough. She assumed that when the chocolate melted, it would make the entire cookies chocolate, but the chocolate bits just melted a little and made a wonderfully good cookie that Ruth's guests ended up liking very much. In fact, people began coming to the inn just to sample Ruth's "Toll House Cookies."

Ruth made a business deal with the Nestlé company. They printed her recipe on the back of their chocolate bars, and she got all the chocolate she wanted to make more delicious cookies at the Toll House Inn. This was before chocolate chips were invented, so Nestlé included a small chopper to help people make their bars into chips for the cookie recipe. In 1939 Nestlé began selling bags of chocolate chips.

Like it says in Proverbs 26:22, rumors and gossip are like those chocolate chips. The words of gossip go right into a person's heart. Rumors can hurt a person so deeply. You know that saying, "Sticks and stones may break my bones, but words will never hurt me"? That's so not true! Words can hurt much more deeply than a bruise.

Let your words be morsels that nourish and strengthen people rather than tearing them down.

Perfect Timing

Bible Blast: Read Proverbs 30:18-19

Promise me, O women of Jerusalem, by the gazelles and wild deer, not to awaken love until the time is right. SONG OF SONGS 2:7

Have you ever stood and watched an eagle or hawk or some other kind of bird flying through the air? Do you ever get amazed by its grace and beauty—and by the perfection of its design? God designed these creatures to be completely aerodynamic. That's a miracle.

So how do you feel about snakes? They're not my favorite animal, but I can't deny that when I see one move along the ground, I can't stop staring. They don't have any legs or arms, but they still move perfectly. Their muscles move in such a way that they can slither around just about anywhere.

And I'll never understand all the science that goes into building a boat, especially those cruise ships! How do those gigantic structures float so effortlessly on top of the water?

The writer of today's Bible Blast found eagles, snakes, and boats amazing too. Then he listed one more thing that he didn't totally understand. His mind had a hard time understanding the love between a man and a woman.

Romantic love is wild, isn't it? Two people are going through life separately. They encounter lots of other people and have lots of friends. But one day they meet each other, and something's different—special. They start to feel all "twitterpated" like the springtime animals in the movie *Bambi*.

Falling in love is such a beautiful mystery, but it's not something you need to be worrying about or even thinking about right now. You're at a great age right now. You get to have fun with your friends. You're figuring out what music you like and what your personal style is. You can go to sleepovers and stay up all night laughing until your stomach hurts. You're growing in your faith every day and figuring out why you believe what you believe. It's a fabulous time!

If you love Jesus and live for him, some day you just might fall in love and it will be in God's perfect timing. Like the focus verse says, don't rush into it. There's plenty of time for getting "twitterpated." For now, just be God's girl!

Girl Gab: Pray with your mom that you would enjoy being a girl and not get distracted by trying to fall in love.

16 December

Living on the Edge

Bible Blast: Read 1 Peter 2:9-12

Dear friends, I warn you as "temporary residents and foreigners" to keep away from worldly desires that wage war against your very souls. 1 PETER 2:11

Girl Gab: Tell your mom what some of the "big" sins are that you would never do. What are some of the "little" sins you need God's strength to stay away from?

When you see other people around you doing wrong things, it can be hard not to do those things too—especially if it looks like they're having fun while they do it.

Since you're a Christian girl, there are some activities you just have to stay away from. Remember how we said earlier in the year that when you know what you should do but don't do it, it's sin? (See James 4:17.) That's really true, and that commitment to doing what's right will be tested as you grow up.

I've talked to Christian girls and guys who think they can do whatever they want as long as they don't do any of the "big, really bad" sins. For instance, they feel like they can say inappropriate things and dirty words as long as they don't say any of the really, really bad words that could get them into deep trouble. But Ephesians 5:4 says those things shouldn't be a part of a Christian's life at all. It says that dirty stories, foolish talk, and inappropriate jokes aren't for you at all.

Part of living for Christ is making choices that are different from what everyone else in the world is doing. You can't just stay away from the really bad things and then expect God to be pleased with that. Love God with your whole heart and your whole life. Ask him what you should and shouldn't do, and he'll show you, especially through his Word. There's a danger in letting yourself get really close to sin. Let me share a story with you to explain what I mean.

Jack Ackerman was a golfer. One day in 1934 he was playing golf in Belleville, Ontario. He hit the ball, and it landed right on the lip of the hole that he was shooting for. It was so close to being a hole in one. Then a butterfly came fluttering by and decided to take a rest on that golf ball. It was just enough to knock the ball into the hole![4]

When we live our lives really close to sin, it doesn't take very much at all to knock us right over that line. So instead of snuggling up close to sin, grab onto the things that please God!

---

4 See *Napoleon's Hemorrhoids (And Other Small Events That Changed History)* by Phil Mason.

Grinchy People

Bible Blast: Read Proverbs 22:24-25

A quick-tempered man does foolish things, and a crafty man is hated. PROVERBS 14:17 (NIV)

Oh, that Mr. Grinch! (Maybe you've seen the movie or read the book *How the Grinch Stole Christmas*.) What do we do with a dude like him? He's green and kind of fuzzy-ish, hates Christmas, steals from nice people, and is really, really angry. Dr. Seuss wrote funny words about Mr. Grinch that were eventually made into a song. They describe the Grinch perfectly. He's foul and nasty wasty. He's compared to unwashed socks, and apparently his soul is full of gunk. Three words describe him: "Stink, stank, stunk!"

Some people are like Mr. Grinch. They're just angry. They look angry. They act angry. They say angry words and do angry things, and they seem to get angrier when other people are *not* angry. Whew! That's a lot of anger! I met up with one of these angry people on vacation not too long ago. He was so mean that he kicked someone else out of the chair she'd been sitting in for one hour. And then he made someone who worked there come clean the chair because he thought the person who was in it was dirty. I'm not kidding. I've never seen anything like it except in movies, but this was real!

When someone is in the middle of being really mad about something, the best thing to do is get out of the way. (Like the person in that chair did!) You can't talk to someone who's acting like that because he's not thinking clearly. His head is too full of "anger stuff" to have room for the truth.

And guess what? If you try to argue with someone who's angry, it makes that person more angry. It's like when you have a campfire. If the flame is burning pretty well but someone wants it to be bigger, she tosses more dry wood onto it. The fire immediately grows. Anger is a lot like fire. It's best to step back until the flames die down.

If you're ever afraid because someone near you is having an anger fit, try to leave the room and pray for that person. Ask God to send his Spirit like water to put out that anger fire.

Girl Gab: Try to write your own verse to the Mr. Grinch song. You could even write one for after he becomes nice and learns to love Christmas. For example, "You're a nice one, Mr. Grinch! You're as smiley as a clown!" Share your verse with your mom, and have a good laugh together. If you know someone whose anger makes you nervous, talk to your mom about it. Be honest with her, and ask her to pray with you.

18 December

Amazing Animals: Monarch Butterflies

Bible Blast: Read Jeremiah 9:23-24

As the Scriptures say, "If you want to boast, boast only about the LORD." 1 CORINTHIANS 1:31

Girl Gab: If you can, look for pictures of monarch butterflies during their migration. At first glance, they look like a bunch of fall-colored leaves in the trees, but then you'll see the effect is actually made by millions of gorgeous monarch butterflies! Ask God for strength to be who he created you to be.

Butterflies are so pretty. I think they look like flying flowers when I see them fluttering around the yard. I especially enjoy monarch butterflies. Their orange and black colors are so eye catching!

Monarchs are amazing for a few reasons, but something they're most famous for is their migration. Every year, 100 million monarchs that can't handle the cold of winter in parts of the United States fly to warmer climates. The amazing thing is that they fly to the same places in California and Mexico every year. They even fly to the same trees, which is really bizarre because butterflies have a very short life span and only migrate once in their life. That means that every year brand-new butterflies are flying to the same trees their ancestors have been flying to for years. The details and intricacies of God's creation plan are so cool!

Before monarchs become butterflies, they are fat, striped caterpillars that *only* eat milkweed plants. Milkweed has stuff in it that makes the monarch poisonous when it's an adult butterfly. So if a predator tries to eat the monarch butterfly, it will get very sick or die. That's one reason why monarchs are so brightly colored. It's a warning that says, "Back off! I'm poisonous!"

There's another butterfly that looks a lot like a monarch but isn't one. It's called a viceroy. It has very similar orange and black markings on its wings with one little black horizontal line that lets us know it's not a monarch. But predators don't know the difference. They stay away from the viceroy thinking it's a poisonous monarch, so both species are protected.

As Christians we need to be proud of serving and loving God. When we're nervous that someone might make fun of us because of our faith, we shouldn't try to disguise ourselves to look like everyone else. God wants us to wear our beautiful "Jesus colors" with joy so that others can see him in our lives and learn more about him.

Mary Said What?

Bible Blast: Read Luke 1:30-37

"Don't be afraid, Mary," the angel told her, *"for you have found favor with God!"* LUKE 1:30

 The story of Christmas begins with a young girl named Mary, and when I say young, think not much older than you! A lot of people believe she was probably a young teenager. God sent an angel whose name was Gabriel with a message for Mary. The message was a big deal. Mary was going to give birth to the Savior of the world. She was surprised and a little confused because she had no husband yet. (She was engaged to Joseph.) She answered something like, "How can I have a baby if I'm not even married yet?" The angel told her that God would place the baby inside of her.

Let's pause for a moment. Can you even imagine receiving a message like that? "Hi, Mary. I'm Gabriel, and I'm an angel. You're going to give birth to the Son of God." I think I would have about a hundred million questions, but do you know what Mary said? She said, "I am the Lord's servant. May everything you have said about me come true" (Luke 1:38). The angel left, and everything he had told Mary came true.

Now we've got Joseph to think about.

There he was, engaged to be married to the lovely Mary and—bam!—she's pregnant. He had some questions, and God answered them in a dream. An angel visited Joseph while he was sleeping (see Matthew 1:20-21) and let him know that everything was okay. He assured Joseph that the baby in Mary's belly really was God's Son and that his name would be Jesus. The angel told Joseph he should still take Mary to be his wife, and that's what Joseph did.

What a wild beginning to this story! Two angels visit and two people decide to trust God and obey him even though everything felt kind of crazy.

When we look at Mary and Joseph, we can be encouraged to know that God uses ordinary people to do big things. He knew the young couple loved each other and loved God, so he could trust them to carry out this very important mission of bringing his Son into the world.

Girl Gab: Mom, share your favorite part of the Christmas story with your daughter today. Daughter, what is yours? Pray together. Ask God to teach you something new while we study Christmas together.

Baby Born in a Barn

Bible Blast: Read Luke 2:1-7

She gave birth to her first child, a son. She wrapped him snugly in strips of cloth and laid him in a manger, because there was no lodging available for them. LUKE 2:7

A census is a way of collecting information about a group of people. Maybe you remember the census of 2010 when your mom or dad filled out the paperwork that reported how many people lived in your home, who they were, and how old they were. The government likes to know how many people it is responsible to protect.

Mary and Joseph traveled to Bethlehem from their small town because of a census. Emperor Augustus called for it. This big count of the people gave him an idea of how his people were doing. The census required men to go back to the city they were born in and take their families with them, so Joseph took Mary and headed to Bethlehem. (It was a much bigger deal then than it is today!) It was during their stay in Bethlehem that Mary gave birth to Jesus, but it sure wasn't a birth for a king!

Because the city was packed with visitors from the census, Mary and Joseph couldn't find an inn or hotel to stay in. The available accommodations were all full of guests. Poor Mary! She was exhausted from the trip, and her body was starting to tell her, "It's time for this baby to come!" If you've ever been around women during those last days of pregnancy, you might know just how uncomfortable they can be. As a woman's body begins to press the baby out, she can feel the muscles in her stomach tightening and loosening. That can feel like bad cramps in the back and belly. It's not a great time for a woman to be without a bed and some comfy pillows!

Joseph managed to find room in a barn of some sort, and that's where Jesus was born. Mary wrapped him up and laid him down in his first crib, an animal's feed bin. It sure wasn't very luxurious. There's a good chance that aside from Mary's and Joseph's voices, the first noises the infant Jesus heard were the animal sounds of cows, sheep, chickens, and goats.

How perfect is that? The first sounds Jesus heard were the sounds of the animals his heavenly Father had created.

Girl Gab: Talk this out with your mom. Why do you think God arranged for his Son to be born in a barn? If you are able to, visit a barn nearby. While you're there, notice everything you can. Close your eyes. What do you hear? What do you smell? What's the sound under your feet as you walk? Is it breezy or cozy? Are there birds in the rafters? What's the barn used for? What would be some of the cool things about being born in a barn? What would be difficult?

Baby's First Visitors

Bible Blast: Read Luke 2:8-12

They hurried to the village and found Mary and Joseph. And there was the baby, lying in the manger. LUKE 2:16

After Jesus was born, the first visitors to arrive on the scene were the shepherds. An angel had told them to go see the baby who would be wrapped up in cloths, lying in a manger. The shepherds hurried off and found the baby just as the angel had said. After they visited with the little family, the shepherds went back to their sheep, telling everyone what had happened and praising God along the way.

The next group of visitors was a group of wise men from lands east of Bethlehem. They had followed a star to find Jesus. When they arrived in Jerusalem, they started asking around, wondering if anyone knew where the "newborn king of the Jews" was. The words "king of the Jews" bothered King Herod a lot. After all, Herod was the king, and he didn't want anyone else to try and take that from him. He told the wise men to let him know when they found Jesus so he could "go and worship him too" (Matthew 2:8). God warned the wise men that King Herod was lying about wanting to worship Jesus, so they didn't tell Herod anything when they did find Jesus.

Many people believe Jesus wasn't a tiny baby anymore when these wise guys found him. He may have been two years old by then. When they found Jesus with his mom, they bowed down and began worshiping him and giving him gifts. (You'll learn more about those gifts in the next few days.)

After the wise men left, Joseph had another angel dream, this one instructing him to get up and take his family to Egypt because King Herod was looking for them because he wanted to kill Jesus. Another wildly surprising message! But Joseph took his family and left that very night for Egypt.

Herod was not a good guy. When he found out the wise men had tricked him, he sent out an order that all boys two years old and under in the Bethlehem area would be killed. After Herod died, Joseph had angel dream number three, telling him it was safe to go back to Israel. The family settled in the town of Nazareth.

Girl Gab: Are you blown away by the circumstances surrounding the coming of Jesus? Keep these things in mind as you enjoy Christmas this year. In fact, try to do everything you can to focus on the truth of Christmas rather than all the gifts and packages!

This is a trustworthy saying, and everyone should accept it:
"Christ Jesus came into the world to save sinners."
1 TIMOTHY 1:15

Girl Gab: So what's the answer? Tell your mom what you learned about why Jesus came to the earth. Remind each other of that reason as you go through the holiday season.

Christmas day is so incredibly soon! Woot! Woot!

Even though I'm sure you're really excited, I want you to take a Meditation Moment today to discover why Jesus came to the earth in the first place.

He didn't come so we could get lots of presents.

He didn't come so we could find good deals at the mall.

He didn't come so that we could feel warm and fuzzy while we sing Christmas carols.

He didn't come so we could enjoy our grandmother's homemade apple pie.

He didn't come so you could have time off from school for Christmas vacation.

The reason he did come is found in 1 Timothy 1:15. This verse says that he came to save you. Remember how he did that? He died on a cross in terrible pain so that you and I don't have to be separated from our God but can live with him eternally. Pray and ask God to give you even more understanding about why he sent Jesus to the earth and what that means for you during a very commercialized Christmas season. After you read the verse, hang out for a bit with God, and let him talk to you. When you feel like he's told you something during your meditation time, go ahead and write it down.

Receiving Is Believing

Bible Blast: Read John 1:10-14

To all who believed him and accepted him, he gave the right to become children of God. They are reborn—not with a physical birth resulting from human passion or plan, but a birth that comes from God. JOHN 1:12-13

Don't you just love the beautiful packages under the Christmas tree? I like to stare at the ones with my name on them and try to figure out what's inside.

Gifts certainly are a big part of Christmas, and it all began with the wise men who came to visit Jesus after he was born with their gifts. Can you name all three presents they brought? Matthew 2:11 records that the gifts were gold, frankincense, and myrrh.

I've often heard it said that Christmas is a season for giving. And, you know, that's so true. I have few greater joys than buying the perfect gift for a loved one or providing presents for a family who is in a hard place financially. And, of course, when we read John 3:16 and Romans 6:23, we're reminded that Christmas is about the greatest gift, Jesus, who came so we could have eternal life.

But Christmas is also a season for receiving. Don't worry! I'm not talking about trying to get all the presents you possibly can! I mean that a gift isn't complete or useful or enjoyed unless it's received by someone.

Think about it. God sent his only Son, Jesus, to die for everyone's sins. If we choose to believe in him and live for him, we will spend eternity in heaven with him and all other believers. If we don't, then we will spend eternity in hell—totally apart from God. Those of us who have received that gift of eternal life are enjoying our relationship with God, and we always have hope because heaven is our home. But those who don't believe have no idea what riches are waiting for them—if they would just receive the gift.

This Christmas, every time you open a gift or a card, let it be a beautiful reminder of your decision to receive the greatest gift of God. Be a joyful receiver this holiday season.

Girl Gab: What's the best gift you've ever received? Did you ever receive something that you didn't really want? Thank God for the perfect gift of his Son, Jesus.

24 December

Girl Gab: If you could be one of the wise men today and you had the opportunity to give the baby Jesus a gift, what would you bring him? Something you made? Something you already have? Talk with your mom for a minute about what you think Mary and Joseph must have felt or thought when they saw these symbolic gifts given to their baby.

Not Your Typical Baby Gifts

Bible Blast: Read Isaiah 9:6-7

They entered the house and saw the child with his mother, Mary, and they bowed down and worshiped him. Then they opened their treasure chests and gave him gifts of gold, frankincense, and myrrh. MATTHEW 2:11

Have you been to a baby shower? It's a fun time of lots of "oohs" and "aahs," while a very uncomfortable but delighted pregnant woman opens oodles of really cute presents. She gets teeny-weeny baby socks, cozy blankets, brightly colored toys that jingle and squeak, and anything else a baby could possibly need. So when I read the gifts the wise men brought for baby Jesus, I thought, "Huh? Wouldn't a toy have been more appropriate?"

As always, when we read something in Scripture that isn't easy to figure out, we just have to dig a little deeper to understand. Gold, frankincense, and myrrh were appropriate gifts for this particular baby. Here's why.

1) Giving gold to baby Jesus signified that he is King. Gold is a symbol of royalty, and the wise men knew this little toddler was the King of kings.

2) Giving frankincense to baby Jesus meant that he is God. Priests in those days used frankincense as part of their worship of God. Exodus 30 describes the specific instructions God gave Moses about using frankincense to make a particular type of incense sacred for the Lord. God says, "Do not make any incense with this formula for yourselves; consider it holy to the LORD" (verse 37, NIV). The wise men knew that, when they presented the frankincense to this baby, they were presenting it to God.

3) Giving myrrh to baby Jesus meant that he came to die. Myrrh was used for embalming someone after the person died. (Embalming is a process they used to preserve the body.) In fact, John 19:39 says that myrrh was one of the substances used to prepare Jesus' body for burial after the Crucifixion. Right away the wise men knew why this most special baby Jesus had been born—to die for their sins and for the sins of the world.

Language Lab:
What Does "Immanuel" Mean?

Bible Blast: Read Deuteronomy 31:6

Look! The virgin will conceive a child! She will give birth to a son, and they will call him Immanuel, which means "God is with us." MATTHEW 1:23

It's Christmas day! How much sleep did you get last night? Did you stay awake all night long because you were so crazy excited about this special day?

It seems appropriate to take a moment between the celebrations to focus on the name Mary gave to Jesus as declared in Matthew 1:23. *Immanuel!* Sometimes you'll see it spelled "Emmanuel," and sometimes it's spelled "Immanuel." It means the same thing either way. The name means "God is with us." Emmanuel is Jesus. Jesus is Immanuel. When Jesus came to the earth as a human, he brought God closer to us. God was really and truly "with us" in a human, visible, touchable form.

That name of Immanuel must have really blown Mary and Joseph away when they held that little baby in Bethlehem. God was with them. Immanuel—right there in their arms.

When you sing the Christmas song "O Come, O Come Emmanuel," you can know it's all about Christ coming to set people free. When you see the word *Israel*, you can stick your own name in there, because he came to set you free from the power of sin, too!

> O come, O come, Emmanuel
> And ransom captive Israel
> That mourns in lonely exile here
> Until the Son of God appear
> Rejoice! Rejoice! Emmanuel
> Shall come to thee, O Israel.

Today's a busy day, but you can still remember Immanuel when you're opening presents, giving gifts, eating great food, visiting relatives, and watching football. All day you can know that because of Jesus, God is always with you.

Girl Gab: Grab a few minutes with your mom today, maybe while you help her prepare food or clear the table, and talk to her about the word *Immanuel*. Tell her what it means. Ask her questions about it. Thank God together that he is always with us.

Kickin' Kraft:
Bow-Licious Wreaths!

(Check out p. 378 for a great mother-daughter craft that helps reinforce today's devo!)

Kickin' Kraft: Beautiful Thoughts

Bible Blast: Read Luke 2:16-20

Mary kept all these things in her heart and thought about them often. LUKE 2:19

We've learned a lot about Mary over the last week, haven't we? Today's focus verse gives us another clue into the kind of girl Mary was.

The shepherds were totally pumped up about what had happened. They told everyone they met about the angels' visit and their discovery of the baby Jesus. The people were amazed by their story. It probably became the talk of the town. It may have been tempting for Mary to join in all the talk and to let people know who she was. She could have gone around Bethlehem saying, "I'm Mary! I just gave birth to God's Son! My baby boy is the Savior of the world!" But instead she kept everything in her heart.

What Mary had experienced was more intimate and miraculous than you and I could ever imagine. God had chosen her, nobody very grand or important, to be the one to bring his Son into the world. There is no doubt Mary had a lot to think about. I like to think that, as she held that precious infant, she was having conversations with God in her heart about him. She probably had a lot of thoughts that she needed God's help with, and it sounds like he did help her in the quiet place of her heart.

Now that Christmas Day is over, take time to talk with God in your heart about Jesus and about the holiday you have just experienced. Spend some quiet time with him today.

Banana Fingers

Bible Blast: Read 2 Corinthians 9:6-9

This same God who takes care of me will supply all your needs from his glorious riches, which have been given to us in Christ Jesus. PHILIPPIANS 4:19

Give me a hand, will you? I mean a hand of *bananas.* That's what a cluster of bananas is called, and the bananas are called fingers! The next time you see a bunch of bananas, you'll notice it really does kind of look like a group of yellow fingers.

I learned that the way I've always eaten a banana may not be the best way. I usually hold it by the bottom, dig my fingernail in the stem part, and peel it like that. But did you know banana experts say to eat it differently? You *do* know who the banana experts are, don't you? Monkeys, of course! If you watch a monkey eat a banana, it holds the stem part like a handle and peels it from the other end. If you try it, it's actually a lot easier! The other reason I like eating a banana like that is because that little seed part is exposed right away so you can get rid of it if you don't like to eat it.

Americans eat more bananas than any other fruit. We each eat about five thousand bananas in our lives! Even if you don't appreciate the sweet taste of a banana, you have to admit that God designed them perfectly. They have their own cases to protect the fruit from getting nasty. You don't have to wash it, because you only eat the inside. Bananas aren't juicy, so you don't have to worry about dripping on your clothes. We can buy them all year long. They're packed with some good vitamins. And a banana has a perfect handle so your hands don't have to get dirty. That's pretty wonderful!

The banana is just one small example of God's perfect provision for us. He gives us everything we need and more. When he provides something, it's always exactly right.

So if you ask God for a friend and the person he brings you isn't the kind of person you would typically hang out with, remember that God's gifts are good. Get to know that girl, and discover why God brought her into your life.

Girl Gab: Eat a banana like a monkey with your mom today. Spend some time talking about God's perfect provision for you and your family.

28 December

Just like You

Bible Blast: Read James 5:16-18

Elijah was as human as we are, and yet when he prayed earnestly that no rain would fall, none fell for three and a half years!
JAMES 5:17

Girl Gab: Ask God how he wants to use you today; then obey him. Pray that he would help you and your mom to help others in the power of the Holy Spirit.

There was a time in Bungoma, Kenya, when some of the leaders of the churches didn't think kids could minister powerfully to others. They even thought that people should wait until they are adults to accept God's gift of salvation. But God was speaking to the other leaders and saying, "Those kids are important! I need them to do great things in Kenya!" So those leaders started working with the children and helping them grow in Christ and in the power of the Holy Spirit.

As the children learned more about Jesus and his love, they started going to hospitals and other places to help others learn more about him too. One time a group of children went to a hospital, and their leader told them to obey whatever God told them to do. A boy said, "I think God wants me to sing," so he did. When the people heard the song, God's Spirit touched their hearts. Soon the sick people were crying and asking the children to show them the way to Jesus! That boy's simple song was used by God to open hearts!

Seeing God use them for his purposes and his glory made the children want to do more and more for their city. They felt that God wanted them to march through the city for seven days. They began praying, telling people about Jesus, and having special meetings where the kids led worship and preached messages to everyone who came. During those seven days, the Kenyan children went to hospitals and prayed for the sick. One time more than one hundred people were healed, and they all left the hospital and went back to their homes! At another hospital, so many people were healed that the hospital had to close! It's used as office space now.[5]

I love that James 5:17 says Elijah was "as human as we are." In 1 Kings 17-19 you can read about all the miraculous things God did through him. God can do awesome things through you, too.

---

5 Story taken from *Here Comes Heaven! A Kid's Guide to God's Supernatural Power* by Bill Johnson and Mike Seth.

No Chance

Bible Blast: Read Psalm 139:13-16

You made all the delicate, inner parts of my body and knit me together in my mother's womb. PSALM 139:13

Have you ever played Scrabble? I have some friends who are great at that game. They even know weird little words like *Xi*, *Za*, and *Quag*. (Those are actual words in the *Scrabble Dictionary*!)

Do you know who invented Scrabble? An architect named Alfred Butts created the game during the time of the Great Depression, which was a time of big money problems, when people didn't have a lot of money to spend on extra things like board games. He made a bunch of the then-unnamed games and just sold them to neighbors and people he knew.

Alfred started working with another guy, and they renamed the game "Scrabble" since you have to dig around for the letters that you play, but it still wasn't selling very well, and Alfred needed some cash soon. Then a guy who worked for New York's department store, Macy's, played Scrabble while he was on vacation and decided to sell it in the store. When that happened, Scrabble started flying off the shelves.

The thing with Scrabble and lots of other games is there's a lot of chance involved. Yes, you employ your wits and skill to use the letters you get to make words that earn big points, but you don't have any choice over which letters you pick up.

With God there is no such thing as luck or chance. He created you on purpose. He knew what you would look like right now even before you were born. He also knew what gifts, talents, likes, dislikes, fears, and loves you would have. When he made you, he didn't close his eyes and randomly pick you. He knows where you'll be ten years from now and where you'll be fifty years from now. He created you to do specific things for him because you're the perfect one to do them.

God doesn't make mistakes, and he doesn't make anything for "no reason." You can walk around today with your head held high because you know that your Creator wants to use you for his great work!

Girl Gab: If you have Scrabble, ask your mom to play it with you sometime. It could be a little hard because your mom probably knows more words than you, but maybe you could ask her to take it easy on you! Praise God that you both were made on purpose!

30 December

Don't Give Up

Bible Blast: Read James 1:2-4

You know that the testing of your faith develops perseverance.
JAMES 1:3 (NIV)

Girl Gab: Do you have goals you want to set for this next year? See if, with your mom's help, you can come up with one goal for each of these categories:

1) Your family

2) Your talents and gifts

3) How you spend your time

4) Your relationship with God

Pray that God would remind you of these goals throughout the year. You can write them on a piece of paper, and when the end of next year rolls around, you can read what your goals were.

There's only one more day left in this year! That's kind of exciting, isn't it? Lots of people see this as a time to start something new or to try something different or to kick a bad habit. Does your family make New Year's resolutions like that?

For some people the end of this year might be difficult because they wanted something to happen that didn't. Maybe a man didn't get the job he was hoping for or a woman wasn't able to get pregnant. Maybe instead of getting healthier, someone only got sicker. It's hard to understand why some things don't happen when we want them to, especially when we're praying about it.

Frances had a brother who didn't love Jesus, but she still really loved her brother. She prayed and prayed and prayed for him. She asked God to help her brother to give his life to Christ. She didn't want him to die without knowing Jesus because she wanted him to go to heaven with her. Do you know how long Frances persevered in her prayers for her brother? She prayed for him for *seventy-two years!* Finally, her brother died. But soon after that, someone came to her and told her that her brother had accepted Christ into his heart shortly before he died! I bet Frances was so thankful then that she had never given up on praying for her brother. When she died at the age of ninety-six, she knew she would see her brother again in eternity with Jesus.

Is there a prayer you've been praying this year that hasn't been answered yet? Don't give up! Perseverance means you keep on trying and keep on going even if you get discouraged. When your faith is put to the test, you develop more perseverance in you. Just because the year is ending, don't give up on your prayers. God is definitely listening.

An Ending and a Beginning

Bible Blast: Read Philippians 1:3-11

I am certain that God, who began the good work within you, will continue his work until it is finally finished on the day when Christ Jesus returns. PHILIPPIANS 1:6

Girl Gab: Mom, pray today's Bible Blast over your daughter as a blessing for the year ahead.

It's New Year's Eve! Do you have special plans with your family tonight? Do you get to stay up until midnight? Does your mom cook a special meal for New Year's Eve or New Year's Day? It's our family's favorite night to spend playing games with friends. We love games, especially card games. So we make a table full of snacks, invite friends over, and start playing! Before we know it, it will be time to turn on the television to watch the ball drop in Times Square. And then we fall asleep dreaming of tomorrow's big pork and sauerkraut dinner!

Today I want you to sit down with your mom and answer these questions about this past year:

- What's something really funny that happened?
- Did anything difficult happen?
- What new thing did you start doing?
- What's the best book you read?
- What is one thing God taught you?
- What was the most fun thing your family did?

It's so good to remember what has happened. Even if you experienced something hard, it's great to look back and see how God helped you through it. He's done a lot of things in you and through you this year, hasn't he? And he has big plans to use you next year, too. Are you excited for that?

Kickin' Krafts

January 7
Radical Reflections!

Supplies:
- Any size mirror. (Find an old one in Mom's makeup drawer!)
- Puffy paints or markers

1. Think of what your new label is, and write it on that mirror. You can use marker if you want, but puffy paints are awesome for making it look really funky.

2. Decorate the frame, too, if the mirror has one.

Then every day when you check out your hair in that mirror, you'll be reminded that any silly names someone called you when you were little aren't the truth. You have a new name, so go conquer some giants!

January 31
Excellent Ebenezer Stones!

Supplies:
- A few cool stones (Smooth river stones work well, but anything you find outside works.)
- Craft paint
- Puffy paint or permanent markers
- Paintbrushes
- Glue and sequins or stickers or other small decorations

1. Paint each stone a different color. Let them dry.

2. Use puffy paint or permanent marker to write a word on each one from the list of "Ebenezers" you came up with earlier. For example, if you thought of a time when God helped you tell the truth when you really wanted to lie, you could write, "Truth!" on one stone.

3. Decorate the stones any way you want.

When you're finished, you'll have a handful of happy little Ebenezer stones to put on your desk as reminders that "up to this point, the Lord has helped you!" As you experience more times of God's provision and help, you can add more stones to your collection. How cool would it be to have words like *Truth*, *Meals*, *Friends*, and *Sleep* in front of you while you do your homework? One thing to remember: When Samuel set up the Ebenezer stone, it didn't mean the stone had any power or magic to it. It was just a reminder for himself of God's goodness. If you lose the stones, it's no big deal. God's power is still the *greatest!*

February 4
A Slammin' Sunglasses Case!

Supplies:
- An old T-shirt or pair of jeans that doesn't fit you anymore
- Ruler
- Fabric scissors
- Needle and thread or glue
- Stuff to use for personalizing your case

1. Cut the T-shirt or jeans into a long rectangle. When you fold the rectangle in half, it needs to be big enough to hold your shades, so do some measuring before you cut! It will probably be something like eighteen inches long and six inches wide.

2. Fold the rectangle over lengthwise and either sew or glue the two long sides together so there's an opening at one end for your sunglasses to slip into. Let that dry.

3. Decorate your Slammin' Sunglasses Case with fabric glue or craft glue and beads, yarn, photos, or old jewelry to make it personal!

February 19
Jazzy Jars!

Supplies:
- A clear glass jar or vase with no labels on it
- Craft paint (not watercolor)
- Glue
- Paintbrushes

1. Make sure your jar is clean and dry.

2. Mix your paint with some of the glue so it will stick to the glass jar. Make sure it's not too runny.

3. Paint a fabulous design on the jar.

4. Let the jar dry completely. If you want, paint over your design with a clear glaze to seal it.

5. Fill the jar with flowers, pencils, marbles, or even flour! Write today's focus verse on a card and give the Jazzy Jar and card as a gift to remind someone of God's provision.

March 1

Bodacious Bookmarks!

Supplies:
- Two pennies
- Scissors
- Poster board or heavy paper in your color of choice
- Craft glue
- Markers

1. Cut the poster board into the size and shape you would like for a bookmark. A typical bookmark is about two inches wide and six inches long, but you don't have to be typical!
2. Glue the two pennies onto the bookmark at the top, and wait for it to dry completely. Craft glue dries clear, so don't worry if it looks white when it's wet.
3. Using your markers and any kind of fancy writing you want, write today's focus verse underneath the two pennies.
4. Decorate the bookmark anyway you like. This would be a great bookmark to keep in your Bible!

March 22

Egg-Stravagance!

Supplies:
- An egg
- A pin
- A small bowl
- Glitter
- Craft glue
- Paintbrush
- Wax paper

1. Wash the egg and hold it over a bowl. Gently twist and push the pin into the smaller end of the egg so that it makes a tiny hole in the shell.
2. Flip it over and do the same thing in the bigger end of the egg. Push the pin through and break the yolk.

3. Using your pin, make the second hole a little bigger.

4. Blow into the smaller hole until all the egg comes out of the larger hole. (You can fry up the egg and eat it!)

5. Brush glue all over your empty egg and roll it in glitter until it's covered.

6. Let the egg dry on waxed paper.

April 5

Million-Zillion Journals!

Supplies:
- A single-hole puncher
- About five sheets of paper, any colors or designs you like
- An inexpensive journal
- Craft glue
- Small bowl
- An old paintbrush
- A marker

1. The first thing you need to do is go to town on the paper with that hole puncher! Pop a movie in and just punch, punch, punch the paper until you have a good pile of multicolored hole-punch dots!

2. Dump some glue in a small bowl, and use the paintbrush to brush a thin layer of glue on the front cover of your journal.

3. Scatter and sprinkle the dots all over the glue before it dries. You may need to adjust some of them so they're laying flat. Doing this over a sheet of newspaper makes for easy clean up! (You can also do this to the back cover once the front has dried.)

4. Let the glue completely dry. Now write "God's Thoughts about Me Outnumber the Sand!" somewhere on the cover.

5. Let the dots remind you of all the grains of sand and how much God loves you!

April 22

Quick-Change Butter Jars!

Supplies:
- A small jar with a tight-fitting lid (baby-food jars are great)
- Heavy cream

1. Fill your jar a little over halfway with heavy cream.

2. Secure the lid tightly.

3. Shake, shake, shake that jar until your cream turns into butter! This can take up to ten minutes, so get ready! Take turns shaking if you get tired.

4. Take off the lid and pour off any excess liquid.

5. Put the lid firmly back on the jar.

You've turned ordinary heavy cream into a *new creation!* Now grab some crackers or bread, and start munching!

May 10
Poppin' Calendar!

Supplies:
- A calendar (Larger calendars will be easier to kraft.)
- Ruler
- Bubble wrap
- Scissors
- Glue that dries clear

1. Measure the size of the square for one date on your calendar.

2. Cut out squares of bubble wrap to match the size of the square.

3. Apply glue to the smooth side of a bubble wrap square and stick it on each date of the month, making sure you can still see the actual date.

4. You can just do it one month at a time or a few months at a time, depending on how puffy you want your calendar to be.

5. Now instead of putting an X on each day as you count down to the last day of school, pop the bubble-wrap square. It will make the countdown a lot more enjoyable!

May 28
Slick Bath Salts!

Supplies:
- Small bottle or jar
- Bowl (Make sure it won't stain.)
- Epsom salts
- Food coloring
- Perfume or essential oil
- Waxed paper

1. Figure out how much Epsom salts you'll need to fill your jar and pour them in a bowl that won't stain.

2. Add a little food coloring and mix it into the Epsom salts until the color is evenly distributed. You don't want the salts to be solid with color, just enough to make them pretty.

3. Mix in your fragrance to be as strong as you would like.

4. Spread the salts out onto waxed paper and let them dry completely.

5. Pour the bath salts into the bottle or jar.

6. The fragrance will be best if you wait a week or two before using the bath salts.

7. Add a tablespoon or two to your next hot bath and relax!

June 5
Punky Pins!

Supplies:
- Safety pins (any size)
- Beads (all kinds of beads that will fit onto your safety pins when the pin is closed)

1. Being careful not to stick yourself, open a safety pin.

2. Thread the pin through the holes of the beads. You can create any patterns you want.

3. Give some pins to your friends. Make a special one for your mom. Stick these Punky Pins on your backpack, purse, hats, dog's collar, or shoelaces!

June 16
Boomin' Beach Bag!

Supplies:
- One onion bag (the plastic mesh bag that comes full of onions from the grocery store)
- Scissors
- One piece of thick string (about eighteen inches long)
- One plastic clip or carabiner to clip it onto your backpack or wherever

1. First, make sure your mom's done with the onion bag. Then, cut off the top so it's pretty much even.

2. Weave the plastic string in and out of the mesh bag around the top to form a drawstring, threading it through the clip or carabiner. Tie the ends together.

3. Toss your sunglasses, sunscreen, and favorite book into your Boomin' Beach Bag, and pull the drawstring closed. You're off to the beach!

July 3

"Quick" Sand Stuff!

Supplies:
- 6 cups of play sand (You can get different colors if you want.)
- 3 cups of cornstarch
- 1½ cups of cold water
- Large bowl

1. Mix the water and cornstarch together really well. It will take a couple of minutes to get it nice and smooth.

2. Using your hands, slowly mix in the sand, one cup at a time. This requires a lot of finger strength!

3. Mess with it! It's such cool stuff! When you're all done, store it in an airtight container.

4. When you get it out again, you'll need to zap it with 2-3 tablespoons of water. Just sprinkle the water on and work it in.

July 29

Campin' Cookie Dough Sticks!

Supplies:
- 1 cup butter
- 2 cups all-purpose flour (You can also use half whole wheat flour.)
- 1 teaspoon baking soda
- ¾ cup brown sugar
- 1 (3½ ounce) box of instant vanilla pudding mix
- ¼ cup milk
- 1 teaspoon vanilla
- 2 cups chocolate chips
- Popsicle sticks

1. Using a mixer (ask Mom), cream the butter and sugar until it looks fluffy and lighter.

2. Mix the pudding in.

3. Stir in the vanilla and the milk.

4. Add the baking soda and the flour ½ cup at a time, combining as you go.

5. Stir in those yummy chocolate chips.

6. Stick balls of dough onto the ends of popsicle sticks. Keep them in the fridge or freezer.

7. Share them and eat them! And your mom doesn't have to worry because there are no raw eggs!

August 7

Groovy Garbage Can!

Supplies:
- A garbage can that mom says is okay to decorate
- Tacky glue (craft glue) or a hot glue gun
- Stuff to decorate with from around the house

The idea with this Kickin' Kraft is to turn your boring garbage can into something beautiful! Here are some ideas:

1. Use a feather boa from your dress-up days, and glue it around the top edge of your garbage can.

2. If you have a bunch of plain, circle stickers (like the ones people use for pricing items at garage sales), place them on your garbage can in a pattern.

3. Make little balls out of aluminum foil, and glue them around the top and bottom of your garbage can.

4. Glue buttons in the shape of the first letter of your name on the side of your garbage can.

August 30

Dazzling Doorway!

Supplies:
- A plastic shower curtain (any color or pattern that you like)
- A spring rod that will fit in your bedroom doorway
- Some kind of hooks to hang your curtain on the spring rod
- Scissors
- A ruler

1. Measure the width of your doorway, and cut the shower curtain to that same width.

2. Measure how long you need the curtain to be for your doorway, and cut the curtain to that length. (You may not need to cut it at all.)

3. Starting at the bottom of the shower curtain, cut the length of the curtain into two-inch-wide vertical strips. Leave about six inches at the top of the shower curtain uncut.

4. Hang the curtain on the spring rod, and get your mom to help you fit the rod securely into your doorway, making sure your bedroom door still closes.

5. You could also use this to dazzle up a window in your room!

September 11

Treasure Hunt Bottles!

Supplies:
- A clear plastic water bottle
- Enough sand to fill half of the bottle. (You could also try using salt.)
- Tiny cool things for someone to find
- An index card and marker

1. Make sure the bottle is clean and dry, inside and out.

2. Put the sand in the bottle. Do this outside or over a trash can.

3. Add the little trinkets. You can use buttons, tiny figures, erasers, barrettes, coins, and beads.

4. Screw the lid on tightly, and shake the bottle so the items get scattered throughout the sand. You can add more sand if you need to.

5. Write the list of "treasures" down on the index card, like "One red button. A cow eraser. A 1974 penny." Give the bottle and card to a friend as her very own Treasure Hunt Bottle! Encourage your friend to try to find everything in the jar by shaking it around.

September 20

Bucket o' Thoughts!

Supplies:
- A bucket, box, or bag that you can decorate
- Glue, tape, or stapler
- Stickers, pom-poms, photos, magazine cutouts—anything to make this your own!
- Markers or paint

1. The instructions for this Kickin' Kraft aren't very difficult. Somewhere on your container write "Bucket o' Thoughts," so that you know not to use it for a garbage can, pencil holder, or basketball hoop!

2. Now decorate your container with whatever Krafty items you have around the house. This is going to be your Bucket o' Thoughts, so make it as special as you like! If you're going to keep it in your room, you may want to decorate it to match your bedspread or a favorite poster.

3. Over the next week, write down a thought you're having, like "Today Chelsea was saying mean things behind Anna's back. Why is she doing that if she's supposed to be her best friend?" Put that thought into your Bucket o' Thoughts. At the end of the

week, arrange a time to sit down with your mom and empty your bucket. Just tell her what's on your mind about whatever you wrote down.

4. Enjoy your time with your mom. She loves you so much!

October 4
David's Disco Ball!

Supplies:
- A Styrofoam ball from a craft store
- Spray paint (to be the background color of the ball)
- Hot glue gun or duct tape
- Lots of old CDs (Make sure you ask before you take these!)
- Heavy-duty scissors (Your dad might have some.)
- String or yarn

1. Take your Styrofoam ball outside and spray paint it. Ask a parent for help.

2. While that dries, very carefully cut the CDs into random shapes and sizes with the scissors. If it's too hard for you to do, ask an adult for help.

3. Using the glue gun or small pieces of duct tape, cover the ball with the CD pieces. Make sure the shiny, mirrored sides of the CDs are facing out.

4. Glue one end of the string to the Styrofoam ball, and wait until it dries completely.

5. Hang up your David's Disco Ball, shine a light on it, and jam to your favorite Jesus tunes!

October 17
Sticky Word Game!

Supplies:
- An empty mint or candy tin (like the one Altoids come in)
- One sheet of sandpaper (The 100-grit kind works well.)
- 3-D paint
- Paintbrushes
- Acrylic paint
- Old magazines or books
- Scissors
- Self-adhesive magnetic sheets (You can get these at craft stores.)
- Tweezers

1. Use the sandpaper to rough up the entire mint tin. This will help the paint stick to it better.

2. Draw a line around the outside of the top of the tin with the 3-D paint.

3. Paint the rest of the tin with the acrylic paint. (You don't need to paint the inside of the tin.)

4. Cut out lots of words from magazines and old books.

5. Peel the backing off the magnetic sheet and lay it on the table, sticky side up.

6. Use the tweezers to place the words on the sticky side of the magnetic sheet.

7. Cut the words out carefully with the scissors.

8. Put the Sticky Words inside the tin and—voilà!—you have a Sticky Word Game!

9. Use the top of the Sticky Word Game tin to make sentences and stories out of your Sticky Words. When you're not playing, keep the Sticky Words safely stored inside the tin.

November 12

Happy Hair Clips!

Supplies:
- Small pieces of fabric. Tulle or lace works best!
- A needle and thread
- Glue
- An old hair barrette or clip

1. Cut the fabric into 6" x 3" rectangles.

2. Layer the rectangles however you like, and then tie a piece of thread around the middle of the pile. It should look like a funky bow.

3. Either sew the bow to the hair clip or glue it. Just make sure the clip will still work when the bow is attached.

4. Snap that Happy Hair Clip into your hair, and smile big!

November 21

Pollyanna's Thanksgiving Turkey!

Supplies:
- Construction paper in all different colors
- Scissors
- Glue stick or tape
- Markers

1. Draw the outline of a turkey (with no tail feathers) as big as you can on a brown piece of paper, and cut him out.

2. Use other colors of paper to make his feet, beak, and eyes, and then glue him together.

3. Hang your turkey up somewhere where the whole family can see him.

4. Cut a whole bunch of feather shapes out of different colored paper and place them near your turkey, along with a glue stick or roll of tape and a marker.

5. Every time someone in the family is thankful for something, have him or her write it on a feather and stick it on the turkey. By the time Thanksgiving comes, Pollyanna's Thanksgiving Turkey will be covered in "thankful feathers"!

December 2
Perfectly Plump Pillows!

Supplies:
- Scissors
- An old pair of tights
- Fiberfill stuffing or some other kind of fluffy stuff
- An old pair of jeans or pants
- Yarn or ribbon

1. To make the pillow, cut one leg off an old pair of tights. Stuff it full of whatever fluffy filling you're using, making a tube-shaped pillow that's about twelve inches long. Tie the other end off in a knot.

2. Cut the leg off an old pair of jeans or pants (ask Mom first) about eighteen inches long. If you cut both ends off, the ends will fray over time and look really cool.

3. Stuff the pillow you made out of the tights into the center of the jeans leg.

4. Using ribbon, yarn, or even hair elastics, tie off each end of the jeans leg, with the pillow in the middle. It should look kind of like a big piece of puffy candy.

5. Put your Perfectly Plump Pillow on your bed, and chill out with a great book!

December 26
Bow-Licious Wreaths!

Supplies:
- Leftover Christmas bows
- Foam wreaths from the craft store (Any size will do.)
- Glue (Hot glue works great.)
- Construction paper
- Markers

1. Leftover gift bows from Christmas make excellent wreaths for other holidays.
   - Use red and white bows to make a Valentine's Day Wreath.
   - Use green and silver bows for a St. Patrick's Day Wreath.

- Use white and yellow and purple bows for a Happy Easter Wreath.
- Use bows of the colors of your favorite sports team to make a Team Spirit Wreath.

2. All you have to do is gather the bows and separate the colors for whatever wreath you want to make. Glue the bows all over the foam wreath. You can use the paper and markers to make a little sign like "Go Falcons!" depending on which theme you choose.

3. Ask your mom for a box, and store your wreaths in the attic or somewhere until it's time to use them! You could have a cute Bow-Licious Wreath for every holiday!

Wacky Appendix

This is not an appendix, as in a wacky blind-ended tube in the human anatomy. This is an appendix, as in a wacky collection of fun stuff moms and daughters can do together. As I was writing this devo book, I realized that sometimes I mentioned things that I wanted you to be able to do or explore together. So here's all that fun stuff in one great spot, plus some other great ideas. On a rainy day or during a school break, you might want to just pick up this Wacky Appendix and have some wacky mother/daughter time. Be sure to start with the cake!

Radical Recipes to Try

Janet's Chocolate Cake with Peanut Butter Filling

The Cake
2 c sugar
1¾ c flour
¾ c Hershey's cocoa powder, unsweetened
1½ tsp baking soda
1½ tsp baking powder
1 tsp salt
2 eggs
½ c milk
½ c sour cream
½ c vegetable oil
2 tsp vanilla
1 c boiling water

Grease and flour two 9-inch round pans. Combine dry ingredients in the mixing bowl. Add eggs, milk, sour cream, oil, and vanilla. Beat on medium speed for two minutes. Stir in the boiling water. The batter will be extra runny. Pour it into two pans. Bake at 350° F for 30-35 minutes. Cool ten minutes before you remove the cakes from the pan to cool completely on wire racks.

The Peanut Butter Filling
¼ c butter, softened
½ c smooth peanut butter
About 1½ c powdered sugar (until it is the thickness of a peanut butter egg)
A tablespoon or two of milk (keep it thick)

Beat the butter until it's smooth. Add peanut butter and blend well. Add most of the powdered sugar, and then a little milk. Just work it until it is the consistency of a peanut butter egg and you have the taste that you want. After the cake is completely cooled, use all of this mixture between the two layers. It's a lot. You'll love it.

The Chocolate Frosting

½ c butter

2/3 c Hershey's cocoa powder, unsweetened

3 c powdered sugar

1/3 c milk

1 tsp vanilla

Melt butter. Put it in the mixing bowl and stir in the cocoa. Alternately add powdered sugar and milk, beating on medium speed until frosting is a good spreading consistency. Add more milk, as needed. Stir in vanilla. After you fill the cake with peanut butter filling, have fun icing it with this rich chocolate icing.

Refrigerate the cake. It's yummier when it's just a little cool, with a tall glass of cold milk.

Missionary Sherri's Warm Mango Muffins with Whipped Topping

Mango Muffins

1 large ripe mango, diced small

2 c all-purpose flour

½ c sugar

1 tbs baking powder

½ tsp salt

1 c buttermilk

¼ c vegetable oil

2 large eggs, beaten

1 tsp almond extract

Combine flour, sugar, baking powder, and salt in a large mixing bowl. Combine milk, oil, eggs, and almond extract in a medium bowl; whisk until smooth. Add the milk mixture to the flour mixture; stir just until moistened. Stir the chopped mango gently into the batter. Divide the batter evenly into twelve prepared muffin cups.

Bake at 400° F until golden, about 20-25 minutes. Remove the mango muffins from the cups and place on a wire rack to cool slightly. Eat them while they are warm with both butter and freshly whipped cream.

Whipped Cream

1 c whipping cream
2 tbs powdered sugar
1 tsp vanilla

Add ingredients together in a cooled glass bowl. Whip on high until the liquid firms to create peaks. Dollop on top of a warm muffin just before you bite into it!

Anna Marie's Sassy Southern Sweet Tea

*Since this recipe involves using the stove, definitely get your mom's help!

Fill a medium saucepan ¾ full with cold water.
Add 8 tea bags.
On medium heat, bring to a boil.
Once it hits a rolling boil, turn it off and remove the pan from the burner.
Put 2 cups of white sugar into a gallon-sized pitcher.
Add the hot tea. (Don't add the tea bags, though!)
Stir until the sugar is dissolved.
Add enough cold water to fill the pitcher.
Stick it in the fridge to get it nice and cold.
Enjoy!

Luscious Lemonade

6 lemons
6 cups cold water
1 cup sugar

Using a juicer or your bare hands, squeeze all the juice out of the lemons. You should get about a cup of juice. Remove any seeds. You can use lemon juice from a bottle, but using fresh lemons makes the lemonade taste extra refreshing.
Put the lemon juice, water, and sugar in a pitcher, and mix it really well.
Pour it over ice in a glass and enjoy!

Movie to Rent

Faith like Potatoes

This captivating and heart-wrenching South African production is a story of one man's struggle for a better life for himself and his family. Angus Buchan is a Scottish farmer living in Zambia when the area's constant political turmoil finally leads him to believe he must settle in a new country if he ever hopes to be truly prosperous. But, after settling into the agriculturally fruitful KwaZulu Midlands, the Buchan family come to realize that starting a new life isn't necessarily going to be easy. Angus starts on a downward spiral of despair from which only a momentous restoration of faith can save him. Told partially in the Zulu language, *Faith like Potatoes* is a remarkably life-affirming film.

Fun Stuff to Do

Bloomin' Butterflies

You can buy kits that enable you to watch the wonder of metamorphosis together. Some places to shop include

> www.carolina.com
> www.sciencekit.com
> www.nature-gifts.com

Super-Secret Handshake

Use high-fives, pinky links, and fist bumps to create the coolest handshake in the world just for you and your mom to do together!

Language Laughs

Have you ever wanted to learn another language? It's much easier to do when someone else in your house does too. Get a beginner's language workbook and start going through it with your mom. You might want to check up on each other's progress once a week. You could even teach your dog to obey commands in that language!

Topsy-Turvy Holidays

Plan to celebrate a holiday in the wrong month! That's right! Why not put up some Christmas decorations in the heat of the summer and celebrate Jesus' birth again? Or you could have an Easter egg hunt in the snow!

Mixed-Up Mealtime

Plan a meal that's totally flipped around! Eat your meal in this order: dessert, main course, salad. How cool to eat dessert first!

Loopy Latch-Hooks

Latch-hooking is a really cool, totally retro type of craft that's super easy to do. See if you can find a funky latch-hook kit at the craft store, and buy an extra hook to go with it so you and your mom each have one. (See if you can find a kit that's on clearance!) You and your mom can work on it together or take turns until it's done.

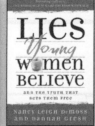

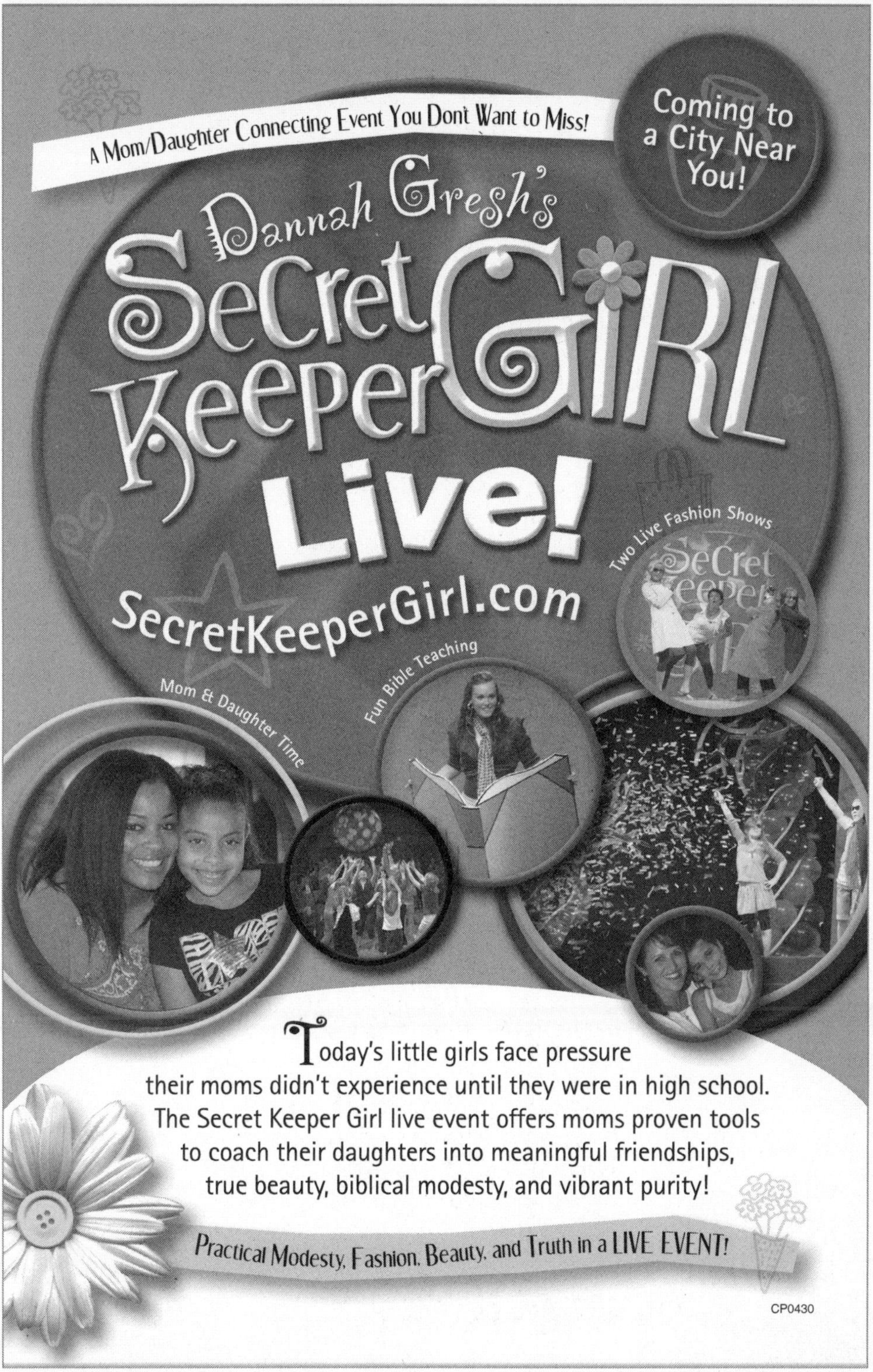